Performance Management Workbook

E. James Brennan

PRENTICE HALL
Englewood Cliffs, New Jersey 07632

Prentice-Hall International (UK) Limited, *London*
Prentice-Hall of Australia Pty. Limited, *Sydney*
Prentice-Hall Canada Inc., *Toronto*
Prentice-Hall Hispanoamericana, S.A., *Mexico*
Prentice-Hall of India Private Limited, *New Delhi*
Prentice-Hall of Japan, Inc., *Tokyo*
Simon & Schuster Asia Pte. Ltd., *Singapore*
Editora Prentice-Hall do Brasil, Ltda., *Rio de Janeiro*

© 1989 *by*

E. James Brennan

10   9   8   7   6   5   4   3

Library of Congress Cataloging-in-Publication Data

Brennan, E. James.
   Performance management workbook / by E. James Brennan.
      p. cm.
   Includes index.
   ISBN 0-13-658634-1
   1. Personnel management. I. Title.
HF5549.B798   1989   89-8680
658.3—dc20   CIP

ISBN 0-13-658634-1

PRENTICE HALL
BUSINESS & PROFESSIONAL DIVISION
A division of Simon & Schuster
Englewood Cliffs, New Jersey 07632

Printed in the United States of America

About the Author

E. James Brennan is president of Brennan, Thomsen Associates, Inc., a personnel management and pay practice consulting firm headquartered in Chesterfield, Missouri (a suburb of St. Louis), with a West Coast office in Newport Beach, California.

Brennan held human resource management positions at **Rexall Drug and Chemical Company, Dart Industries** and **Mallinckrodt, Inc.**, before founding the midwestern office of **Sullivan, Eisemann and Thomsen, Inc.**, shortly followed by **Brennan, Thomsen Associates, Inc.**. Over the past two decades, he has consulted on personnel management and pay systems for organizations of all types and sizes throughout the U.S. and Canada, from national governments and major corporations to small businesses and non-profit agencies.

He is an internationally recognized expert on direct pay, executive compensation, job evaluation and merit pay systems; he is retained by government agencies and private firms as an expert witness in court cases dealing with human resource management issues. A popular speaker at professional symposiums and conferences, he is the author of over fifty professional articles and the compensation editor of the *Personnel Journal*.

Brennan is a long-term member of the **American Society for Personnel Administration**, the **American Compensation Association**, the **Administrative Management Society** (President, St. Louis chapter) and the **National Committee for Pay Equity** (also a member of their job evaluation task force). He holds a bachelors degree in human resource management from Webster University, completed at night after Vietnam-era military service.

TABLE OF CONTENTS

WHAT THIS WORKBOOK WILL DO FOR YOU

This book is a practical working guide for everyone who manages people or is concerned with performance.

It provides complete and clear step by step instructions for all supervisors, whether experienced veterans or beginners, on how to handle daily issues of performance management. It is designed to reduce pressure, prevent panic, avoid omissions and eliminate mistakes when confronted by a serious and urgent performance problem. It also gives a structured format for choosing and implementing appropriate long-term steps to increase mutual success in the workplace; heading off big problems by catching and correcting them while they are still small. It is a universal process for unique performance management needs of all kinds.

Every person whose job deals with (and depends upon) the work of others will find a wealth of information to magnify the effectiveness of both supervisor and subordinates. This workbook gives specific action plans and decision guides to upgrade skills, to save time, to isolate and identify deficiencies or problems and to select among a wide variety of possible solutions. It is presented in a manner that gives concise summaries of broad major areas of concern, followed by detailed checklists, diagnostic questionnaires, tables, worksheets, cross-references, remedial steps and sample forms and procedures, dissected and analyzed for simple imitation or customizing.

This is a supervisor's "cook-book," offering practical yet highly sophisticated solutions to performance management challenges. Those with extensive academic credentials in human resource management will find short but comprehensive applications of the most effective modern management concepts and theories, stripped of scholarly jargon and without superfluous historical background discussions. All will recognize common-sense guidelines, time-saving decision aids and real-life "how-to" prescriptions that are distilled from the best elements of successful performance management practice.

The book was written to give people-managers a complete but extremely specific process for handling their most valuable and most troublesome resource - their employees. It emphasizes the logical, rational steps to take in order to minimize problems with subordinates (and superiors). It helps supervisors assure that every aspect of a situation is swiftly audited, examined and taken into account before a decision is made; and it dramatically increases the probability that the preventive or remedial action will be timely, appropriate, effective and accepted.

In over twenty years of corporate personnel management, as both in-house executive and out-house (sometimes that is a necessary part of the role) external consultant, the author has found a great need for clear and uncomplicated generic performance management tools and techniques for the general reference and daily use of supervisors in every location and industry.

Those who manage people lack the time to sift through hundreds of courses and thousands of books ranging from philosophical musings to "rah-rah" inspirational sermons in the hope of finding a few items of practical utility. Even when they discover a promising new performance method or management tool, experienced executives know that what succeeds "there" may fail "here." Some performance programs, practices and procedures work excellently in one environment but do not "travel" well into other environments. On the other hand, performance management techniques that are so diluted of substance that they can apply anywhere often become little more than slogans or broad concepts that are better suited for posters on the wall than for inclusion in an operating manual. Neither first-line supervisors nor senior executives can easily reconcile arcane and general (if not downright contradictory) academic theory with the urgent demands for immediate, consistent and workable specific applications on the job.

Pressured by the fast pace of modern business, it is all too common to find supervisors forced to either do nothing at all or take action that may well be inappropriate, because they do not feel that they have enough time to satisfy themselves about exactly what is going on with their people and how to best handle it. Whether their decision is to act or not to act, supervisors can and do make performance management decisions that frequently aggravate problems and come back to haunt them and the entire organization later.

The need for results can lead managers into a chaotic atmosphere where performance targets are attacked by a method best described as "Fire!, Fire!, Fire!" And when the targets are missed, the response is all too often just another hysterical order to "Fire!, Fire!, Fire!" once again.

There is a better process: "Ready, Aim, Fire, Score, Adjust." This workbook gives operational guidelines and procedures for that more rational and sensible approach to performance management.

- READY - audit your resources and prepare information.

- AIM - identify needs and plan future action.

- FIRE - take action to hit the performance target.

- SCORE - review performance results and provide feedback.
- ADJUST - counsel on performance, changes and improvements.

Each element involves a different aspect of performance: organizing resources, making plans, putting them into action, appraising and communicating performance results (as they were planned and they actually happened), along with appropriate consequences, and making corrections to improve the next try. The core of this workbook is therefore the different types of performance management communications, how to prepare, select and use them, applying the right kind of plans, evaluations, adjustments, remedies, improvements, etc., for each unique circumstance.

This book will instill in its readers a greater recognition, appreciation and mastery of solid, practical and proven performance management techniques through concise discussions and ready-to-use decision guides, forms and examples.

The increased effectiveness of supervisory performance management actions will have a direct impact on the immediate bottom line, with beneficial results that multiply into the future. Supervisors will also gain a new sense of comfort and security by knowing that a quick and comprehensive decision process that specifies options, remedies and action plans for any performance issue is right at hand.

For example, many supervisors and managers of people see performance management as nothing more than an annual performance review: a situation typically described as stressful, difficult and essentially subjective. The occasion can create such tension that there is a joke about it in the human resource management profession: the supervisor cannot sleep the night before the review interview and the employee cannot sleep the night after.

There is no need for such anxiety. The evaluation of employee performance does not require a "surprise party" where no one is prepared for the comments or reactions of the other.

The Interview Planning Guide in this workbook, alone, will defuse much of the volatility of such merit reviews. Likewise, the Performance Problem Diagnosis process will simplify and streamline investigations into the causes of less than ideal work results, while guaranteeing a more comprehensive inquiry and more effective remedial prescription than ever before.

Readers will see new horizons of achievement in performance management excellence exposed by this material, which will also provide a clearer path and easier journey to their ultimate goal.

Chapter 1:
HOW TO DEVELOP EFFECTIVE PERFORMANCE MANAGEMENT HABITS

Five Key Rules to Manage the Work Climate

Five conditions must be present for a positive work climate that will provide fertile ground for practical performance management.

Employees Must:

1. Know **what is expected** of them on the job.
2. Know **how to do** their jobs.
3. Be given a **supportive work environment** free of unproductive interference and system problems.
4. Receive **appropriate consequences** for the work they do.
5. Be given accurate and timely **feedback** about their job performance.

These basic conditions are quite reasonable and sensible. Everyone will agree that they are fundamental to group success. Failure to achieve these simple objectives is at the root of most performance problems. And the effective remedial solutions to performance management problems are usually found by analyzing where the basic principle is violated and correcting the mistake with appropriate action.

What Effective Performance Managers Know

Who Is Responsible for Supervision and Management

Everyone who works is involved in performance management.
The work climate affects every person who exists within it.
At the very least, you must manage your own work. No matter how many bosses you may have above you, it is you, not they, who must perform your duties.

While superiors can provide guidance, direction, training and assistance, the individual worker is still accountable for his or her own personal performance.

Even the lowliest worker is in some respect a self-manager. Only robots perform tasks in a manner that permits absolutely no variable choice in methods and procedures. Human beings are constantly faced with choices that require judgment to decide the best response. The action which results is the performance that affects the worker, the boss and the entire organization. It makes sense to assure that the performance action is the product of a clear and conscious process of planning, review, communication and feedback. Otherwise, performance "just happens" rather than being "managed."

What Makes Someone a "Manager"

One does not have to carry an organizational job title with the word "manager" in it to have a vested interest in performance management.

A manager can be in charge of people, data or things. Someone who controls the investment of corporate funds, for example, is generally considered to be a manager, even though he or she may have no direct subordinates reporting to them. Such a manager of data or things (in this case, a money manager) is primarily concerned with personal performance: how well he meets his investment earnings goals or how well she predicts the movement of the market.

The manager who supervises no one must still be aware of practical performance management techniques. They apply to this individual, to the boss and to the wider world of people whose actions affect the individual manager's work. You need to be able to interact effectively with other people, whether you have been placed in command of them or not. Indeed, no matter how solitary your work, as long as you are either using or producing goods or services which involve other people in any way, you will have to deal with performance issues.

Likewise, the individual worker needs to know the basic methods of performance management. He can apply them to himself, to better manage his own responsibilities, duties and tasks. She can use them to have a positive influence on the work of other people that contributes to her success and that of the organization.

How All Workers Depend on the Performance of Others

There is hardly any kind of work that does not depend on the performance of other people besides the one individual worker. Those other people whose performance is important include co-workers, customers, suppliers, regulators, and so on. While it may not be the official responsibility of the worker to "supervise" or "manage" those people, it is certainly in the worker's own interest to behave in a way that permits and encourages others to be a help rather than a hindrance. It is quite possible to be a "performance manager" without being an executive or a supervisor.

The Unique Characteristics of a Supervisor

If you are a supervisor, your work requires you to be responsible for the performance of others. One who is designated as a supervisor, a leader of others, faces extra challenges.

Where a "solitary" worker or manager follows orders, directions or procedures, the supervisor must both follow the directives from above and pass them on to subordinates. He is the link between higher management and his work group. She must plan and schedule work for others as well as for herself. He must make decisions about and for a number of jobs rather than just one. She is employed to exercise a wider and longer overview (a "super vision") of work issues than the individual worker.

Why Supervisors Must Take Special Efforts to Manage Performance

It is often difficult enough just to keep your own tasks under control. When the responsibility for supervising the work of other people is added, it can become too much for the supervisor who is unprepared.

Being prepared for supervisory responsibilities is not just a matter of education, training, experience, skill or instinct... although all those factors play a part. Effective performance management requires practical actions that are appropriate for the situation. It's not just "know-how." That can remain theoretical. Performance management calls for action.

Unfortunately, there can be a big difference between thought and action. Intellectual knowledge is not always carried through into actual behavior. Despite a large body of knowledge on useful practical methods of performance management, relatively few people apply those principles well or consistently.

Beware of Bad Performance Management Habits

Regardless of prior training or good intentions, bad management habits are found among the executives and employees of even the best firms.

- People are not told what management expects them to do and criticized when they ask for clarification.

- Employees are given projects they couldn't handle if their lives depended on it.

- Conflicting tasks are assigned to be completed simultaneously.

- Good work is punished and bad work is rewarded.

- Workers are kept in the dark (or even misled) about the adequacy of their performance.

Most people become supervisors only after spending a period of time proving their abilities as a subordinate or technical specialist. They observe many examples of poor management, even in the most successful organizations. Confidence in theoretical concepts or "enlightened" beliefs about human relations can be severely shaken by exposure to successful bosses who ignore those methods.

The passage of time and the pressures of modern business take a toll, as well. The academic lessons on modern management techniques studied years ago are easily forgotten when immediate decisions must be taken on the job today. Management skills that have not been exercised regularly can atrophy and shrink purely because of lack of practice on the part of the individual.

The organization plays a vital part, too. Official company policies can either help or hurt performance management efforts.

Well-constructed formal personnel management policies will reinforce the effective personal actions of good managers, enhance the skills of indifferent supervisors by providing constructive guidance, and limit the damage that can be done by poor leaders. The best official policies, however, are no proof against abuse by people who refuse to apply them properly. But good policies poorly implemented are still better than no policies or bad ones.

Self-Destructive Organizational Practices To Be Avoided

Some firms permit or even force managers to act in ways that are literally destructive to the very goals of the company.

- Job descriptions are discouraged out of fear that employees will "only" do what is on the description; or documentation is prepared by an outsider and filed away for years, despite major changes in the actual tasks, objectives and priorities. In either case, chaos reigns, with people sincerely acting on the basis of fundamental misunderstandings of their responsibilities.

- Employment decisions are made without regard for competence but according to superficial impressions about criteria like physical appearance. Even if it is a modeling agency, the organization can't easily survive when staffed by people who please the eye but lack other skills to do their jobs.

- Performers are denied adequate equipment to perform their duties. Imagine a secretarial pool with typewriters that break down every day or a delivery service running on the cheapest and most unreliable tires. Such task interference is magnified when the maintenance and purchasing systems are slow and unwieldy.

- The largest rewards are given to those who stroke the boss's ego while those creating the profits go unrecognized, without positive encouragement or reinforcement. Or try paying a sales force according to seniority when the most junior employees routinely out-perform the senior ones.

No matter how ridiculous these situations appear, they do happen. Counterproductive management policies and practices are found in almost every organization. It rarely happens because of deliberate malicious intent; most commonly, inappropriate and destructive methods are the result of carelessness, short-sighted thinking and a failure to set and communicate priorities.

Poor practices repeated over time become bad habits. And if the firm has survived thus far, the bad habits can be very hard to break. There is a tendency for people to cling to those behaviors that have made them what they are today. Organizations are composed of human beings, so organizations demonstrate the same kinds of coping mechanisms as their individual members. The thinking is, "If it worked in the past, it will be successful in the future," or "If it ain't broke, don't fix it." The questions left unasked are: how well did it really work in the past? ...and how defective does a method have to be before it is worth fixing?

It is remarkable how many performance problems can be identified that are constant and recurring handicaps on organizational efficiency. These nuisances distract employees, waste energy, divert scarce resources from major objectives, and require time, talent and money to overcome. If one were cynical, you could conclude that the majority of employees would have to learn new jobs if everything worked right. On the other hand, life is much better for everyone ...employees, managers, organizations, customers and the general public... in work climates where managers actually plan, communicate, review and reward positive performance.

What Makes A Good Performance Manager: The Actions They Take

The characteristic behaviors of effective performance managers are more than personality traits. Good managers are not necessarily outgoing, friendly people. Attributes like patience, humility, a sense of humor, benevolence, good-will and open-mindedness are valuable interpersonal skills for popularity; but they will not make you an effective manager. Mastery of the technical or professional field you manage, coupled with the ability to think quickly and be articulate also enhances your prospects for managerial success; but brains and a glib tongue are not the measure of leadership quality.

The Five Habits of Effective Supervisors

It is the things they do that characterize effective performance managers. They regularly and habitually act in ways that provide a positive work climate.

1. They give leadership, guidance and direction to their subordinates. They make sure that everyone knows what they are expected to do; and they involve employees in the planning, inviting their contributions and encouraging their input.

2. They select qualified competent workers. They provide practice, training and counseling and assure that their group knows how to do their jobs when methods, equipment or circumstances change.

3. They clear roadblocks that can interfere with successful performance by employees. They use their overview position to spot sources of task interference that come from conflicting or contradictory instructions, competing assignments, shortages of equipment or other resources; and they remove or reduce those distractions that prevent or inhibit proper

performance.

4. They see that their workers are properly rewarded and given positive reinforcement for job success. They act to discourage employee actions that hurt progress towards the group goal. They encourage desired performance by fair and equitable treatment, tied to the attainment of desired work output objectives.

5. They let people know where they stand and how they are doing at all times. They communicate relevant information about performance adequacy in a positive and timely manner. They solicit employee observations, opinions and suggestions. They take pains to assure that employees can plan, perform, "score," correct and improve their own performance with minimum dependence on "the boss."

The Five Steps for Successful Management Performance

The effective performance manager believes in following the steps for success:

- GET READY   (prepare properly);

- TAKE AIM   (plan carefully);

- FIRE   (perform, take action);

- SCORE   (review the results, appraise performance);

- ADJUST   (communicate the results, give feedback on the degree of success, provide meaningful reinforcement and corrective or remedial guidance).

He repeats the cycle constantly; it can be a daily process for some tasks, or an annual one for others. It is applied to the performance of his own management duties and to her interactions with her subordinates.

Some do these things better than others and still remain effective performance managers. Few use exactly the same methods and approaches; but they all follow a similar process, no matter what they call it.

Why You Need to Know Your Personal Management Habits

Everyone can improve; but improvement requires self-knowledge so you can choose the methods best suited for your personality and that of your organization.

How Your Personality Fits in with the Personality of the Organization

Since an organization is a human enterprise, it exhibits a "personality" of its own.

Remember that the effectiveness of your behavior is affected by the unique personality style of your organization.

Methods that work in one company may not work in another with different customs and traditions.

Performance Management Tip

Carefully observe the management styles used by the most successful executives/managers in your firm. The more consistent the pattern you see, the more likely that it is considered the ideal method in your organization and is the standard against which all managers are measured.

It is easier to swim with the current than against it. As long as the "company style" is reasonable, effective and within your power to adopt, **do so.** Unless any unique personal management style can be quickly and clearly proven to be far superior to the accepted organizational style, the person who insists on acting in a way that flies in the face of conventional behavior runs the risk of being labelled a maverick.

As the Japanese say, "The nail that sticks up will be hammered down."

There are many excellent methods for the detailed analysis of the specific management styles that are found in the world of work. The identification and study of what habitual style you exhibit as a manager or experience as a worker can be a complex and expensive exercise. For the present purpose of illustrating what is meant by "good" and "bad" performance management behaviors, a short summary review will be enough to make the point.

Why Supervisors Do <u>Not</u> Manage Performance

(Where Performance Management involves the planning,
communication and appraisal of work, giving feedback about
work and career and providing appropriate consequences for results.)

1. ☐ No time – too busy doing other things to plan work, discuss progress, evaluate results, coach and reward employees.

2. ☐ The supervisor's boss sets a poor example and he concludes, "If I don't get clear direction, an appraisal, counseling or a raise, why should my employees?"

3. ☐ The supervisor is unwilling or afraid to pass on bad news or handle the type of necessary conflict that comes from levelling with people.

4. ☐ She is not honest with herself, employees or superiors.

5. ☐ He feels he will be criticized if higher management learns of employee performance deficiencies or improvement needs brought to light through documented appraisals.

6. ☐ She fears she will lose her good people if they or others become aware of their capabilities and value.

7. ☐ He is not really concerned with employee communication or development: he focuses all attention on personal work output and prefers doing things himself to supervising others.

8. ☐ Because of her emphasis on short-term production, she is not sold on the idea that appraisals are an essential part of her job.

9. ☐ He is not really aware of their performance or the results required. He takes performance one day at a time, reacting only after disasters occur.

10. ☐ She sees no value in appraisal or counseling, feeling that "People can't really be changed anyway."

11. ☐ He has received little or no training in how to appraise, evaluate, counsel or coach and uses that as an excuse.

12. ☐ She prefers to keep people in the dark: besides avoiding conflict situations, silence protects her position and authority from question.

13. ☐ He is afraid of competition for his job – wants to be indispensable by denying information to subordinates and superiors.

Why Supervisors Do Manage Performance

(Where Performance Management involves the planning,
communication and appraisal of work, giving feedback about
work and career and providing appropriate consequences for results.)

1. ☐ It is the responsibility of a supervisor to know your people and their abilities, even if you do not have a formal appraisal system. Whether your formal performance evaluation system uses the traditional chain of command approach or a peer review process, the immediate supervisor is still the member of management officially designated to oversee the employee's work.

2. ☐ All employees, including supervisors, like to know where they stand. Employees resent "the mushroom management style" (to keep people in the dark, pile natural fertilizer on them and then expect them to grow).

3. ☐ Performance appraisal and counseling increases employee motivation. Demonstrating interest in employees and helping them improve encourages them to contribute and achieve the productive results needed by the supervisor.

4. ☐ Supervisors get valuable feedback from their employees. They hear about employee problems, get reactions to company policies and procedures, and receive information that helps them assess their leadership abilities and effectiveness.

5. ☐ Supervisors achieve results through people. The better the results, the better the performance and reputation of the supervisor.

6. ☐ When employees know their improvement needs and are helped to develop, the results they achieve (on this job and future ones) reflect credit on both the supervisor and the team.

7. ☐ Employees can direct their work performance and skill development towards clear predetermined objectives. Both the supervisor and the employee know what is to be achieved and where the employee is going.

8. ☐ The supervisor can make more accurate assessments of progress towards business plan goals and more objective evaluations of performance by comparing actual results with the planned objectives.

9. ☐ The information documented in a formal appraisal is a vital record of performance history. Without such a record, the organization may be unable to make effective and enforceable decisions about discipline, pay, promotion, etc.

10. ☐ Performance documentation helps develop possible replacements for supervisors. A recorded history is developed on employee performance so that a "pool" of potential backup candidates is available when employees must be selected for promotion. Having one or more possible replacements can free a supervisor for promotion, as well.

Why Actively Managing Performance is in Your Best Personal Interest

Note that none of the reasons given "for" managing performance assume that the organization requires it. Even if top management appears indifferent or hostile to performance planning, feedback, appraisal, etc., those activities still pay off for the manager, the supervisor and the employee. And they should make more money for the owners, or at least create more efficient and productive operations in a non-profit enterprise.

Very few organizations will consciously prevent someone from using management methods that make a greater contribution towards group success. On the contrary, when superior actual results flow from practices and procedures that surpass current requirements, the person who initiated the improvements should experience enhanced career prospects.

How to Best Use This Workbook to Improve Your Management Skills

This book is a working guide for supervisors who manage the performance of others. Sections follow a logical sequence by topic, with cross-references noted. The **Index** at the end of the text is extensive, showing all pages where each subject and key phrase or word is covered.

Refer to the Techniques and Examples for Better Performance Results

The chapters that follow provide clear definitions of key performance management techniques. You will find specific methods and procedures, accompanied by sample forms, program documentation examples and discussions of various options. The examples have been chosen to provide the best approaches, rather than a history of discredited or less effective methods.

How the Forms Will Assist and Guide You

Forms are not the point, in themselves. Forms are aids to objectives and are not the objective in themselves. Small firms managed by one individual may have little need for the kind of elaborate and detailed documentation required in corporate conglomerates. It is the results prompted by the forms and procedures that are important.

Every organization should always document certain vital decisions that could have legal consequences. A negative performance appraisal, for example, should be recorded as a basic defensive measure in case there might be a challenge to an eventual termination.

Why the Documentation Samples Are So Valuable

A large organization must carefully document and record many more personnel actions than a small firm, just to maintain smooth operations. It becomes vital to keep both current and historical data on recruitment actions, job content and objectives, performance appraisals, training and career development, counseling, discipline, terminations, and so on. The reasons are not just legal ones. New executives and supervisors need to know what has occurred before they arrived. Employees deserve to have their past achievements and growth made known to their new bosses who may not have been aware of their merit. You can't maintain continuity in any organization undergoing change unless you have access to information about past practices and current plans.

Adapt and Use the Wide Variety of Practical Tools for Unique Needs

Organizations, like other human organisms, have variable needs and circumstances that demand a customized approach to decide the precise methods best suited to them.

This workbook is designed to give you the practical tools to learn and apply effective performance management techniques in your daily actions. A wide variety of proven methods are offered, to assure a universal application; and the pros and cons of options for special cases are regularly presented for your consideration. Where a number of techniques are possible, the best proven methods are summarized or detailed; and the dangers of certain types of actions are clearly set forth.

Understand and Practice the Techniques Until They Become Automatic

Up to this point, you have received a frame of reference on what must be done to create an effective work management climate that promotes positive performance. You have been presented with an overview of various performance management habits. You have considered the pros and cons of different views and approaches of people-management. You have seen practical reasons for developing effective habits.

Now it is time to study those principles in detail and learn how to apply them in practical and specific ways. The repeated application of the simple, effective and complete performance management techniques will soon fix them in your mind and make them habitual.

Chapter 2:

HOW TO QUICKLY DIAGNOSE
PERFORMANCE MANAGEMENT NEEDS

Why Problem Diagnosis Comes First

No matter what the job description says, solving problems always seems to get the first priority in every organization. Those "problems" can range from urgent emergencies to long-standing annoyances; but they share one common element: actual results do not match the positive performance expectations.

When that happens, the attention of the performance manager must focus on solving the problem, to the exclusion of everything else. Since problem-solving is so important and potentially time-consuming, the first chapter of this text dealing with detailed techniques and methods concentrates on identifying the true causes of problems that can be solved by the various steps covered in later chapters.

Why Diagnosis Is Needed to Keep "Solutions" from Becoming New Problems

People are always yelling, "FIX it!" when something goes wrong, but the first solution that comes to mind is not always the right one... especially when you are dealing with people problems.

Like a doctor, the performance manager must conduct a diagnosis before giving out a prescription; otherwise, your organization may only get sicker, just as the doctor's patient will get sicker if the wrong solution is applied. A good performance problem diagnosis does not have to take a lot of time, but it is essential to assure that you have identified the problem, its cause and the proper solution. The few minutes spent in diagnosis may save you from a quick failure. A premature super-fast corrective response that is not on target may also cost you days or weeks of back-tracking and apologies to reverse the undesirable effects of the wrong remedial action.

Performance Management Tip

Even under ideal circumstances, every management decision can only be made according to the Best Available Data.

Every decision will be a B.A.D. decision, made on the basis of the Best Data Available at the time.

It therefore makes sense to do everything possible to make sure that you analyze the performance problem **before** you act. The better your information on the nature and extent of the problem, the better your decision will be. If you fail to check out rumors and confirm assumptions before making a hasty decision, you run the risk of making a choice based on **B.A.D.** information that is inexcusably incomplete.

A Real-Life Example of the Importance of Targeting

Performance management needs are rarely obvious, or they would not exist for long. What first appears to be "the problem" often, upon closer examination, turns out only to be a symptom of a deeper problem.

A while ago, a major transportation firm experienced high turnover in its data processing department. Almost every programmer quit the company "for a better job opportunity offering higher pay" after no more than three years of service.

The problem had existed for a long time and had serious negative effects on the efficiency of the department. The constant turnover disrupted the continuity of programming projects, destroyed work schedules and forced the frequent reassignment of tasks.

In the past, the organization had raised salaries in the computer section to attract and retain these professionals whose work was vital to the company's coordination of national shipments. They had no trouble hiring new people, but they could never hold them for long. Consultants were called in, this time, to review the pay rates and make appropriate recommendations to correct the turnover problem.

But the problem was not pay. The consultants applied the conventional problem diagnostic techniques to study the work climate and discovered that:

1. performance plans and work objectives were clear and well-communicated;
2. the data processing personnel (current employees and past departed ones, as well) were highly qualified and competent experts, with a

disproportionately large number of Ph.D.s and advanced degrees in mathematics and computer science;

3. they worked in lovely offices in a suburban campus environment, using the most modern and most powerful advanced computer equipment, with unlimited support resources;

4. they received the highest rates of pay for their work that could be found in the country; they were all personally aware that they were grossly "overpaid" for their duties, compared to the pay practices of other organizations;

5. they received accurate and timely feedback about their job performance; their boss was closely involved in all phases of their work and no one was kept in the dark.

The problem was certainly not pay, even though that was the solution that had been consistently applied to reduce turnover for years. The employees were happy to accept the ever-escalating pay rates, but they still routinely left after a few years. They felt that they had to leave to preserve their hard-earned professional skills.

The big boss to whom they all reported had an aversion to the more modern computer programming languages and higher-level expert systems which were standard in business use and in academic instructions. He was far more comfortable using the old autocoder and assembly languages for computer programming than the more current Cobol and PL-1 languages. So he required programmers to convert the modern computer programs and commercial programming packages back into the old-fashioned obsolete languages he best understood.

Not only was this inefficient (the converted programs required from ten to fifteen times more computer space and more time to run than the modern programs), but it was also extremely difficult. The programming staff was highly trained in modern methods; but they were required to re-design modern systems so they would run in the old ways which were only briefly covered in college. It was like requiring diesel locomotive engineers to convert their diesel machines into wood-burning steam engines. They were routinely lined up outside their boss's office every day, seeking assistance and guidance on "ancient" methods which were no longer in general use anywhere else.

Despite the lovely offices, modern equipment and high pay, the programmers still experienced a defective work climate. Specifically, they did not work in an environment that supported their desire to apply the latest programming technology. Instead, they were forced to work in an unproductive manner.

They were paid a fortune to withstand the frustration and pressure, so they would build up a nice nest egg before finally quitting for another job that would allow them to use the modern skills they could not apply at the transportation firm. The programmers felt compelled to leave before they had spent so much time working in the technology of the past that they might forget the skills of the modern present. The turnover was due to an unproductive interference in their work environment that threatened to make them technically obsolete if they stayed. In a way, their compensation was inadequate. No sum of money could make up for the long-range career opportunities they risked losing as long as they were denied a chance to practice and maintain their modern computer skills.

Instead of increasing the payroll, the old boss was moved aside (kicked upstairs, since the only way he had been able to so cripple the efficiency of his department was his long and close friendship with the Chairman of the Board). A new manager from a related department who was competent in modern methods of computer technology and performance management techniques was given his supervisory responsibility. She unleashed the suppressed talent of the programming staff and all was well from then on. Of course, the consulting firm was fired for embarrassing the Chairman's old friend, but that's what consultants are for... to get the job done and go away.

Three Tools to Diagnose What Is Wrong

The previous example illustrates the importance of careful diagnosis.

Three diagnostic methods are provided here for your immediate use. The first is an expert system that concentrates on "the performer," which may be the individual employee, a department or the corporation. The remaining two are audit techniques (one using a semi-narrative format and the other a checklist) to identify, confirm and assess how performance management systems are working.

Performance problems interfere with mutual employee/organization excellence. When actual work results do not match expectations (whether those expectations are high or low), there is a "performance problem."

It may be a minor deficiency, a series of failures, a gradual reduction in productivity or a loss of effectiveness. It may be an inability to reach desired objectives or a lack of progress towards certain goals. It may only be uneven and inconsistent work output...sometimes great and sometimes not so great. Whatever the specific reason, a "performance problem" is here defined as any gap between management expectations and actual employee performance.

Big problems grow from little ones, so the far-sighted supervisor does not wait until disaster has struck. As soon as a "performance problem" is noticed, a diagnosis should be conducted to determine the probable cause and to select the most effective prescription. Prompt and appropriate corrective action (a vital part of "super-vision") is necessary when either the individual employee or the organizational system is not working properly.

How to Identify Performance Problems with Tool #1

What Precise Questions to Ask to Find and Fix the Causes of Problems

The **Performance Problem Diagnosis** is a multi-purpose analytical tool that filters your observations to spot problem areas and indicate solutions. This diagnostic exercise is a quick procedure to identify possible causes of inadequate or improper behavior. The diagnosis can be applied to the organization as well as to the individual. You can apply it to yourself as well as to a subordinate. It asks a series of multiple-choice questions. The answer you select will either tell you to:

- continue and proceed to the next question,
- confirm your answer, making sure it is correct,
- or take a specific action to remedy the problem.

The **Performance Problem Diagnosis** questionnaire on the following pages is a simple but sophisticated tool to identify potential causes and probable solutions for performance problems of all kinds. It simplifies the pursuit of excellence by prescribing precise actions to improve or correct performance.

The user should either make a copy of the pages, so the answers can be marked without obscuring the original text, or note down on a separate sheet of paper the questions whose answers call for a specific remedial response action.

Details of the various **Remedial Methods**...training, practice, improvement, development, feedback, reinforcement, and so on... which appear in italics follow in later chapters. A quick look at the comprehensive **Index** in the back of the book will show you exactly where to find the details of each remedial method.

Performance Problem Diagnosis Questionnaire

Answer each question about the performer(s). The recommended remedial action for each **yes** or **no** answer follows the ☞. If you are not sure about any answer, investigate and confirm before acting.

Do the Performers...

1. know **what** the desired action is?
    - ☐ **no** ☞ *instruct*;
    - ☐ **yes** ☞ *confirm* and continue.

2. know **they** are supposed to take the desired action?
    - ☐ **no** ☞ *instruct*;
    - ☐ **yes** ☞ continue.

3. know **when** to take the desired action?
    - ☐ **no** ☞ *instruct*;
    - ☐ **yes** ☞ continue.

4. know the relative **priorities**?
    - ☐ **no** ☞ *instruct*;
    - ☐ **yes** ☞ *confirm* and *monitor*.

5. know **how** to take the desired action?
    - ☐ **no** ☞ continue;
    - ☐ **yes** ☞ *confirm* and *monitor*.

    - ↳ have they ever done it successfully before?
        - ☐ **no** ☞ *train*, *replace* or *change expectations*;
        - ☐ **yes** ☞ continue.

    - ↳ have they done it well recently?
        - ☐ **no** ☞ give *practice* and *re-evaluate*;
        - ☐ **yes** ☞ continue.

6. know the **standards** or level of performance expected?
    - ☐ **no** ☞ *inform* and confirm understanding;
    - ☐ **yes** ☞ continue.

    - ↳ are there standards?
        - ☐ **no** ☞ set *standards* and give *feedback*;
        - ☐ **yes** ☞ continue.

    - ↳ does everybody agree on them?
        - ☐ **no** ☞ create *agreement* and *clarify*;
        - ☐ **yes** ☞ continue.

    - ↳ is anyone meeting them now?
        - ☐ **no** ☞ *review expectations*;

       ☐ **yes** 🖝 *compare* and analyze.

7. know **whether** they are doing it right or not?
       ☐ **no** 🖝 provide *feedback*;
       ☐ **yes** 🖝 continue.

8. know **how to interpret** feedback information in order to correct their performance?

      ✔ if given good information, can they figure out how to change and improve?
         ☐ **no** 🖝 *instruct, plan corrective/remedial action...*or *replace*;
         ☐ **yes** 🖝 continue.

9. have adequate **resources** (time, equipment, people, money, information) to do it?
       ☐ **no** 🖝 provide *resources* or change *expectations*;
       ☐ **yes** 🖝 continue.

10. have productive physical **accommodations** for work?
       ☐ **no** 🖝 provide better accommodations or change *expectations*;
       ☐ **yes** 🖝 continue.

11. have significant **distractions** that interfere with concentration and disrupt work?

      ✔ interruptions?
         ☐ **no** 🖝 continue;
         ☐ **yes** 🖝 reduce/eliminate *interruptions* or change *expectations*.

      ✔ higher-priority tasks?
         ☐ **no** 🖝 continue;
         ☐ **yes** 🖝 clarify relative *priorities* or change *expectations*.

12. **suffer from some condition** or circumstance that limits their work effectiveness?
       ☐ **no** 🖝 confirm and continue;
       ☐ **yes** 🖝 investigate, *counsel* employee, take *remedial/corrective* action or *replace*.

13. receive **negative consequences** (punishment, hostility, resistance, loss of status or power) for taking the desired action?

      ✔ consider such sources of consequences as superiors, peers,

subordinates, family and the reward system...
- ☐ **no** 🖙 continue;
- ☐ **yes** 🖙 provide stronger positive *consequences* and reduce the impact of negative *consequences*.

14. receive **no consequences** for taking the desired action?
- ☐ **no** 🖙 continue;
- ☐ **yes** 🖙 provide *consequences* and positive *reinforcement*.

15. receive **immediate, positive consequences** for doing something other than the desired action?

- ✔ do "good" things happen when they act improperly?
  - ☐ **no** 🖙 continue;
  - ☐ **yes** 🖙 remove *rewards* (and increase negative *consequences*) for wrong action, and/or increase positive *consequences* for correct action.

- ✔ is negative reinforcement or corrective feedback long delayed?
  - ☐ **no** 🖙 continue;
  - ☐ **yes** 🖙 give immediate *warnings* and *guidance* on *improvement*.

16. receive **no information** on the consequences of taking the desired action?
- ☐ **no** 🖙 continue;
- ☐ **yes** 🖙 provide *feedback*.

- ✔ do they know it makes a difference to do it right?
  - ☐ **no** 🖙 *instruct* and provide *feedback*;
  - ☐ **yes** 🖙 continue.

17. receive **wrong information** on the consequences of their actions?

- ✔ is the feedback inaccurate?
  - ☐ **no** 🖙 continue;
  - ☐ **yes** 🖙 make the *feedback* accurate.

- ✔ is the feedback confusing (contradictory, complicated or too much to interpret)?
  - ☐ **no** 🖙 continue;
  - ☐ **yes** 🖙 simplify the *feedback*.

- ✔ does the feedback lead them to conclude they are doing OK when they are not?

      ☐ **no** ☞ continue;
      ☐ **yes** ☞ correct the misleading information.

18. receive information on progress, results or consequences that is **not sufficient** (i.e., not clear, not specific, too late, too infrequent) for them to correct their performance?

     ↙ do the performers get direct, frequent and timely information?
        ☐ **no** ☞ continue;
        ☐ **yes** ☞ give fast and direct *information* to the performer.

     ↙ do they get enough information to know how to correct their performance?
        ☐ **no** ☞ provide more *feedback* information;
        ☐ **yes** ☞ continue.

     ↙ do they get precise information that identifies needs and possible solutions?
        ☐ **no** ☞ provide precise *feedback*;
        ☐ **yes** ☞ continue.

19. receive information on desired action that **communicates confidence** in the performer?
        ☐ **no** ☞ *communicate* confidence and positive *expectations*;
        ☐ **yes** ☞ continue.

20. receive proper **authority** to take action?

     ↙ have the necessary authority to take the desired action?
        ☐ **no** ☞ delegate authority and clarify responsibility;
        ☐ **yes** ☞ continue.

     ↙ is the authority clear?
        ☐ **no** ☞ clarify authority and responsibility;
        ☐ **yes** ☞ continue.

     ↙ is the authority consistent with that granted for similar previous responsibilities?
        ☐ **no** ☞ explain changes and confirm understanding;
        ☐ **yes** ☞ continue.

21. give **upward feedback** on progress towards objectives and needs?

     ↙ keep superiors properly informed?

    ☐ **no** ☞ clarify *expectations* on upward *feedback*;
    ☐ **yes** ☞ continue.

✓ identify deficiencies to be corrected?
    ☐ **no** ☞ reduce employee anxiety, offer *help* with problems;
    ☐ **yes** ☞ continue.

✓ specify solutions planned and actions to be taken?
    ☐ **no** ☞ ask for *reports* on *plans*;
    ☐ **yes** ☞ continue.

✓ suggest options requiring higher management approval?
    ☐ **no** ☞ ask for *suggestions*;
    ☐ **yes** ☞ continue.

✓ "pass the buck" unnecessarily or improperly?
    ☐ **no** ☞ continue;
    ☐ **yes** ☞ clarify responsibility and accountability.

✓ exceed their authority to act, without management approval?
    ☐ **no** ☞ continue;
    ☐ **yes** ☞ clarify limits on freedom to act.

Summarize, classify and analyze the answers. Look for patterns in the prescribed actions. They will show where the problems originate and what kinds of solutions are best. Remember: if you do not take action, the deficient performance will continue.

How to Use Diagnosis Questionnaire Answers

The problems identified and the remedies specified will usually tend to be concentrated in a few general areas.

If employee competence is an issue, for example, you will find that the recommended remedial actions may include the statements:

- *confirm* that he knows what he is supposed to do;
- *communicate* her responsibility for producing the desired results;
- *monitor* his ability to perform the task;
- increase and improve *feedback* information on how she is doing;
- provide *training* or *practice*;

- consider *transfer* or *termination*.

The words in italics are keywords that refer to subjects, topics, methods and techniques that are explored in great detail in later sections of this workbook. The chapter headings alone will tell you where to find the principal treatment of those recommended methods. If you want to locate every spot where the italicized keyword method can be found, just refer to the index at the back of the book.

All of the suggested remedial actions are covered in great detail in the relevant chapters that follow. These examples will show, discuss and illustrate corrective measures for any problem you face.

How to Identify Performance Problems with Tool #2

Ways to Spot Organizational Reinforcement Problems with an Audit Survey

Superior work results come from employee strengths which are supported and used by the organization.

No employee, no matter how brilliant or talented, can excel up to his or her full potential without organizational support. And the effectiveness of the organization depends directly on the competence of its employees. Both the employee and the total organization affect each other.

The performance of the individual should be directed towards the objectives of the organization, following the priorities and methods the organization prescribes for the attainment of those various goals. If the goals, objectives, methods and priorities are not clear, then the employee is inhibited, handicapped and sometimes completely thwarted in the attempt to perform properly.

Before you conclude that all performance problems can be solved by dealing with the workers alone, it is a good idea to review the organization's reinforcement and reward system.

It may well be that employees are being negatively affected by influences that are imposed from above and whose solution is beyond their control.

What you think is a problem may be exactly what top management wants. What you consider a disastrous situation may be of relatively little importance and low priority to the firm. Or the company may be unwittingly using reward and reinforcement methods that undercut, contradict or interfere with your efforts.

The effectiveness of your remedial actions can be diminished by formal performance management and compensation programs that continue to reward and reinforce the very actions that you condemn. Sometimes, the formal systems even punish performance that is truly in the best interest of the organization.

If employees are paid by the volume of their work output without regard for quality, you must wrestle with a problem in the balance of consequences. Asking workers to slow down their production quantity and to voluntarily accept a cut in pay just to satisfy you will not work. To persuade people to produce higher quality widgets or to sell more expensive items with less volume count but a higher profit margin, you must arrange more positive consequences and fewer negative ones for the behavior change. Unless you personally control the total reward system, you must apply the **Remedial Methods** in such a masterful manner that you either persuade your superiors to change the formal reward system to support your goal or you convince your subordinates that it is in their own best interest to pay less attention to the formal rewards.

It is also possible that the official reward systems will be of little use in providing an incentive to employees for changing their behavior. Organizations that pay according to seniority alone find that wages and salaries cannot be easily used as a motivator in their reward environment.

While some of these difficulties can be overcome merely by better **Planning and Communication**, it is wise to review all the potential sources of performance management problems, lest you miss some as you concentrate on the obvious ones. There are a number of diagnostic techniques to identify performance problems that may be caused by organizational practices and procedures that run contrary to your understanding of overall policies, philosophies and objectives. Two types of organizational diagnostic reviews are offered here.

What You Can Discover Through a Compensation Audit

The review of "compensation" here involves much more than just looking at money. Compensation covers what employees get for what they do; and it should be directly related to what top management wants people to do. The reward, pay and reinforcement systems of the organization should operate to support and encourage the achievement of organizational goals.

It is therefore vital to know what those goals and objectives are, in terms of performance management actions. The narrative audit form that follows next was created to review the philosophies and goals of top management, to document their perceptions of relative importance and the degree of successful attainment, to discuss their views of actual practices and the difficulty encountered. This particular survey form was designed to identify the beliefs of a number of individual decision-makers in a confidential format.

It is constantly amazing to see the wide variety of responses one gets to the same questions from key executives in the same organization. The answers become even more interesting as the same questions are asked at different layers of management. Company policies are rarely as clear as senior executives would like to believe. Even the senior managers themselves seldom agree on what those policies are, their priority, their intent and their degree of success and difficulty.

Any confusion on these matters can cripple the effectiveness of the enterprise. If one executive believes that the company intends to pay top dollar to new hires, while another thinks that he is supposed to offer the lowest possible starting salary, the performance of both individual employees and the whole organization will suffer. Conflicting messages are being sent to workers. They will complain of pay inequities, suspect favoritism, and perhaps even accuse their bosses of dishonesty and deception. That affects performance.

Even if the top echelon of the organization agrees on all aspects of their system for rewarding positive performance (usually only after an intensive process of soul-searching, discussion and clarification), they must communicate it to lower levels of management. Unity at the top is only the first step: it must be translated into a message transmitted throughout the enterprise before all employees can be expected to know and understand the "official" position. Until then, there is always a strong possibility that people-managers will be innocently out of step with the true intent of policy makers. There is no sense in allowing managers to waste time, effort, energy and money trying to achieve an objective that is not actually desired by the organization.

PHILOSOPHY AND OBJECTIVES

The reasons for using various compensation approaches fall into 10 categories. The organization's philosophy and objectives in these ten areas indicate what results should be achieved when the compensation program is working properly. Also, the kind of programs you need depend on the unique objectives of the organization.

The anonymous perceptions, impressions and comments of key individuals such as you will help us determine what the actual compensation philosophy is, how the actual practices meet those philosophical objectives, and what is needed to close any gaps while maintaining programs that are already working well.

Please describe policy IMPORTANCE as high (3), medium (2) or low (1).

#	CATEGORY AREA	PERCEIVED OBJECTIVE OR POLICY OF THE ORGANIZATION	IMPOR-TANCE
1	*Competitiveness*: to be above, below or just at competitive pay levels.	Pay above community average and always stay close to major competitors.	3
2	*Pay for Performance*: to motivate good or improved performance through variable compensation rewards.	"Committed to merit increases and performance bonuses..." (that's what they say, anyway)	2
3	*Internal Equity*: to maintain a fair, defensible relationship between salaries in the organization.	Differences in base salary should be related to job value and long-term personal performance.	3
4	*Government Compliance*: to satisfy EEOC, FLSA and other governmental requirements.	Meet requirements, comply with the law, avoid negative publicity.	1
5	*Cost Control*: to maintain cost/expense control and stay within budget.	Stay within authorized budget limits.	2
6	*Communications*: to use pay rewards as feedback to communicate the organization's strategic goals, objectives and philosophy.	Rewards are supposed to be incentives for better work, a source of motivation, etc.	2
7	*Turnover*: to maximize retention of productive employees and keep turnover rates low.	Keep the very best employees and let the others leave if they want to.	1
8	*Cost Effectiveness*: to provide the maximum value for each dollar spent for compensation.	Payroll and personnel costs are constantly being reviewed to squeeze more bang for the buck.	1
9	*Social Concern*: to protect employees from catastrophe and to provide post-employment security.	Employees are covered against disaster	1
10	*Administrative Ease*: to provide useful information and results without taking much time away from other management duties.	Keep paperwork to a minimum! Only the most essential records are filled out.	3

ACTUAL PRACTICE.....and OPINIONS AND COMMENTS

Once you have described what you believe to be the intended policy or objective of the organization,

- please state the **degree of success** you believe has been achieved,
- briefly describe the **actual practice**,
- and give your estimate of the **degree of difficulty** involved in meeting the policy objective.

As before, *please describe SUCCESS and DIFFICULTY as high (3), medium (2) or low (1).*

SUCCESS	ACTUAL PRACTICE OF THE ORGANIZA- TION	DIFFICULTY	OTHER OPINIONS OR COMMENTS
2	*Competitiveness:* We keep pay a bit above local rates but tend to fall far behind our major competitors	3	Very difficult to get reliable survey data on what out-of-town major competitors plan to pay. We always react late.
1	*Pay for Performance:* Little difference in merit increases between so-so performers and the best. Bonuses seem based more on seniority than on current work results.	3	It's hard to be tough and firm on your people when others ignore merit when distributing bucks.
1	*Internal Equity:* No one really understands why people are paid what they are!	2	The official line is "shut up" — so all we hear is gossip and gripes. Dunno what's true.
2	*Government Compliance:* Satisfy the letter of the law.	1	Doing the minimum in this area may catch up with us in the future. Attitude now is "don't get caught".
3	*Cost Control:* Budgets are pretty flexible. With a good argument, you can get the budget limit raised and look good.	2	Policy looks strict, but actual practice is quite rational & reasonable.
1	*Communications:* $ Rewards are all about the same. Nobody explains exactly why you got what you did, unless it's a promotion.	2	Plenty of communication with "recognition" rewards, but not much said about the more common cash rewards.
3	*Turnover:* Rarely lose anyone we want to keep — if we know they're good and they consider leaving, we can make counter-offers.	2	We do lose a lot of new people before we have time to judge them. And when key workers want extra money, they let us know they're looking.
2	*Cost Effectiveness:* Salary budgets and benefit plans get changed a lot, supposedly to save money!.... but we never seem to get extra value.	2	All the changes are confusing.
2	*Social Concern:* The life & disability insurance is great. After 20 years, pension is ok. Medical benefits are worthless unless hospitalized.	2 ?	Not my area — I don't know how tough/expensive better coverage would be.
3	*Administrative Ease:* Not much personnel paperwork to do.	1	Never get much "useful info" from personnel records.

The example shows the kind of important information that can be discovered by a simple questionnaire.

In the illustration, the person who answered the questions identifies some key points. For instance, he sees *"Competitiveness"* as extremely important to top management; he defines it in his own words, briefly discusses the mixed success he has observed, rates the achievement as very difficult and comments about the problems he has seen.

His or her perceptions are valuable because they show:

- whether the "correct" policy/objective has been successfully communicated;

- what various managers and employees see as the relative importance of certain subjects;

- whether others see the actual practices as successful;

- how people "in the trenches" view the practices of the organization;

- what others see as the degree of difficulty experienced in trying to achieve the organization's objectives, and why.

The question of whether the employee is "right" or "wrong" (particularly about overall company policy) is worth considering, even though this is not a formal test. One can expect different people to have different experiences and perspectives, as far as actual results are concerned; but they should have a clear and accurate understanding of management intent.

The main point is whether the employee has the same idea about goals, objectives and philosophies as top management. If not, it identifies areas where the organization needs to improve its internal communications; or it may expose facts that prove that the employee has a better idea about what is going on than top management does.

In addition, such answers can expose a wealth of valuable information about the real problems that rack the organization, particularly when the questionnaire can be submitted anonymously. Employee suggestions for improvements can also be quite helpful and are often more practical and realistic than theoretical solutions presented by people who are far removed from the real action.

Sometimes the knowledge that the company can't correct problems immediately keeps management from trying to discover just what the problems are. The fear that asking a question about problems will lead employees to expect a prompt solution often stifles communication.

An audit questionnaire provides a structured way to open up new lines of communication without necessarily implying that there will be quick solutions to every problem discovered, or even a detailed report on the audit findings.

Performance Management Tip

If you want to discover what is on the minds of employees without conducting a formal "employee attitude survey" which requires you to report what could be embarassing results, slip a few questions dealing with opinions into an audit instrument.

As long as the "attitude" questions are related to the "factual" areas being studied and are not given a lot of emphasis and attention by the investigator, employees will tend to answer them frankly. This maneuver may produce valuable information that shows whether you have any serious problems that require special action or more data gathering.

Best of all, you can get suggestions, opinions and answers without having to make a commitment that management will take prompt action to correct employee dissatisfactions.

How to Identify Performance Problems with Tool #3

Ways to Use the Compensation Audit Checklist for Quick Answers from Many People

A longer checklist version of the audit follows next. It does not require narrative answers, but asks for selections among multiple choices. The questions and answers can be computerized, to simplify repeated use and to facilitate the analysis of group responses.

This detailed checklist focuses on key action areas where policies, practices, priorities and needs become apparent. No writing skills are needed to complete this form. It will identify views of

- how the employer intends to treat employees,

- what kind of policies are being communicated by organizational actions and circumstances,

- whether actual practices support, ignore or contradict stated policy objectives,

- if management decisions produce the desired results,

- what kind of behavior is being reinforced by the formal policies of the company,

- how important the subject area is,

- how much success has been attained and with what difficulty.

As a survey, it only measures the perceptions of the person answering it; but if it is completed by a number of "knowledgeable" managers, it will produce valuable insights. The checklist is a tool to quickly spot areas where the system may be the problem, or where confusion exists on the nature or intent of the management system.

Compensation Audit Checklist

A. COMPETITIVENESS

A-1.   Can you find competent people willing to work for the same salary you pay to current employees?
    ☐ Always   ☐ Sometimes   ☐ Never   ☐ Unknown

A-2.   Are competent people willing to start work at salary rates below those paid to current employees?
    ☐ Always   ☐ Sometimes   ☐ Never   ☐ Unknown

A-3.   Do you have competitive data on the pay rates for similar jobs at other organizations that compete with you for employees?
    ☐ Always   ☐ Sometimes   ☐ Never   ☐ Unknown

A-4.   Compared to other like enterprises, you want your competitive pay structure position to be:
    ☐ High   ☐ Medium   ☐ Low

A-5.   What is the level of importance you place on maintaining your desired competitive structure position?
    ☐ High   ☐ Medium   ☐ Low

A-6.   What degree of success has been achieved in maintaining your desired competitive position?
    ☐ High   ☐ Medium   ☐ Low

A-7. What was the degree of difficulty encountered in attaining that level of success?
  ☐ High   ☐ Medium   ☐ Low

Other comments: _____

B. PAY FOR PERFORMANCE

B-1. All else being equal, should better performers get better pay?
  ☐ Always   ☐ Sometimes   ☐ Never   ☐ Unknown

B-2. Should better performers get dramatically larger pay increases?
  ☐ Always   ☐ Sometimes   ☐ Never   ☐ Unknown

B-3. Are better performers treated as specified above?
  ☐ Always   ☐ Sometimes   ☐ Never   ☐ Unknown

B-4. Do employees believe that? Would they agree with your last answer?
  ☐ Always   ☐ Sometimes   ☐ Never   ☐ Unknown

B-5. Are supervisors able to effectively evaluate the performance of their subordinates?
  ☐ Always   ☐ Sometimes   ☐ Never   ☐ Unknown

B-6. What is the level of importance you place on reinforcing better performance through variable compensation rewards?
  ☐ High   ☐ Medium   ☐ Low

B-7. What degree of success has been achieved in reinforcing better performance through variable compensation rewards?
  ☐ High   ☐ Medium   ☐ Low

B-8. What was the degree of difficulty encountered in attaining that level of success?
  ☐ High   ☐ Medium   ☐ Low

Other comments: _____

C. INTERNAL EQUITY

C-1. Are employees told the average value or the pay range (minimum to maximum) for their job?
  ☐ Always   ☐ Sometimes   ☐ Never   ☐ Unknown

C-2. Are employees informed of the job values/ranges for other jobs in the organization?
    ☐ Always   ☐ Sometimes   ☐ Never   ☐ Unknown

C-3. Do employees understand why the organization pays different amounts to different people in different jobs?
    ☐ Always   ☐ Sometimes   ☐ Never   ☐ Unknown

C-4. Should there be clear and consistent reasons for pay variances between different employees and different jobs?
    ☐ Always   ☐ Sometimes   ☐ Never   ☐ Unknown

C-5. What is the level of importance you place on maintaining a fair and defensible relationship between salaries in the organization (internal equity)?
    ☐ High   ☐ Medium   ☐ Low

C-6. What degree of success has been achieved in meeting your internal equity objective?
    ☐ High   ☐ Medium   ☐ Low

C-7. What was the degree of difficulty encountered in attaining that level of success?
    ☐ High   ☐ Medium   ☐ Low

Other comments: _____

D. LEGAL COMPLIANCE

D-1. Do you intend to be an ideal, model employer in terms of how well you comply with the spirit (as well as the letter) of laws affecting discrimination, overtime pay, etc.?
    ☐ Always   ☐ Sometimes   ☐ Never   ☐ Unknown

D-2. Do personnel records consistently support pay decisions or disciplinary/termination actions?
    ☐ Always   ☐ Sometimes   ☐ Never   ☐ Unknown

D-3. Are protected classes (women, minorities, handicapped, those over 40) treated and rewarded exactly the same as others?
    ☐ Always   ☐ Sometimes   ☐ Never   ☐ Unknown

D-4.   What is the level of importance you place on legal compliance activities that exceed minimum government requirements?
     ☐ High   ☐ Medium   ☐ Low

D-5.   What degree of success has been achieved in meeting your intended legal compliance objectives?
     ☐ High   ☐ Medium   ☐ Low

D-6.   What was the degree of difficulty encountered in attaining that level of success?
     ☐ High   ☐ Medium   ☐ Low

Other comments: _____

E. COST CONTROL

E-1.   Do you prepare annual budgets for wage and salary expenses?
     ☐ Always   ☐ Sometimes   ☐ Never   ☐ Unknown

E-2.   Do your actual pay expenses match the budgeted (or otherwise anticipated) amounts each year?
     ☐ Always   ☐ Sometimes   ☐ Never   ☐ Unknown

E-3.   Do supervisors who recommend or authorize "excessive" pay expenses encounter effective controls and receive quick feedback?
     ☐ Always   ☐ Sometimes   ☐ Never   ☐ Unknown

E-4.   Do productivity or profit increases match or exceed the cost of payroll increases?
     ☐ Always   ☐ Sometimes   ☐ Never   ☐ Unknown

E-5.   Do you intend to maintain careful controls over personnel/payroll/benefit costs and expenses?
     ☐ Always   ☐ Sometimes   ☐ Never   ☐ Unknown

E-6.   What is the level of importance you place on the above objective?
     ☐ High   ☐ Medium   ☐ Low

E-7.   What degree of success has been achieved?
     ☐ High   ☐ Medium   ☐ Low

E-8.   What was the degree of difficulty encountered in attaining that level of success?
     ☐ High   ☐ Medium   ☐ Low

Other comments: _____

F. COMMUNICATIONS

F-1.   Are salary increases and performance rewards clearly explained in terms of the employee's individual contribution to overall goals?
        ☐ Always   ☐ Sometimes   ☐ Never   ☐ Unknown

F-2.   Do performance appraisal interviews produce surprises or expose major misunderstandings between supervisors or employees?
        ☐ Always   ☐ Sometimes   ☐ Never   ☐ Unknown

F-3.   Do you intend to use pay rewards as feedback to communicate the organization's strategic goals, objectives and philosophy and to reinforce those who best achieve them?
        ☐ Always   ☐ Sometimes   ☐ Never   ☐ Unknown

F-4.   What is the level of importance you place on the above objective?
        ☐ High   ☐ Medium   ☐ Low

F-5.   What degree of success has been achieved?
        ☐ High   ☐ Medium   ☐ Low

F-6.   What was the degree of difficulty encountered in attaining that level of success?
        ☐ High   ☐ Medium   ☐ Low

Other comments: _____

G. RETENTION AND TURNOVER

G-1.   Do you retain the employees you want to keep?
        ☐ Always   ☐ Sometimes   ☐ Never   ☐ Unknown

G-2.   Are you able to terminate the employees you want to replace?
        ☐ Always   ☐ Sometimes   ☐ Never   ☐ Unknown

G-3.   Are key performers likely to get offers of more pay from other organizations?
        ☐ Always   ☐ Sometimes   ☐ Never   ☐ Unknown

G-4.   Did your top executives come up from the ranks of your organization?
        ☐ Always   ☐ Sometimes   ☐ Never   ☐ Unknown

G-5.   Are the advancement opportunities of valuable workers blocked by the presence of unpromotable superiors?
☐ Always   ☐ Sometimes   ☐ Never   ☐ Unknown

G-6.   Do you test the ability of employees to handle new responsibilities before they are promoted or reassigned?
☐ Always   ☐ Sometimes   ☐ Never   ☐ Unknown

G-7.   Have you identified backups for key positions?
☐ Always   ☐ Sometimes   ☐ Never   ☐ Unknown

G-8.   What is the level of importance you place on restricting turnover to only those employees you are happy to lose?
☐ High   ☐ Medium   ☐ Low

G-9.   What degree of success has been achieved?
☐ High   ☐ Medium   ☐ Low

G-10. What was the degree of difficulty encountered in attaining that level of success?
☐ High   ☐ Medium   ☐ Low

Other comments: _____

H. COST EFFECTIVENESS

H-1.   Do you regularly confirm that your total compensation package (pay, life & health insurance, pension, perquisites, etc.) is valued by your employees?
☐ Always   ☐ Sometimes   ☐ Never   ☐ Unknown

H-2.   Do you regularly review the cost-efficiency of your fringe benefit and perquisite programs, to know the price is reasonable?
☐ Always   ☐ Sometimes   ☐ Never   ☐ Unknown

H-3.   What is the level of importance you place on providing the maximum value for each dollar spent on compensation?
☐ High   ☐ Medium   ☐ Low

H-4.   What degree of success has been achieved in getting your money's worth for the compensation you pay?
☐ High   ☐ Medium   ☐ Low

H-5.   What was the degree of difficulty encountered in attaining that level of success?

☐ High   ☐ Medium   ☐ Low

Other comments: _____

I. SOCIAL CONCERN

I-1.   Are employees reasonably well-protected from financial catastrophe and provided post-employment security by your "safety net" fringe benefit programs?
       ☐ Always   ☐ Sometimes   ☐ Never   ☐ Unknown

I-2.   What is the level of importance you place on offering reasonable protection for sick, disabled or retired employees?
       ☐ High   ☐ Medium   ☐ Low

I-3.   What degree of success has been achieved in delivering the intended level of care?
       ☐ High   ☐ Medium   ☐ Low

I-4.   What was the degree of difficulty encountered in attaining that level of success?
       ☐ High   ☐ Medium   ☐ Low

Other comments: _____

J. ADMINISTRATIVE EASE

J-1.   Do supervisors demonstrate, by their actions, a clear and accurate understanding of the personnel/pay policies they must follow and apply?
       ☐ Always   ☐ Sometimes   ☐ Never   ☐ Unknown

J-2.   Are supervisors able to handle their personnel management responsibilities without diverting too much time from other essential tasks?
       ☐ Always   ☐ Sometimes   ☐ Never   ☐ Unknown

J-3.   What is the level of importance you place on keeping personnel and pay management systems and procedures simple and easy to administer by supervisors?
       ☐ High   ☐ Medium   ☐ Low

J-4.   What degree of success has been achieved in keeping personnel and pay management systems and procedures sufficiently easy to administer?
       ☐ High   ☐ Medium   ☐ Low

J-5.   What was the degree of difficulty encountered in attaining that level of success?

☐ High   ☐ Medium   ☐ Low

Other comments: _____

How to Turn Checklist Answers Into Practical Solutions

The answers to the checklist can be computerized, word-processed or otherwise summarized for comparison. It is simpler and easier to complete than the narrative form, with specific questions whose answers point to problems and remedies.

Questions of fact are asked before broader opinions are requested. For example, if the answers in the COMPETITIVENESS section (A), show that

- the manager can't hire competent people at the rate paid to current employees,

- the organization has no idea what other competing firms pay,

- *and* it is considered vital for your pay to be highly competitive,

then it becomes rather obvious that the company has not been very successful in achieving success in "pay competitiveness." The likely causes of the problem and the potential solutions now become clear: you need to survey your competition and find a way to either increase your hiring rates or persuade job candidates that your lower-paying jobs are actually more attractive than the immediate cash would suggest.

What All Three Diagnostic Techniques Have in Common: They Identify Needs

Both the narrative and the checklist audit forms will confirm areas where general agreement exists, will expose inconsistencies and will identify areas where the most urgent remedial action is required.

Applied to a representative sample of managers or other employees, these audit forms can give an interesting picture of how people view the management systems and techniques of the firm. Such perceptions must be dealt with. You can have the best programs, forms and procedures in the world and still fail to meet your goals if employees (and particularly managers and supervisors) lack confidence in them.

How Correctly Identifying the Causes of Performance Problems Permits the Proper Solutions

Managers cannot afford to act in the dark. These audit procedures are examples of how you can shed light on the actual perceptions and beliefs of key decision-makers. Until those at the top have agreed on the course of action to be followed by others and communicated the objectives and their priority, no one can manage performance effectively ...because the desired performance has not yet been identified.

Once senior management is united in its concept of primary goals and their relative priorities, then people-managers can proceed to direct action towards those objectives. Both the diagnostic and the audit procedures will help to verify whether managers and supervisors truly understand what is wanted; these methods will also point to areas where things are not going right and will suggest the steps to correct problems.

The next chapter shows how you to set, communicate and review performance plans that will correct existing problems and, by anticipating, prevent others in the future.

Chapter 3:

PLANNING TECHNIQUES FOR SUCCESSFUL PERFORMANCE

Why Careful Preparation Pays Off

There are always more ways to do something wrong than there are to do it right. So, let people know what is wanted from them.

Merely turning people loose to "do their thing" can be an invitation to chaos when "the thing" that needs doing requires specific results or close cooperation. People are far more likely to produce the right results with the benefit of planning, communication and feedback review by a thoughtful manager.

This chapter shows how performance planning, communication and review can be done to increase the probability that effective performance will take place. The simple steps will provide information for action and create opportunities to improve work results.

The Three Parts in a Successful Performance Plan

What you need is not just a piece of paper, but a living plan. Like any other living organism, an effective plan requires constant care to keep it alive throughout the entire period for which it was initially created.

First, recognize that there are three parts to the performance planning process.

1. Planning

The Nature and Purpose of Planning

Planning involves preparation and direction. It is the process of identifying goals and objectives which will be targeted for achievement by employees. Without planned targets, employees may act aimlessly or inaccurately; and information on performance results will be impossible, meaningless or misleading. Workers must know their target, where the bulls-eye sits and what the margin of acceptable error is. Without a plan that defines the goal, there is no way to change performance in a way that assures that the adjusted future performance will actually be better than before.

How to Plan When Making a Plan

With a plan, you are pointing out what must be done and how. The actions employees take and the results they produce can be compared against what was planned, communicated through feedback (sometimes resulting in the plan itself being reviewed and altered), and adjustments made in either the plan or the work methods to be followed. Those adjustments can be alterations in the target objectives, actions to remedy employee competence issues, steps to gather more data for analysis, improvements in the resources dedicated to the work goal, more appropriate consequences for proper performance, or new methods to give and receive feedback.

2. Communication

The Role of Communication in the Planning Process

Communication flows through all aspects of performance management. The exchange of information is basic to the planning process; it is often part of the performance action itself; it is essential to appraisal and training steps. Communication is absolutely integral to goal planning, process and output review, performance feedback and appraisal, counseling, rewarding, disciplining, terminating, etc. Managing performance is basically a series of communication actions.

The Types of Communications Used in Planning

Communications can take all sorts of forms: written, verbal, body language, pictures, graphs, etc. It can come from the manager or from the daily work itself. The point is that the employee is kept informed of his or her work expectations and how he or she is doing against the planned results required for organizational success.

3. Review

How Reviews Keep Plans Alive and Well

Review is the observation and communication of work results. Every management step is subject to review; and the review process is at the core of actions to provide feedback, appropriate consequences and corrective measures.

Once a performance plan has been made, it must be regularly reviewed to assure that it remains valid and realistic. If circumstances change and the objectives must be modified, the plan should be updated to match the new reality. For the plan to have any value, the current version must also be communicated to the affected employees. Even the best plan will be ineffective if it is merely filed away as a historical document rather than kept up to date as a current action plan.

Performance Management Tip

A valid current Performance Plan is both a **positive** and a **defensive** tool of great value.

It confirms understanding of what should be done and how it should be accomplished, so both parties will know what is expected and how success is defined.

It also documents mutual expectations, protecting the supervisor from charges that "you never told me what you wanted." A reasonable and legitimate performance plan that has been communicated to the employee in advance is invaluable; if used as the basis for periodic reviews, it will support personnel management decisions and reduce argument.

To get maximum value from a performance plan, top management must endorse it as an accurate statement of their desires and must allow you to keep the specific details of the plan current.

What to Do When Detailed Plans Are Discouraged

If you anticipate resistance or difficulty in defining or renewing initial plan details, take the initiative by submitting a "tentative" working plan for others to review, edit and correct. Make it clear that unless they have specific alterations or changes to suggest, the tentative plan will be put into effect on a certain date.

It is important (particularly when the organization has little experience or a high degree of discomfort with detailed plans) to present the performance plan to both upper management and the employee as a general outline of initial expectations, subject to modification and change as circumstances warrant.

In a fast-changing work environment, highly detailed plans can have a very short life span. Initial plans that contain elements which depend on conditions that are likely to change must be closely monitored and regularly updated to reflect reality.

Never promise what you cannot deliver. Unless you are confident that you will have enough time and information to periodically revise and re-communicate plan details that are likely to change, it is safer to keep the performance plan broad enough to last through a year without substantial revision. A brief general plan can always be expanded or made more specific, but it is much harder to do the opposite without losing credibility.

The Way to Make Performance Plans that Work

Performance Plans can be as simple or as elaborate as you want them to be. Experience shows that you should start with simple plans. Once the utility of simple performance plans has been proven and established, you can always refine them, expand their scope, add more complex detail and embellish or customize them as you please.

How the Planning and Goal Setting Cycle Operates

Overall strategic plans are created to define the goals and objectives for the entire organization. After endorsement by the top executives, the "official" goals are passed on down to a succession of lower levels in the enterprise. As the goals filter down, they are refined into increasingly more specific terms and detailed form.

Why Goals Are Like a Waterfall

The flow of goals and objectives through an organization is much like a "cascade" of water over a cliff where the water splashes on rocks below and separates into more separate streams and finally into tiny rivulets. No matter how unique the eventual trickle may appear, it came from the same original source and still operates to nourish the thirsty ground. To continue the analogy, the water will collect and eventually be absorbed to condense again into moisture that returns as rain to once more feed the cascade. In the same way, the results of small work groups provide feedback which affects the strategic planning of the top management group.

Business planning or goal setting provides the direction needed to keep performance oriented towards the right objectives. Corporate goals are broken down into division goals which are divided into department goals which are translated into section goals which are refined into individual worker goals, plans and tasks. The process is simple and logical.

How Goals Change Form and Require Different Plans as They Are Passed Down to Different Levels

When a goal such as "a higher return on stockholder investment" is defined at the top of the organization, each level of management modifies that overall goal into increasingly smaller, more specific goals. And each of those specific goals are addressed by increasingly detailed plans that define the precise results needed from each operating level. Just watch what happens...

Shareholders	Want a higher return on their investment.
Board of Directors	Sets a goal of increasing stock dividends by 5%.
Chief Executive	Plans to increase profits by 3% and cut costs by 2%.
Sales Manager	Sets a goal of increasing sales by 6%, planning to accept slightly lower unit profit margins, while reducing the cost of sales by 8%.
Area Sales Representative	Sets a goal of 10% more sales with 10% lower expenses by pushing low-margin products and cutting travel expenses by telephoning rather than visiting repeat customers who do not require a sales pitch in person.

Notice that GOALS are statements of *what* will be accomplished, while PLANS are the descriptions, blueprints and action steps of **how** it will be done.

There is a clear progressionary cycle. Each goal requires an action plan. Each action plan produces new, more specific goals which must be achieved to fulfill the larger plan. Each specific goal calls for more detailed plans, etc., until you reach the level of individual tasks and activities; and even the smallest, most routine task is also subject to goals and plans as to its objectives and methods.

Techniques to Define Meaningful Performance Goals

Goals are targets. They are the objectives you pursue. In the work world, they are the performance results for which someone is responsible or accountable.

Goals and objectives are the conditions that are desired to exist in the future. They are descriptions written today of what tomorrow should look like.

The Three Best Ways to Organize and Describe Goals

There are a number of ways to classify, describe and define performance expectations. Three of the best methods are illustrated here.

1.   Break Goals Down Into Areas of Responsibility

Goals and objectives (desired outcomes) are usually set in terms of major responsibility areas. Organizing your thoughts according to the types of results that are expected will greatly simplify the goal setting process.

Return on Investment	Cost Control	Labor Relations
Sales Volume	Administration	Shipping
Profit	Marketing	Data Processing
Training	Purchasing	Maintenance
Manufacturing	Safety	Engineering
Employment	Customer Relations	Budgeting
Product Development	Supervision	Quality
Inventory Control	Personnel Development	Advertising
Facilities	Communications	Gov't Compliance
Lobbying	Product Management	Research
Patents	Records	Legal Affairs

The list is endless. There are as many ways to describe areas of responsibility and accountability as there are organizations that expect results. Every employee has numerous areas of responsibility; each contributes a piece to the total of all actions that exist in the enterprise.

2. Consider the Types of Goals

Goals can also be classified, for the sake of convenience, into **routine, problem-solving, innovative** and **personal** types. This is another way to organize your thoughts and stimulate ideas about how you can best describe what a job demands.

1. **Routine** goals are the typical basic objectives and tasks that are standard expectations for the job.
   - Get to work on time.
   - Meet the daily production schedule.
   - Answer the phone before the second ring.
   - Satisfy contract specifications.
   - Prepare the weekly expense report.
   - Make twelve sales calls a month.
   - Submit an annual budget.
   - Approve time cards.

2. **Problem-Solving** goals deal with activities that require substantial problem resolution, remedial steps or improvement efforts to change the current situation. When something goes wrong with the performance of a routine goal, it can quickly move into the problem-solving category.
   - Handle employee grievances at the second step.
   - Investigate high product reject rates within two days.
   - Reduce turnover among key employees to 5%.
   - Hold travel expenses to $2,000 a month.
   - Negotiate mutually-acceptable budgets.
   - Represent the company during tax audits by the Internal Revenue Service.

3. **Innovative** goals involve creative efforts directed towards special challenges (opportunities, of course) that require imagination or unique approaches to produce results. These assignments are never routine or repetitive.
   - Prepare the company's first emergency evacuation plan.
   - Write a new employee discipline policy by year-end.
   - Design a plan to prevent hostile take-over of the corporation.
   - Improve on Einstein's start towards a unified field theory.
   - Research the market prospects for new products in the year 2000.
   - Cut fabrication costs by 25% this quarter.

4. **Personal** goals are individual employee development actions to increase competence, improve skills, enhance career growth prospects, etc.; they are

generally recommended and encouraged by the organization as valuable for both current performance and future potential promotions. Employees are usually not held accountable for the completion of personal goals unless they are required to be met as a valid condition of employment.

- Attend a course on personal computer use in June.
- Begin work on an advanced degree.
- Prepare a personal career plan.
- Improve interpersonal communications skills.
- Become active in a local professional society.

Every job does not automatically involve every type of goal, nor is there necessarily any required balance, proportion or ratio of one type to another. A receptionist might have no **innovative** goals or objectives, while a legislator will have many.

3. How to Classify Goals by Subject Matter

Another way to classify goals is in terms of their subject matter: whether they deal primarily with people, data or things. Of course, such goals overlap. Everyone works with people to some extent; handling data or information requires contact with people and dealing with things; working with things also involves using data and dealing with people. But the prime object of a goal can usually be associated with one area more than the others.

People goals call for interactions with human beings and other creatures.	**Data or Information** goals deal with thoughts, facts, ideas, observations.	**Things** goals deal with materials, objects, machines, tools.
Manage	Compute	Manipulate
Help	Design	Repair
Lead	Improve	Use
Guide	Organize	Transport
Counsel	Evaluate	Operate
Consult	Plan	Produce
Advise	Research	Paint
Persuade	Solve	Build

Ways to Use All the Category Methods

Thinking of how goals fall into these different kinds of categories will help you identify all the things that must be accomplished for work output to equal "proper performance."

These goal-setting methods can be used individually or all together. Each classification method may suggest the same kind of objective. For example, "Enforce company attendance rules" is a **supervisory** responsibility involving a **routine** goal which **deals with people**.

The Three Steps to Turn Goals into Effective Performance Plans

Taking goal statements and converting them into performance plans that make sense is a three-step process.

1. **Use the short summary goal statements to define plan needs:**
   - what should happen,
   - what should be the outcome or the end result,
   - what condition should exist after effective performance has been delivered.

2. **Specify measurement criteria for goal attainment:**

Quality	the degree of accuracy, maximum error rate, indicators of subjective satisfaction, etc.
Quantity	number, volume, rate, percentage, ratio, proportion, count, frequency, etc.
Time	length of time in seconds, minutes, hours, days, weeks, months, etc., deadlines and temporal sequences ("before...", "when..." or "after..."), etc.
Cost	amount of money, budget, profit, margin, investment, cost of materials or resources, etc.

3. **Communicate the final goals and objectives, along with their relative priorities. Stating Priorities is a High Priority.** If all the planned goals have equal importance, their priority levels will all be the same. But if a few goals are far more important than others, be sure that their relative priorities are clarified to the employee. **When all things are not equal....**
   - Separate goals into "must" and "want" categories: those which absolutely must be achieved and those you want done but whose

achievement is not essential.
- Rank goals and objectives in order of importance.
- Use weights to show the relative priority.
- Tie rewards values to specific outcomes in a way that reinforces the communication of goal priorities: i.e., "continued employment depends on..."; "promotional qualification is contingent on..."; "raises will be based on..."

Some of those elements were applied in the goal samples shown under the **Types of Goals**.

Why You Should Show Importance With Priorities

Some jobs carry more responsibility for certain "standard" activities than other jobs. While all employees may share a general obligation to pay attention to some common goals, the degree of attention required and its importance to the organization varies.

For example, everyone may have to be concerned about *cost control*, but that particular goal category is much more important to a budget analyst than it is to a clerk-typist. *Cost control* goals and objectives are vital to the budget analyst job. They are the reason that particular position exists. But cost control opportunities are more limited for the clerk-typist, whose job is rarely exposed to the kinds of activities that can make a major impact on total organizational costs.

The way goal importance varies by job should be reflected by different weights or priorities. Objectives dealing with cost control might be identified as "A" priorities for the budget analyst, with those work results weighted to constitute 75% of the overall performance evaluation. On the other hand, cost control goals might be "C" priorities with a 10% overall weight for the clerk whose opportunities to affect costs are strictly limited. The clerk-typist is more likely to have the highest priorities and weights placed on production activities that deal with quality, quantity and timeliness, rather than cost.

Performance Management Tip

Never underestimate the ability of people to misunderstand your priorities. Document and communicate the primary goals and objectives of each job, so there can be no doubt or question about what comes first.

You can't afford to allow employees to guess about what is most

---

important when the wrong guess will cripple productivity.

Failure to plan, communicate, confirm and review priorities makes the manager at least partially responsible for the well-intentioned errors of subordinates.

Positive results are much easier to produce when employees who are constantly faced with a large number of tasks know what is most important.

How to Create Clear and Measurable Goals That Are Easier to Understand

Goals and objectives become more real and attainable when they are defined and communicated in terms of the measurable outcomes that will be visible when they are completed. In other words, make sure the worker will know when the work has been done right!

The Best Goal Statements Identify Standards of Performance

The preferred goal statement contains clear and **measurable** standards of performance. Other terms used for *performance standards* include *criteria, result levels, expectation categories, indicators of performance adequacy, levels of achievement, evaluation definitions* and *output classes.* Any term can be used. The idea of *measurement* means to identify the overt signs by which all parties will be able to recognize the nature and the value of the work results.

Illustrations of How Measurement Criteria Make Goals Crystal-Clear

You will notice how much clearer goals appear when measurement criteria are added to define specific expectations. "By October 1, hire three new clerks whose combined salaries do not exceed $50,000" is far more meaningful than "Handle hiring."

The goal statement, "By October 1, hire three new clerks whose combined salaries do not exceed $50,000,"

- ▸ has an implied **quality** standard (pick people good enough to pass the competence screening tests and win the management approvals for employment)
- ▸ specifies a **quantity** of **three** clerks to be hired
- ▸ identifes a **time** frame ("by October 1") for completion

▸ defines the **cost** limit at $50,000.

Why "Measurements" Do Not Always Have to Be Numbers

Numbers are not always necessary as a measurement criteria. Numbers are nice because they appear to be so precise and final; but accountants and statisticians know better: numbers can be "fiddled" and are affected by many factors. If proper performance absolutely must match a numeric figure, like a budget limit, then a number is the best standard of measurement.

Many performance criteria cannot be easily subjected to numeric analysis. How can you measure the quality of a flavor chemist's work with numbers? Well, you can put numbers on some work outputs:

- the number of tests conducted
- the budget limit for lab equipment
- the time schedules for project completion
- the percentage of new flavor products approved for sale

As shown, even the quality of work can, in some senses, be expressed in numbers. But **subjective measures** are also possible and often preferable, such as:

▹ how well the chemist complied with government regulatory standards
▹ the quality of detailed research documentation that would permit another flavor chemist to take over the project with little lost time or effort
▹ the degree of approval received from flavor judges and critics
▹ whether the scientist is sufficiently articulate and poised enough to persuade the Board to approve additional expenditures for new research facilities

Whatever Can Be Mutually Understood is "Measurable"

Anything that can be described so that the boss and the subordinate both understand what it means can be used as a *measurement* criteria. **Mutual agreement on the understanding** is the desired end when you set performance standards for goals and objectives. As long as all parties involved have the same performance expectation, then the work plan is clear enough to use.

It is not uncommon for a boss to tell a subordinate, "I don't know exactly what will constitute satisfactory performance of this goal right now, but let's discuss it as the year progresses." That is perfectly acceptable, since both parties understand that the performance plan criteria will be refined in the future.

A decision to defer the precise definition of plan success measurements may be necessary when, for example, the goal is to "satisfy the Vice President," and it is yet unclear just what she wants. In that situation, the best course of action is probably to make a **problem-solving** plan to achieve the goal of finding out what will satisfy the Vice President.

Further details on ways to clarify goals and objectives so everyone will know how to recognize successful performance are in the chapter on communications and feedback.

Examples That Make Goals Come Alive

A Sample Combining General and Specific Objectives

A large electric utility separated their goals into three major performance areas: GENERAL PERSONAL PERFORMANCE OBJECTIVES, GENERAL MANAGEMENT PERFORMANCE OBJECTIVES, and SPECIFIC POSITION OBJECTIVES.

The GENERAL objectives were all stated in broad terms that could apply to all employees, while the SPECIFIC objectives varied according to the individual job and position. And each goal performance area carried a fixed weight throughout the organization.

All Goal Performance Areas, With Priority Weights

GOAL PERFORMANCE AREA	AREA WEIGHT
A. General Personal Performance Obectives	3
B. General Management Performance Objectives	4
C. Achievement of Specific Position Objectives	5

Since their fixed weights added up to 12, it meant that general personal objectives (dealing with individual "input" skills and behaviors) received the smallest overall priority. General management activities were slightly more important; but the specific bottom-line objectives which were customized for each individual were given the highest priority.

This was deliberately done to emphasize the critical importance of achieving exactly what each position was expected to do in order for the success of the entire organization. How each performer did it, in terms of management techniques and personal strengths, was given less importance.

Each performance goal area was subdivided into standard objective statements that could be further detailed for all management jobs, most professional/clerical jobs, and many labor jobs. Sub-weights ranging from a low of 0 (not applicable) to a high of 5 (critical to this area) were specified to control how much relative importance could be placed on each element within an area.

A. GENERAL PERSONAL PERFORMANCE OBJECTIVES
Total Area Weight = 3

Objectives	Sub-Weight
1. Maintain and improve technical skills	3
2. Show knowledge of all operations of own unit and relevant operations of other groups	4
3. Relate all work to corporate goals	4
4. Demonstrate recognition of group/section role in the overall corporate mission	5
5. Represent group/section needs and interests to senior management	2
6. Personally provide authoritative advise and effective reports to other groups	3
7. Communicate a positive image of the Company in dealings with people outside the organization	4

B. GENERAL MANAGEMENT PERFORMANCE OBJECTIVES
Total Area Weight = 4

Objectives	Sub-Weight
1. Develop policies and implementation strategies	5
2. Plan work and set priorities	5
3. Organize and coordinate group efforts	5
4. Establish specific goals and objectives	4
5. Improve overall organization strength	4
6. Develop subordinates	4
7. Maintain positive work environment for optimum employee productivity	3

C. ACHIEVEMENT OF SPECIFIC POSITION OBJECTIVES

Total Area Weight = 5

Objectives	Sub-Weight
1. Position accountabilities from Position Description	5
2. Contribution to corporate goals	3
3. Achievement of section goals	4
4. Contribution to corporate performance indicator objectives	2
5. Achievement of section performance indicator objectives	3

This approach gave all managers clear guidelines on what performance areas top management considered most important. It also suggested the types of goals managers were expected to create and how much weight could be placed on each.

The objective with the highest sub-weight in the goal area with the highest weight was C-1, Position accountabilities from Position Description. That broadcasts the message that the specific detailed duties that define the job are expected to carry the greatest priority. At the other extreme, A-5, lobbying senior management for your group, is the lowest priority: it has the lowest sub-weight in the area with the lowest area weight.

That particular approach has the advantage of consistency, paid at the price of detailed clarity. It permits managers to start their goal-setting process with the benefit of standard information on what top management expected, leaving the precise details of exactly what constitutes successful performance up to the managers and supervisors.

A Sample That Specifies Measurement Criteria

The next example goes beyond the previous one to better identify exact performance criteria.

One engineering design firm decided that all their goals and objectives fit into four broad categories: PROFIT, QUALITY, CUSTOMER SATISFACTION and CORPORATE COOPERATION.

Next, for each type of job, they identified exactly what they meant by those general terms: the things that would indicate success or failure in each category and where they would find information to measure the level of achievement.

This sample shows how their broad goals were applied to a supervising consulting engineer in a branch office.

Sample Goal Objectives and Performance Criteria

GOAL CATEGORY AREA	SOURCE OF PERFORMANCE INFORMATION
Profit	profit contribution reports return on assets reports reports on net fees billed
Quality	reviews of project design proposals panel judgments of completed projects accuracy of forecasts data on subordinate development reports on procedural compliance
Customer Satisfaction	direct feedback from clients amount of referral business requests for this individual
Corporate Cooperation	records of assistance to other offices amount of business referred to others degree of service on corporate committees responses to information requests

Next, the company proceeds to assign priorities to the goals and to define specific performance standards.

In this case, the degree of importance or priority for the goal category is shown by a numeric weight, although it could also be illustrated by a letter (A,B,C) or a phrase (High, Medium, Low). The advantage of numeric weights is that they can be multiplied against overall performance evaluation scores to precisely assure that rewards will be granted proportional to the importance and value of the results.

Once the sources of information about performance are identified as they were above, it is easy to set specific objectives, defined in terms of the performance indicators.

Here are some specific objectives and performance standards for the PROFIT goal area, using only a few of the sources of performance information that could be applied as indicators.

Sample PROFIT Goal Ojectives and Standards

GOAL CATEGORY	WEIGHT	PERFORMANCE INDICATOR	OBJECTIVE(S)	STANDARDS OF PERFORMANCE
Profit	40%	profit contribution reports	$200,000	under $200 K = 0 $180-220 K = 1 over $220 K = 3
		% increase in net fees	10% increase	increase under 8% = 0 increase around 10% = 1 increase over 12% = 3

Objectives can be further refined within goal categories to show just which specific objectives are considered most important.

For instance, if QUALITY goals carry 30% of the weight for this job, management can clearly communicate what types of work quality are emphasized by breaking down the QUALITY objectives into smaller pieces, each given a sub-weight. That demonstrates the relative importance of each separate objective that fits into the overall QUALITY goal category.

Quality Objectives Which Add Up to 30% of the Overall Rating

PERFORMANCE INDICATORS FOR QUALITY	SUB-WT	QUALITY OBJECTIVE(S)	STANDARDS OF PERFORMANCE
panel judgments of completed projects	25%	win approval and recognition	criticism = 0 approval = 1 award = 3
data on subordinate development	75%	develop competent subordinates who qualify for promotion	over 80% are promotable at year-end = excellent (3) 40-80% are promotable at year-end = good (1) under 40% are promotable at year-end = marginal (0)

That partial example shows a case where the supervisor will be notified that the development of promotable subordinates is three times more important than winning project competitions. The wise employee will recognize that if he or she wants to do well in the achievement of QUALITY goals, qualifying subordinates for promotion will carry more weight with the organization than a project award.

The exercise of boiling goals down into clear results you want to see, in terms everyone can recognize, will save time and trouble in the future. This step of the process gives the manager the opportunity to test preliminary ideas about goals and objectives before they are discussed with the employee.

The last example shows a situation where the initial version of the *standards of performance* for QUALITY objectives place a premium on subordinate development. But what if the supervisor has been assigned a group of subordinate employees who have truly reached the highest level their skills can support? If the raw material is not there, the supervisor might not be able to prepare the employees for promotion under any circumstances! Such a QUALITY objective would be patently unfair to the supervisor in that case and should be either given much less weight or restated in more reasonable terms. For instance, developing even one or two subordinates for promotion after they have been written off as "dead-ended" by others could be an outstanding performance result.

A Lesson on Reasonable Performance Expectations

The sports commentator Heywood Hale Broun covered the Boston Marathon every year for over twenty years. He said that there were always about a dozen contenders who had a realistic expectation of coming in first. But, back towards the end of the pack, there would be two middle-aged amateurs. Each year, as they bent over to tie their shoe laces, one would say to the other, "Well, Harry, I'll bet this year you throw up before I do!" That is a case of reasonable expectations.

Performance Management Tip

Never assign an objective whose achievement is impossible or beyond the control of the worker.

Be cautious about giving all people the same specific performance expectations, unless their circumstances are identical.

A Sample of Clerical Goals and Performance Objectives

The final example covers a typical clerical position. Every job, even that of a secretary whose duties vary according to the manager's needs, exists to produce output results which can be analyzed and converted into goals and performance objectives.

Performance Plan for a Secretary

Goal, Objective or Duty	Criteria for Satisfactory Goal Performance	Weight
1. Prepare double spaced manuscripts with occasional tables and figures, in a timely manner	Average number of pages produced per hour	.15
2. Complete manuscripts with a high degree of accuracy and minimal required revision	Average number of drafts before an acceptable final version was produced	.15
3. Produces single spaced letters, memos and correspondence less than one page long	Average number of complete sets (including envelopes and copies) per hour	.1
4. Sends accurate unreviewed final drafts, signing on behalf of manager	Average number of errors per letter/memo reported by recipients	.2
5. Keeps budget records; submits monthly summary to Accounting	Completeness and timeliness of reconciliation reports	.1
6. Maintain accurate budget records	Accuracy of reconciliation statements	.2
7. Performs other general secretarial duties (answers phone, makes appointments, orders supplies, etc.)	Accuracy, timeliness and feedback from visitors, clients and others contacted	.1

Again, the first step is to identify performance criteria that will serve as a mutually agreed-upon source of information about how well the task was completed. Then, specific performance standards can be established to confirm the type of actual results that will be considered good, bad or indifferent.

In the secretarial example, let's assume that a wide span of performance quality is possible and the organization asks for (or permits the manager to use) five different levels to measure performance:

If Performance is...	the Rating is...
Outstanding - results consistently far exceed satisfactory levels	4
Excellent - results clearly exceed satisfactory levels	3
Satisfactory - results meet the standards	2
Marginal - results only meet the minimum acceptance level	1
Unsatisfactory - results are below the minimum acceptable level	0

Then specific levels of work output results can be defined and associated with each performance level, to assure clear understanding of what constitutes what level of performance in each objective/duty area.

For example, for Goal/Objective/Duty number 1, dealing with the preparation of double spaced manuscripts, the standards of performance can be stated as in terms of the average number of pages completed per hour:

No. per Hour	Performance Level	Rating
under 5	Unsatisfactory	0
5	Marginal	1
6	Satisfactory	2
7	Excellent	3
8 or more	Outstanding	4

In the same way, the value of variable levels of goal achievement can be clarified in each of the other goal/objective areas.

The performance against Goal 6 objectives, dealing with the accuracy of budget reconciliation reports, could be measured by the number of months per year when the secretary's reports matched Accounting's records without any errors.

Perfect Months	Performance Level	Rating
5	Unsatisfactory	0
6	Marginal	1
8	Satisfactory	2
10	Excellent	3
12	Outstanding	4

It is always worth while to clarify goals, but clarifying goals and simultaneously describing each level of performance multiplies the effectiveness of the message. As shown in later chapters, the process of assigning ratings to different performance levels strengthens communications; it also improves feedback and permits more powerful motivation through reward reinforcement that is tied to pre-established performance expectations.

How to Put Goals Down on Paper

Once you have a good idea of the items that should be included in a performance plan, it is time to organize them on paper, so they can be revised, approved, documented and communicated.

Ways to Draft Goals and Objectives with the Accountability Management Worksheet

The **Accountability Management Worksheet** is a simple format for planning performance goals or objectives over a fixed period of time. The period of time it will cover is usually a fiscal year or the length of time before the employee's next overall performance review. If employee duties are expected to change soon, it may only cover the period of time during which the employee is on the current assignment or project.

It can be initially drafted by either the manager or the employee, but it should be discussed, revised and understood by both before being formally submitted for approval by the necessary levels of management. Even if it is not used as a formal "contract" covering all duties, such a document is an invaluable aid to confirm mutual understanding about what the employee is expected to do.

A Sample Detailed Objective Plan

A sample plan of objectives, citing the responsibility area, priority, general expectations and specific performance standards, with timetables for completion, illustrates the process.

You will note that priorities are identified as both alphabetically and numerically. The alphabetic scale used here is: A (vital/essential), B (important) and C (valuable). The numeric scheme further communicates the precise relative importance of each goal, showing how much weight the area will have in the final overall rating. Use either method (or both) to assure that the performer will know where her primary priorities lie.

Accountability Management Worksheet

Name: *R. Simpson*	Title: *Office Manager*
Department: *Administration*	Immediate Supervisor/Title: *G. Henson, Controller*

This Performance Objective Plan should be updated whenever a major change occurs.

Type of Goal or Objective	Performance Results that are expected and, if possible, the standards in terms of quality, quantity, time and/or cost.	Importance or Weight
1. Hold expenses to $175,000	Below $160,000 = Outstanding $170,000 = Exceptional $175,000 = Satisfactory Above $180,000 = Poor	A 30%
2. Supervise staff training	All trained by June = Outstanding All trained by December = Satisfactory	B 10%
3. Design new billing system	If accepted = Satisfactory (Detailed standards to be worked out later)	A 20%
4. Review subordinate work	Satisfactory = Written performance reviews submitted by November Exceptional = (above) + formal quarterly reviews Outstanding = (both above) + formal weekly reviews	B 10%
5. Keep performance plans current	Revisions communicated to employees and filed with boss when requested = Satisfactory Revisions made without prompting = Exceptional (last above) + alerted boss when/how old plans threatened to become obsolete = Outstanding	B 10%

6. Prepare plans for next year	Satisfactory = all plans approved by November	B
	Exceptional = all plans approved by Nov. with only minor changes	10%
	Outstanding = all plans approved by Nov. with no changes	
7. Participate in staff meetings	Rating will depend on attendance and quality of input, as determined by senior management observers	C
		5%
8. Other special assignments	(Specific goals and performance standards to be established and documented when needed)	C
		5%

Planned by	Date	Approved by	Date	Reviewed by	Date

The Kind of Messages That Can Be Sent With a Detailed Plan

This example makes it clear that the office manager should watch the budget carefully, since "expense control" is the top priority item, with 30% of the the overall performance rating riding on that one objective area.

On the other hand, "staff meetings" are clearly identified as being at the lowest priority level. If the office manager is forced to choose between attending a staff meeting and completing the design of a new billing system on time, it is obvious that the new billing system is far more important.

Performance Management Tip

Stick to 5% increments in Performance Plan priority weights. No one can tell the difference between an 18% and a 20% weight, so make life easier by rounding off weights to the nearest 5%.

Any goal or objective that is worth less than 5% of the total overall evaluation or priority weight in the Performance Plan is not worth listing separately.

If the activity is important enough to include in the plan but not, by itself, worth 5% of the whole job, then combine it with other minor expectations in a special section. For instance, a *Personal Development* category could list a number of goals like *improve attendance, pass professional certification test, stop smoking*, and *complete one approved night school course*; while none of those alone might be a significant portion of the job, together they could easily combine to be worth 5%.

What All the Planning Methods Have in Common

All the examples that have been presented show various ways to plan positive performance. Each sample demonstrates a different degree of specific information that can be communicated in a performance plan. Some are more elaborate and more detailed than others. In general, the more credible data the organization has about goals and performance criteria, the more specific the plan can be.

The samples also illustrate that planning must be accompanied by ongoing review, creating a cycle. The results of periodic reviews may lead to modifications in the performance plan. Interim progress against the objectives of the modified plan are again in turn periodically reviewed to assure that the plan remains reasonable and attainable, the performance standards are relevant and appropriate, and proper steps are taken to continue, improve, correct or remedy actual performance results. The cycle culminates in a year-end performance review summarizing the past performance and a new plan for the next year.

How Performance Is Planned and Reviewed Through a Year

A more complete example of an entire planning and review process, applied over the course of a year, is seen next.

The **Performance Planning and Review Sequence** describes the steps to taken through a typical year by a major corporation. While the demonstration example deals with an employee at a level far above that of "secretary," the principles are exactly the same for all jobs. The planning and review process can be applied in the identical manner for any kind of performance plan review. The only changes would be limited to the detailed job duties, goals and objectives. Reviews can be conducted for the purpose of a merit increase, a bonus award, a promotional decision, or merely to measure and communicate how much each employee contributed to total organizational results.

A Schedule of Eight Sequential Steps for Planning and Review

The Performance Planning and Review Sequence

What You Do at the Beginning of the Year

1. Establish performance objectives in each goal category, according to organizational needs and individual circumstances.
2. Place a priority weight on the overall goal categories and any subordinate performance objectives within each category.
   a. The weight shows the relative importance of each goal or objective and will be multiplied times the year-end rating to produce a weighted score for overall goal performance.
3. Prepare, discuss, set and communicate the weighted objectives and related standards of performance for all employees.
   a. Standards of performance are the conditions that must exist by year-end to earn each of the following descriptions:

Rating	Adjective	Level of Results Achieved
0	Inadequate	Below minimally acceptable levels
1	Good	Adequate, competent, satisfactory, at or slightly above required levels
3	Exceptional	Far above required levels

What You Can Do on an Optional Basis

1. (optional) Assign current position values to each job.
   a. A position value is a standard dollar amount selected for consistent internal equity and external competitiveness which applies to all people holding the same job without regard for the actual salary of any individual job-holder. It is the average value of the job to the Company, no matter who holds it.
   b. Final decisions on position values require the approval of the Human Resources/Compensation Department.
2. (when applicable) Explain that performance rewards will be distributed according to

    a. the size of the total merit/bonus budget pool (the "pie"); and

    b. the weighted overall performance scores times position value (each employee's "slice of the pie").

What You Must Do During the Year

6. Periodically review actual performance against objectives. Conduct periodic reviews whenever work output slips or at least once every three months.

    a. Make sure that the goal objectives and standards of performance remain valid; alter or adjust them as required/permitted, communicate any new or changed expectations.

    b. Confirm clear employee understanding of performance expectations and knowledge of how current performance results compare to standards.

What You Must Do at Year-End

7. Document overall performance, scoring and computing ratings; communicate and discuss results with employee; file annual review summary with Human Resources to support pay actions.

8. Plan, discuss, revise and communicate new performance objectives and weights for next year.

Detailed Procedures for the Plans Made at the Beginning of the Year

What the Initial Plan Should Contain

Shortly before the beginning of the performance period (usually a twelve-month year), the supervisor must establish and document the critical elements of the employee's performance plan:

☐ Goal Categories or Responsibility Areas
    o Financial/Profit
    o Quality
    o Customer Satisfaction
    o Compliance with Corporate Policies
    o Productivity
    o Employee Relations

- o (..or whatever other major categories/areas defined as vital by the Company)
☐ The priority weights (if any) placed on each Goal Category or Area.
☐ The specific objective(s) in each Area and the objective weights, if there is more than one objective in each Area.
☐ Performance indicators that will be used as sources of information on the adequacy of results: where one can look to track progress against goals and objectives.
☐ The levels of performance results (standards of performance) that will bring "exceptional," "good" and "inadequate" ratings.

This information must be communicated to the affected employee at the beginning of the performance period to assure a clear understanding of expectations. A copy shall be filed with corporate Human Resources for the same reason.

What the Plan Looks Like at the Beginning of the Year

A sample of the kind of information to be communicated at the beginning of the performance year follows, using only one Responsibility Area or Goal Category (Quality) as an example.

THIS DATA TO BE COMMUNICATED TO EMPLOYEE
AT THE BEGINNING OF THE   PERIOD.

OVERALL CATEGORY PERFORMANCE RATING WORKSHEET for _____

GOAL CATEGORY	CATEGORY WEIGHT	PERFORMANCE AREA	PERF. OBJECTIVES	STANDARDS OF PERFORMANCE	Obj. Weight	Obj. Rating	Wtd. Obj. Score
QUALITY	20	Project design excellence	Win approval and recognition	criticism = inadequate (0) general approval = good (1) public award = exceptional (3)	70		
		develop subordinates	achieve high relative ranking in a) number promoted on your recommendation b) subsequent performance of those promoted on your recommendation	To be determined by end-of-year relative ranking of all managers — bottom 1/4 = inadequate (0) top 1/4 = exceptional (3)	30		
					100		
					Total Obj. Weights	Total Wtd. Obj. Scores	

The sample **Overall Category Performance Rating Worksheet** details the 20% weight placed on "Quality" goals, defines the specific performance areas involved and lists the objective(s) in each. It also describes specific outcomes that will earn certain performance ratings under the "Standards of Performance" column and specifies the relative weights for each objective.

In this case, the highest priority in the Quality category is "Project design excellence," which carries 70% of the weight. "Develop subordinates" only gets 30% of the weight for the Quality area.

When the employee has this kind of information in hand at the beginning of the performance period, he or she knows what will be expected.

Detailed Procedures for the Year-End Review of Actual Plan Results

What the Final Review Should Contain

At the end of the performance period, the supervisor must document and communicate:

- ☐ The actual performance results for each goal/objective, compared against the expectation standards.
- ☐ Any narrative comments, particularly explanations of *how* and *why* the actual outcome took place and any special circumstances that should be taken into consideration.
- ☐ The final rating of performance against each objective and the overall rating. (In this case, using 3 for "exceptional," 1 for "good" and 0 for "inadequate").

Samples of How the Final Review Is Prepared and Documented

The expanded information on the fully completed PERFORMANCE APPRAISAL WORKSHEET is primarily intended for the use of the supervisor. It provides a place to organize observations, to document findings in detail and to explain the rating judgments that will be discussed and later summarized in a concise overall rating.

This information shall be:

- ☐ Reviewed and approved by the next management level above the supervisor performing the review.
- ☐ Reviewed and discussed with the employee.
- ☐ Entered onto the OVERALL CATEGORY PERFORMANCE RATING WORKSHEET for weighted scoring of the various ratings.

TO BE COMPLETED AT YEAR-END FOR DISCUSSION AND TO DETERMINE
RESULTS AND RATINGS FOR OVERALL CATEGORY PERFORMANCE RATING WORKSHEET.

PERFORMANCE APPRAISAL WORKSHEET for _____
FOR ANALYSIS OF RESULTS AGAINST OBJECTIVES

Area	Objective	Performance Indicators*	Results	Comments	Rating
Quality	Win approval of project design quality criticism = 0 award = 3	corporate design board opinion; peer reviews news/magazine stories; positive comments by architects & critics in other firms	liked by board; peers unimpressed; rave reviews; won two design awards	While the project was not up to the highest state-of-the-art design capabilities, that was due to budget restrictions. The final design was still much better than the public and our competitors are used to seeing.	3
	develop subordinates	year-end rank among managers on a) #promoted b) success of those recommended for promotion	Ranked in upper 50% of a) number promoted on his recommendation. and Ranked in top 10% in subsequent b) success rate of protogés.	Willing to invest time in training & development of subordinates for transfer and promotion to other units. His commitment to grooming future corporate talent has distracted him from achieving better short-term financial results with his unit. His rare gift for acting as an effective mentor should be encouraged by giving him more "development" and fewer "financial" responsibilities.	3

*sources of information on quality, quantity, time and/or cost
results which can be compared to expectations for performance appraisal.

This appraisal worksheet has space for expanded discussion points and comments that will back up and support the ratings on individual objectives.

It guides the supervisor in making each decision. It also allows more space for discussion notes and observations that explain and qualify the ratings, one by one, without being influenced by weights.

Next, the OVERALL CATEGORY PERFORMANCE RATING WORKSHEETS are completed, using the objective ratings detailed in the PERFORMANCE APPRAISAL WORKSHEETS.

Two of those worksheets are shown, documenting results in two areas, "Quality" and "Profit."

OVERALL CATEGORY PERFORMANCE RATING WORKSHEET for _____

GOAL CATEGORY	CATEGORY WEIGHT	PERFORMANCE AREA	PERF. OBJECTIVES	STANDARDS OF PERFORMANCE	Obj. Weight	Obj. Rating	Wtd. Obj. Score
QUALITY	20	Project design excellence	Win approval and recognition	Criticism = inadequate (0) general approval = good (1) public award = exceptional (3)	70	3	210
		develop subordinates	achieve high relative ranking in a) number promoted on your recommendation b) subsequent performance of those promoted on your recommendation	To be determined by end-of-year relative ranking of all managers — bottom 1/4 = inadequate (0) top 1/4 = exceptional (3)	30	3	90
					100		300
					Total Obj. Weights		Total Wtd. Obj. Scores

Overall Category Performance Rating =

Total Wtd. Obj. Scores __300__ divided by

Total Obj. Weights __100__ = __3__ times

Category Weight __20__ = __60__.

OVERALL CATEGORY PERFORMANCE RATING WORKSHEET for _____

THIS TO BE COMPLETED AT YEAR-END.

GOAL CATEGORY	CATEGORY WEIGHT	PERFORMANCE AREA	PERF. OBJECTIVES	STANDARDS OF PERFORMANCE	Obj. Weight	Obj. Rating	Wtd. Obj. Score
PROFIT	60	% increase in net fees	10% increase	increase under 8% = inadequate (0) / of 10% = good (1) / over 12% = exceptional (3)	25	1	25
		profit contribution	$20,000,000	under $20M = inadequate (0) / $20-25M = good (1) / over $25M = exceptional (3)	10	3	30
		return on assets	30%	under 22% = inadequate (0) / over 40% = exceptional (3)	15	0	0
		% profit improvement	8%	under 8% = inadequate (0) / 9-12% = good (1) / 13+% = exceptional (3)	50	3	150
					100		205
					Total Obj. Weights		Total Wtd. Obj. Scores

Overall Category Performance Rating =
Total Wtd. Obj. Scores **205** divided by
Total Obj. Weights **100** = **2.05** times
Category Weight **60** = **123**.

These sheets are the same ones used at the beginning of the year; but now they have *Objective Ratings* and *Weighted Objective Scores* from the supervisory review of actual year-end performance results.

For example, in the PERFORMANCE APPRAISAL WORKSHEET for the "Quality" goals, the supervisor detailed the reasons for ratings of "3" (exceptional) in both performance objectives. Those ratings were transferred onto the OVERALL CATEGORY PERFORMANCE RATING WORKSHEET for Quality, where the various *Objective Weights* were multiplied against the *Objective Ratings*.

The first quality objective was weighted as "70," which was multiplied times the rating of "3" to produce a *Weighted Objective Score* of 210.

The second quality objective was weighted as "30," which was multiplied times the rating of "3" to produce a *Weighted Objective Score* of 90.

The *Total Weighted Objective Scores* for the Quality goal category was 210 plus 90, which equals 300. The *Total Objective Weights* for the Quality goal category was the first weight, 70, plus the second weight, 30, which equals 100.

As shown on the bottom left of the Quality Category Worksheet, the Overall Category Performance Rating is the Total Weighted Objective Scores (300) divided by Total Objective Weights (100) times the Category Weight of 20, which comes out with a total category rating of 60.

The same procedure was followed with for the Profit Category, where there were four objectives with various weights and ratings for an overall Profit Goal Category weighted at 60. That computation produced an Overall Category Performance Rating of 123.

How Overall Total Performance Is Computed

The Way to Use Separate Ratings for a Summary Appraisal

Finally, the Summary Performance Appraisal can take place, using the weighted ratings from each OVERALL CATEGORY.

In the examples using weights, overall performance against goals and objectives is computed by adding the Overall Category Performance Ratings from each Goal Category and dividing that number by the sum of the Category Weights.

For the sake of simplicity, let's assume that the Profit and Quality goal categories covered in the previous examples were the only ones used for the entire year. That gives us the following data:

Goal Category	Category Weight	Overall Category Performance Rating
Quality	20	60
Profit	60	123
Totals	80	183

How a Little Math Yields an Impartial Weighted Score

The total Category Performance Ratings (183) are divided by the total Category Weights (80) to derive the final overall weighted performance rating of 2.2875, which is well above the 1 for "good" performance and just below the 3 for "exceptional" performance.

Of course, adding more goal categories with additional weights and extra objectives will change the numbers; so will a different rating scheme than 0, 1 and 3. The procedure for computing a precise overall weighted rating remains the same. No matter how many goal categories and objective areas you create, as long as you use one consistent rating scale for actual performance results against objectives, you can follow this same method to come up with a summary performance rating that accurately reflects the value of performance against goals with various priorities and weights.

The Advantages of Weighting Performance Goals

This "mathematical" goal review method is extremely useful for a supervisor who wants to assure that people are aware of the different priorities (weights) placed on different tasks they must perform.

The weighting process gives credit (and emphasis) where it is due, preventing employees from getting the wrong message about the importance of attaining various goals. Instead of letting people believe that complying with the dress code is just as important as completing vital projects on time, it allows you to distinguish between objectives, placing a higher priority/weight on one when it is first announced and when it is last evaluated.

It is also a valuable tool for supervisors and managers who want to take pains to assure employees that they will be evaluated and rewarded in the most objective and impartial manner possible.

Making Plans That Fit Your Unique Work Environment

Performance plans can be general or precise, broad or limited. The format that is chosen as "right" depends on the philosophy and environment of the organization.

Some firms exhibit a strongly authoritarian style summarized in Frederick the Great's statement, "Nobody thinks, everybody executes." For them, performance plans are detailed blueprints specifying exactly how a prescribed list of tasks are to be completed.

Why Detailed Plans Are Preferred by Some Firms

Highly detailed and specific plans are found in organizations where:
- decision making is centralized;
- authority is closely limited and jealously guarded;
- performance results must meet certain exact requirements;
- survival depends on predictable employee actions;
- failure to follow standard procedures has caused major problems in the past;
- the work output and process is repetitive and subject to little change;
- uncertainty is addressed by a laborious process of simplification;
- initiative is limited or discouraged;
- the work force is unskilled and/or not trusted;
- large numbers of employees perform similar tasks;
- a high degree of employee turnover is anticipated;
- rigid procedure manuals abound;
- operating circumstances are consistent or controllable;
- market share is stable;
- deviation from standard procedures could be disastrous.

Why General Plans Are Preferred by Other Firms

Other more entrepreneurial companies see plans as broad outlines whose details are to be filled in at the discretion of employees who are expected to exercise wide discretion.

Vague or general plans are characteristic of enterprises where:
- authority is decentrallized;
- key decisions must be made without formal guidance;

- specific performance needs are unknown or unpredictable;
- creativity and initiative are required and encouraged;
- employees are highly trained and experienced;
- people work in small but extremely competent teams;
- there have been few problems in the past;
- unique jobs are common, few people hold similar positions;
- employees have wide discretion to design their own jobs;
- there is little turnover;
- those closest to work information are trusted to use it properly;
- training and manuals provide guidelines rather than rigid rules;
- improvisation is the rule rather than the exception;
- flexibility is cultivated;
- there is high morale and inter-group cooperation;
- work conditions change rapidly and constantly;
- the organization is growing;
- there is a wide margin of acceptable error in work output needs;

What Your Particular Work Environment Demands in a Plan

While neither list is expected to be complete or final, it is clear that there are dramatic differences between the characteristics of companies that use different performance planning styles. Neither approach is necessarily right or wrong; that is relative to the needs and circumstances. The lists demonstrate why certain business conditions may require or permit a certain approach to performance planning.

In the real world, planning differences between these arbitrarily extreme examples are often not as polarized as they seem. Even the most flexible creative firm which prefers a "general direction" rather than a detailed plan needs to achieve specific financial objectives to survive; and the most rigid government contractor must face highly ambiguous challenges where exact performance needs cannot be precisely predicted in advance.

Also, terms like "precise" and "general" can be deceptive.

How Identical Words and Phrases Mean Different Things to Different Firms

"Follow standard operating procedures" can call for quite a lot of discretion when the procedural rule merely reads "make the best decision under the circumstances"

"Satisfy the boss" can be extremely easy to understand when the boss tells you every day exactly what is expected in your work results

The point is that plans must be made, communicated, reviewed, updated and fufilled for organizational goals and objectives to be achieved with some degree of efficiency by the workers. When those plans are clear and realistic, *from the viewpoint of the workers*, the work results will usually be better.

Chapter 4:

HOW TO CONDUCT PERFORMANCE REVIEWS AND APPRAISALS

The Purpose of Performance Reviews and Appraisals

While no one wants to upset or antagonize well-intentioned employees, careful and objective evaluations of work plans and results are essential. The organization has a right to know what it is getting for its investment in human resources. Management is responsible for directing, monitoring and controlling work performance. This is particularly important when the product or service provided by the organization depends on the work of a number of people, each doing their part to contribute to the overall success of the enterprise.

Employees, too, have a right to know what is expected from them, how well they meet those expectations, and what their prospective future is within the organization. The desired work output specified in the performance plan must be reviewed and appraised to give management sufficient information to answer those employee questions.

What Review and Appraisal Means

To "review" is to examine or inspect.
To "appraise" is to evaluate for a judgement.

The Secret to Avoiding Conflict: Focus on Work Results

The key to Performance Review and Appraisal is focusing on **work results**, not the personality of the worker. An effective supervisor uses Performance Appraisals to achieve work objectives, not to express personal feelings or to trade subjective accusations. The idea is to improve the excellence of the work team, not to vent, blame or condemn.

A businesslike and non-threatening approach gives the supervisor more flexibility and control over a mutually stressful situation. When you focus on specific facts rather than imputed personality traits, actual work results rather than broad behavioral characteristics... then the employee is more relaxed, receptive and encouraged to offer comments and suggestions. People have greater respect for a supervisor who shares information, treats them as adults, responds to their concerns and considers their opinions.

Where a **review** is commonly identified with a factual investigation and study, an **appraisal** is generally perceived to involve more subjective conclusions.

Why Performance Appraisals Are Important

Performance review and appraisal is necessary to establish and maintain the essential conditions for positive performance management.

Other names for the process are

- [ ] performance plan review
- [ ] accountability analysis
- [ ] status check
- [ ] audit of results
- [ ] performance evaluation
- [ ] progress report

It confirms understanding of job duties, evaluates work results, checks for problems in the work environment, produces information for rewards and provides feedback. It determines the extent to which work results are due to the individual employee or due to other forces.

One of the goals of a performance appraisal system is to encourage regular job-related discussion between the employee and the supervisor. A supervisor must realize that evaluation of performance takes place whether or not it is done formally at regular intervals. It is to everyone's advantage to handle it in a professional and objective manner. All too often, supervisors operate on a "no news is good news" philosophy. An employee is expected to assume that he/she is doing a good job and is appreciated as long as the boss does not complain. However, employees need feedback to know where they stand and to adjust their performance to meet expectations.

How to Conduct a Sound and Fair Appraisal

The Characteristics of Good Appraisals

The Performance Appraisal is **most likely to be sound** if:
□ its purpose is well defined;
□ it is based on information that is relevant and accurate;
□ it is sufficiently complete that no important information has been overlooked.

The appraisal process will be **fair** if the employee knows:
□ why he or she is being appraised;
□ what goes into the evaluation judgement; and
□ how it will be used.

General Guidelines for Performance Appraisals

Listed below are guidelines to be kept in mind prior to, during and after any appraisal. These guidelines may require some modification depending on the situation, but they are always worth reviewing each time you prepare to conduct an appraisal.

1. □Take one thing at a time; don't try to cover too many areas in one session.
2. □Compare actual results achieved to the results expected.
3. □ Appraise on the basis of relevant, representative and sufficient information.
4. □Make an honest appraisal; be prepared to explain questionable items.
5. □Open the appraisal process to employee input and subsequent correction.
6. □Avoid any comments on age, sex, race, national origin, etc., that could suggest prejudice or violate discrimination laws.
7. □Keep written and oral appraisals consistent.
8. □Present your appraisal as opinion, based on your observation.
9. □Make written appraisals available to employees.
10. □Identify needed areas of improvement and specify remedial action.
11. □Support the employee's effort to improve.
12. □Give the employee feedback about improvement and performance needs.
13. □Never imply the existence of communication that has not been made.

14. ☐ Provide a right of appeal to the employee.
15. ☐ The employee must acknowledge your evaluation; they should understand it; but they do not have to agree with it.

How to Select the Right Type of Appraisal for the Situation

There is more than one type of appraisal, and each has a different purpose calling for different methods and timing.

The Five Kinds of Appraisals: What They Are and How To Use Each

The principal types of appraisals are:

1. Planning Review

Supervisor and subordinate meet to study, discuss and maintain/update/restore the integrity of the current performance plan. They pause to check whether their direction has changed and whether they are presently on course.

1. Identify what the organization needs from the job.
2. Compare current needs to the last documented performance plan.
3. Modify the plan to accurately reflect any changed goals/objectives, priorities, timetables or standards of performance.
4. Assess the degree of success accomplished so far.
5. Check the information and resources allocated for job completion to assure that they are adequate for the updated expectations.
6. Agree on ways to maintain future plan integrity (how to know when objectives change or when performance is off target).
7. Confirm mutual understanding of the new, revised or revalidated performance plan.
8. Set a date or conditional cue for the next meeting to review the performance plan.

2. Coaching Appraisal

The manager appraises the employee's performance in an effort to help the employee improve performance. This should be done whenever you notice that

work results are not meeting standard expectations.
1. Examine each goal/objective/task and determine the skills required.
2. Evaluate the skills and proficiency of the employee.
3. Isolate those areas where improvements would be helpful or are needed.
4. Discuss your analysis with the employee and confirm the need for change.
5. Select the "best" method to correct or improve performance.
6. Create an action plan: what both you and the employee will do and when it will be done.
7. Implement and monitor the action plan.

3. Salary Appraisal

The manager appraises the value of the employee's work results before recommending suitable salary action. This should be done on a 10-14 month schedule depending on your salary system and competitive market.

1. Notify the employee of the time and date for a formal salary review and (optional) solicit a self-evaluation of their own performance.
2. Organize and document your observations and comments.
3. Rate employee performance.
4. Review your rating and the reasons (as supported by your documented observations and comments) with higher management (if any). Confirm the appropriate salary increase before discussing it with the employee.
5. Hold a private meeting without interruptions to discuss the performance review.
6. At that time or shortly afterwards, establish specific performance objectives or expectations for the next year.

4. Growth Potential Appraisal

Managers and supervisors meet privately to evaluate the future potential of subordinates. They consider the anticipated needs and forecasted growth opportunities in the organization against the abilities, interests and expectations of employees. These assessment decisions, manpower plans and development recommendations are **highly tentative**, subject to change and must be periodically reviewed.

1. Assess future organizational needs:
   a. forecast what positions and skills will be needed;
   b. review the relevant talents, abilities and interests of employees.

2. Match people with the current and projected organization needs. For each position, identify the candidates for backup, succession or promotion, stating their status:
    a. immediately ready
    b. ready in one or two years
    c. ready in three to five years
    d. far from ready but the best available candidate
    e. not promotable or transferable
3. Diagnose what is needed to prepare and qualify candidates.
4. Create action plans to close any gaps.
5. Apply action plans to individuals through **Coaching Appraisals** or **Career Development Discussions**.
6. DO NOT PROMISE anything you can't guarantee. **Growth Potential Appraisal** results do not create commitments and are often never communicated to the employee, lest a change in plans might create impatience or disillusionment.
7. Monitor and track individual progress against growth objectives.
8. Regularly update status records and plans.
9. Do not let growth predictions unduly affect **Salary Appraisals**. Unless promotability or transferability is an important part of the current job assignment, it should not be a factor in evaluations of how the person performs in the current job.

5. Career Development Discussion

The supervisor and the employee discuss the employee's interests, aspirations and questions about his/her future in the firm. This should be done on a 12-18 month cycle for all employees.

1. Prior to the meeting the employee should be given some method of self-inquiry about skills, interests and aspirations.
2. The supervisor's role is to discuss the realism of the employee's self-analysis and to help establish workable career development plans.
3. The employer should have a good understanding of the employee and know the qualification for other positions or where to refer the employee for more information.
4. In holding the discussion, the employer needs to listen, avoid hasty judgements, answer questions and offer thoughtful opinions about the realism of an employee's career plans.

5. Do not promise anything you cannot guarantee. Keep in mind that conditions may change in the future.
6. Conclude with some plan.

Important Points About Self-Appraisal

Just as in setting initial goals and objectives, the more employee participation in the plan review and performance appraisal processes, the better the results. Self-appraisal cannot hurt and usually helps. When an employee volunteers to submit an optional self-appraisal before the supervisor conducts the formal appraisal meeting, it assures better mutual understanding of the employee's view point and expectations. It also reduces supervisory anxiety about employee perceptions and lets both parties focus on areas where they disagree.

Given a voice, employees will often be much more critical of their own performance than the supervisor, who can then reassure them. Likewise, when people are asked to recommend goals and objectives for themselves to accomplish, they frequently overestimate how much can reasonably be attempted; and again, the supervisor can clearly define reasonable management expectations. Employee input improves the process and increases their "ownership" of the final result which management issues.

Some organizations merely give the employee the same form that the supervisor will use; they then ask the employee to put him/herself in the place of the boss and rate their own performance. An example is found at the end of this chapter. Other firms use separate worksheets, so they can ask for employee input and feedback about subjects that are not normally documented on the appraisal form.

Special worksheets for employee involvement and self-appraisal are included among the sample forms at the end of this workbook.

Performance Management Tip

To avoid surprises in the appraisal, ask the employee to conduct a self-appraisal for your review.

You, the supervisor, are not bound by the employee's opinion of how good her work was; but it will reveal what she thinks **before** you document your observations and hold any appraisal or review of actual performance, whether it is a periodic informal review or a formal year-end appraisal. Her self-appraisal will show:

1. where she is too harsh on herself, so you can head off unnecessary anxiety and guilt feelings;
2. where she agrees with your observations, so you can confirm her self-knowledge and encourage improvement without having to spend a lot of time on an area where you both agree;
3. where she is too easy on herself, so you can concentrate on these areas to emphasize your confidence in her ability to improve;
4. where she does not understand her job priorities, so you can clarify them and confirm that she correctly recognizes the proper relative importance of goals and objectives now and in the future.

A Guide to Choosing the Right Time for Each Kind of Appraisal

Each appraisal type has a different purpose. Ideally, they should be done at different times. Otherwise the employee may become confused, listen selectively (not hear everything you say) or be reluctant to speak frankly. It is quite difficult to shift mental gears between topics like past performance (covered in **Salary Appraisal**) and future potential (emphasized in **Career Development Discussion**).

For example, during a **Salary Appraisal** employees will not feel as free to admit shortcomings and improvement needs as they will **after** pay increases have been announced. Likewise, the details of a pay raise may distract an employee from important points you need to make about their career future.

There are different **timing options** for each type of **Performance Appraisal**.

1. **Planning Reviews** should occur as often as necessary, but at least twice a year. It is unfair and unwise to let an entire year pass without formally reviewing the original performance plan for adequacy and appropriateness. Quarterly performance reviews should be scheduled in the typical organization, but may be held more frequently:
   - to make timely plan adjustments in response to new organizational imperatives, avoiding wasted or misdirected effort;
   - to confirm correct mutual understanding of goals and objectives between supervisor and subordinate;
   - to check whether questionable performance results stem from issues of competence, system problems or plan deficiencies;
   - to provide feedback on actual performance against goals, letting both parties know what in the mind of the other;
   - to emphasize the importance of the clear mutual expectations

documented in the performance plan;
- to improve mutual knowledge about actual results and operating conditions;
- to permit effective corrective actions before minor problems become major disasters.

The **Coaching Appraisal** should be conducted **as soon as** a performance deficiency is suspected and a **plan review** has been completed (to assure that the difficulty is not merely one of plan misunderstanding). Do not wait until performance becomes a serious problem.

The **Salary Appraisal** should take place **at a specific time:**

Annual/Fiscal Year	Best for programs using actual vs. budget results as one measure of performance, or for programs in which it is important to get a clear picture of how the performance among a group of employees compares at one particular point in time.
Annual/Anniversary Date	Conducting appraisals on the employee's anniversary date of hire gives the appraisal an individual focus that is important in the employee development type of appraisal programs.
Semi-Annual/Quarterly	It is highly desirable to regularly monitor and formally review performance quarterly or semi-annually, using either fiscal or anniversary cycles. Then you need only summarize your periodic appraisals at year-end.

Further details on the relative advantages and disadvantages of different salary action timings are covered in the chapter on **Pay.**

The **Growth Potential Appraisal** takes place **at least** every year or whenever long-term business plans are made or changed.

The **Career Development Discussion** can be conducted **at any time.** For the most effective career counseling, first conduct a **Future Growth Potential Appraisal** to confirm what options are practical. The **Career Development Discussion** often takes place shortly after a salary increase decision has been made and communicated. Separating the two appraisals in time is desirable, to prevent confusion between "actual past" and "potential future" issues.

Later chapters concentrate on employee growth and career development actions.

Invaluable Technical Tips on Appraisals

What You Must Do to Avoid Major Problems

Be alert to some frequent **sources of difficulties** in performance appraisals than can come from the system or process used by the manager.

"Performance" Must Be Defined

It is critical to identify and communicate what constitutes the performance that is to be requested and appraised.

Clear details of desired results must be communicated in advance to employees, before they can be expected to direct their efforts in the right directions. Only then can they be fairly evaluated on their level of achievement. If they don't know what is wanted, they cannot be held accountable for their efforts.

Factors to Be Rated Must Be Valid

Good management practice and the law requires that employees should be rated on factors relevant to their jobs.

Whenever possible, use work results and performance accomplishments rather than irrelevant subjective opinions on traits, style or personality attributes. Measure outputs instead of inputs.

For example, baseball players are not paid according to how articulate they are on TV interviews, their ability with mathematics (none of them seem to realize that you can't "give 110% of your maximum effort"), how well they dress off the field or their knowledge of baseball glove manufacturing methods. Instead, they are paid according to fielding percentage, error rate, batting average, runs-batted-in statistics, won-lost record, etc.

If an "input" characteristic has any relevance to "output" performance, it is the **output** rather than the input that should be requested, measured and rewarded. That produces results instead of only "show." Now, if you were hiring a sports **broadcaster**, you WOULD care about verbal skills, their ability to count and their appearance; because those attributes would then be highly relevant to their work results.

What defines the performance factors for rating is unique to each situation, but it should always be directly connected to the achievement of the job objective; and the closer, the better. Another way to test factors for appropriateness is to ask,

"Is it possible for the individual to score high on this factor and still not get the job done properly?": if so, then the factor cannot be assumed to be particularly relevant and will expose the employer to risk.

"Standards of Comparison" Must Be Clarified

Effective performance appraisal programs require clear standards of comparison on the value of results. All must agree on what "good" means in a given context.

Otherwise, supervisors may take the stance that "all my people are outstanding" or "no one is average." The organization must assure that both supervisors and employees have a common understanding of what constitutes different levels of performance (i.e., how they will know when results are *excellent* rather than *good* or *outstanding* versus *satisfactory*).

Employees also can easily fall into the trap of thinking that merely meeting the minimum required standard of performance will win them "exceptional" ratings. The best approach is to define the limits of each performance rating term or scale, as it applies to a certain objective: for example, "anything below 80% is grounds for termination," "between 90% and 105% is satisfactory," and "over 105% is exceptional." That way, clear guidelines on what the ratings mean are assured; and the parameters, limits or boundaries can be adjusted in line with operating realities as the performance plan evolves.

Supervisors Must Be Trained

Successful appraisal programs require training for supervisors who must carry them out.

Those who conduct plan reviews and performance appraisals need knowledge, practice and confidence. Formal training also emphasizes the vital importance of the ongoing process of review, evaluation and appraisal. Refresher training should be periodically offered to confirm competence and upgrade skills with new methods.

An entire chapter is dedicated to the **Communications Techniques** that are vital for reviews and appraisals; and there is a structured INTERVIEW PLANNING GUIDE in the final chapter, **Manager's Tool Kit.**

Forced Distribution of Ratings Must be Avoided

Manipulating performance evaluations and changing ratings to match arbitrary past projections or fixed budget limits can destroy the credibility of merit programs.

"Forced distribution" is the process of setting quotas on various summary performance appraisal categories that will be used for merit, promotion or developmental decisions. It limits the number of people who can be identified as "outstanding," "superior," etc., usually because of budgetary constraints on the maximum permissable cost of pay increases.

Managers confronted by arbitrary limits on appraisal ratings can be faced with a difficult choice between either defying the policy and making an honest performace rating or artifically downgrading the employee for budgetary purposes.

Organizations that compel supervisors to make false performance rating decisions in order to assure budgetary compliance do not show much confidence in supervisory appraisal judgments; nor do they realize that they have discouraged excellence by creating (and enforcing) a self-fufilling prophesy about how many "excellent" employees they will have. It is a far better idea to let the salary budget vary or "flex" according to actual unit performance results instead of short-changing employees for doing better than was expected when the original budget was created.

An extensive discussion of this subject by the author can be found in "The Myth and the Reality of Pay for Performance," in the March, 1985, issue of the **Personnel Journal**.

If faced with the issue, it is recommended that the manager first make an honest performance appraisal; then award pay increases as you can afford them. Budgetary contraints on pay increases can remain sacred, if the company insists, but the validity and integrity of the performance appraisal system need not be compromised.

How to Spot and Avoid Causes of Bias in Performance Ratings

As human beings, we all have our blind spots that can permit bias to creep into performance appraisals. Some people show bias deliberately, for reasons that make sense to them. Others intend well but slip into error without even knowing it.

A quick review of the different kinds of bias and their causes might correct the mistaken ideas of those who deliberately abuse their management powers; and it will certainly help the honorable manager to police his/her own habits and to alert subordinates of improper tendencies.

Performance Management Tip
Review the **Bias List** before every appraisal, to make sure that the review is not based on a biased or prejudiced perception.

What To Do About the Halo Effect, Stereotypes, Subjective Standards, Central Tendency, Recent Behavior, Leniency & Opportunity Bias

The most common **causes of bias in Performance Ratings** include:

Halo Effect

The tendency to let one observation affect all others. Rating someone high or low in all categories just because he/she is high or low in one or two areas. Allowing the fact that the employee is the Chairman's favorite son to influence evaluation decisions. Best prevented by sticking to valid performance standards and priorities.

Stereotypes

Basing appraisals on fixed conceptions of what was expected rather than on all the facts that actually occured. Often reflects managerial favoritism or prejudice, a closed mind and a selective review process that excludes anything that would contradict the preconception. Typical of *inductive* (looking for facts that fit your theory) rather than *deductive* (create a theory to match the facts) reasoning. A manager guilty of stereotyping usually ignores or distorts information on performance. A close review of the application of objective performance standards will expose improper stereotyping. Requiring supervisors to apply objective performance plan measurement criteria will discourage stereotyping and reduce its affect on appraisals.

Subjective Standards   Evaluation terms or appraisal criteria whose meanings vary between individual users. Such phrases as good, adequate, satisfactory and excellent can be interpreted differently. Average is generally misunderstood. Expectations based on another person's un-defined feeling of satisfaction are essentially subjective. Can be avoided by clarifying in advance what results will earn what adjectival label.

Central Tendency   Rating everyone the same and denying the existence of significant differences between employees. Seen when a manager cannot notice variations in results that are great enough for clear distinction; or when differences are ignored, in the interest of over-simplification or because of an inability or unwillingness to explain/defend conclusions about differences. Can be prevented by better training or improved feedback to the rating manager about significant performance differences.

Recent Behavior   Over-emphasizing the most recent behavior while forgetting consistent past problems or important "older" accomplishments. Letting the most proximate action overwhelm or outweigh previous ones. Generally found when the manager does not conduct or record periodic reviews during the year. Documenting the results of periodic reviews allows supervisors to refresh their memories about major performance results at year-end. Also, attention to the appraiser's compliance with priority or weighting scales on performance plans will prevent recent behavior from being improperly weighted.

Leniency Bias   The rater gives the employee "the benefit of the doubt" to an extreme, exaggerating the positives and minimizing the defects and improvement needs. A lenient manager may anticipate a negative employee reaction to a low rating or critical comment and therefore inflate the rating higher than deserved. Or the appraisal is softened to avoid conflict or hurt feelings that might damage the working relationship. Sometimes, the manager merely lacks confidence in her ability to fairly rate performance, or he does not feel that the company's expectations are fair. In a few cases, the bias is a conscious decision to "give them a break," to compensate for something else or to express favoritism. Leniency bias, like excessive harshness, can only exist to the extent that the performance plan and appraisal standards permit it.

Opportunity Bias

An employee receives an inappropriate rating because of circumstances that have nothing to do with actual performance. The supervisor who received a promotion may wish to leave a parting gift to his old crew. The boss whose automobile was just dented may take her annoyance out on innocent subordinates. There is plenty of money in the merit budget, so everyone is scored higher to expend the available funds while they last. Appraisal ratings and conclusions that do not match reality will show up as unsupported by specific performance result criteria. Correctable by closer management reviews of evaluations and remedial training for offenders.

Why Mistakes in the Appraisal Process Can Be Expensive

Avoidance of gross errors will not guarantee complete success in performance appraisal; but it will help to prevent failure and to avoid court appearances.

Failure in the performance appraisal process hurts the employee, management, owners, and the total organization. It can also be embarassing and expensive.

What the Judge Said to Management

The following words by the judge in the court decision against the company in *Mistretta v. Sandia Corporation*, U.S. District Court, District of New Mexico, October 20, 1977, shows what can go wrong:

"The (employee performance evaluation) system is extremely subjective and has never been validated. Supervisors were not told to consider specific criteria in their ratings. Like the systems criticized in (citations), the evaluations were based on the best judgment and opinion of the evaluators, but were not based on any definite identifiable criteria, e.g., quantity or quality of work measures that were supported by some kind of record."

"Courts have condemned subjective standards as fostering discrimination. Thus they have declined to give much weight to testimony when a company's justification of its decision or policy is based on subjective and nonvalidated criteria. (Citations.)"
15 FEP Cases 1980 (1977); 24 FEP Cases 316 (1980).

The materials in this workbook were carefully designed to keep you from ever experiencing such an outcome.

Sample Performance Appraisal Forms

A large number of performance appraisal forms and procedures, including an INTERVIEW PLANNING GUIDE that summarizes the key points of this and other chapters, as they apply to interviews, are found in the **Manager's Tool Kit** which is the last chapter in this text.

Methods to Deal with the Unique Aspects of Salary Increase Appraisals

Because they involve pay decisions, **Salary Appraisals** are more sensitive than others and require special care.

How to Separate "the Person" from "the Job"

Evaluate and appraise the work of the **person** against the normal standards of the job. Remember that Job Evaluation measures the general value of the job that is to be done (reflecting the normal relevant competitive salary paid for this kind of work), while Performance Appraisals measures the relative adequacy of the work results actually produced by a specific individual.

Don't let the value of the job influence your appraisal of the performance of the person. The fact that one job is extremely important (and typically highly paid) does not mean that whoever performs it should automatically be rated high in performance. They will be judged against higher standards of performance if the job is critical.

More important jobs always carry higher pay than less important jobs, no matter who does them or how well they are done. Performance Appraisal focuses on how well each employee does his or her own job, regardless of how valuable the job is. A file clerk can be an exceptional worker, while a senior professional may be only marginally productive; but the financial value of their various outputs will usually result in more dollars going to the low-performing senior professional than to the high performing file clerk.

The Basic Information Every Manager Needs Knows to Know About Merit Pay

When **Salary Appraisals** take place, performance ratings must be used wisely to assure fair and equitable pay treatment. There are many special, complex and highly technical features of merit pay administration. Without going into great detail, here are a few important concepts that summarize the basic principles of merit pay...

Merit pay means:

- ▶ paying rates that are both externally competitive and internally equitable (fair);
- ▶ hiring people at salaries that reflect their anticipated competency level (i.e., minimum rates for minimally qualified people, average competitive rates for those expected to perform the full job right away, and above-average pay for people who surpass the norm in proven abilities);
- ▶ providing differential pay progression that, over time, results in employees earning pay that is proportional to their sustained performance (so the consistently marginal workers will earn less than the average competitive rate, the consistently competent workers will earn average pay, and consistently outstanding workers will earn well over the average).

If this does not happen in your organization, the fault may be in the salary increase methods rather than the Performance Appraisal process. An excellent appraisal process can be sabotaged by poor salary administration practices.

Further details on salary practices are covered in the chapter on **Pay**.

Sample Policies and Procedures for Performance Appraisal

What You Will Learn from Real-Life Examples

While a section of the **Manager's Tool Kit** chapter at the end of the book contains many examples and discussions of forms and procedures for appraisals, a few real-life examples are useful here, to demonstrate the range of recommended versions.

Two sets of instructions and three sets of forms illustrate

- how performance appraisal can be used for multiple purposes
- how different appraisal elements can be emphasized with different employee groups
- how the performance appraisal form can evolve

Simple Appraisals Using the Most Basic Methods

Not every organization (or supervisor) is ready for the advanced methods of performance review and appraisal.

Performance Management Tip

If managers are reluctant, afraid or untrained in the appraisal process, **start with the most simple formats.**

Once people gain confidence in their ability to perform basic performance reviews, they can be introduced to more sophisticated and refined methods.

When supervisors (or employees) suggest improvements in the simple methods, that is a clear sign that they are ready for more advanced techniques.

Simple means what is easily understood by the people who have to use the procedures. A method does not have to be *dumb* to be *simple*. Simplicity in performance reviews also does not require blind consistency in the matter of irrelevant details: a simple but appropriate process can be achieved by giving supervisors samples of review formats and letting them adapt and alter them as needed.

For those who want to start with simple forms and procedures, a set of four examples from a factory operation where supervisors were encouraged to experiment follow.

A Sample of a Completed Supervisor Review

This first example shows how Harry, a supervisor, is rated in ten areas of responsibility.

The form itself shows how five levels of ratings are defined, from OUTSTANDING (with a score of 4) down to UNSATISFACTORY (with a score of 0). The Overall Rating is the average of the nine individual area ratings that were scored; the tenth and last responsibility area, "Progress towards Goals," was not scored, because specific performance goals had not been established and communicated before the review.

SUPERVISORY/PERFORMANCE REVIEW

Name _Harry_

Position _Shipping Receiving Supervisor_

Rating   A   Outstanding (4)

        B   Above Average (3)

        C   Average (2)

        D   Below Average (1)

        E   Unsatisfactory (0)

1. Job knowledge (as pertains to your primary job function).   RATING ___B___
Indicate areas of strength.

Harry is generally knowledgeable of the warehouse area.

Indicate areas that may be strengthened.

knowledge of freight rates, freight terms, etc.

2. Initiative (makes or proposes improvements frequently to   RATING ___B___
improve operations).

Harry frequently looks for ways to organize and improve.

3. Planning and organizing of work and subordinates so   RATING ___C___
efforts are properly directed.

Harry generally plans his work.

4. Follow up (performs tasks assigned or discussed without   RATING ___C___
being reminded).

Harry generally follows up on assignments.

5. Delegating (effectively discharges duties so that work on   RATING ___C___
important projects/tasks can be done).

Has shown ability to designate. However, sometimes waits until problems arise before assigning duties or pitching in to help.

6. Quality of work (strives to improve quality of his/her area;   RATING __C__
   plans rather than reacts). Note major accomplishments.

   Quality of Harry's work is good. Harry's occasional paperwork errors can be avoided.

7. Communicating (frequent two-way discussions with   RATING __C__
   employee/subordinates to get to know them).

   Communication with them can be very good or be absent.

8. Works as a team member (looks out for overall good, even   RATING __D__
   if his/her area may suffer as a result). *Harry has difficulty working as a team player. He strives to make shipping / receiving a success. However, does not inspire people to want to work with him.*

9. Management ability—stimulates and guides people to   RATING __D__
   achieve desired results—challenges people to contribute
   (list examples).

   Harry is a hard worker but has not learned how to stimulate others to want to work hard.

10. Progress toward goals.   RATING __N/A__

    List major accomplishments.

    Harry has generally done well with receiving and shipping functions. He has worked to contain freight expense and supply expense.

    List major areas that could be handled better in the future.

    Work as a team member and learn to communicate with peers in a manner that promotes and stimulates cooperation, not dislike and contempt.

    OVERALL RATING: __C__ (2)

    Reviewed by _____ Date _____

    Career planning comments:

    _____

    _____

    _____

    _____

A Sample Completed Review of a Staff Professional

The Buyer/Planner review shows a very similar appraisal of a support staff professional with indirect management powers who does not have anyone directly reporting to her.

A careful comparison with the previous example will show a few differences in the review criteria. "Delegating" and "Management Ability" responsibility areas were deleted as irrelevant to this job; the reviewer could just as easily have kept them on the form and marked those areas as "Not Applicable."

Few comments are documented, so a third party would not learn much about Violetta's performance from this form alone.

PERFORMANCE REVIEW/INDIRECT (NO DIRECT REPORTS)

Name _Violetta_

Position _Buyer / Planner_

Rating A Outstanding (4)

    B Above Average (3)

    C Average (2)

    D Below Average (1)

    E Unsatisfactory (0)

1. Job knowledge (as pertains to your primary job function). RATING _A_
   Indicate areas of strength.

   Violetta is most knowledgeable of plant's components and planning activities.

   Indicate areas that may be strengthened.

   None

2. Initiative (makes or proposes improvements frequently to RATING _B_
   improve operations).

   Violetta continuously makes refinements to her area of responsibility.

3. Planning and organizing of work and subordinates so RATING _A_
   efforts are properly directed.

   Very well organized

4. Follow up (performs tasks assigned or discussed without RATING _A_
   being reminded).

5. Quality of work (strives to improve quality of his/her area;   RATING ___B___
   plans rather than reacts). Note major accomplishments.

   Quality is very good.

6. Communicating (frequent two-way discussions with co-   RATING ___B___
   workers to assure good working relationships).

7. Works as a team member (looks out for overall good, even   RATING ___A___
   if his/her area may suffer as a result).

8. Progress toward goals.   RATING ___N/A___

   List major accomplishments.

   Violetta has organized her work very well
   and is respected for her knowledge and
   ability to perform.

   List major areas that could be handled better in the future.

   OVERALL RATING: ___A (3.6)___

   Reviewed by _____ Date _____

   Career planning comments:

   _____

   _____

   _____

   _____

   _____

A Sample of a Completed Foreman Review

The Foreman Review shows an example where the supervisor expanded the rating categories to double the number of levels used in the last two examples. Ten levels are used and applied to ten performance criteria.

The criteria themselves vary: some are broad functional goals; some are fairly specific objectives; some are personal goals; and some are merely areas of responsibility.

The evaluating supervisor assigns a score between 0 and 10 to each of the ten criteria areas and averages the result for an Overall Rating.

FOREMAN REVIEW CRITERIA

	Rating
	0—no achievement
	10—excellent

Updated production sheet with scrap and down time

Needs to improve accuracy in counting, pay closer attention.   8

*Daily follow-up with Q.C. asking about quality of work on line

~~is~~ *is developing a technique for working with Q.C.*   8

*Talk to each line worker to know their problems and suggestions

Talks to a few, needs to be more open to everyone.   6

Increase overall production *This staying the same due to the overall operation.*   5

*Promote team spirit *Needs to improve, develop a line of communication with employees*   5

Reduce scrap *Overall operation has improved.*   8

*Improve self-image *Needs to dedicate himself to improve. It has to come from him.*   7

*Set example for people to follow; on time, helpful, positive

Needs to be more helpful; needs to establish a positive attitude.   7

*Technical knowledge and expertise *Needs To read some additional materials to gain knowledge*   6

*People skills *These are improving, and with more time ~~~~ will become strong in this area.*   6

Overall Rating *66%   C*

Rated by _____

Date _____

A Sample Completed Review of an Inspector

The Quality Control Inspector is reviewed on still another set of performance criteria. Some of the areas are similar to ones seen earlier, but the supervisor has broken a number of them down into smaller and far more specific functional responsibility areas. Each sub-area is rated on the 0 to 10 scale and those ratings averaged to give the category area rating score. The eight major category ratings are totalled and divided by 8 to yield the average as the Overall Rating.

This supervisor has altered the general form to make the relevant appraisal factors quite clear to the inspector. Although details about actual work results are not shown, the supervisor's ratings certainly show the areas of strength and the areas that need substantial improvement.

QUALITY CONTROL INSPECTOR/REVIEW CRITERIA

Rate each point as 0 thru 10 (0 being no ability to 10 excellent ability)

1. Job knowledge　　　　　　　　　　　　　　　　　　Rating ___6.3___
    A Inprocess　　　　　　　　　　　7
    B Raw Materials　　　　　　　　　8
    C Computer Systems　　　　　　　4
    D Testing　　　　　　　　　　　___

2. Accuracy of work　　　　　　　　　　　　　　　　Rating ___8.0___
    A Batch record errors　　　　　　8
    B Batch record omissions　　　　8
    C Test data　　　　　　　　　　　8
    D　　　　　　　　　　　　　　　___

3. Communication　　　　　　　　　　　　　　　　　Rating ___5.0___
    Ability to comunicate in an effective manner

4. Works as a team member with all departments　　Rating ___5.0___

5. Uses time effectively　　　　　　　　　　　　　　Rating ___3.5___
    Uses free time effectively ___4___
    Seeks assignments when caught up ___3___

6. Locates quality problems before scrap is generated.　Rating ___6.5___
    In manufacturing ___6___
    In raw materials ___7___

7. Innovation—uses imagination in problem solving.　Rating ___4.0___

8. Decisiveness—willing to make and stand by decisions.　Rating ___2.0___

LIST MAJOR ACCOMPLISHMENTS
Can fill in on computer in my absence.

Work & cooperation with other departments has improved markedly in last 2
　months.

Can handle all routine lab tests.

LIST MAJOR AREAS THAT COULD BE HANDLED BETTER IN THE FUTURE
Wastes more time than most others (talks too much).

Seems reluctant to use his own judgment to make decisions.

Overall rating ___5.0　C___

Reviewed by _____　　Date _____6/10/88_____

CAREER PLANNING COMMENTS

Note: As discussed elsewhere, using the term *average* is not generally recommended, since it implies a relative norm that does not always exist (or can't be clearly defended) in reality. This organization chose to use that term because it did have a clear meaning to its supervisors and employees.

Likewise, the firm chose to give each and every major performance criteria area the same equal weight, rather than putting a higher priority (or multiple factor) on some areas than on others. As long as each criteria area/cagegory is truly of approximately equal importantance, there is nothing wrong with that.

Performance Management Tip

Never adopt a particular performance review form just because someone said it was the best in the world. It may be the most sophisticated and elaborate, but that alone does not make it the most appropriate for your needs.

There are many "good" and "better" forms to review and appraise performance. The value of each is relative to your situation.

Review the wide variety of samples in the **Manager's Tool Kit** in the final chapter to see the many options you have.

Use the methods that work best in your organization. As the organization and its people change, be prepared to change performance management methods.

Performance Appraisals for Exempt/Management Employees

An Example of a Participative Process

More ambitious review and appraisal methods require more documentation and consistent written guidance to evaluators.

The first example shows how an employer can make performance appraisal an open participative process covering planning and goal setting, with reviews of actual work output compared against objectives, remedial and developmental actions and career aspirations.

It uses a self-appraisal approach to involve the employee. In fact, the instructions that follow are for the **employee** to use in preparing for his or her own performance review.

This format was created for employees who meet the Federal requirements for exemption from the overtime pay provisions of the Fair Labor Standards Act. The employees labelled "exempt" and covered by this procedure would typically be executives, managers, supervisors, degreed professionals and scientists.

Actual Instructions Given to Employees: A Sample

UNITED VAN LINES
EXEMPT EMPLOYEE'S INSTRUCTIONS FOR PERFORMANCE APPRAISAL

I. INTRODUCTION

The performance appraisal accompanying this set of instructions is designed to be used by you for:

1. assessing your job performance for the preceding twelve months, and

2. gaining some insight into your career path at United Van Lines.

By honestly reviewing and documenting the performance of your job responsibilities, and sharing these with your supervisor during your appraisal discussion, a clear understanding between you and your supervisor of how your job performance is viewed will emerge.

Also, an assessment of your performance can offer considerable insight into your career path by identifying your strengths which then enables you to explore where and how they can best be utilized within the company. Any specific areas of your performance that need improvement can be seen as challenges that you need to meet in order to maintain the growth of your career.

When preparing your performance appraisal, please keep in mind that your supervisor is available to help you with your questions. If you and your supervisor need further assistance, please contact the Personnel Department whose staff is always ready to help you with your inquiries.

II. IMPLEMENTATION

All new employees will receive a performance appraisal following their first six months of employment with United and will thereafter be reviewed on an annual basis on their anniversary date. The Personnel Department will send your

---

by permission of United Van Lines, Inc.

performance appraisal packet to your supervisor as the time for your review approaches, and your supervisor will then initiate the appraisal process with you.

III. PREPARATION

It is strongly recommended that you keep a file of your activities during the year. In this file you can keep your own notes of such things as:

- when you were out sick
- memos from your supervisor and other departments that verify your good performance
- circumstances surrounding incidents when time was lost or targets were not met
- those times when you put forth unusual effort in order to accomplish a task
- documentation of creativity, initiative and long-range planning

The above suggestions are only a guide, and not all-inclusive. The reason that it is recommended that you keep a file of such documentation is that for most of us it is difficult to remember those things that happened almost twelve months in the past. Since you will be appraising yourself for twelve months of effort, these notes will serve as reminders that enable you to complete a balanced and honest appraisal. The time that you take to keep your file up to date will be rewarded when you sit down to complete your appraisal.

In addition to keeping your personal file, the following suggestions are made to help you in completing your performance appraisal:

- Review the attached job description with your supervisor to insure that it is accurate and that you both agree on the duties on which you will be evaluated.
- Be receptive to what your supervisor says about your performance, and be sure to discuss, and reach an understanding, on those areas in which you do not agree or are unclear.
- Be as specific as you possibly can, both in your discussion with your supervisor and what you write on your appraisal form.
- Make a copy of your performance appraisal for your records.

IV. COMPLETING THE FORMS

1. Cover Sheet

This page identifies you and where you work. It also provides ample space for you to write your comments following the appraisal process, and spaces for the signatures of the members of your line of management. Please note, in the middle of the page, that your supervisor signs your copy. You will sign your supervisor's copy.

2. Performance Measures

Your performance is always measured by the degree to which you achieved specific measurable goals. At United Van Lines, these goals will always represent the objectives as stated in the company's Three Year Business Plan. For this reason, and to insure that you can measure your performance accurately, great care needs to be taken in forming the objectives in your business plan. Each objective should be carefully analyzed to make sure that it meets the following criteria:

Specific   It relates to a particular area for which you will be personally responsible.

Measurable It specifies what conditions will exist when the objective has been successfully met.

Individual   It relates to your contribution in meeting a goal.

Realistic   It describes a performance level that is both attainable and challenging.

Output   It describes a tangible result or product, not the process used to achieve the result or product.

Target Dates The date upon which the objective, or part of the objective, is to be achieved.

With goals that are clear, specific and measurable, it becomes possible to assess your performance in a fair and balanced manner.

A. Departmental Objectives

These are the objectives of your department for the current year as listed in the Three Year Business Plan. If necessary, the objectives from the previous year's plan will also be included in the appraisal.

Under the area entitled, "Departmental Objective," list a departmental objective for which you were personally responsible, being as specific as you possibly can.

Under the area entitled, "Results Accomplished," describe the degree to which the objective was achieved on the agreed upon target date, again being as specific as possible.

After the area entitled, "Comments/Evaluation," you can write specific supporting statements of how you performed toward the achievement of your objective. If an objective was not achieved in a timely manner, this would be the appropriate place to state your explanation.

Finally, in the box provided for "Rating," assign a numerical score that reflects your assessment of the degree to which you achieved the particular objective and/or the quality of the result. The rating scale is listed at the bottom of the appraisal form. List each of your departmental objectives separately, using additional pages, if necessary. Extra forms are available in the Personnel Department. NOTE: In determining a rating on your performance, it is important to remember that it is not you as a person who is being evaluated, but how you performed in achieving your agreed upon objectives as listed in the business plan. For this reason, it is again important to emphasize that your objectives be clear, specific and measurable. Also, as stated at the top of the appraisal form, you can substitute your Quarterly Status Report on the Business Plan for this page. You must, however, still rate your performance and state the results accomplished on each objective.

B. Personal Objectives

There are objectives that you have chosen either because they are a routine part of your responsibility or because they relate to your development as an employee. Follow the same format as you did in evaluating your departmental objectives.

3. Management Skills Rating

On this page you are asked to rate your performance with regard to specific managerial skills. There are three categories:

Managerial	those skills that relate to the effective flow of work through your area of responsibility.
Personal	those skills and characteristics that you need in order to manage your responsibilities in an effective manner.
Working with people	those skills that you must develop in order to accomplish goals through others.

4. Management Skills Improvement Section

This section emphasizes those areas in your management skills rating in which you assigned a rating of two (2) or less.

In the area labeled, "Skill needing improvement," write a specific statement that describes the management skill that you feel you need to improve or perform differently, and then after the heading "Steps I will take to ensure this improvement," list the specific action steps that you will take to improve the specified skill area, along with a projected target date for completing your action steps.

When you have your appraisal discussion with your supervisor, the two of you will work out the final format of your improvement plan. It is important to remember that this does not constitute a formal probationary measure, but is intended to serve as a management mechanism for identifying and improving skills needing attention.

5. Attendance

The total number of personal and sick time that you have accumulated during the year should be noted in the appropriate space, and the corresponding rating written in the box for this purpose. Any extenuating circumstances for poor attendance should be written in the provided space. A less than satisfactory (over 6 days) rating can negatively affect the amount of your merit increase.

6. Punctuality

Being punctual is a necessary part of day to day departmental operations. This includes coming in to work and leaving at the proper time. Rate yourself accordingly, and comment on your punctuality record if you feel the need to document a non-punctual trend.

7. Additional Job-Related Strengths and Accomplishments

In this section you are asked to list any strengths or accomplishments that you have that relate to your present job, or could be utilized on your present job if you brought them to the attention of your supervisor. Also, these additional strengths and accomplishments can point toward other opportunities for you at United Van Lines. The list that you develop can include such things as working well with people, demonstrating initiative and enthusiasm, technical knowledge and skill, and exercising good judgment. List any job-related strengths that you have, and be sure to provide specific examples of what you mean.

8. In the area entitled, "I could improve my performance if:" list specific things that you can do to improve your performance, which can include better organization of your time, acquiring new skills, or other things that you know you could do to improve your performance. Also, list specific things that your supervisor could do to improve your performance, which might include closer supervision or changing the procedure of how things are accomplished in your department. You can also include specific things that you feel the company could do to improve your performance. In all cases, please be as specific as possible and provide examples, and indicate exactly how these examples would improve your performance.

V. Returning the Forms

After you and your supervisor have discussed your performance appraisal, and all parts of the appraisal have been completed, you will give your original copy to your supervisor, who will obtain all necessary signatures. Your supervisor will then return all forms to the Personnel Department before the 15th of the reviewing month.

Performance Appraisals for Non-Exempt/Non-Management Employees

A different set of instructions and a separate form are used to evaluate performance for employees who are paid "on the clock" (clerks, laborers, technicians, etc.), according to how many hours they work.

An Example that Concentrates on Current Work Results

The instructions given to supervisors are shown to give a bit less emphasis to skill potentials and career development than the previous example. The actual form does ask for "strengths and weaknesses" and calls for specific action plans to remedy any performance deficiencies.

The Actual Instructions Given to Supervisors: A Sample

SUPERVISOR COPY
UNITED VAN LINES
INSTRUCTIONS: NON-EXEMPT PERFORMANCE APPRAISAL

The non-exempt performance appraisal is designed to be utilized as a tool for measuring, applauding and/or criticizing an employee's performance over a specific period of time. It is the direct supervisor's responsibility to provide each employee with necessary feedback to insure proper communication at all times.

IMPLEMENTATION

U.V.L. Performance Appraisals are implemented on each employee's anniversary date. New employees are appraised after their initial six month probationary period has been satisfied, as well as their anniversary date. If the direct supervisor voluntarily resigns or employee is transferred, an appraisal must be completed (unless an appraisal has been completed in the preceding six months). Reminder notices and the appraisal itself are initiated by the Personnel Department to the appropriate reviewing supervisor.

PREPARATION

It is strongly recommended that each member of management keep a file on each employee who reports directly to you. During the course of a year make short notes to help remind you of incidents which reflect on the employee's performance. It might include such things as:

- days when the employee was out sick
- memos concerning good performance from other departments
- incidents where time was lost or target dates were not met
- incidents where unusual effort was put forth in order to accomplish a task
- indicators of creativity, initiative, long range planning, or other special effort

The objective is to appraise twelve months of performance rather than the previous three months (which is the freshest in our memory). Therefore, some method for refreshing our memory is essential. Use any method which works for you, but have some method for recording events during the year. Although time pressures may vary, poorly completed forms are unfair to the employee as well as having possible future legal ramifications.

In addition to an employee file, the following is a list of suggestions that should prove helpful in preparing for and discussing the completed performance appraisal:

- Review the attached job description to insure its accuracy
- Review the employee personnel file thoroughly noting past performance appraisals
- Have an open mind and be receptive to the employee's comments and suggestions
- Don't generalize, in criticizing performance cite specific examples
- Encourage questions or comments about the review
- End on a positive note

In cases where a new supervisor is doing the appraising, members of the Personnel Department will be available to assist or clarify any questions.

FORMAT

1. Cover Sheet

This page identifies the employee to be appraised and provides for the signature of all those involved in the appraisal process.

2. Major Assigned Duties

Major assigned duties are written statements that convey, in general terms, what responsibilities are assigned to the employee being reviewed. They are the basis for receiving a numerical performance rating. Ratings are a means of measure by which a supervisor and subordinate can measure each duty. Ratings range from a high score of five (5), meaning little if any improvement can be made, to a low of one (1) indicating that performance in a particular area is totally unacceptable. An employee who is performing new duties will receive a rating of N, too new to rate. All ratings must be documented with specific examples of good and/or bad performance. Ratings without supporting evidence will be considered incomplete and returned for further clarification.

3. Attendance

The total number of personal and sick time off should be noted in the appropriate blank and rated in the corresponding box. Any extenuating circumstances for poor attendance should be noted in the space provided.

4. Punctuality

Being punctual is a necessary part of day to day departmental operations. This includes reporting to work, returning from breaks, and leaving work at the proper designated times. A score of Unsatisfactory in Punctuality should be expanded upon in the Performance Improvement Plan.

5. Additional Job Related Strengths and Accomplishments

This list should include, but not be limited to, any strengths or accomplishments that have occurred or continue to occur which can be identified and might otherwise go unnoticed. This list may include such areas as: working well with people, demonstrating initiative and enthusiasm, job knowledge, etc. In the section under strengths and accomplishments, specific examples of performance should be cited that would improve ratings and overall job performance.

6. Performance Improvement Plan

The Performance Improvement Plan is designed to give employees who achieve a rating of two (2) or below in any area a chance to rectify their performance within a specific time frame. It is not a punitive device nor is it a probationary tool. It is designed merely to improve an area of performance. The supervisor completes the "Performance to be Improved" and "Results to be Accomplished" areas while both the supervisor and the employee complete their respective action steps to accomplish the desired results. Realistic target dates (usually 30-90 days) are determined with evaluation of results to be documented upon completion.

After all parts of the appraisal have been completed, the reviewing supervisor must secure all necessary signatures on the cover page and have their respective Vice President return the completed appraisal to the Personnel Department before the 15th of the reviewing month.

Van Lines

(Employee's Copy)

Performance Appraisal

DATE OF HIRE _____

ANNIVERSARY DATE _____

LAST REVIEW DATE _____

NAME OF EMPLOYEE _____

JOB CODE _____ POSITION TITLE _____ PAY RANGE (1–10)_____

DIVISION _____ DEPARTMENT _____

REVIEW PERIOD: FROM _____ TO _____

REVIEW AND DISCUSSION

This Appraisal Form has been completed by: _____

Signature of Supervisor: _____ Title _____

Date: _____

COMMENTS FOLLOWING APPRAISAL: _____

_____

_____

_____

_____

_____

_____

_____

SIGNATURE: _____ DATE: _____
Manager

_____ DATE: _____
Director

_____ DATE: _____
Vice President

_____ DATE: _____
Sr. Vice President

Merit increases will take effect the first day of the month in which the employee's anniversary date occurs. In order for this to be possible the completed performance appraisal must be turned in to the Personnel Department by the 15th of the preceding month. **Non-exempt**

NS-SS-36 7/83

MAJOR ASSIGNED DUTIES

Duty: _____

Evidence supporting rating: _____

_____

_____

_____ ☐ Rating

Duty: _____

Evidence supporting rating: _____

_____

_____

_____ ☐ Rating

Duty: _____

Evidence supporting rating: _____

_____

_____

_____ ☐ Rating

Duty: _____

Evidence supporting rating: _____

_____

_____

_____ ☐ Rating

Duty: _____

Evidence supporting rating: _____

_____

_____

_____ ☐ Rating

Performance Rating Scale: 5 – Outstanding   4 – Highly Satisfactory   3 – Satisfactory
                            2 – Less Than Satisfactory   1 – Unacceptable   N – Too New to Rate

ATTENDANCE

_____ was absent
_____ days during the review period (as stated
on cover page). Extenuating circumstances (if
any, describe)

_____

_____

_____

ABSENCE

Annual Attendance Rating Scale

    0 — 2 days = 5
    3 — 4 days = 4
    5 — 6 days = 3
    7 — 10 days = 2
    over 10 days = 1

RATING

Punctuality:　Outstanding _____　　Satisfactory _____　　Unsatisfactory _____

Comments on punctuality: _____

_____

_____

If attendance or punctuality are less than satisfactory cite circumstances on Performance Improvement Plan.

ADDITIONAL JOB RELATED STRENGTH AND ACCOMPLISHMENTS

_____

_____

_____

_____

_____

_____

_____

_____ could improve her/his performance if:

_____

_____

_____

_____

_____

_____

_____

PERFORMANCE IMPROVEMENT PLAN
(This may be completed during the appraisal interview)

Performance to be improved or corrected:

_____

_____

_____

_____

_____

Goals or results to be accomplished:

_____

_____

_____

_____

_____

Employee action steps:

_____

_____

_____

Supervisor action steps:

_____

_____

_____

Target date: _____

Evaluation of results (to be filled in after
target date)

_____

_____

_____

_____

_____

Performance to be improved or corrected:

_____

_____

_____

_____

_____

Goals or results to be accomplished:

_____

_____

_____

_____

_____

Employee action steps:

_____

_____

_____

Supervisor action steps:

_____

_____

_____

Target date: _____

Evaluation of results (to be filled in after
target date)

_____

_____

_____

_____

_____

An Illustration of Gradual Evolutionary Improvements

With success, the confidence to refine and improve a well accepted appraisal process grows.

Once supervisors and employees had tested, practiced and used the separate appraisal forms for different kinds of employees, the organization felt prepared to incorporate their suggestions into a longer and more complex single form for all employees.

How an Improved Form Changed from the Earlier Version

The new form has a multiple purpose: salary review, performance appraisal, career development and succession planning. The number of possible performance appraisal ratings rose from five to seven, showing that supervisors demonstrated sufficient evaluation skills to be able to distinguish credible differences between so many rating levels. It also illustrates an extremely open and highly participative appraisal process: much of the information is *self-appraisal*, completed by the employee.

Other examples of the various options available and how the evolutionary process operates can be found in the final chapter, **Manager's Tool Kit**.

An Actual Sample of an Improved Appraisal Form

PERFORMANCE APPRAISAL

UNITED UNITED UNITED Van Lines

Name _____

Department _____

Division _____

Anniversary Date _____

Position Title _____

Salary Grade _____

Exempt ☐   Non-Exempt ☐

Appraisal Instructions: Appraise performance in accordance with defined codes shown below:

7 = Far exceeds all job requirements and established goals. Rarely equalled on performance expectations. This rating denotes exceptional performance and is associated with performance that has a significant impact on the department's or the organization's performance. This rating equals 7 points.

6 = Consistently and clearly exceeds job requirements. Contributes significantly to company/department success well beyond job requirements. Goals achieved are well above satisfactory performance of job requirements in terms of completeness, timing, budget, etc. This rating equals 6 points.

5 = Frequently exceeds expectations and demonstrates ability to surpass stated standards. This rating equals 5 points.

4 = Meets all job requirements and all expectations which were established as a basis for the evaluation. By definition, this is satisfactory performance and is the level of performance that is expected of the employee. This rating equals 4 points.

3 = Shows significant progress toward satisfactorily meeting job requirements and expectations. Meets minimum standards. This rating equals 3 points.

2 = Demonstrates sincere effort in achieving job requirements and expectations and is making progress. Does not meet minimum standards. This rating equals 2 points.

1 = Fails to meet job requirements, expectations and minimum standards. Problem areas need to be monitored and documented. This rating equals 1 point.

NA = Objective/Duty is too new to rate, or Management Skill does not apply.

Concluding comments following appraisal interview:

_____

_____

_____

_____

Employee's comments and signature — The contents of this form have been reviewed by me. I understand that this form will be used by the company in connection with salary administration, development and placement activities. My comments on this review are:

_____

_____

Date _____ Signature _____

Supervisor's comments and signature:

I have discussed this appraisal with the employee on: Date _____

Supervisor's concluding comments: _____

_____

Date _____ Supervisor's Signature _____

Reviewer's (next level of management) comments and signature:

_____

_____

Date _____ Signature _____

Optional Signatures: Date _____ Signature _____ Date _____ Signature _____

NS-A-1044 3/86

(1)

Name _____

I. **Objectives (if Exempt)/Duties (if Non-Exempt)** — List major job related objectives/duties; comment on results in terms of job-related standards. Rate results, cite especially how the results met, exceeded or failed to meet job objectives or standards (see rating codes). Distributive points must total 100 with each objective/duty individually weighted.

To be completed by Employee:

	Rating	Distributive Points
1. Objective/Duty _____		
Results _____		
2. Objective/Duty _____		
Results _____		
3. Objective/Duty _____		
Results _____		

To be completed by Supervisor:

Supervisor Agree Disagree	Rating Earned	Distributive Points	Points Earned
	____ ×	____ =	☐
	____ ×	____ =	☐
	____ ×	____ =	☐

(2)

Name _____

To be completed by Employee:

	Rating	Distributive Points
4. Objective/Duty _____		
Results _____		
5. Objective/Duty _____		
Results _____		

(If more than (5) Objectives/Duties are involved, please obtain additional page(s) from Personnel.)

Supervisor's comments:

Supervisor, please comment below on any results or ratings that were lower or higher than employee's listed results and ratings, and record any other additional comments you may have. (If additional space is needed, please use page 8.)

Obj./Duty Number						

To be completed by Supervisor:

Supervisor Agree	Disagree	Rating Earned	Distributive Points	Points Earned
		____ X ____ =		□
		____ X ____ =	100 =	□ □

Total Distributive Points and Points Earned:

Divide Total Points Earned by 100

$$\frac{\quad}{100} = \frac{\quad}{\quad} = \quad$$ Post this number in Item 1 in Section X

(3)

Name _____

II. **Management Skills — to be completed by Exempt Employee only:**

Evaluate the performance in terms of the task-related skills listed below. Cite specific examples which illustrate the proficiency and effectiveness (or lack thereof) in applying these skills to meet the requirements of the job. Rate effectiveness; describe how behavior met, exceeded or failed to meet the requirements of the job. Distributive points must total 100 with each skill individually weighted.

To be completed by Exempt Employee only:

	Rating	Distributive Points
1. Skill in Managing People		
2. Skill in Communicating		
3. Skill in Decision-Making		
4. Skill in Budgeting/Controlling Costs		
5. Skill in Administration		
6. Skill in Problem Solving		
7. Skill in Planning		

To be completed by Supervisor:

Supervisor Agree	Disagree	Rating Earned	Distributive Points	Points Earned
		___ ×	___ =	☐
		___ ×	___ =	☐
		___ ×	___ =	☐
		___ ×	___ =	☐
		___ ×	___ =	☐
		___ ×	___ =	☐
		___ ×	___ =	☐

(continued on next page)

(4)

Name _____

Management Skills — (continued)

To be completed by Exempt Employee only:

	Rating	Distributive Points
8. Skill in Achieving Results _____		

To be completed by Supervisor:

Supervisor Agree	Disagree	Rating Earned	Distributive Points	Points Earned
		X ___ =	100	= ☐
				= ☐

Total Distributive Points and Points Earned:

Exempt Only

Divide Total Points Earned by 100

$$\frac{\text{____}}{100} = \text{____}$$ Post this number in Item 2 in Section X

Supervisor's comments:

Supervisor, please comment below on any management skill ratings that were lower or higher than employee's ratings, and record any other additional comments you may have. (If additional space is needed, please use page 8.)

Skill No.

III. Attendance — To be completed by Supervisor

_____ has missed _____ days in the last 12 months.

Rating: Satisfactory ☐   (If employee has missed more than six (6) days, rate unsatisfactory and ½ % must be deducted from merit increase.)

Unsatisfactory ☐

Comments _____

IV. Punctuality — To be completed by Supervisor

Rating: Outstanding ☐   Satisfactory ☐   Unsatisfactory ☐

Comments on punctuality _____

(5)

Name _____

V. Personal Objectives — T⊃ be completed by Employee

Non-Exempt Employees: Please list the personal objectives you will work to achieve during the next Performance Appraisal period. (This may include increases in quantity and quality of work, better work procedures, more efficient workflow, etc.)

Exempt Employees: Please attach a copy of your Personal Objectives Statement for the next appraisal period.

_____
_____
_____

VI. Document hereon any work-related habits that enhance on the job effectiveness — To be completed by the Supervisor.

_____
_____
_____

VII. Development — To be completed by the Supervisor

This section is to be used to identify employee's developmental needs. This may include improvement in skills, increases in personal effectiveness, additional professional development, or development of improved work habits. (NOTE: If an Exempt Employee receives a rating of 1 on any Management Skill, a developmental goal related to that skill must be established.)

1. Developmental Goal _____

   How this will be accomplished _____

2. Developmental Goal _____

   How this will be accomplished _____

3. Developmental Goal _____

   How this will be accomplished _____

Name _____

VIII. **Document hereon any notable one-time achievements that reduced cost, simplified procedures or increased service or effectiveness — To be completed by the Supervisor**

_____
_____
_____
_____
_____
_____
_____
_____

IX. **Additional Supervisory comments (Additional job related strengths, special contributions, progress since last appraisal, etc.)**

_____
_____
_____
_____
_____
_____
_____
_____

X. **Overall Performance Rating — To be completed by Supervisor**

	Non-Exempt	Exempt
Objectives/Duties Rating (Item 1)	_____ X .67 = _____
Management Skills Rating (Item 2)	N/A	_____ X .33 = _____
Overall Performance Rating	_____	_____

*If Overall Performance Rating is below 3.0, employee must be placed on a formal Performance Improvement Plan.

(7)

Name _____

Continued Comments: Please use this page if additional space is needed to expand on any section of this Appraisal form. Please cross reference Section number and if necessary Entry number (i.e. Duty number, Skill number, etc.)

Section No.	Entry No.	COMMENTS

(8)   (If needed, additional pages for comments may be obtained from the Personnel Department.)

After seeing how performance appraisal can call for corrective and remedial actions, it is time to explore such actions in detail.

Chapter 5:

HOW TO CHOOSE THE
BEST REMEDIAL METHODS

Simple Ways to Pick the Right Problem Solution

Most workers have adequate job skills: they know how to do the job, and usually have done it properly in the past. Ask yourself, could the employee do the job if their life depended on it? If the answer is "no," then training is definitely needed. If the answer is "yes", then knowledge is not the basic problem and some remedial methods other than training may be indicated.

A Quick Test to Confirm Whether Training Is Required

Training is needed when the employee does not know
- Responsibilities
- Goals, Objectives or Standards
- Proper Procedures
- Priorities
- When to Act

Methods for Training, Instruction, Practice, Improvement and Development

The next few pages focus on training methods. Some of them are useful for more than basic instruction or skill training. These methods can also
- provide practice
- improve abilities
- demonstrate knowledge
- create confidence
- test flexibility
- expose strengths and weaknesses
- reveal development needs

If none of the above are relevant issues, skip ahead to the other **Remedial Methods** sections on **Feedback**, **Reinforcement**, **Balance of Consequences** and **Task Interference**.

A Summary of the Major Types of Training Methods for Instruction, Practice, Improvement and Development

No.	Type	Location	Method
1.	On-the-job Coaching	Preferably at the normal place of work.	Personal instruction, guidance, coaching, goal setting and work planning.
2.	Staff meetings	In an area free from interruptions.	Participation in workshop or conference.
3.	Job rotation	Wherever new assignment will achieve objectives.	Give full authority and responsibility (no "assistant" roles).
4.	Emergency fill-in assignments	Where the needed skills will be tested.	Assign full responsibility as long as assignment is in effect.
5.	Special individual projects	Anywhere.	Assign full responsibility and authority.
6.	Task-force assignment	Within or outside the unit.	Assign as task-force member, chairman, consultant or advisor.
7.	Classroom educational courses	At work location; outside schools; professional societies.	Attend courses taught by expert instructors.
8.	Guided reading	Home.	Selected reading list from superiors or library; use books, magazines, reports; organize book reading/review club.

9.	Teaching educational courses	At work; outside schools/societies; community forums.	Teach formal courses; research and prepare special course material.
10.	Outside professional or psychological counseling	Away from work.	Personal conferences and consultations.
11.	Off-the-job activities	At professional societies or community groups.	Practice and demonstrate planning, organizing, etc., through volunteer committee work, election to office, etc.

Each type and method of training has a different purpose and use. Before you prescribe any one kind of training, improvement or development method, **make sure** that it is suitable for what the employee needs. First, diagnose the need (why something should be done); then select the most appropriate method to satisfy that need. For example, if you want someone to kick a drug habit, classroom courses are less helpful than personal counseling (see next page).

How to Select the Best Training Method for Instruction, Practice, Improvement and Development Needs

A Checklist Guide to Choosing Among Eleven Optional Training Methods

Needs ↓

Match the needs with checked options	1. Coaching	2. Staff Mtgs.	3. Job Rotate	4. Emerg. Fill-in	5. Ind. Projs.	6. Task Force	7. Class-room	8. Read.	9. Teach.	10. Couns.	11. Off-Job
Improve or develop ... job skill/ knowledge	✔	✔	✔		✔	✔	✔	✔	✔		✔
...knowledge of other operations	✔	✔	✔	✔	✔	✔		✔	✔	✔	
...problem-solving techniques	✔	✔			✔	✔	✔	✔			✔

Match the needs with checked options	1. Coach-ing	2. Staff Mtgs.	3. Job Rotate	4. Emerg. Fill-in	5. Ind. Projs.	6. Task Force	7. Class-room	8. Read.	9. Teach.	10. Couns.	11. Off-Job
...flexibility			✔	✔	✔	✔			✔		✔
...teamwork		✔				✔					✔
...problem-sharing		✔				✔					✔
...leadership				✔							✔
Discover ... relative abilities		✔	✔	✔	✔	✔					✔
...breadth and versatility		✔	✔	✔	✔	✔					✔
...ability to adjust/perform under pressure			✔	✔	✔					✔	
...barriers to career advancement	✔	✔	✔	✔	✔	✔				✔	✔
...solution to a current work problem		✔				✔					
...specific personal development needs	✔	✔	✔	✔	✔	✔				✔	✔

This worksheet is an important tool. Use it regularly to confirm that the employee's needs are met through the most appropriate remedial method. Don't waste time, money, effort and energy by using the wrong training methods: they will not accomplish the objective efficiently and will only frustrate all parties involved.

Each method has particular strengths. Be sure that you select the method that is best suited to remedy the performance need.

Tips on How to Use the Training Method Worksheet to Pick the Best Remedial Approach

The worksheet on training methods reminds you to first consider the objective before you select the specific remedial exercise method to provide instruction, practice, improvement or development.

Why "Training" Should Not Be Restricted to Classes

"**Training**" is much more than a process of classroom lecture on technical skills. It is a learning process that involves demonstration. That learning and its demonstration are not always limited to the employee; it also involves the manager.

Much training is ordered because the manager needs assurance that the worker is capable of exercising skills not normally called for in her regular job. In such cases, the manager wants to learn the employee's capabilities by having her demonstrate her skills. While that objective might be accomplished in a classroom situation, the employee's practical ability to perform a particular "new" task may just as easily be tested through a special assignment.

The Special Advantages of Each Remedy Option: Coaching, Staff Meetings, Job Rotation, Emergency Fill-In, Individual Projects, Task Forces, Classrooms, Reading, Teaching, Counseling and Off-Job Volunteer Work

The relative advantages of the various training exercises should be carefully considered before one or more methods are chosen.

1. **Coaching** can be provided anywhere, although it usually is best offered on the job, where the most appropriate work resources and "case" examples already exist. Coaching:

   - calls for the investment of time by both coach and worker;
   - may not require time to be lost from regular work;
   - does not require the immediate boss to be the coach, but can use a senior employee (thus "training" and testing them as a supervisor);
   - focuses on specific limited learning needs;
   - gives fast and practical results;
   - allows instruction and guidance to be focused on actual work output;
   - assures close supervision of behavior change;
   - can catch a mistake before it goes into effect;
   - produces immediate value to the organization;
   - has a variable time frame, adjustable to actual needs.

2. **Staff Meetings** combine the talents and insights of team members in a place where they can assemble and share information and ideas without

interruptions. Staff Meetings:

- require absence from normal work activities for a while;
- expose participants to a wide variety of ideas and views;
- permit the simultaneous "cross-training" of a large number of people;
- can focus on a specific work plan, task or problem;
- provide a forum to demonstrate the communication and leadership skills of individual members;
- can enhance group cohesiveness and "team spirit";
- bring a number of minds to bear on a topic where different views or concensus are valuable;
- expose others to the talents of employees they may work with, work under, supervise, or evaluate in the future;

3. **Job Rotation** involves a formal transfer to other duties (usually in the same department or a related area) that will use, hone, sharpen and test employee skills and potentials. Job rotation:

- requires the abandonment of old duties and the assumption of new ones;
- tests employee abilities in a new environment;
- develops new perspectives about work in the employee;
- provides a change for one who is bored and unchallenged;
- may produce a better match between employee skills and company needs than the old job did;
- increases the talent pool by cross-training;
- brings a fresh viewpoint to the new job;
- retains an employee whose ability to perform the old job is still available to the organization;
- demonstrates employee flexibility and ability to handle change;
- develops potential candidates for promotion who have a wider viewpoint of company operations;
- can be cancelled, reversed or continued (depending on its success) without making anyone look bad.

4. **Emergency Fill-In Assignments** fill an urgent need for sudden task completion while testing and demonstrating employee ability to handle a vital temporary project. Emergency assignments:

- can be "planned," in terms of advance contingency planning for who might be available on short notice for certain rush performance needs;

- are a reality test of competence in a new and important project;
- demonstrate employee flexibility and ability to work under pressure;
- offer the same advantages as Job Rotation, but with a shorter time-frame expectancy for the length of the assignment.

5. **Special Individual Projects** can be anything and anywhere you want. Special projects:

    - are custom designed for the mutual needs of the employee and the organization;
    - are as short or as long as desired;
    - need not interfere with regular duties;
    - permit one to combine the advantages of Coaching, Staff Meetings and all other methods;
    - can be completed without affecting other aspects of the job or the organization.

6. **Task Force Assignment** picks the individual to serve on a term selected to address a specific task. As a contributing member of a special group project, the employee may have a different role than in his or her normal job. A Task Force Assignment:

    - contains many of the same advantages of the previous methods options;
    - allows the employee to exercise either greater or less responsibility and authority than on the regular job;
    - can test skills of leadership, technical competence, problem solving, teamwork, and flexibility;
    - makes the specific talents of this individual available to a select group with a special charter to act;
    - completes a project needed by the organization without creating new jobs or departments.

7. **Classroom Educational Courses** are what most people think of as "training." They are the best method for providing individuals with a well-rounded, clear, complete and consistent set of specific skills and body of background knowledge. Classroom courses:

- can be held at work, in schools or on the premises of other organizations;
- are available from public and private sources, from commercial firms and volunteer professional societies;
- come in all sizes and types, from limited technical briefings to extensive post-graduate courses of study;
- provide more expert instruction by educational professionals whose skills many not be accessable through other training methods;
- give a broader overview of a topic area than in-house training methods;
- allow the employee to demonstrate and test his skills outside the real work-world environment, where he can fail safely (or at least without damaging others);
- should result in greater confidence about the credibility of employee abilities by both individual and supervisor;
- require a commitment of time, energy and money;
- can produce "the training effect" (a self-fufilling prophesy that "if I was supposed to do better after the course, I will do better," even when nothing new was learned because confidence and competence were reinforced);
- must produce results proven to be effective in real life.

8. **Guided Reading** is usually a supplemental method applied for limited purposes. Guided Reading can be done anywhere and anytime and:
    - fills gaps in knowledge;
    - maintains current technical expertise;
    - accesses the knowledge of specialists;
    - gives a wider framework and background on topics;
    - can be started and stopped with affecting others;
    - may be combined with Staff Meetings, Classes or other methods;
    - is inexpensive and simple to implement.

9. **Teaching Educational Courses** is an extremely effective way for a competent employee to become an expert. Teaching a Course:
    - forces the employee to learn a broader span of a subject area than she normally encounters on the job;
    - teaches the employee what he or she does not already know;

- demonstrates any needs for better planning, communication, review and evaluation/appraisal skills;
- impresses one with the importance of academic study that applies to work areas;
- develops humility, when the teacher can't answer a simple but important question;
- provides practice in research, leadership and presentation skills that are valuable on the job;
- makes the skills and knowledge of one employee available to many others;
- enhances the prestige and self-confidence of the teacher;
- reflects credit on the employer who selected and developed the teacher.

10. **Outside Professional or Psychological Counseling** encompasses some of the aspects of Coaching and Individual Special Projects; but it is usually conducted by an outside expert or specialist who is not on the company payroll. Outside Counseling:

- is generally offered off the work premises;
- uses a specialized professional expert;
- usually involves complete confidentiality about what the employee says;
- provides an outside perspective of employee needs and problems;
- makes authoritative expertise available for more effective and more credibile management decisions.

11. **Off-the-Job Activities** of various kinds provide many opportunities for employees to learn, practice, rehearse, test and prove abilities that pay off at work. Professional societies, management clubs, community groups, charities, etc., are always hungry for people who are willing to be active in group efforts. Off-the-Job Activities:

- offer in themselves many, if not all, of the training methods mentioned earlier;
- provide a structure and continuity to employee efforts;
- permit workers to discover their weaknesses without directly affecting their employer;
- put employees in contact with a network of other individuals who are interested in achievement;

- broaden the viewpoints of people who only live for their immediate jobs;
- give people a chance to excel in ways that bring a high degree of ego-building praise and approval;
- do not usually interfere with current work;
- offer a subordinate a chance to practice being a manager without any negative consequences to the company.

It is common to see a number of these training methods used simultaneously or in combinations. All have relative strengths and weaknesses; but a quick review should help you select the best for your needs.

Remember to pick the method to suit the need rather than merely applying the same prescription to remedy every problem.

What to Do to Follow Up on Training & Remedial Actions

Why You Need to Check the Success of Training

Training is provided to
- correct actual performance deficiencies;
- prevent potential performance deficiencies;
- produce a positive change in behavior;
- maintain the current level of proper behavior;
- satisfy management that employees are, in fact, competent.

For any of those things to happen, "trainees" must be taught relevant material in a way that they can understand, accept, absorb, and apply. Most importantly, they must also act so that the lesson of the training are actually applied and seen in work results. And the value of the (hopefully) improved work results should be greater than the cost of the training program, including salaries, lost work output, diverted time and other resources.

How to Measure the Results of Instruction, Practice, Improvement and Development

The effectiveness of the training program should be regularly and systematically reviewed to assure that it meets those vital criteria of validity, transferability, acceptance and worth.

The Four Measures of Effectiveness

To measure	The method to use is	Done by
VALIDITY	"Before" and "After" skill tests	Test participants during program
TRANSFER	Observe changes in job results	Survey participants and supervisors after program finished
ACCEPTANCE	Degree of appreciation and use	Follow-up survey of participants
WORTH	Compare program cost vs. benefits	Input from supervisors

How to Measure Program Validity

Validity can be assessed by tests of employee skills before the begin the program and after they have completed it. It answers the question of whether the training program did accomplish its stated learning objectives.

A test of the validity of the training process does not measure how long trainees will retain what they have learned, but it will determine how much hypothetical learning actually took place. It also provides valuable feedback for the course instructors and the participants themselves. Pre- and Post-testing lets the learners discover the extent of their improvement and alerts them to how well they can expect to do when they apply their new knowledge.

How to Measure Whether the Transfer of Skill & Knowledge Took Place

Transfer refers to the degree to which the training affected on-the-job work results after the training program has ended. Transfer tests measure whether the new lessons showed up in later work results.

Once time passes, lessons can be forgotten or neglected; so transfer tests should be repeated at intervals to find out how long the training "sticks" with the trainee, and why.

How to Measure the Degree of Employee Acceptance (with a Sample Questionnaire)

Acceptance is literally that: how well people accepted the training. Did they value it? Did they use it?

Some insight into trainee acceptance can be found by an immediate survey of participant attitudes and opinions at the end of the training session. Again, positive responses do not automatically guarantee that employees will value and use the new material (they might just be reflecting gratitude at getting some time off the regular job); but negative immediate reactions are a bad sign. If trainees disliked and resented the program, their disapproval may lead to rejection of the intended lessons: their performance may not improve and might even decline.

EVALUATION OF TRAINING SESSION

Subject:	*Speaker(s):*	*Date:*

Your observations are important to help us improve our ability to serve you. We continually strive to accurately identify management education needs and to address those subjects in a manner which does, in fact, provide relevant and useful information. We need your comments and constructive criticism to aid us. Please take a moment to complete this Evaluation Form by selecting the answer which best represents your feelings or thoughts.

1. What is your overall impression of the presentation?
   ☐ Excellent   ☐ Good   ☐ Fair   ☐ Poor

2. What is your opinion of the session content (balance of theory and practical advice)?
   ☐ Excellent   ☐ Good   ☐ Fair   ☐ Poor

3. Were the objectives of the session met?
   ☐ Fully met   ☐ Adequately met   ☐ Not adequately met

4. What is your opinion of the instructor's knowledge of the subject?
   ☐ Excellent   ☐ Good   ☐ Fair   ☐ Poor

5. How do you rate the organization and delivery of the presentor?

☐ Excellent   ☐ Good   ☐ Fair   ☐ Poor

6. Did the speaker respond to questions or otherwise interact with the audience?
   ☐ A great deal   ☐ Somewhat   ☐ Seldom   ☐ Not at all

7. How useful were the handouts (if any)?
   ☐ Excellent   ☐ Good   ☐ Fair   ☐ Poor   ☐ Not Applicable

8. How effective were the visual aids (if any)?
   ☐ Excellent   ☐ Good   ☐ Fair   ☐ Poor   ☐ Not Applicable

9. How realistic were the workshop exercises (if any)?
   ☐ Excellent   ☐ Good   ☐ Fair   ☐ Poor   ☐ Not Applicable

10. Were your expectations for the session met?
    ☐ Exceeded   ☐ Fully met   ☐ Adequately met   ☐ Not adequately met

11. Would you recommend this session to others?
    ☐ Yes   ☐ No

12. What changes would you suggest to make the presentation more beneficial?

   Thank you for attending the session and for providing us with your comments.

How to Measure the Worth of the Remedial Program

   Worth is determined by a cost-benefit analysis. The value of the training, practice, instruction or development program is compared to the price paid for it.

   The criteria for such value judgments of "worth" are not simple. There is long-term value and short-term value; the same applies to costs. All actions to remedy, maintain or improve performance have immediate costs: if nothing else, they take time and resources and require employees to experience some (and often much) interference with their normal duties. It can be quite difficult to determine the amount of subsequent performance improvement that can be directly attributed to the "training," particularly over time. And it is even harder to accurately measure the mistakes that **were not** made due to the program, unless you have a highly effective performance feedback system and extensive historical records.

Why Measuring Results Will Improve Remedial Programs

It is important for training courses and remedial/developmental programs to designed with an eye to these issues of **validity, transfer, acceptance** and **worth**, to assure that:

▷ the training method chosen is the one(s) best suited for the needs discovered in the assessment stage;
▷ there is confirmation that participants learned what was needed;
▷ positive changes in job output/behavior resulted;
▷ participants accepted and used what was taught;
▷ the worth of the program was proved to top management.

Training can be valuable even if all these goals are not met. After all, a developmental exercise that makes participants feel more confident has some worth to the organization. But a lack of persuasive information on the precise dollars-and-cents payoff for the company may lead to cancellation of the program when budgets get tight. The proper assesssment of training needs includes an analysis of what top management must know before they will approve the action.

Other Remedial Methods When Training Is Not the Answer

How Practice, Feedback, Reinforcement, and Removing Obstacles Can Be More Effective Than "Training"

Most "deficient" performers do not need training. In the majority of cases, people who perform below expectations **could** do the job if their lives depended on it. They do not need further education or training but need, instead:

Practice	an opportunity to regain old skills by more frequent use;
Feedback	information on what you want and how they are doing it;
Reinforcement	positive consequences when they perform properly;
Balance of Consequences	the consequence of doing what you want is more valuable than the consequence of doing what you

don't want;

Obstacles Removed   the elimination of obstacles to proper performance which cause task interference.

How to Give "Practice" by Adapting Training Methods

The first of those needs (**practice**) can be satisfied by using some of the eleven optional training/improvement methods on the previous pages.

Practice differs from conventional classroom **training** in its emphasis on repetition that refreshes the memory and increases the ease with which skills already learned are applied. While training provides new skills, practice merely sharpens the performer's ability to use skills learned long ago which may not have been used for a while. The rest of the remedial methods that may be needed (feedback, reinforcement, etc.) are discussed in greater detail here.

Feedback Techniques to Guide Progress

An Example of the Importance of Mistakes

The British comic actor John Cleese of *Monty Python* and *Fawlty Towers* fame heads the largest training film production company outside the United States. In a 1987 speech to American training and personnel executives, he paid tribute to the vital importance of **feedback** about what goes wrong. He pointed out, quite amusingly, that "mistakes" are essential to progress: without the feedback we get from errors, it is quite difficult (if not impossible) to ever get things right.

Very few human beings are ever able to do everything perfectly correctly on the first try. The rest of us mortals make our plans, set our sights, do our best, note the results, correct our aim and adjust our actions to improve the probability that our next attempt will be more successful. We GET READY, AIM, FIRE, SCORE and ADJUST.

Ways to Give Feedback Information on Progress

But we are only able to SCORE and ADJUST because of feedback on how the result of our action compared to the desired goal or performance expectation. Even the preliminary steps of preparation, planning and action are extremely difficult without feedback. Information that confirms or corrects our initial independent assumptions and guesses is required for effective performance at all levels.

A List of the Types of Feedback You Can Use

Some of the types of feedback are

praise	criticism
cheers	jeers
smiles	frowns
rewards	punishments
suggestions	objections
encouragement	complaints
observations	hints
promotions	terminations
appraisals	silence
attention	neglect
report cards	progress reviews
raises	bills
bank statements	alarm bells

What Feedback Is All About: Information

Feedback can be positive, negative or simply neutral. It always gives information about a condition or situation that exists before, during or after an action. Feedback provides the road signs that guide our journey to a performance objective. It tells you where you are, whether you are on course and how far you still have to go.

Without feedback, the performer is like a blindfolded golfer. He won't know the score unless someone tells him. In fact, he won't even be able to find the golf ball to strike, much less aim for the green, on his own.

In the work environment, the failure to provide for feedback is a form of feedback itself: "no feedback" communicates the message that no one cares about performance or the performer. Denial of feedback frustrates basic human needs. People want to excel, and to know how they are doing, they need feedback information.

The performance manager will find feedback one of the most valuable tools in his kit of skills.

Proper feedback can eliminate or at least identify many common performance problems. It also helps unleash the talents of employees by giving them information on how they are doing so they can adjust and correct before disaster strikes.

Characteristics of a Good Feedback System: The PERFORMERS Anagram

P - Performance standard oriented:
    Actual vs Expected Performance.
  E - Easily understandable:
    Simple, clear and easily interpreted feedback.
    R - Routed to the right person:
      Feedback should go back to performer without delay.
     F - Frequent:
      Feedback should be frequent enough to assure desired performance.
      O - On target:
        Feedback should focus on correct performance.
       R - Relevant:
         Feedback should focus on what the employee needs to know.
        M - Measurable:
          Provides the employee with specific information for measuring
            performance and progress.
          E - Expressed positively:
            Feedback should be used to reinforce desired behavior.
           R - Real and Honest:
              Feedback will only work if it is accurate.
             S - Self-Administered:
                Employees should be able to guide and correct their own
                  performance.

Vital Information About Feedback Characteristics

The feedback information should give specific details about **how close the actual performance came to the target.** It is not enough to know that you missed the objective; you need to know how far off you were to correct your aim. Merely telling people that they "did right" or "did wrong" leaves a lot of questions unanswered. People should be notified of their relative degree of success, so they can properly adjust their behavior accordingly.

Feedback must be **simple, clear and understandable** to be useful. If the information on performance is complex, confusing, overwhelming in volume and detail, or otherwise difficult to comprehend, it will frustrate and demotivate employees and waste organizational resources. No one wants to spend a day searching through a large computer printout for the one piece of data that will save them one hour's work in the future. Information overload paralyzes decision making and effective performance.

The **performer** must get the feedback in a **timely** manner. Reports containing essential information for improved performance should reach the worker in time for corrective action. Telling the boss is fine, but the feedback must be received by the performer before it can be used.

Frequent feedback is needed when corrective adjustments must be taken quickly. The proper frequency is relative, depending on the situation; but if the performer doesn't know how she's doing at any time, then the feedback is not frequent enough.

Keep it **on target**. Focus feedback on **correct performance** rather than what was wrong. Otherwise, you may distract, discourage or antagonize the employee by an over-reliance on negative criticism. The idea is to do it right, not to dwell on all the ways to do it wrong. Success is more likely to come from the active pursuit of excellence rather than from the mere avoidance of failure.

Provide **relevant** information. Unnecessary data and excessive detail waste everyone's time. It's easier to see a diamond on piece of black velvet than on a sandy beach.

Give **measurable** feedback that helps the employee see exactly where his work stands.

Express positive performance reinforcement with positive feedback, encouraging the repetition of the behavior you want. Expectations tend to be self-fufilling prophesies. People will generally try to live up to (or down to) the performance expecations of those they respect; so emphasize positive consequences: they are far more powerful than negatives, anyway.

Be **real** and honest, about your management style and the feedback you provide. Inconsistent or "unnatural" personal behavior by the boss can be just as disturbing to subordinates as being given false information: both situations communicate dishonesty, deception and manipulation. For optimal performance results, your employees don't have to like you, but they must be able to trust your honesty and predict your reactions.

Self-administered feedback is the most effective kind. Strive to create ways for employees to know how well they are doing even before the boss knows. The more steps, chains and filters there are between the feedback information and the performer who needs it, the more difficult it is to provide. Employees will usually become their own toughest critics when they become personally involved in reviewing and evaluating their own performance.

Performance Management Tip

For fast and easy effective feedback, have employees keep a graph showing how their actual work results match up to the objective.

A chart or plot of actual daily/weekly output, maintained **by the employee** will focus attention on how things stand, particularly if the graphic method shows positive results with a scale that moves up.

An upward-curving line or a box with an ascending series of ladder-like steps has an innate instinctive positive appeal to people. It makes them feel better about doing better.

Reinforcement Methods to Direct and Strengthen Performance

A Summary of the Kinds of Reinforcement

Reinforcement is any action that comes as the consequence of behavior. The long list of standard reinforcements used in the business world illustrates that they can be either positive or negative. They can be used to encourage proper behavior or to discourage (extinguish) negative performance.

There are many kinds of reinforcement. **Training** and **feedback** are forms of reinforcement, because they are steps that follow behavior and are used to affect future actions. A pay increase, for example, is both a reinforcement and a feedback: it sends a message that the employee's performance has been recognized as worth more money to the company.

Details of formal compensation methods for reinforcement are covered in the **Pay** chapter.

Reinforcement methods are also forms of feedback that communicate the **consequences** (see the next section) of performance.

Most people tend to forget how many types of reinforcement are available for their use. Managers place an unnecessary handicap on their effectiveness when they neglect the full range of reinforcement techniques and place all of their reliance on only a few, like wages and promotions.

A Partial List of the Types of Reinforcement You Can Use

REWARDS	PUNISHMENTS
recognition	withholding rewards
job security	no raises
wage/salary	small raises
raises	no promotions
bonuses	no bonuses
benefits	no recognition
perquisites	
promotions	negative actions
preferential assignments	criticism
psychological stroking	demotions
merchandise	bad assignments
prizes	undesirable transfers
services	termination

Rewards That Have No Financial Cost

There are many reward and reinforcement methods available at your fingertips that do not cost a penny.

No-Cost Rewards

- public compliments for a job well done
- delegating authority for enjoyable projects
- recommending someone for promotion
- giving personal attention
- sharing information

Such actions can be taken swiftly and usually do not require special organizational approvals. Keep in mind that all the principles on effective feedback techniques apply to reinforcement. As a form of feedback, rewards and punishments are most effective when they are clear, fast, appropriate, positive, etc.

The Reinforcements That Are Most Powerful

Certain reinforcements have advantages over others.

How Carrots Beat Sticks

Positive rewards are intended to satisfy employee desires, while **negative punishments** are barriers to (or attacks against) satisfaction of a need. Punishments are usually a withholding or denial of the rewards people seek: instead of being praised, he is criticized; instead of getting a raise, she is fired, and so on.

Rewards are more effective than punishments.

Basic psychology teaches us that when behavior directed towards the satisfaction of a need meets with an obstacle (like punishment), frustration results. Frustrated people become unhappy, anxious, childish, passive, resentful, stubborn, angry or aggressive... often exhibiting many of these states. Punishment will stimulate negative reactions, only a few of which promise to support positive performance.

While punishments have a role in management, it should be a minor one, primarily reserved for disciplinary actions that may end in termination of employment. Punishment is an act of failure. Organizations that want to excel do not focus on failure but on success; and success is a positive goal that rarely comes from dwelling on past failures.

When Non-Cash Rewards Are Better Than Money

Rewards that take a form other than money have particular advantages over cash. Of course, only money will pay the rent or put food on the table; but it has limitations, too.

Pay increases have to wait until the proper time; word of praise can be granted instantly after performance.

You can't brag to your neighbor about how much money you make without appearing offensive; but you can rave about the snazzy company car that came with your promotion without seeming quite as crass.

Paychecks go into the pocket or the bank account to be mixed with other cash, with no intrinsic identity associated with the action that earned it; a handsome engraved plaque on the wall will forever remind the employee of the specific performance that won it.

Bonus money can be spent by the individual without him even remembering where it went; but a company-paid family vacation in Europe will never be forgotten... and such a prize directly rewards the entire family for employee performance, so they share in the benefits accruing from his hard work and are likely to become more positively involved in his career.

Cash rewards create an expectation of repetition. When people get a raise or a bonus one year, they rely on it to be repeated again next year (and with a higher pay-out amount). Non-cash rewards are usually not seen as automatic. They are easier to change or abolish without violent employee reaction. And they do not compound the base and total compensation costs like pay raises.

As long as employees earn enough cash for their disposable income needs, non-cash awards and prizes can be extremely cost-effective and flexible ways to provide supplemental rewards.

The Four Basic Rules that Govern Human Behavior: How People Weigh the Balance of Consequences

1. Reinforcement encourages repetition

If one behavior is desired but a different behavior is reinforced, the reinforced behavior is more likely to be repeated.

Also, punishment discourages repetition... or at least leads to behaviors which avoid punishment.

2. The faster the response, the stronger the effect

The more immediate the consequences of a behavior, the more effective it will be in influencing subsequent behavior. The longer you delay the response, the more you weaken the perceived relationship between the original behavior and the consequence (a reward or a punishment).

A long delay between action and consequential result weakens any reinforcement, positive or negative.

3. Importance is subjective

People have their own motivations. The consequences that influence a behavior are those that have value to the individual. People always act according to their own perceptions of maximum self-interest, and their values may not be the same as yours. Offer "carrots and sticks" that mean something to your employees.

Remember that a need, once satisfied, is no longer a motivator. Rewards that were effective in the past may not work as well if those rewards are designed to meet needs that are now already met.

And a need, once satisfied, is no longer a motivator.

4. Positives are better incentives

The more positive the consequences of a behavior, the better the chances of the behavior being repeated.

Negative reinforcement (punishment) may extinguish undesirable behavior, but it rarely works well all by itself. If negative consequences for the "wrong" actions are not combined with greater positive consequences for the "right" actions, people can be tempted to cover up and avoid punishment while continuing to do what they please rather than what you want.

How Understanding the Consequences of Behavior Will Make You More Effective

Performance managers must work through others to achieve organizational objectives. That calls for very different skills than doing all the work yourself; many would say that managing, leading and guiding people is far more difficult, too. It depends on how well you know and use principles of human behavior like those key ones summarized under the heading, **Balance of Consequences.**

Some of the most authoritative research on human behavior was done by Harvard professor B. F. Skinner, who is widely known as "the father of behavioralism." It is said that it was some of Dr. Skinner's graduate students who formulated what is now referred to as the Harvard Law of Behavior.

Under carefully controlled laboratory conditions where all outside influences are monitored to prevent interference with the experiment, the experimental subject will do as it damn well pleases.

It is both amusing and true. All the research studies with people running through mazes and taking tests agree on one overwhelming fact: People do what they WANT to do. It is not necessarily good or bad; it is just a fact. And it is not a new discovery but one that has been known for thousands of years by all effective performance managers.

You must recognize that people seek their own best self-interests (and those are not always "selfish" in the conventional sense) before you can begin to deal effectively with people. You must remember that proper performance will only become a reality when employee desires are served by the achievement of organizational needs.

Everyday problems can be avoided by those who are aware of motivational principles and apply them properly. Improved productivity comes from the practical use of these basic laws of human behavior.

Motivation

You will not learn how to **motivate** people, because no one can motivate someone else.

Motivation is not a substance one person can inject into another. As the "Harvard Law of Behavior" shows, motivation is internal. People have their own motivations. There is no sense in your trying to create motivations for others; they have developed their own in childhood. Unless you are their parents in their formative years, you have little hope of changing their motivations; and some would deny that even parents have that power. You can, however, make use of motivations in ways that do not involve manipulation but result in mutual advantages.

As a manager, you must find ways to align the motivations of others with your needs, to create a belief that achievement of organizational goals will satisfy their motivations. Thus, you can increase the probability that people will perform in a positive manner for mutual need satisfaction.

Performance management demands that you recognize how future employee behavior is affected by the **consequences** of past behaviors: what kind of feedback they get, the type of rewards or punishments, etc. It is an application of **exchange theory**, which deals with the cost-benefit decisions people make when they are asked to compare the cost of an action with the benefit which results. Here, it is discussed as a balancing of consequences.

Making Use of the Four Key Principles of Motivation

The first principle is **Reinforcement Encourages Repetition.** When people do a good job, you want to reinforce that good job performance. When behavior is rewarded, that behavior tends to be repeated.

A simple pat on the back, a word of praise, a mark of status, a promotion or a salary increase are all rewards that can reinforce positive performance. Most of those reinforcements are very easy to use and many are quite inexpensive.

There is another important point about reinforcement. IF ONE BEHAVIOR IS DESIRED, BUT A DIFFERENT BEHAVIOR IS REINFORCED, THE REINFORCED BEHAVIOR IS MORE LIKELY TO BE REPEATED.

If you tell people to do one thing, then reward them for doing something else, which do you think they will repeat more often in the future? If you tell your employees to keep you informed about problems, to notify you when something goes wrong... but then you lavish your praise and approval ONLY on those employees who NEVER come to you with any problems, what kind of behavior are you reinforcing?

People tend to do what is rewarded. In this case, they soon get the message that only good news is rewarded. So they will simply stop bringing you bad news; and you will think that everything is going fine until the roof caves in around your head.

Likewise, line foremen whose salaries are based on the pay rate of their union subordinates can find themselves in a conflict of interest. Although they are supposed to identify with management, they are rewarded when the union wins high pay increases and their own pay jumps. If foremen think their pay will go up more if the union negotiates a richer labor rate, they are tempted to undercut management efforts to control labor costs. They receive a greater reward by helping the union than by helping management.

If reinforcement encourages repetition, the opposite of that is also true: PUNISHMENT DISCOURAGES REPETITION.

One of the best examples involves a U.S. government agency whose agents were frequently offered bribes. The government decided to initiate a very strict policy, ordering agents to report any bribery attempts immediately. But, when they did report bribery attempts, they were instantly relieved of duty, suspended and flown to Washington for cross-examination and formal depositions. They were accused of soliciting bribes and were treated as though THEY were the criminals. So what happened? The number of bribery attempts reported by agents suddenly and dramatically declined. Of course. One behavior was desired, but then it was punished. Agents were given more reinforcement to keep their mouths shut then they were given to follow instructions. When they did follow instructions, they were punished, while, if they ignored instructions, they were left alone to do their work.

Reinforcing positive performance is vital. Your employees pay more attention to what you DO than to what you SAY. If your people say to themselves, "the way to get ahead around here is not based on performance, it's based on something else," then you're in big trouble; because people will always tend to do those things that lead to reward and avoid punishments... even though those actions may not be in the best long term interest of the organization.

The second principle of behavior is **The Faster The Response, The Stronger The Effect.**

Long delays between employee action and company reward or punishment reduce the psychological effect of company response. THE MORE IMMEDIATE THE CONSEQUENCE OF BEHAVIOR, THE MORE EFFECTIVE IT WILL BE IN INFLUENCING SUBSEQUENT BEHAVIOR. Although this seems obvious, formal management systems are notorious for their failure to provide immediate feedback.

What do you do with the employee whose pay increase comes in January and who does his best work in February? That poor unfortunate must wait eleven months to receive a formal reward. In many cases, by the time his next pay increase rolls around, the company may have forgotten what a great job he did, way back last February. And even if you remember, and give him a hefty increase next January, don't expect him to be very grateful. The long delay between the original positive performance and the eventual reinforcement will have robbed the reward of much of its meaning.

You should try to respond immediately, because the shorter the time span between the action and the consequence, the more strongly the two are linked. Personnel departments may not give you much help in this area. Most formal reward systems require long time delays before meritorious performance can be reinforced. Nevertheless, as a manager of people, you have both the responsibility and the opportunity to respond immediately. A mere word of praise upon completion of an important project is more effective than a formal letter of commendation six months later.

The third principle of human behavior: **Importance Is Subjective.**

Remember the Harvard Law of Behavior? Your people have their own value systems, their own priorities, and they may well not be the same as yours. THE CONSEQUENCES THAT INFLUENCE A BEHAVIOR ARE THOSE THAT HAVE VALUE TO THE INDIVIDUAL.

Arthur Burns once described an economist as someone who would marry Farrah Fawcett for her money. That is an excellent example of different motivations. What turns you on may not be of the slightest interest to someone else.

You probably see this principle in action every day. You offer an out-of-town transfer and promotion to one employee and receive an enthusiastic reaction. You offer the same transfer and promotion to another and receive a negative, anxious response. One feels flattered and pleased, and the other feels threatened. One person wants a bigger salary, a fancier title, and a chance to see the world. Another wants security, stability, doesn't want to interrupt his night school courses or take his kids out of a familiar school... doesn't want to move.

Sometimes the conflicts over personal reward values are less extreme and more subtle.

You have a senior worker whom you are considering for promotion. But you are concerned over this individual's habit of socializing after work with co-workers who are now her peers, but who may be her subordinates in the future. You would like to create a little distance between this senior person and the rest of the group; so you tell her to stop being so friendly with her co-workers or she might lose the promotion. What do you think she will do?

Her eventual choice will depend upon which is more important to HER. If she is more interested in friendship than she is in organizational status, she may reluctantly pass up the opportunity for a promotion because it holds a lower priority in her personal value system. This is why it is so important for you as a manager to know your people.... to know their values, their priorities, and their subjective motivations.

Human motivations can be very complex. Samuel Clemens once commented that the difference between a man and a dog is that a dog will never bite the hand that feeds it. When people act in a way that appears irrational to you, you must remember that they always have a reason that makes sense to them, even though you may not understand it, and they might not fully understand their subconscious reasons themselves.

Most often, the reasons are simple. What you consider to be a valuable reward may not be appropriate for the recipient. If you are trying to hire a dedicated bachelor, you can't expect him to become too excited about your generous maternity benefit coverage.

Speaking about hiring people brings us to another aspect of this principle. A NEED ONCE SATISFIED, IS NO LONGER A MOTIVATOR. The same job applicant who is anxious to please and eager to do anything necessary to get the job shows a completely different attitude when his first pay increase comes due. Last year, getting that job was the most important thing in his life. Today, he takes the job for granted and wants to know what kind of increase he is going to get. He will no longer be satisfied with the statement, "Well, you've got a job, don't you?"

The fourth principle of human behavior, **Positives Are Better Incentives**, focuses on the relative power of various kinds of consequences.

Did you ever try to get an employee all charged up by telling her, "If you do this assignment right, you can keep your job?" Unless that employee is extremely insecure, the promise that you will refrain from punishment is not going to generate much enthusiasm. On the other hand, if you can say, "There will be a $500 bonus in your paycheck next week if you finish this project Friday," you may see some real action. THE MORE POSITIVE THE CONSEQUENCES OF A BEHAVIOR, THE BETTER THE CHANCES OF IT BEING REPEATED.

If a money-hungry supervisor works three hours of unpaid overtime every night and comes in to work every Saturday for a year, only to be told at increase time that his hard work and self-sacrifice has earned him only 1% more in his salary increase than the average granted to clock-watchers... then you can't expect him to work as hard next year. That 1% difference between his 7% increase last year and an 8% increase this year will not even cover the cost of responding to his wife's divorce petition.

Again your formal personnel practices may not give you much assistance. When the difference in the annual base pay increase between a barely adequate and a really good performer is rarely more than 2%, you don't have much opportunity for conventional pay incentives. You may have to use your imagination and use some non-traditional approaches or find non-monetary positive rewards that will stimulate the desire to excel in your employees.

A lot of corporate protocol is a response to this challenge. Status symbols are rewards... who gets what parking space and whether or not his name is on it. Are you assigned to a cubicle, do you have an enclosed (or corner) office, a secretary, the type of furnishings or expense authority you are allowed, and so on. There are many perquisites which cost very little but which can produce a substantial return on your investment.

The Problem with Punishment

Those who rely on negative consequences (punishments) to influence behavior will find that punishment alone, without counterbalancing rewards, can have unforeseen results. Instead of extinguishing undesirable behavior, punishment may increase resentment, stimulate more negative behavior, and merely make offenders more careful.

People are not stupid. If they know that discovery of misbehavior brings punishment, they also know that they have not one but two options: to stop the misbehavior or to prevent its discovery.

Although tough managers would like to believe that fear creates compliance, they may be kidding themselves and providing a source of entertainment to their employees. It is relatively simple for a group of employees to make a mockery of a harsh supervisor by continuing to "misbehave" while covering their tracks and avoiding punishment.

The tough manager who places his or her reputation on the line by ordering all subordinates to report even the most petty personal use of company materials (copiers, pencils, pens, rubber bands and paper clips) by co-workers, threatening dire punishment for all offenders, runs the risk of becoming an office joke.

Some employees may begin to smuggle supplies home as lark. As long as discovery and punishment can be avoided, disobedience will bring a greater reward in amusement and revenge, not to mention peer approval in an "us-against-them" environment, than it will bring obedience.

Manipulation Is Resented

It is not unknown for manipulative managers to deliberately foster a group spirit of peer loyalty by using unfairly harsh treatment (usually at the hands of a third person) to bind together a group of individuals who previously had little in common. Fraternity and sorority hazings, basic military training, and the strikes that often accompany union organizational drives are all examples of practical application of the psychology of human behavior.

While such Machiavellian "games" may work at times, they are dangerous. If employees ever suspect that they are being manipulated or deceived, they will react with anger, distrust, and scorn. This often leads to the complete destruction of morale and increased rebellion, quitting, and even deliberate sabotage.

Legitimate management requires honorable methods that treat people with respect and dignity. Rewards and reinforcements can easily be tailored to the needs and preferences of employees for the mutual benefit of labor and management without violating ethical standards.

Remember those four main principles of human behavior! They work best when used in combination. If you promptly reinforce positive performance with rewards which have substantial value to your employees, you will dramatically increase the probability of getting the maximum performance from your people.

How to Identify and Solve Task Interference Problems

What the Five Typical Obstacles to Positive Performance Are

Task Interference is the most common reason for inadequate performance. It places obstacles in the way that prevent or discourage people from doing the job right. There are five major types of task interference obstacles that haunt every workplace.

1. Incorrect or Incomplete Instructions

The employee does not "get the message" and therefore does not know what is actually expected or how to do it properly.

2. Competitive Tasks

The employee is expected to do conflicting tasks at the same time.

3. Distractions

Something pulls attention away from the job being done and interferes with desired work results.

4. Changing Priorities

People are continually being taken off assignments before they are completed, told to drop the current task and start on something new.

5. Inadequate Support People, Services, or Equipment

The employee is expected to do the job without enough resources.

Why Task Interference Obstacles Are So Dangerous

The obstacles classified as **task interference** wreak havoc with employee performance. They are particularly insidious and frustrating because they are often not recognized as causing or contributing to ineffective work results.

Task interference has more negative effect on work than any other source. It can make proper performance impossible, as when the employee is given bad instructions or conflicting orders. It can make success possible but highly unlikely, as when the work environment contains annoying distractions or unnecessary changes.

Task interference can easily escape the attention of both manager and employee as a critical drag on efficiency. When that happens, confidence is eroded: neither the boss nor the performer can figure out why the worker can't perform properly. And yet, the answer may be right under their noses, in the form of interference with successful task completion.

How to Recognize the Signs and Causes of Task Interference

The Symptoms of Incorrect or Incomplete Instructions

- The employee could do the job right if he or she knew what the boss really wanted, but the objective is never properly communicated.
- The goal seems clear, but a vital piece of information on the process, the timetable, the budget limits, the people or equipment resources is missing or wrong.
- Standards of performance that would permit recognition of complete/correct project success are not communicated.
- Feedback on who, where, when, how and why to apply corrective measures during the job is inadequate.

The Signs of Competitive Tasks

- The employee is expected to do two mutually exclusive tasks **at the same time** such as interview an applicant and finish a report.
- Being expected to answer the phone before the second ring and keep your fingers constantly flying over the computer keyboard.
- Scheduling the same person to make personal visits in Los Angeles and New York in the same afternoon.

- Making a physician perform brain surgery on himself.

Examples of Common Distractions

- A disruptive work environment filled with background noise and people walking by.
- Suddenly pulling an employee off a project calling for deep concentration.
- Trying to conduct a counseling interview with a disturbed employee in the middle of Times Square at 11:59 p.m. on New Year's Eve.
- Being notified, just before making a sales pitch to a prospective client, that you will be laid off next week.

What You Will See When Priorities Change Too Often

- Continually being pulled off unfinished assignments to do other tasks.
- Spending a weekend working on the action plan for a project that was cancelled last month, without your knowledge.
- The identity of the most important goal changes every day.
- The employee faithfully begins evey task suspecting that the boss will redirect his efforts before it is half finished.

How You Can Tell When Support People, Services, or Equipment Are Inadequate

- The employee is expected to do the job without the proper resources.
- People must spend excessive time to get the resources needed.
- Untrained employees are assigned to complex jobs beyond their competence to perform.
- The maintenence department only works the first shift, while most of the equipment breakdowns occur on the second shift.
- You must recruit essential workers from outside who can begin production immediately, but your starting salaries are too low to attract qualified candidates.
- The organization **must** hire and retain far more expert people than competitors need, because here it requires more talented people to overcome the low level of support/resources they will receive to get the job done.

Everyone has seen situations that could be added to the list.

How Hiring Superhuman Performers Can Backfire

Task interference can be a deceptively elusive problem, because super-competent and extraordinarily dedicated people can sometimes fight their way through difficulties that will stop an ordinary average person dead in their tracks.

The very fact that *someone* once found a way (through rare genius, tremendous energy or even blind luck) may blind everyone to the truth that the prior success was an abberation from the norm. Unless the organization is prepared to adjust its employment practices to select only exceptional personnel (who are, by definition, rather scarce), something must be done to permit ordinary human beings to perform effectively. Otherwise, perfectly competent and dedicated normal workers will be thwarted, frustrated, puzzled and demotivated by their failure to overcome task interference obstacles.

Performance Management Tip

Design jobs that can be performed by normal human beings.

If the successful performance of job duties regularly requires extraordinarily talented people, the organization can be held hostage by those super-stars (who are very rare, hard to find and even harder to replace).

It is better to break a tough job that can only be done by one in a million people into two simpler jobs that can be effectively performed by a large number of people. That way, there will be less stress on both the company and the worker and a higher probability that each can continue to survive without the other.

The Solutions to Task Interference Problems

Better planning and improved feedback will cure most task interference problems.

How to Plan a Path to Detour Obstacles

The first step to overcoming task interference is to carefully diagnose the nature and cause of the obstacle. Then you can create a remedial plan with feedback elements to track results and warn of danger.

Job and task analysis, situation analysis, problem analysis, etc., may be required to clearly identify the primary sources of the interference. Further studies may be needed to discover which problems or handicaps are inherent in the work situation and which can be rectified by management or employee action.

Questions that must be answered before an effective remedial plan can be made include:

- ▸ What is the problem? What is the nature of the deviation from desired results? What is supposed to happen and what is happening instead?
- ▸ Specify the *what, where, when, why* and *how* of the interference. Who has information, and what do they think?
- ▸ Is the obstacle only encountered by this one performer? If so, why? ... what are the unique conditions?
- ▸ What are the possible and most probable causes of the obstacle(s)? Which can be investigated and considered?
- ▸ Which among the choice of possible causes could account for all the specific cases of interference?
- ▸ Is the obstacle avoidable or something that must be accepted as an inevitable part of the job?
- ▸ How can the interference be ended or the obstacle be avoided?
- ▸ What changes or additions in instructions, training, feedback or resources are needed to make the remedial plan work?
- ▸ Is it simpler and more practical to merely modify or qualify performance expectations, rather than end the interference?
- ▸ If others can function in this obstacle/interference situation, at what point should consideration be given to selecting another person to do the task?

A person torn between two activities that cause constant distraction and conflict over how time is spent may be the victim of a kind of task interference that is very difficult to cure. It is possible that both tasks are indeed vital parts of the job. For example, a policeman cannot respond to an emergency call and conduct routine patrol activities at the same time.

If the obstacle involves something that is not required by the job, then it can be easy to remove. A research analyst, for instance, does not have to work in a crowded office, located far from the information reference sources and filled with loud, raucous shouts from exuberant salespeople; he should be given a work place that is quiet, close to the data library and free from distractions and interruptions that would break concentration.

A supervisor who officially reports to two managers, on the other hand, is bound to experience task interference. Both managers will want her to concentrate on their assignments and time may not permit simultaneous performance of two tasks which must be done immediately. A remedial plan in this case might require the two managers to reach an agreement between themselves about the priority or time to be given to their projects **before** the supervisor is given assignments.

Remedial methods should first focus on the removal of the obstacles, barriers, roadblocks, distractions, shortages and so on that are diagnosed as the source of the interference.

Unnecessary obstacles should be eliminated. Any "necesary evils" must be identified and taken into consideration for the remedial plan. Priorities should be set and clearly communicated. Performance expectations may have to be altered or even lowered to more realistic levels if difficult obstacles remain inevitable.

How Feedback Helps a Detour to Successfully Avoid Obstacles

The second stage in the remedial solution is the design and implementation of supportive methods, intervention techniques and fall-back measures. These are secondary plan elements which anticipate what could go wrong with the remedial plan. They act to prevent future obstacles, to head off plan failure, to add extra levels of remedial effort when the simpler efforts don't work, and to act as contingent plans which minimize the negative effects when task interference cannot be avoided.

The success of those plans depends on accurate and timely feedback. Information that shows whether the primary remedial plan is working must be identified, collected and studied. When the feedback indicates that problems remain, secondary remedial methods are triggered and put into effect. The actual results are examined regularly until the feedback information proves that the solution has worked.

Effective feedback is information that answers questions like:
▷ How will we know when results are at, below or above planned levels?

▷ Can the performer get fast, accurate and clear information of plan progress?

▷ Does the person demonstrate an ability to implement the plan?

▷ Will everyone understand when the next step in the plan should be implemented or when it has proven successful?

▷ What conditions will exist when the obstacle/interference has been eliminated or overcome? Have those things happened?

If the feedback shows that none of the primary or secondary remedial plans has been effective, then the diagnosis must be repeated and the remedial plan must be revised in the light of the new information about what did **not** work (which is important *feedback* in itself).

Chapter 6:

COMMUNICATION TECHNIQUES THAT BRING POSITIVE RESULTS

Communication Techniques

Communication is never a one-way flow of information. The very Latin root of the word means "coming together"; so the ideas or data being transmitted must be received and understood before any kind of communication actually takes place.

The Three Basic Types of Communications

It is helpful to remember that most communications, both written and oral, can be separated into one of three categories: TELL, SELL and RESOLVE.

1. TELL ... to present facts, data, information, feelings or opinions where the objective is merely to have another understand what you have said and where the communication is expected to have neutral emotional content;
2. SELL ... to offer benefits for a change of behavior, to convince someone to change, to persuade with arguments why something is in the other person's interest, to win acceptance of an idea when opposition, skepticism or indifference is expected;
3. RESOLVE ... to explore, investigate, to question, to seek understanding through the exchange of information about facts, feelings, perceptions and opinions when you need to know what is going on in another person's mind.

For example, suppose that you want a senior employee who is single and has no children to change his scheduled vacation from June to September. You have many choices about how you can communicate your message.

You can TELL him, "I want you to change your vacation from June to September." That may risk a response in which he will tell you where to go (and not on vacation, either). A milder TELL statement would be a simple exposition of your need, "I have reason to prefer that you change your vacation to September."

You can SELL him: "If you change your vacation to September, you would miss all the summer crowds at resorts"; or, "If you would be willing to change your vacation period this year, I will give you first choice on vacation times next year." Of course, the advantages you offer must be seen as real to be persuasive.

You can RESOLVE by investigating the possibility of opposition to your goal: "Would it be any problem or inconvenience for you to change your vacation to September?" From there, you can proceed to TELL him your problem, explain your need and present your SELL arguments, if necessary.

In any given conversation, you will find yourself moving from one mode to another all the time: at one moment, telling your view, then soliciting the other's opinion before responding with another "tell" and perhaps a persuasive suggestion. The point is not pure introspection but practical technique: different modes or types of communication are called for to achieve different objectives.

Giving orders (a TELL communication) will not usually resolve a dispute between employees. When disagreement occurs, the best solution typically requires you to discover (RESOLVE) the cause of conflict and create mutual commitment (SELL) for a cooperative plan acceptable to all parties. After proper agreement has been reached on the facts and the optimal solution, then it may be time to TELL the parties that they are expected to implement that solution.

Going into a long presentation on the advantages of satisfying customer needs (a SELL action) may be unnecessary when all you want to do is to inform the shipping department that a certain order must go out today. Of course, if they hem and haw, you might have to investigate and explore (RESOLVE) their reasons for delay. You may even have to SELL another manager to let your shipment go out first, instead of hers. Then you can TELL shipping that your same-day priority has been approved.

When a customer declares that he wants to buy your product or service, that is not the time for a sales pitch on its advantages. As it is said in the sales field, "When the customer decides to buy, **stop selling!**" Instead of PERSUADING him to continue his purchase, you might only lead him to change his mind by raising new questions about whether your product is really as appropriate as he thought. If that happens, then you will have to RESOLVE his objections and SELL him that your TELL statements do address his needs.

How to Use Each Communication Type

The things you must do to communicate effectively vary according to the kind of communication you are using. There are different characteristic behaviors associated with each mode of communication.

How to TELL Facts Clearly

> In TELL, you must
> 1. be clear in the purpose of your message,
> 2. be organized in its presentation,
> 3. be accurate, factual and complete,
> 4. provide emphasis on key points,
> 5. summarize, and
> 6. confirm that you have been understood.

You are the active party to the communication; the recipient's response is required only to the extent that it confirms their understanding of your message.

It is wise to prepare a TELL communication in an outline format.

How to SELL a New Idea

> To SELL, you must
> 1. be seen as sincere, truthful and honest,
> 2. be seen as understanding the other person's point of view,
> 3. offer benefits and advantages that are appropriate and meaningful to the other party,
> 4. be sensitive to their reactions.

Note that you must "be seen" to exhibit certain traits. It is certainly preferable to actually possess them, but if the subject doesn't **believe** that you do, then your persuasiveness ability will suffer accordingly. The perception of the viewer is critical in SELL situations. The most virtuous person on earth will look rather suspicious standing over a body with a smoking gun. Less drastic examples are seen every day. A manager who has just fired three people for "speaking their mind" at his invitation will find other subordinates reluctant to talk frankly to her on the same day. It is difficult to persuade a subordinate that you value his suggestions when you never ever seem to be able to make time for an uninterrupted discussion.

Whenever you behave in a way that contradicts your stated position or avowed intent, you undercut the credibility and believability of your words. That strikes at the heart of persuasiveness, when your communication must be accepted as valid before the recipient can even consider whether it serves their own interest.

As an advocate for a position, an idea or an action that is not likely to be endorsed without some resistance, you must have some insight into the other party's interests; otherwise, they might not see any advantage in what you present as "sales points." You must also be sensitive to your audience's reactions and alter your persuasive pitch accordingly.

Keep in mind that the goal of a SELL communication is to get the other party to accept, as valuable to them, something that you want them to do. Don't fall into the beginner's trap of repeating and emphasizing the advantages **you** will receive if they act the way you wish (unless your personal satisfaction is in fact very important to the other person). The best persuaders are not always salespeople, but they are individuals who present such advantages to the "buyer," the subject of their pitch, that he cannot refuse the proposition without feeling that he is acting against his best interests.

Although passionate intensity, high sound volume and rapid-fire patter may sell a lot of turnip twaddlers on late-night TV, such extreme demonstrative theatrics are only rarely seen (and then only as a source of comic relief) in the business world of productive executives.

How to RESOLVE Conflicts

The RESOLVE mode of communication is the most complex.

> To RESOLVE, you must:
> 1. solicit the views of the other party, actively involving them in the communication,
> 2. listen to what others say and observe what they show,

3. reflect your understanding of the other's message (both their speech content and their emotional feeling) without judgment,
4. confirm your own understanding of what you have heard or learned,
5. remain neutral until all the facts and opinions are collected,
6. let the other person do most of the talking,
7. express your own opinion,
8. ask for (and give) feedback,
9. identify areas of agreement,
10. work to establish a positive solution or resolution to areas of disagreement.

When you RESOLVE, you are trying to gain information to identify or explore a problem or create agreement. You are asking others to TELL you what they know or what they believe, to open up and expose their thoughts and feelings on an issue that is sensitive or provokes anxiety. You invite them to SELL you, so you can learn what they think is important to you and them. You ask for their views, listen calmly and dispassionately, give periodic feedback on what you understand them to mean, express your respect for their thoughts and feelings.

Do not commit yourself by stating your personal opinion until both parties are satisfied that mutual understanding of what has been said has been reached. After that has been confirmed, then you should give your views, ask the other to "play back" what you said, to confirm that they understand what you mean (just as you did with their statements). Once areas of agreement have been established, you can work to resolve differences over subjects where you disagree.

Special Methods to Control the Communication

A large degree of control can be exercised over communications by the simple use of **questions, answers, probes** and **reflections**. These are rhetorical devices used to lead and direct the communications process.

When and How to Use Questions to Learn More

How to Use Open Questions to Get People Talking

Open Questions are leading statements or broad and open general questions that invite and encourage the employee to freely express his thoughts and feelings. Use them when you want others to speak their mind in whatever detail they choose.

- I expect you have had a hard day.
- Tell me about your ambitions.
- How do you feel about working here?
- What would you suggest we do in the future?

When to Limit Answers with Closed Questions

Closed Questions are narrow, specific and focused questions (also sometimes phrased as statements) which limit, restrict or control the response to the precise area you desire. Use them to ask for particular answers on a given topic or more detail about a general comment; they demand precise responses with clearly defined limits on the freedom of the other to choose their answers.

- How did the machine break?
- What time is it?
- Give me some detail about the travel requirements of your last job.
- Why can't we do that today?

How to Restrict Responses to a "Yes" or "No"

Yes/No or **Binary Questions** are much more focused forms of closed questions that are phrased and expressed so that they ask for a simple *Yes* or *No* response. Use them when you only want a *Yes* or *No* answer, without detail. They are preferred when you want a short answer with no qualifications or discussion.

- Are you ready to go?
- Did you hear the phone ring?

- Do you want to keep your job? (Actually, there is probably only one likely answer to that one.)

Performance Management Tip

Never ask a **Binary Question** that solicits a simple *Yes* or *No* answer when you want more information than a single syllable in response.

"You can do better than this, can't you?" invites a short answer, while "What could you do to improve your performance?" demands a longer and more complete response.

Methods for Selecting the Kind of Answers You Want to Get or Give

Answers to questions can be stated as TELL, SELL or RESOLVE statements.

If neutral factual information is requested, a straightforward TELL statement should suffice as your answer.

Question	TELL Answer
Where is the exit?	The exit is through the first door to the right.

If the question shows reluctance or resistence and you wish to persuade another course of action, an answer shaped as a SELL statement would be in order.

Question	SELL Answer
Why do I have to do this?	This task is a vital part of your job and its completion is important to your next merit increase.

If the question raises issues that must be identified or problems that must be solved, use an answer that applies the RESOLVE method.

Question	RESOLVE Answer
What's wrong with filing complaints in the trash can?	Tell me how you think a customer will react when you ignore their complaints instead of correcting the problem.

Ways to Use Probes to Uncover What People Think

Probes are reactions, neutral responses or questions that prompt an employee to continue and say more. They communicate your interest and involvement in the conversation, without demonstrating any judgment or conclusion on your part.

- Oh.
- Really!
- Really?
- (Kinesthetic body movements or gestures like a nod, a smile, a frown, wrinkling the brow, waving a hand to continue, etc.)
- I see.
- Hmmmmm.
- (Silence ... sometimes called "the pregnant pause" that pressures the other to speak ... is also a probe)
- My goodness!

Questions, answers and probes are both invitations and messages. They prompt others to respond and provide feedback to the listener about your own thoughts and feelings. There are some other valuable special ways you can give the employee feedback to check and confirm your understanding of the meaning and implications of what they said. They fall under the category of reflection feedback.

How to Confirm Understanding with Reflections

Reflection feedback operates like a mirror. You re-state your understanding of what the other said. Reflections demonstrate your perception of their message, in terms of either factual content or emotional feeling.

Using reflection feedback will permit correction of any misunderstanding and assure the employee that you are listening carefully; it will also encourage others to continue talking. Demonstrating that you have accurately received their message and have insight into their attitudes or feelings makes for a more effective communication process. It creates confidence on both sides that the intended message is being sent and received.

What You Should Know About Reflecting Content and Feeling

There are two major kinds of reflections: those that reflect content and those that reflect feeling.

1. **Reflect Content** by re-stating the information you heard, summarizing the message you received and saying it back to the speaker, providing a mirror of your understanding of the facts, ideas, or thoughts expressed by the other.
   - So you agree with that decision.
   - You like the second method.
   - It is your view that we should cancel the order.
   - You intend to work late tonight.
2. **Reflect Feeling** by identifying the emotional content or feeling transmitted in the message you heard, summarizing the attitude you noticed and commenting on it to the speaker, providing a mirror of your understanding of the feelings expressed by the other.
   - You seem happy with the new equipment.
   - You look depressed.
   - It's clear to me that you take a lot of pride in your work.
   - You're upset over the delay in getting your paycheck.
   - I can see that you are concerned about your future.
   - You're confused about the conflicting results of the test.

Why Reflecting Feeling Is Difficult But Powerful

The feeling reflected should be the **employee's** feeling, as you interpret it, re-stated by you for correction or confirmation. When you express your **own** feelings independent of the other person's, you are talking and no longer listening. That's all right to do once the employee has become actively involved in the discussion (in fact, it's highly recommended for the final stages of RESOLVE conversations to assure fully open communications and mutual understanding). But if you fail to let the employee know that you accept and understand their feelings, a premature statement of your opinions and feelings may discourage them from continuing in the face of your rejection.

Reflecting another's feeling is not the same as agreeing with it. Be sympathetic to their emotions and respect their right to "feel" a certain way, even if you do not feel the same way as they do. Feelings are not subject to a "right or wrong" analysis. They are always considered appropriate by the person feeling them. Feelings will not respond to direct orders by outsiders; they are emotions internal to the person experiencing them and must be considered valid for that person. The only way you can get beyond the emotion to address the causes for it is to acknowledge the other's feeling before resolving the underlying problem.

It should be noted that people raised in the "macho" or "impassive/authoritarian" styles of management are notoriously weak in **reflecting feeling**. That can be a crippling defect. Employee performance is affected by the heart as well as by the mind. Performance managers who are sensitive to what employees feel, who literally seek and confirm an understanding of emotional attitudes, are far more skilled in human relations matters than those who treat people like machines.

The reflection of feeling is your best tool for defusing emotional crises. When someone is terribly upset, anxious or furious, the last thing they want to hear is that the other person is not listening to them: you must "listen" to their feelings (and acknowledge them) as well as their words and actions.

Performance Management Tip

When someone is upset, **first** deal with their feelings and emotions.

Only after you have shown sympathy and comprehension for their feelings will they calm down enough to give you a good chance of dealing with facts, ideas and logical solutions.

The manager who is confronted by an enraged employee pounding on his desk should IMMEDIATELY reflect feeling: "You are obviously very upset about something"; or he can reflect feeling with action rather than words, by showing concern and closing the door to provide privacy. A cold or indifferent response by the manager (like a yawn) will only convince the upset employee that she will never get a full hearing or satisfactory resolution to her problem here, because the boss clearly doesn't show any appreciation of how important this subject is to her.

When managers or supervisors reflect feeling, they establish a powerful connection with the employee; they confirm that the **entire** message ... which includes emotion ... is getting through. Once the employee accepts that the boss recognizes, respects and accepts her emotional feelings, some of the barriers to effective communication fall. Then the discussion can move to the exchange of opinions, factual data, etc., and problem resolution plans can be made. You must RESOLVE blockages caused by feelings before you can proceed to TELL, SELL or RESOLVE anything else.

How to Combine Communication Methods for the Most Powerful Results

The Way Questions, Answers and Feedback Overlap

Reflection feedback can be combined with other **questions** and **probes**. The **reflections** can be **answers** to employee comments or questions, just like **probes**.

Answers are responses; but they can also continue the conversation, further involving the employee with **questions, probes** and **reflections**.

Reflection answers can easily be phrased to request further information, to confirm factual understanding or to invite more input from the employee.

Examples of Messages that Contain Other Communication Elements

- Yes, that is very interesting.
- I would like to know more about your idea to increase production.
- No, you are not in trouble, but I want you to understand what we need you to do.

A Sample Communication, Demonstrating All Methods

All these communications techniques can and will be used together and in succession. The typical conversation will move from one mode to another, with the people using various different techniques at different times.

When it is done well and the techniques are chosen to match the situation, the performance manager can quickly and efficiently handle delicate communications problems.

The sample communication illustrates the process in a situation where the performance manager had not prepared a formal communications plan anticipating what do at each stage or how to do it; but the supervisor listens carefully to each employee comment and responds with words and techniques designed to produce answers to specific information needs.

Sample Communication

Supervisor's Communication Plan at Each Stage	What the Supervisor Says	What the Employee Says	*Supervisor's Next Thoughts*
Greet a subordinate with an Open Question	How are you, Ed?	I guess I'll survive. *(Sigh!)*	*Is there a problem?*
Reflect Feeling to see if there's a problem to Resolve	You seem unhappy about something.	I just feel depressed.	*Yes, there is a problem.*
Try to involve him for a Resolution	Want to talk about it?	No.	*Oops! Used a Binary Question that let him close the door.*
Start the Resolve process correctly by Telling purpose	When a key worker is bothered on the job, it's my responsibility to see what I can do.	Yeah, sure. That what my old boss used to say. But he … oh, never mind.	*He's seems afraid to level.*
Tell him his opinion is valued. Persuade (Sell) him to open up.	Since I took over the section, I've always found your ideas sensible. Maybe I can help.	Well, no matter what I do, I never get ahead.	*What does he mean by that?*
Seek clarification with a Closed Question.	What do you mean by "getting ahead?"	The old boss said my work was great, but I needed more academic background for a promotion.	*Now he's talking. Keep the information coming.*
Encourage him to continue with a Probe.	And?	After I finished my degree at night, then he said I was too important for the section to spare me. I was already senior here, and whenever a chance for a promotion elsewhere came, he killed it.	*Aha!?*

Check understanding by Reflecting Content and Feeling.	You feel that you have done what was asked of you to prepare for advancement. Now you are frustrated because nothing happened.	You got it! I can't win.	*What does he plan to do?*
Explore his general thoughts with an Open Question.	What do you see as your options now?	Since doing the "right thing" didn't work, I can either stay at the same level forever here or take one of the outside offers I have.	*Has he decided yet?*
Discover his specific ideas with a Closed Question.	Do you really want to leave the company?	No, not after my investment of all these years. I have a lot to offer this outfit, but they won't let me grow because I'm too vital in one spot!	*Hmmm.*
Confirm insight with a Reflect Content.	You want to grow here but you think the company would rather lose you to a competitor than make better use of your skills here.	It does sound stupid, doesn't it?	*Yes, it does.*
Offer a suggested solution with a Closed Question.	Could you help me find and train a back-up for you, so I can put you up for promotion without destroying my section?	You bet!	*Now I see why the old boss was kicked upstairs.*
Summarize Resolution with a Tell and a Sell.	It might take a while, but it would expose you to some management challenges.	Great! I don't mind waiting as long as I know I really have a chance to advance.	*Could be a win-win solution.*
Reflect Feeling and Content about the proposed plan.	So you feel good about making a plan to make the section less dependent on you.	Yes. In fact, I feel good about having you as my supervisor here, Sue. I won't let you down.	*We'll see.*

What started as a simple greeting to a surly employee ended with a plan and produced a happy and highly motivated employee. A problem previously unknown to the new supervisor was discovered and hopefully solved, to the benefit of the supervisor, the employee and the whole company. Future action is still needed in this case, but it would not be surprising if Ed finds his expanded involvement in section management so satisfying that he changes his mind about a transfer or promotion.

This sample conversation could have gone many ways. It is presented to illustrate how the conscious knowledge of simple communications techniques can be put to practical use in situations you face every day.

Knowing and understanding these principles and techniques is only a start: you must **practice** them before they can be added to your repertory of performance management skills.

Chapter 7:

CAREER PLANNING AND DEVELOPMENT FOR PERSONAL & ORGANIZATIONAL SUCCESS

When you consider all the important aspects of human resource management, career planning and development must come first, even before employment. As the primary goal-setting activity that determines long-term people-needs, it should have a top priority for organizations. Individual employees should likewise give careful thought to seeking the kinds of work activities that allow them to use their strengths, express their talents and fulfill their life ambitions in productive and employable careers.

No one can know what kind of employees to recruit, what kind of jobs to seek or what kind of academic career curriculum to offer (much less study) until decisions have been made about what is needed in terms of work careers.

It is a GET READY and TAKE AIM activity within the context of overall performance management; and it is, in itself, a process that demonstrates how people and organizations GET READY, AIM, FIRE, SCORE and ADJUST to achieve goals and to meet employment needs.

Who Is Responsible for Career Planning? Everyone!

Career planning is done by everyone, although employers, employees and academics have different reasons for doing it.

The managers in each company are responsible for overall manpower planning in their enterprises. They must make their own assessments of the future personnel needs of their organizations and take appropriate action to identify the skills, jobs and people required to meet the objectives.

Each individual employee is personally responsible for planning his or her own career. The individual must decide what field of study will provide the best preparation to satisfy future work ambitions.

The educational establishment also has a major role in career planning. Schools teach courses designed to meet the employment and career development requirements of the future, as projected by employers and as pursued by students who hope to become employees.

What Managers and Employees Must Do About Careers

This chapter will focus on the activities typically required of employees and managers. Some of the steps recommended for individual employees to take are also taken by management, from a slightly different perspective. Where the individual is concerned with his or her personal career direction, company management must be concerned with their ability to match the work needs of the total organization with the career interests and aptitudes of its employees.

The great industrialist Andrew Carnegie once said, "You could take away all my factories and all my money, but if you left me my people, I could build it all up again."

The **Career Planning Guide** that follows is a typical example of how an organization that truly believes that their people are their most valuable resource would encourage them to plan their own destinies. That process is similarly applied by managers to the organization itself. Organizational needs are then matched with the aspirations and potentials of employees, as seen by themselves and as perceived by managers, to provide the information for **Personnel Inventories**, **Manpower Plans** and **Succession Plans**.

A Detailed Career Planning Guide

How to Start a Career Plan

When you start a vacation trip, do you just jump in the car and start driving in any old direction? Of course not. You plan your vacation. You think about what you would like to do, where you want to go, the resources available, and the best route to get you there. If you go to all that trouble to plan a few weeks of your time off work each year, it seems logical that you should invest at least the same amount of care and effort in planning your future at work. After all, you owe it to yourself to make your business career as personally satisfying as possible.

The Company is committed to providing an environment in which you may develop your potential and realize your personal goals, while making a positive contribution to the company's objectives. The reason is simple. When your work uses your talents, satisfies your needs, and allows you to achieve your aspirations, both you and your employer grow.

Both parties must take different actions to make the potential mutual benefit become reality. The company must provide the opportunity, and the employee must provide the response.

The Company provides opportunity by cross-training and promoting qualified candidates from within. We also believe that good people-decisions must be responsive to the interests of the people. For instance, employees should not be forced to take jobs they do not want. Supervisors are therefore required to solicit the career interests of their employees, who are encouraged to make their aspirations known.

Part of the company's obligation is to give you guidance on how to apply the career planning process, information about the career fields that exist in the organization, and assistance in seeking resources for special needs.

These are some of the ways the Company provides opportunity. But the primary responsibility for career planning rests with you.

Although there are many factors you cannot control, such as business needs, technological change, economic conditions, and qualified job competitors, there are more factors that only you control. Only you can state your preferences, choose your goals, and develop your qualifications. Only you can plan your career.

This **Career Planning Guide** exists to

- provide some thoughts, observations, and suggestions on the career planning and self-development process;
- supply information on career fields in the Company;
- explain the resources that are available to help you develop yourself.

If you are perfectly satisfied with your present job or with your long-term career plans, this material may seem unnecessary. Please bear with us. One of the objectives of this guide is to stimulate your thinking about your career plans. If the only result is to confirm your earlier thoughts, at least you will have tested and re-examined your assumptions in the light of today's information. That is a valuable result.

There's no guarantee that your career plans will be fulfilled. But the failure to plan will handicap your chances for success. With a plan for career self-development, you can affect critical factors that only you control and increase the probability of reaching your goal.

The Six Steps in the Career Planning Process

Your part of the career planning process has six steps:
1. Self-appraisal
2. Examine career options
3. Review "fit" of self and career
4. Set goals
5. Establish Work plans
6. Implement Work plans

How to Conduct a Self-Appraisal

You should start by asking yourself such questions as:
▷ What does career growth mean to me?
▷ Where have I been? Where am I now? Where do I want to be?
▷ What do I want to make of myself?
▷ What have I always liked to do?
▷ What do I want to do in the future?
▷ What do I do well?
▷ What are my talents?
▷ What gives me satisfaction and sense of involvement?
▷ What skills, knowledge or abilities do I have to work with?
▷ What things have I least enjoyed?
▷ What knowledge, skill or experience do I lack?
▷ What aspects of myself do I want to develop through my work?

Your answers are unique to you. More importantly, the answers should be known to you, so you can act on them.

A Series of Exercises to Review the Past and Project the Future

Draw a straight line. (Yes, really) Mark the beginning of the line as your birthdate, and the end as the end of your career. place an "x" at a point on the line that represents where you are now. You should have a diagram that looks something like this:

Born _____ X _____ End of career

Put a plus sign above the line and a minus sign below the line. Trace the "ups" and "downs" in your life from its beginning up to today. Extend the line from the present into the future. (For example)

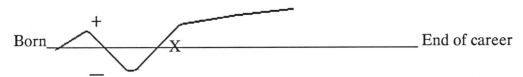

Why did you draw your line the way you did for the period from birth up to today? What have those experiences taught you? Why did you draw your line the way you did for the period from today to the end of your career? Do you want your future to go that way? What do you have to do to make tomorrow go the way you want?

Start with a review of your past experiences. Examine what you have done on each job, from your first up to the one you hold today. Keep it brief and honest ... You are the only one who will see this, anyway.

<u>Section I - Job Responsibilities:</u> Describe your job as you see it in terms of key responsibilities. Other words meaning about the same are: result areas, primary duties, or important functions. Here are some questions to help you identify the key responsibilities of your job: What important results were expected of you? what did your supervisor emphasize? On what things did you spend a lot of time and effort?

Job 1	Job 2	Job 3

<u>Section II - Major contributions:</u> Review each job responsibility and note any contributions you have made. These may include an important problem solved, an idea successfully implemented, an improvement in your job, or accomplishing a particularly difficult objective or assignment.

Job 1	Job 2	Job 3

Section III - Performance Difficulties: Since we all have some difficulties with particular aspects of our job, review each job responsibility and note trouble areas, things that happened that made you less effective than you could have been.

Job 1	Job 2	Job 3

Section I - Job Responsibilities: Describe your job as you see it in terms of key responsibilities. Other words meaning about the same are: result areas, primary duties, or important functions. Here are some questions to help you identify the key responsibilities of your job: What important results were expected of you? What did your supervisor emphasize? On what things did you spend a lot of time and effort?

Job 4	Job 5	Job 6

Section II - Major contributions: Review each job responsibility and note any contributions you have made. These may include an important problem solved, an idea successfully implemented, an improvement in your job, or accomplishing a particularly difficult objective or assignment.

Job 4	Job 5	Job 6

Section III - Performance Difficulties: Since we all have some difficulties with particular aspects of our job, review each job responsibility and note trouble areas, things that happened that made you less effective than you could have been.

Job 4	Job 5	Job 6

Identify Your Likes and Dislikes

An awareness of your present values, interests and abilities is necessary before you can decide "who I will be" or "what I will do." Ignore job titles in your self-appraisal. concentrate instead on the things you have done that stimulated your interest, gave you a feeling of involvement or commitment, and produced a sense of satisfaction and accomplishment. Discover what it is that turns you on about work.

What were the things you liked best about each job?

What did you like least about each job?

As you examine past experiences, look for consistent patterns that characterize things you like to do and work you do well. You may also find other patterns among things you disliked, or did not do particularly well.

True vocational interests are usually consistent over the years. Again, don't focus on titles. A study of past job changes may show that what first appeared to be the most dramatic changes in direction were actually attempts to maintain your pursuit of the same objectives in each case. Likewise, you may have had jobs with substantially identical titles which "felt" completely different to you. The important thing is to identify the elements of each job which you liked or disliked. (People generally *DO* best the things they *enjoy* best.)

Your preferences are important, but so are your skills. What skills, experience, and training do you have that can be applied in a career that will bring you satisfaction?

Skills Audit Worksheet
to Identify Skills/Training/Experience

Check the categories where you have substantial skill/training/experience.

□ accounting   □ tax law

□ finance   □ SEC regulations

□ economics   □ foreign trade

□ insurance   □ postal regulations

                           □ worker's compensation

▫ OSHA

▫ mathematics

▫ law enforcement

▫ statistics

▫ transportation regulations

▫ product quality regulations

▫ technical product knowledge

▫ psychology

▫ field sales experience

▫ industrial relations

▫ advertising

▫ counseling

▫ marketing

▫ government relations

▫ political science

▫ personnel administration

▫ manufacturing processes & eqpt.

▫ industrial engineering

▫ oral & written communication

▫ materials control

▫ multiple languages

▫ transportation

▫ negotiating

▫ traffic

▫ teaching

▫ graphic arts

▫ organization structure

▫ formal education in law

▫ formal education in engineering

▫ formal education in science

▫ formal education in medicine

▫ skilled trades knowledge

▫ health/safety technology

▫ schematics & blueprints

▫ laboratory technology

▫ clerical skills

▫ data processing

▫ computer science

▫ telecommunications

Methods to Evaluate Your Skills

Your success generally depends on your skills. Look over this list of skills and evaluate how they contribute to your work performance.

1. First, evaluate your current proficiency in all skill areas as *High* (**H**), *Medium* (**M**), *Low* (**L**) or *Unnecessary/unknown* (**U**).
2. Then use the same codes to identify the relative importance of each skill
   - to the tasks you must complete
   - to your current position in general
   - to another position or career
3. Compare your current proficiency to the level needed by the situation.

This process will help you determine your skill strengths and weaknesses. Save this information; you can use it later, when you prepare **Career Development Plans**.

Skills Evaluation Worksheet

	Proficiency	Job Tasks or Various Positions			
BUSINESS SKILLS					
1 **Problem Analysis:** Identifying problems; analyzing the causes of problems.					
2 **Decision Making:** Making judgements after an analysis of the information at hand; responding with a decision in a timely and effective manner.					
3 **Planning:** Your own work; work of others; business direction; priorities.					
4 **Organizing/Coordinating:** Your own work; work of others; deciding the time, place and sequence of activities.					
5 **Controlling:** Setting standards; evaluating quality; following-up for results.					
6 **Innovating:** - By modifying or adapting existing designs, procedures, methods; -By new direction, new approaches.					

	Proficiency	Job Tasks or Various Positions			
COMMUNICATION SKILLS					
7 **Oral:** Speaking clearly and concisely in a one-on-one or small group.					
8 **Written:** Presenting written ideas in a clear and concise manner.					
9 **Presentation:** Orally presenting information and ideas in a clear, concise and convincing manner.					
10 **Listening:** Understanding what has been said; probing for understanding.					
PEOPLE SKILLS					
11 **Sensitivity:** To own impact on others, to needs of others, to consequences of own actions, to timing.					
12 **Developing Subordinates:** Identifying needs; coaching; appraising; counseling.					
13 **Handling Conflict:** Performing effectively in spite of stress, conflict or pressure.					
14 **Persuading:** Influencing others in favor of a product, idea or point of view.					
15 **Consulting:** Serving as a source of ''technical'' information; providing ideas to define, clarify or sharpen programs, procedures or plans.					
16 **Interviewing:** Gathering and evaluating information about individuals or situations.					
TECHNICAL					
17 **Job Content:** Knowing the technical and professional aspects of the job.					
OTHERS					
18 _____					
19 _____					
20 _____					

How to Target Your Ideal Ultimate Job

At this stage, you may need your supervisor's help to check the validity of your self-appraisal. Your supervisor, or someone else in management or personnel, may be able to add important factors you may have overlooked, especially areas of strength.

Now design your ideal job. List the job elements and characteristics that best match your present interests and abilities.

Next, shift your attention to the future. What would your ultimate job look like?

You should now have two "ideal job" lists – one for the short term and another as your long-range objective.

The Techniques to Explore Career Options

Apply the results of your self-appraisal to the real world of work. What fields of work promise the closest match to your ideal job today, and the best prospects for tomorrow? Don't limit yourself to specific jobs or particular positions. Keep in mind that career development is a process in which you and the work environment will continue to evolve.

Be flexible. Avoid "tunnel vision" that blinds you to other opportunities. Seek out sources of occupational and vocational information. Some information and advice on other sources is contained in later parts of this guide, but you are certainly able to discover additional facts on your own.

Check your assumptions. Don't make guesses when you can seek out answers that may make the difference in how you decide to spend your life at work. Verify your ideas of what certain jobs are all about. Take your time, and choose your career carefully.

If you had to choose some other career besides the one you currently work in, what would it be?

Would this new field use your knowledge and abilities?

What new skills would you have to acquire to be successful in this career?

Turn to the **Major Salaried Careers** section that follows later and carefully read the descriptions of the career fields you have selected so far.

How to Check the "Fit" of Your Chosen Career

Review your suitability for the career you have chosen.

How does your chosen career match your interests, skills, and abilities?

Turn ahead to the **Major Salaried Careers** section that follows. Use your **Audit Worksheet** answers and examine the degree of correspondence between the skills/training/experience you feel you have, and the characteristics normally held by people currently working in that field.

Note the areas where you need to learn more, and attack them by setting goals and making practical work plans to achieve the goal objectives.

Use the worksheets to test your talents against the demands of other fields of work as well. You may discover that your background applies to more fields than you may have originally thought.

Another approach to the same process is to compare your Audit Worksheet answers with the information on the Knowledge/Requirements Matrix on pages 226-227.

Remember that careful reading of the **Major Salaried Careers** section will provide information on the general activities of specific fields of work and their requirements.

Return to your **Skills Analysis Worksheet**, where you rated your current proficiency in general business skills, communication skills, people skills, and technical skills. Determine the relative importance of those skills in the career you want. Compare your proficiency against the requirements for that career. How do your skills match the needs of that field of work?

Methods to Review Your Personal Self-Assessment

Challenge your initial reasons for focusing on one area over another.
Ask yourself:

- Is this what I really want to do?
- Can I really do it?
- Will this field meet my needs and interests?
- Will this career use my strengths?
- Am I willing to exert myself to improve in this field?
- Is this choice reasonable? Is it realistic? Do others who know me agree with my answers to the above questions?

If the answer to any of these questions is "no," you need to repeat the initial steps again.

Avoid letting others make your life choices for you. You have special skills, and abilities, unique interests and potentials, your own strengths and weaknesses. Don't feel obligated or pressured by anyone else's expectations. Others, such as your supervisor or the personnel department, may help with advice; but you should make your own decision.

Be honest with yourself. Not everyone wants to be a top executive. Not everyone is qualified to be a company president. Be fair to yourself. Focus on a career that will make maximum use of your strengths.

How to Set Long and Short Term Career Goals

Goal setting is a process of describing today what tomorrow should look like.

How would you like your retirement testimonial statement to read? Complete this paragraph the way you would like to hear it when you retire.

_____ retires on _____ at the age of _____.

He was working on _____.

She had always dreamed of _____.

He had just completed _____,

which will _____.

The thing she always wanted to do but never did was _____

_____.

He will be remembered for _____.

People will most miss _____.

She will continue to _____

_____.

What do your answers tell you about what you must do in the remainder of your work life, so your testimonial will actually read the way you wish today? Identify your career ambitions.

- Describe your next position:
- Describe your ultimate last position:

Now consider the steps you should take in the short-term to make your dream become reality.

Start with your current job. Ask yourself:

- How can I create a closer relationship between my desires and my ability to produce?
- How can I improve on my weaknesses and develop my strengths?
- What needs to be done?
- What specific goals can I set?

Think of the next position you want. Make sure it will help move you in your career direction. Follow the same procedures as you did for your current job, above.

At this point, be sure to review your career analysis with your supervisor. He or she may have additional valuable information that will help you create a better plan. Futhermore, your supervisor must know your goals before the organization can take them into account in its plans.

Keep your ultimate long-term goal in mind. It will serve as your point of reference and help place your short-term goals in perspective.

List your answers below.

What must I do to improve or develop my qualifications for my...
Current Position?

Next position?

Ultimate position?

How to Establish Plans to Improve & Develop Your Career

Work plans are the tasks and activities you must complete to achieve your goals. Each goal, whether it is short-term or long-term, whether it is characteristically a routine goal, a problem-solving goal, or an innovative goal, must have specific work plans.

Work plans answer the question "What are you doing about your goals today?" They are specific, concrete, and measurable. They are the steps you must take to reach each goal. And they will help you measure your progress.

Good work plans will keep you moving steadily towards each and every goal you set. If your goals are thought of as blueprints, your work plans can be considered the mortar and bricks that transform the idea into reality.

Review all the information on improvement and development actions you need to take, which you have accumulated through the previous exercises.

Then review the **Development/Improvement Worksheet**.

Development/Improvement Worksheet

Areas of action for improved effectiveness at your current level of responsibility or enhanced potential/readiness for greater responsibilities fall into the following general categories:

If your need is...	On the job coaching	Staff meetings on current problems	Job rotation within component	Job rotation outside component	Emergency fill-in assignments	Special one-person assignments	Task-force assignments	Company education courses	Courses outside company	Guided reading	Teaching courses	Professional counseling	Extra-curricular activities
☐ Job Knowledge	✔	✔						✔	✔	✔	✔		
☐ Performance Skill	✔	✔			✔	✔	✔	✔	✔	✔	✔		
☐ Leadership		✔	✔	✔	✔		✔					✔	✔
☐ Communications	✔	✔				✔	✔	✔	✔				
☐ Personal Traits	✔							✔	✔			✔	
☐ Versatility/Breadth		✔	✔	✔	✔	✔	✔	✔	✔	✔	✔		✔
☐													
☐													

(Expanded descriptions of the suggested development/improvement methods cited above are shown in the Remedial Methods chapter).

Once the areas needing work have been identified and the most relevant action methods chosen, establish specific objectives with time schedules, using the Career/Development Plan form that follows.

How to Put Your Career Development Plan into Final Shape

This plan should be based on the needs for improvement or opportunities for development identified through:
- performance appraisal evaluations and discussions;
- counseling appraisals and remedial planning discussions;
- human resource planning activities;
- individual career planning activities and discussions;
- other pertinent evaluations and recommendations.

Plans can be limited to experience actions or educational actions, or plans can be a combination of all action areas listed in the **Training Methods** section of the **Remedial Actions** chapter.

A Format for Your Completed Development Plan

Areas of skill or knowledge to be Improved or Developed	EXPERIENCE ACTIONS	Due by	EDUCATION ACTIONS	Due by

Finally, put your work plans into effect. The best intentions in the world will come to nothing without action.

Advice on Implementation and Change

As you have seen, the career planning and personal development process is not easy. It offers no quick answers or guaranteed solutions. It requires considerable effort, both in planning and implementation; and changes will have to be made as you face new circumstances, challenges and opportunities. The results will come slowly, even if you remain persistent, patient, and flexible.

So is it worth it? You decide–it's your life.

Summary Descriptions of Major Salaried Careers

It is advisable to check the menu before you order your meal. In the same manner, it is a good idea to familiarize yourself with the kinds of careers that are available in the work world before you fix on one prematurely. A little research at the beginning can save you a lot of trouble over the long run.

This section contains short descriptions of the major fields of work likely to be found in a typical corporation.

The distribution of jobs in this sample company are shown in the "pie chart." The examples demonstrate the career options typically found in a drug, chemical and food products conglomerate. Some employers publish similar lists for their workers. The most comprehensive source of detailed job content information is the massive *Dictionary of Occupational Titles*, published by the U.S. Department of Labor.

For each functional area, there is a list of
- principal areas of responsibility and typical tasks, duties and activities
- the normal skills, training and experience possessed by people working in the area
- some representative job titles

MAJOR SALARIED CAREERS

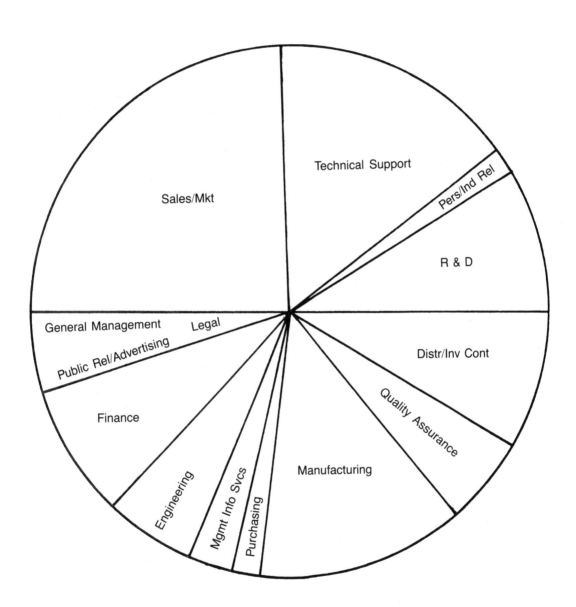

100100 FINANCIAL-GENERAL. Includes all sub-functions listed under: auditing, financial planning, systems and procedures; cost, general, tax and control accounting; payroll, insurance, credit, plant accounting, and treasury operations.

Skills/training/experience possessed by people working in this major function include all the criteria specified under the financial sub-functions.

Typical positions include ... Vice President ... Director of Finance ... Financial Manager.

100101 AUDITING. Examines, verifies, and analyzes business records and transactions concerning financial status and operating procedures. Reviews procedural performance and writes compliance reports.

Skills/training/experience possessed by people working in this function include public accounting, finance, economics, mathematics, oral and written language skills, knowledge of corporate and divisional accounting policies and procedures, knowledge of tax legislation, knowledge of data processing systems, clerical skills.

Typical positions include ... Director of Audit ... Audit Manager ... Sr. Auditor ... Sr. EDP Auditor ... Auditor ... Audit Clerk

101102 FINANCIAL PLANNING. Administers company budgets and makes fiscal forecasts based on historical costs. Analyzes and reports on actual versus budgeted expenses and conducts profitability studies.

Skills/training/experience possessed by people working in this function include accounting, finance, economics, mathematics, oral and written language skills; knowledge of corporate and divisional accounting policies and procedures, knowledge of tax legislation, knowledge of data processing systems, clerical skills.

Typical positions include ... Manager, Financial Planning ... Manager, Profitability Analysis ... Sr. Financial Analyst ... Financial Analyst

100103 COST ACCOUNTING. Prepares and analyzes cost of operations. Conducts inventories, estimates product costs and conducts cost/sales analyses. Develops monthly cost-of-sales reports.

Skills/training/experience possessed by people working in this include accounting, finance, economics, mathematics, oral and written language skills; knowledge of corporate and divisional accounting policies and procedures, knowledge of tax legislation, knowledge of data processing systems, clerical skills.

Typical positions include ... Director, Operations Accounting ... Manager, Cost Accounting ... Supervisor, General Cost ... Supervisor, Physical Inventory ... Accounting Clerk

100104 SYSTEMS AND PROCEDURES. Develops and implements fiscal operating policies and procedures.

Skills/training/experience possessed by people working in this function include: public accounting, finance, economics, mathematics, oral and written language skills, knowledge of corporate and divisional accounting policies and procedures, knowledge of tax legislation, knowledge of data processing systems, clerical skills.

Typical positions include ... Director, Accounting Procedures & Systems ... Manager, Accounting Systems Development ... Manager, Financial Reporting Systems ... Sr. Financial Analyst

100105 GENERAL ACCOUNTING. Performs traditional functions such as accounts receivable, accounts payable, and general ledger.

Skills/training/experience possessed by people working in this function include: accounting, finance, economics, mathematics, oral and written language skills, knowledge of corporate and divisional accounting policies and procedures, knowledge of tax legislation, knowledge of data processing systems, clerical skills.

Typical positions include ... Manager, General Accounting ... Manager, Special Projects ... Supervisor Accounts Receivable ... Supervisor, General Accounting ... Sr. Accountant ... Accountant ... Bookkeeper ... Associate Accountant ... Accounting Clerk

100106 TAX. Prepares tax returns; performs accounting functions related to city, state, and federal tax matters and advises management on tax consideration.

Skills/training/experience possessed by people working in this function include: public accounting, finance, economics, mathematics; oral and written language skills; knowledge of tax legislation, forms and procedures; negotiating skills, knowledge of data processing systems, clerical skills.

Typical positions include ... Director of Taxes ... Tax Manager ... Supervisor Tax Accounting ... Sr. Tax Accountant ... Tax Accountant ... Secretary

100108 PAYROLL. Processes time cards, issues hourly and salaried paychecks, maintains pay records, administers payroll deductions, compiles reports.

Skills/training/experience possessed by people working in this function include: knowledge of data processing systems, accounting, finance, mathematics, oral and written language skills; knowledge of corporate and divisional accounting policies and procedures, knowledge of payroll tax legislation, clerical skills.

Typical positions include ... Manager, Insurance ... Insurance Analyst ... Secretary

100120 CONTROL ACCOUNTING. Provides a wide range of accounting services to a specific unit. Activities encompass budgeting, financial planning, tax, cost, and general accounting. Responsible for unit compliance with corporate fiscal policies and procedures. Conducts cost analyses related to the product and sales. May have additional administrative responsibility for local payroll, insurance, credit, purchasing, and office services.

Skills/training/experience possessed by people working in this function include: knowledge of accounting, finance, economics, mathematics, data processing; oral and written language skills, knowledge of corporate and divisional accounting policies and procedures, knowledge of tax legislation, clerical skills.

Typical positions include ... Group Controller ... Division Controller ... Plant Controller ... Sr. Accounting Clerk ... Bookkeeper ... Accounting Clerk

100121 CREDIT. Researches and analyzes credit information and establishes customer's credit limits. Sets up and monitors special credit arrangements and payments schedules. Establishes and applies collection tactics.

Skills/training/experience possessed by people working in this function include: knowledge of accounting, finance, economics; oral and written language skills, negotiating skills, knowledge of sales and marketing policies and procedures, clerical skills.

Typical positions include ... Credit Manager ... Assistant Credit Manager ... Associate Credit Manager ... Credit Analyst ... Sr. Credit Assistant ... Credit Assistant ... Credit Clerk

100122 PLANT ACCOUNTING. Provides a narrow range of accounting services to a production unit. Prepares tax and cost reports, conducts physical inventories; may perform various other financial or administrative duties of limited scope.

Skills/training/experience possessed by people working in this function include accounting, mathematics, oral and written language skills, knowledge of corporate and divisional accounting policies & procedures, clerical skills.

Typical positions include ... Manager, Plant Accounting ... Supervisor, Plant Accounting ... Plant Accountant ... Associate Accountant ... Bookkeeper ... Sr. Clerk

100123 TREASURY OPERATIONS. Distributes and deposits cash, selects corporate investments; manages trust funds, credit cards, and leases.

Skills/training/experience possessed by people working in this function include finance, economics, accounting, mathematics, banking and investment, knowledge of tax and securities legislation, knowledge of data processing and corporate accounting policies and procedures; oral and written language skills, negotiating skills, and clerical skills.

Typical positions include ... Manager, Treasury Operations ... Supervisor Cash Control ... Cash Management Analyst ... Cashier.... Clerk

100400 SALES/MARKETING-GENERAL. Includes all sub-functions listed under: marketing research, field sales, product management, inter- national sales, customer service and sales training.

Skills/training/experience possessed by people working in this major function include all the criteria listed under the sales/marketing sub-functions.

Typical positions include ... Business Manager ... Director of Marketing ... Director Business Development ... Director Marketing/Sales ... VP Sales ... Director Planning & Administration

100403 MARKETING RESEARCH. Analyzes market conditions to determine potential sales of a product. May provide marketing, advertising, and sales promotional materials.

Skills/training/experience possessed by people working in this function include statistical analysis, mathematics, computer science, psychology, marketing, field sales experience, product knowledge, oral and written language skills, clerical skills, knowledge of advertising, and graphic arts training.

Typical positions include ... Director Marketing Research ... Manager, Market Planning ... Manager Market Research ... Market Research Specialist ... Sales Information Assistant ... Secretary

100404 FIELD SALES. Sells products; calls on customers, demonstrates products, prepares forms and sales paperwork.

Skills/training/experience possessed by people working in this function include oral and written language skill, public speaking and negotiating skills, technical product knowledge, formal training in science, knowledge of sales policies and procedures, psychology.

Typical positions include ... National Sales Manager ... Field Sales Representative ... Accounts Manager ... Clinical Lab Specialist ... Contrast Media Specialist ... Sales Trainee

100405 PRODUCT MANAGEMENT. Directs and coordinates marketing activities for a specific product or product line. Sets prices and establishes profit plans; selects advertising and promotional methods, and coordinates their implementation by the field sales personnel.

Skills/training/experience possessed by people working in this function

include technical product knowledge, business administration, formal training in science, oral and written language skill, field sales experience, accounting, economics, marketing, mathematics, advertising, psychology, and knowledge of sales policies and procedures.

Typical positions include ... Product Group Manager ... Product Manager ... Director Product Management ... Promotional Materials Supervisor ... Stenographer ... Clerk

100408 INTERNATIONAL SALES.
Performs marketing research, field sales, and product management functions in markets located outside the United States.

Skills/training/experience possessed by people working in this function include knowledge of foreign business customs, culture, psychology, and trade legislation; multiple language skills, and the other criteria listed under Marketing Research, Field Sales and Product Management.

Typical positions include ... Area Manager ... Marketing Manager ... Director of Marketing ... Export Office Manager ... Sales Supervisor ... Medicinal Representative

100420 CUSTOMER SERVICE.
Expedites orders, investigates customer complaints, provides liaison between customer and sales/production/distribution functions, may take orders directly from customer.

Skills/training/experience possessed by people working in this function include oral and written language skills, field sales experience, technical product knowledge, psychology, knowledge of sales policies and procedures, mathematics, computer science, and clerical skills.

Typical positions include ... Manager, Customer Service ... Supervisor Sales Service ... Customer Service Specialist ... Customer Service Representative ... Technical Service Representative ... Customer Order Processor ... Account Representative ... Secretary ... Clerk

100421 SALES TRAINING.
Develops and conducts training programs for sales personnel. Teaches product knowledge, sales policies and procedures, selling techniques.

Skills/training/experience possessed by people working in this field include science education, teaching experience, field sales experience, technical product knowledge, oral and written language skills, public speaking skills, psychology, knowledge of sales policies and procedures, knowledge of audio/visual techniques, clerical skills.

Typical positions include Manager Sales Training ... Sales Training Associate ... Regional Trainer

100500 LEGAL. Provides legal advice, draws up legal documents. Prepares applications for patents and copyrights and protects same against infringement.

Skills/training/experience possessed by people working in this function include oral and written language skills, the required education for the practice of law, knowledge of legislative and judicial process; knowledge of corporate and divisional plans, policies, and procedures; experience in directing court cases, negotiating skill, experience in directing court cases, negotiating skill, experience in dealing with government and public agencies, clerical skills.

Typical positions include ... General Counsel ... Attorney ... Patent Attorney ... Patent Agent ... Patent Assistant ... Senior Secretary ... Stenographer

100600 PUBLIC RELATION/ADVERTISING. Plans and directs programs to promote favorable publicity and create goodwill. Writes scripts and news releases, writes and edits organizational publications, assigns and approves art work, buys media space or time; plans exhibits and promotional campaigns, participates in community and civic affairs.

Skills/training/experience possessed by people working in this function include oral and written language skills, public speaking skills, journalism, psychology, marketing, political science, graphic arts training, technical administration, negotiating skills, clerical skills.

Typical positions include ... Manager Advertising ... Director Public Relations ... Editor ... Editorial Assistant ... Sales Promotion Specialist ... Promotional Materials ... Advertising Production Clerk

100700 PERSONNEL/INDUSTRIAL RELATIONS-GENERAL. Includes all activities listed under the functions of employee benefits, industrial relations, employment, safety/health, training & development, compensation, and security.

Skills/training/experience possessed by people working in this function include all the criteria specified under the Personnel/IR sub-functions.

Typical positions include ... Group Personnel Director ... Personnel Manager ... Supervisor Personnel ... Personnel Administrator ... Personnel Representative ... Personnel Assistant

100701 EMPLOYEE BENEFITS. Designs, establishes, and administers pension plans, life and health insurance policies, leave of absence plans, service and suggestion award programs.

Skills/training/experience possessed by people working in this function include finance, insurance, business administration, psychology, industrial relations, oral and written language-skills, counseling skills, mathematics, knowledge of legislation, clerical skills.

Typical positions include ... Benefits Manager ... Benefits Assistant ... Junior Clerk

100702 INDUSTRIAL RELATIONS. Negotiates labor agreements, interprets and administers labor contract provision, adjust grievances, and prepares arbitration and appeal cases.

Skills/training/experience possessed by people working in this function include oral and written language skills, knowledge of law and labor agreements, formal training in industrial or labor relations, knowledge or skilled trades work standards and manufacturing processes, business administration, psychology, economics, negotiating skills, clerical skills.

Typical positions include ... Director, Industrial Relations ... Manager Industrial Relations ... Supervisor Industrial Relations

100704 EMPLOYMENT. Recruits, interviews, investigates and selects candidates for employment.

Skills/training/experience possessed by people working in this function include clerical skills, psychology, oral and written communications; formal education in personnel administration, public speaking ability; knowledge of company policies, operations, organization structure and job requirements.

Typical positions include ... Supervisor of Employment ... Professional Employment Representative ... Employment Representative ... Sales Recruiter ... Supervisor Clerical Employment ... Secretary ... Stenographer

100705 SAFETY/HEALTH. Plans and administers health, accident prevention, fire prevention and protection programs. Conducts safety/ health training. Provides emergency treatment and physical examinations, monitors and inspects work environment for hazards, issues permits and procedures for potentially dangerous operations, deals with government safety agencies and private insurers. May provide professional counseling and employee assistance on chemical abuse problems.

Skills/training/experience possessed by people working in this function include engineering, medical technology, fire and accident prevention, first aid, health physics, chemistry; knowledge of manufacturing processes, psychology, worker's compensation laws, safety legislation; the required education and certification for medical practice or counseling, oral and written language skills, clerical skills.

Typical positions include ... Manager Health & Safety ... Supervisor Health Physics ... Manager Plant Safety & Loss Prevention ... Safety Engineer ...

Emergency Response Specialist ... Industrial Hygienist ...Health Physicist ... Industrial Nurse ... Medical Director ... Medical Technician ... Safety Assistant ... Employee Assistance Program Coordinator

100706 TRAINING & DEVELOPMENT. Designs and conducts programs to improve employee performance and maximize effective management of human resources. Conducts classes to increase employee skills and knowledge, establishes and administers performance measurement systems, coordinates manpower planning programs, placement, outside education programs, counseling, and career planning.

Skills/training/experience possessed by persons working in this function include oral and written language skills, public speaking skills, classroom education skill, formal teaching experience, psychology, personnel administration, knowledge of company operations and job requirements, counseling statistics, clerical skills.

Typical positions include ... Manager Personnel Development ... Supervisor Training ... Personnel Associate ... Secretary

100707 COMPENSATION. Evaluates jobs; establishes and administers wage and salary systems. Approves personnel changes and pay increases, monitors unemployment insurance claims, conducts pay survey, prepares reports from records.

Skills/training/experience possessed by persons working in this function include oral and written language skills, statistics, mathematics, personnel administration, psychology, knowledge of company operations and job requirements, knowledge of personnel policies and procedures, computer science, knowledge of legislation, clerical skills.

Typical positions include ... Supervisor Salary Administration ... Compensation Analyst ... Compensation Clerk

100800 SECURITY. Protects employees and property from physical damage.

Skills/training/experience possessed by people working in this function include oral and written language skills, knowledge of manufacturing processes and physical layout, law enforcement, fire safety, first-aid, psychology, and clerical skills.

Typical positions include ... Guard Supervisor ... Fire Marshal & Security Officer ... Security Officer

100900 MANAGEMENT INFORMATION SERVICES - GENERAL. This

major function includes Building services, office supplies services, auditing, manpower planning and control, records management, and all activities listed under Data Control, Computer Operations, Programming Systems Analysis, and Operations Research.

Skills/training/experience possessed by people working in this function includes all the criteria listed under the above sub-functions.

Typical positions include ... Director Data Processing ... Manager Planning & Administration ... Director Manpower Planning & Control ... Manpower Planning & Control Analyst ... Secretary

100902 DATA CONTROL. Prepares records for entry into computer and distributes completed reports, keeps records of computer transactions, monitors reports for data integrity, applies security procedures.

Skills/training/experience possessed by people working in this function include computer science, oral and written language skills, mathematics, business administration, clerical skills.

Typical positions include ... Supervisor Data Control ... Data Control Clerk ... Distribution Clerk

100903 COMPUTER OPERATIONS. Enters and verifies entry of data to computer, schedules and controls operations of computer and peripheral data processing equipment.

Skills/training/experience possessed by people working in this function include computer science, mathematics, oral and written language skills, business administration, computer services operation skills, clerical skills.

Typical positions include ... Manager Computer Operations ... Supervisor Data Entry ... Computer Scheduler ... Tape Librarian ... Computer Operator ... Data Entry Operator ... Clerk

100903 PROGRAMMING/SYSTEMS ANALYSIS. Designs, programs, and maintains data processing systems. Writes programs and narrative descriptions, revises tests, and debugs programs; documents procedures for users.

Skills/training/experience possessed by people working in this function include computer science mathematics, oral and written language skills; statistics, business administration, clerical skills.

Typical positions include ... Manager Computer Operations ... Supervisor Data Entry ... Computer Scheduler ... Tape Librarian ... Computer Operator ... Data Entry Operator ... Clerk

100905 PROGRAMMING/SYSTEMS ANALYSIS. Designs, programs, and maintains data processing systems. Writes programs and narrative descriptions, revises, tests, and debugs programs; documents procedures for users.

Skills/training/experience possessed by people working in this function include computer science, mathematics; oral and written language skills, statistics, business administration, clerical skills.

Typical positions include ... Manager Systems & Programming ... Project Manager ... Programmer/Analyst ... Supervisor Maintenance Programming ... Lead Programmer ...Programmer

100908 OPERATIONS RESEARCH. Analyzes management information problems, converting them to mathematical models for computer solution; evaluates statistical results and issues nontechnical reports on alternatives and options.

Skills/training/experience possessed by people working in this function include computer science, mathematics, statistics, oral and written language skills, business administration, economics, industrial engineering, analytical and clerical skills.

Typical positions include ... Management Sciences Analyst ... Science Information Specialist

100110 PURCHASING. Buys equipment, services, materials, and supplies. Compiles specifications, selects vendors; negotiates price, contract terms and conditions.

Skills/training/experience possessed by people working in this function include oral and written language skills, negotiating skills, technical product knowledge, understanding of data processes, knowledge of law and governmental regulations, foreign trade, multiple language skills, clerical skills.

Typical positions include ... Director of Purchasing ... Purchasing Manager ... Purchasing Supervisor ... Purchasing Agent ... Buyer ... Purchasing Assistant ... Purchasing Clerk

101200 DISTRIBUTION/INVENTORY CONTROL. This function includes all activities listed under warehousing/shipping, traffic, inventory planning & control, order entry/billing control, and fleet operations.

Skills/training/experience possessed by people working in this function include all the criteria listed under the sub-functions.

Typical positions include ... Material Manager ... Manager Distribution ... Distribution Supervisor

101202 WAREHOUSING/SHIPPING. Receives, stores and issues finished goods, supplies, materials, and equipment. Plans storage and location procedures, keeps inventory records, prepares merchandise for shipping, checks invoices and bills of lading, and loads outgoing shipments.

Skills/training/experienced possessed by people working in this function include oral and written language skills, labor relations, industrial engineering; product knowledge, knowledge of government regulations, mathematics, material control, knowledge of transportation industry, clerical Skills.

Typical positions include ... Supervisor Shipping ... Shipping Foreman ... Warehouse Foreman ... Shipping Coordinator ... Warehouse Expediter ... Shipping Clerk ... Bill Of Lading Clerk

101203 TRAFFIC. Investigates options and plans procedures to insure that materials and finished goods are transported efficiently and economically. Selects carrier, quantity and route; monitors delivery schedules and compliance with government regulations; computes tariffs, negotiates rates, service contracts and damage claims.

Skills/training/experience possessed by people working in this function include oral and written language skills, negotiating skills, economics, insurance, transportation, knowledge of data processing, product knowledge, knowledge of government regulations, clerical skills.

Typical positions include ... Director Traffic ... Traffic Manager ... Traffic Supervisor ... Traffic Specialist ... Traffic Expediter ... Freight Rate Clerk ... Office Clerk ... Secretary

101208 INVENTORY PLANNING AND CONTROL. Determines items and quantity of goods and materials required to be produced to supply sales demand.

Skills/training/experience possessed by people working in this function include oral and written language skills, knowledge of data processing. mathematics, industrial engineering, knowledge of production processes and materials procedures, business administration, economics, statistics, clerical skills.

Typical positions include ... Director Inventory Control ... Manager Inventory Planning ... Supervisor Planning and Inventory Control ... Supervisor Inventory Administration ... PIC Coordinator ... Document Control Clerk ... Video Operator ... Inventory Control Clerk ... Video Poster ... CRT Operator

101209 ORDER ENTRY/BILLING CONTROL. Processes orders for materials or goods, edits for price and specifications, notifies customers of receipt, shipping date, and price. Issues invoices for orders accepted.

Skills/training/experience possessed by people working in this function include written language skills, accounting, knowledge of contract law, data processing, clerical skills; knowledge of corporate administrative practices for purchasing, inventory, pricing, sales traffic, and shipping.

Typical positions include ... Manager Order Entry & Billing ... Supervisor Order Entry ... Supervisor Invoicing ... Pricing Coordinator ... Billing Cost Clerk ... Order Taker ... Order Editor ... Order Clerk

101211 FLEET OPERATIONS. Schedules use of company cars, trucks, aircraft. Purchases vehicles and related services.

Skills/training/experience possessed by people working in this function include oral and written language skills, accounting, transportation, traffic, insurance; formal training and licensing to operate or maintain vehicles; knowledge of safety procedures, governmental regulation and company procedures.

Typical positions include ... Fleet Administration ... Fleet Maintenance Manager ... Chief Pilot ... Co-Pilot ... Dispatcher/driver ... Chauffeur ... Driver

101300 ENGINEERING - GENERAL. This major function includes technical support services, environmental engineering, and all the activities listed under construction, maintenance, utilities and electrical engineering.

Skills/training/experience possessed by people working in this function include all the criteria listed in the above sub-functions.

Typical positions include ... Director Environmental Affairs ... Coordinator Pollution Control ... Energy Conservation Coordinator ... Director Engineering Services ... Manager Project Services ... Manager Drafting Services ... Project Manager ... Manager Plant Engineering ... Principal Project Engineer ... Sr. Project Engineer ... Drafter

101303 CONSTRUCTION ENGINEERING. Designs building facilities, coordinates with building contractors; monitors for building safety and compliance with building codes and other regulations.

Skills/training/experience possessed by people working in this function include engineering, oral and written language skills, mechanical drawing, mathematics, knowledge of environmental and safety standards, building codes, knowledge of manufacturing processes, industrial engineering, clerical skills.

Typical positions include ... Project Manager ... Principal Project Engineer ... Sr. Project Engineer ... Engineer ... Sr. Secretary ... Secretary

101306 MAINTENANCE ENGINEERING. Installs, maintains, and repairs machinery. Repairs existing buildings and equipment or selects contractor.

Skills/training/experience possessed by people working in this function are trade skills such as carpentry, machine repair, electrical, pipefitting and millwright, plus engineering, mechanical drawing, oral and written language skills, mathematics, industrial relations, knowledge of safety codes, manufacturing processes, clerical skills.

Typical positions include ... Maintenance Superintendent ... Maintenance Supervisor ... Maintenance Foreman

101307 UTILITIES ENGINEERING. Operates, inspects, and maintains, building utility equipment such as furnaces, boilers, air compressors, generators and motors.

Skills/training/experience possessed by people working in this function include mechanical and electrical engineering, formal training and licensing as stationary engineer; oral and written language skills, knowledge of environmental and safety codes, power systems, manufacturing processes, mathematics, clerical skills.

Typical positions include ... Supervisor Utilities ... Power Plant Engineer ... Utilities Engineer

101300 ELECTRICAL ENGINEERING. Designs and directs installation of electrical systems for products, process equipment, machinery, or facilities.

Skills/training/experience possessed by people working in this function include formal education in electrical engineering, knowledge of manufacturing processes, experience with power systems, knowledge of safety and building codes, oral and written language skills, experience in drawing and use of electrical schematics and blueprints, mathematics, clerical skills.

Typical positions include ... Electrical Project Engineer ... Electrical Engineer

101400 COMMUNICATION SERVICES - GENERAL. This major function includes administration of all the activities listed under Mail Services, Telecommunications, and Printing.

Skills/training/experience possessed by people working in this function include all the criteria listed under the sub-functions.

Typical positions include ... Manager, General Services ... Office Services Coordinator

101401 MAIL SERVICES. Picks up and delivers company mail, circulates internal correspondence and packages, processes material for regular mail, electronic/fax transmission and express delivery; receives and distributes external correspondence.

Skills/training/experience possessed by people working in this function

include oral and written language skills, mathematics, knowledge of postal regulations, shipping procedures, and related machinery and equipment; knowledge of company organization structure, knowledge of names and locations of units and employees, clerical skills.

Typical positions include ... Mail Room Supervisor ... Mail Clerk

101402 TELECOMMUNICATIONS. Administers and operates telephone, data transmission, and teletype communications systems. Arranges equipment installation, prepares directories, operates equipment, maintains records.

Skills/training/experience possessed by people working in this function include oral and written language skills, knowledge of data processing, knowledge of commercial telecommunications technology, experience in cost analysis, knowledge of company organization structure and names and locations of units and employees, clerical skills, manual dexterity. May have multiple language skills.

Typical positions include ... Director Telecommunications ... Communications Analyst ... Switchboard Operator ... Teletype Operator ... Relief Operator

101500 CLERICAL ADMINISTRATION. This general sub-function includes all general administrative clerical activities which support technical, professional. or executive functions. Purchases office supplies, types letters and reports, files, operates standard office machines, takes dictation, keeps records, follows departmental procedures.

Skills/training/experience possessed by people working in this function include oral and written language skills, typing, shorthand, formal training or experience in operation of office machines, knowledge of departmental procedures, clerical skills, manual dexterity.

Typical positions include ... Manager Administration ... Administrative Assistant ... Office Supervisor ... Executive Secretary ... Sr. Secretary ... Secretary ... Stenographer ... Sr. Clerk ... Clerk-typist ... Junior Clerk

101601 PRINTING. Does layout, pasteup, varityping, operates offset printing machines and/or Personal Computers for desktop publishing, makes reproductions.

Skills/training/experience possessed by people working in this function include oral and written communications skills, formal training in graphic art, desktop publishing using PCs, experience on varitype or printing machines, manual dexterity.

Typical positions include ... Manager Print Shop ... Utility Operator ... Varitypist/Paste-up Artist ... Label Press Operator ... PC Operator ... Desktop

Publisher ... Graphic Artist ... Art Clerk

101700 RESEARCH & DEVELOPMENT - GENERAL. This major function includes all R & D activities of specific technologies (Chemistry, Pharmacology, Microbiology, Bacteriology, Physics, Flavor/Fragrance, Pharmacy, Radiopharmaceutical, Radio-chemistry) and the Technical Evaluation, Clinical Development, Regulatory Affairs, and Clinical Diagnosis sub-functions.

(Specific-technology R & D functions)
101701 CHEMISTRY,
101703 PHARMACOLOGY-MICRO/BACTERIOLOGY,
101706 PHYSICS,
101709 FLAVOR/FRAGRANCE,
101730 PHARMACY,
101731 RADIO PHARMACEUTICAL,
101732 RADIO-CHEMISTRY

Activities common to all specific-technology R&D functions are: applies scientific theories and methods to design or develop new products and modify existing products, collects information, conducts experiments, investigates and evaluates data, consults analyses or materials and processes.

Skills/training/experience possessed by people working in specific-technology R&D functions include oral and writtten language skills, knowledge of production and laboratory equipment and processes, knowledge of safety and governmental regulations affecting product, technical product knowledge, supervisory skills, clerical skills.

Typical positions include ... Director R&D ... Director Research ... Manager R&D ... Project Manager ... Group Leader ... Supervisor Research ... Scientist ... Sr. Research Chemist ... Research Associate ... Research Investigator ... Sr. Chemist ... Biostatistician ... Microbiologist ... Flavor Chemist R/P Chemist ... Chief Perfumer ... Technologist ... Technician

TECHNICAL EVALUATION. Analyzes the technological implications of opportunities for acquisitions, new products, and new projects. Evaluates new developments in relation to the state of technology in the company, submits technological impact reports on the long-term implications of various options.

Skills/training/experience possessed by people working in this function include all the specifics listed under R&D-General, as well as marketing, economics, and marketing research.

Typical positions include ... Director Technical Evaluation

101733 CLINICAL DEVELOPMENT. Devises testing plans and methods for proposed new or improved products requiring human test subjects. Selects qualified clinical testing contractors, negotiates contracts, monitors methods and procedures used, compiles results for biostatistical analysis. Writes labelling results to Regulatory Affairs department. Assists in training of product managers and sales representatives, investigates technical complaints from customers.

Skills/training/experience possessed by people working in this function include all the specifics found under R&D-General, as well as negotiating skills and formal training in anatomy, biology and physiology.

Typical positions include ... Project Manager-Biomedicine ... Clinical Development Associate

101736 CLINICAL DIAGNOSIS. Designs laboratory diagnostic test kits and instruments for clinical use. Researches lab procedures, establishes new methods which will use kits/instruments, designs components, conducts product reliability tests, analyzes statistical results; submits research, test, and labelling results to Regulatory Affairs. Assists in training of product managers and sales representatives, investigates technical complaints from customers.

Skills/training/experience possessed by people working in this function include all the specifics listed under R&D General.

Typical positions include ... Supervisor, Clinical Diagnosis

101734 REGULATORY AFFAIRS. Coordinates and compiles technical information on new health products for government agency review. Prepares and submits applications and supplemental reports for governmental approval.

Skills/training/experience possessed by people working in this function include oral and written language skills, technical product knowledge, formal education in science, experience in quality control and research, knowledge of governmental regulations, knowledge of safety and health technology, clerical skills.

Typical positions include ... Manager Regulatory Affairs ... Regulatory Affairs Associate ... Secretary

101900 QUALITY ASSURANCE. Insures that quality control procedures adequately evaluate products. Reviews methods and techniques to determine whether they adequately measure product reliability and compliance within specifications. Establishes standards and methods for quality control implementation. Monitors unit compliance and advises on procedures.

Skills/training/experience possessed by people working in this function

include oral and written language skills, formal education in science, knowledge of government regulations, experience in quality control, knowledge of production processes, technical product knowledge, clerical skills.

Typical positions include ... Director QA ... Manager Quality Assurance ... Supervisor Quality Assurance ... QA Associate ... QA Monitor

101902 ANALYTICAL SERVICES. Performs qualitative and quantitative investigations to determine the properties and accept ability of materials. Provide analytical consultation on technical aspects of projects or products.

Skills/training/experience possessed by people working in this function include formal education science, training and experience in the operation of analytical instruments processes, technical product knowledge, experience in R&D and quality control, knowledge of instrumentation technology, statistics, clerical skills.

Typical positions include ... Director Analytical Services ... Manager Analytical Services ... Supervisor Analytical Lab ... Scientist ... Analytical Development Associate ... Inquiry Associate ... Sr. Chemist ... Technologist ... Instrument Technician

101999 QUALITY CONTROL. Designs, installs and operates inspection and testing procedures for finished products. Establishes quality specification and measurement techniques, and recommends corrective actions to maintain proper compliance levels.

Skills/training/experience possessed by people working in this function include oral and written language skills, formal education in science, technical product knowledge, knowledge of production processes and equipment, knowledge of laboratory and testing procedures, clerical skills.

Typical positions include ... Director of Quality Control ... QC Manager ... QC Supervisor ... Chemist ... Associate Chemist ... Technologist ... Technician ... Sr. GMP Audit Clerk

102100 MANUFACTURING - GENERAL. This major function includes all the activities of Process Engineering, Production Planning, Production and Packaging.

Skills/training/experience possessed by people working in this function include all the criteria listed under the sub-functions.

Typical positions are ... Plant Manager ... Director of Operations ... Director of Manufacturing ... Plant Superintendent ... Manager, Manufacturing ... Superintendent, Operations.

102101 PROCESS ENGINEERING. Evaluates, selects, and applies engineering principles to production process situations. Originates production methods and procedures, designs and develops special equipment processes, test materials, prepares specifications and reports, coordinates implementation of new processes.

Skills/training/experience possessed by people working in this function include oral and written language skills, formal education in science and engineering, knowledge of production equipment and processes, test materials, prepares specifications and reports, coordinates implementation of new processes.

Typical positions include ... Manager Process Development ... Supervisor Process Technology ... Principal Process Engineer ... Sr. Process Engineer ... Process Engineer ... Group Leader ... Process Chemist

102102 PRODUCTION PLANNING. Establishes production schedules; plans production operations to meet requirements for finished products with the maximum usage of available capacity. Coordinates the use of labor and materials.

Skills/training/experience possessed by people working in this function include oral and written language skills, business administration, knowledge of data processing; knowledge of production processes and procedures, experience in production and inventory control, mathematics, industrial engineering, materials management, clerical skills.

Typical positions include ... Supervisor Production Planning ... Sr. Planner ... Production Planner ... Production Scheduler ... Expediter ... Production Data Clerk ... PIC Clerk ... Planning Coordinator

102106 PRODUCTION. Applies resources of labor, materials, and equipment to manufacture a finished product.

Skills/training/experience possessed by people working in this function include oral and written language skills, technical product knowledge, experience in operation production equipment, industrial relations, training or experience in industrial engineering, chemistry or chemical engineering, knowledge of health and safety regulations, knowledge of manufacturing processes and procedures, supervisory skills, clerical skills.

Typical positions include ... Production Superintendent ... Production Manager ... Production Supervisor ... Production Foreman

102111 PACKAGING. Assembles, fills, packs products for shipment or storage. Determines coordinates with purchasing, traffic, quality assurance, etc. for special packaging requirements.

Skills/training/experience possessed by people working in this function

include oral and written language skills, industrial relations, knowledge of safety, health and postal regulations; technical product knowledge, training or knowledge of packaging equipment and processes, knowledge of the transportation industry, supervisory skills, clerical skills.

Typical positions include ... Packaging Supervisor ... Packaging Engineer ... Packaging Foreman

102300 GENERAL MANAGEMENT. Directs the activities of a major unit/enterprise of the Corporation. Although the unit/enterprise may be organized to provide a service or product, general management activities always include planning, organizing and managing unit/ enterprise efforts to yield the maximum results within given financial constraints.

Skills/training/experience possessed by people working in this function include negotiating skills, advanced education or training in both technical and management fields, prior management experience in a variety of functional areas; demonstrated high levels of energy, stress tolerance, and sensitivity; demonstrated skills in written and oral communication, leadership, planning and organization, management control, problem analysis, decision making, and reading speed and comprehension; a wide range of personal interests and broad perspective on issues.

Typical positions include ... Vice President ... General Manager

A List of Research Sources on Careers

A classic source of self-help for career choice and job search activities is **What Color Is Your Parachute?**, an inexpensive paperback manual updated and re-issued **every year** by its author, Richard Nelson Bolles, and published by *Ten Speed Press*. Available at most bookstores, it contains hundreds of exercises to assist individuals who are reviewing career options and hunting new jobs.

For a wealth of detailed information on the full range of the types of formal career planning and development programs popular with employers at any time, the performance manager should contact various professional associations:

American Society for Personnel Administration
606 North Washington St.
Alexandria, VA 22314

International Personnel Management Association
1617 Duke St.
Alexandria, VA 22314

American Society for Training and Development
1630 Duke St.
Alexandria, VA 22313

Association of Training and Employment Professionals
100 Bidwell Road
South Windsor, CT 06074

National Employment and Training Association
P.O. Box 1773
Upland, Ca 91786

A Knowledge/Requirements Matrix to Match Skills with Careers

The detailed chart that follows shows how you can compare your skills, training and experience (or that of a subordinate) to the characteristics of a particular field of work. Such devices to match personal qualifications with specific career applications are easily programmed for interactive computerized use.

Whether the method is manual or automated, it is a simple process to take the results of an employee talent analysis and identify fields of work where such talents are required and highly valued.

	FINANCE-GENERAL	Auditing	Financial Planning	Cost Accounting	Systems & Procedures	General Accounting	Tax Accounting	Payroll	Insurance	Control Accounting	Credit	Plant Accounting	Treasury Operations	SALES/MKTG-GEN	Market Research	Field Sales	Product Management	International Sales	Customer Service	Sales Training	LEGAL	P.R./ADVERTISING	PERS/IND. RELS.-GEN	Employee Benefits	Industrial Rels.	Employment	Safety & Health	Training & Develop	Compensation	Security
Accounting	•	•	•	•	•	•	•	•	•	•	•	•	•	•			•	•												
Finance	•	•	•	•	•	•	•	•	•	•	•		•	•									•	•						
Economics	•	•	•	•	•	•	•			•	•		•	•			•	•					•	•		•				
Insurance									•														•	•	•					
Mathematics	•	•	•	•	•	•	•	•	•	•	•	•	•	•	•		•	•	•				•	•						
Statistics														•	•			•					•					•	•	
Clerical Skills	•	•	•	•	•	•	•	•	•	•	•	•	•	•	•		•	•	•	•			•	•	•	•	•	•	•	•
Data Processing	•			•	•	•	•	•		•	•		•																•	
Computer Science														•	•		•	•					•						•	
Telecommunications																														
Tech. Product Know.														•	•		•	•	•	•		•								
Field Sales Exper.														•	•		•	•	•	•										
Advertising														•	•		•	•				•								
Marketing	•								•					•	•		•	•				•								
Psychology														•	•		•	•	•			•	•	•	•	•	•	•	•	•
Industrial Relations																							•	•	•					
Counseling																			•				•	•		•	•	•		
Government Relations																					•									
Political Science																					•	•								
Personnel Admin.								•	•														•	•	•	•		•		
Oral/Written Commun.	•	•	•	•	•	•	•	•	•	•	•	•	•	•	•		•	•	•	•	•	•	•	•	•	•	•	•	•	•
Multiple Languages														•			•			•										
Negotiating Skills	•					•			•					•		•	•			•	•	•				•	•			
Teaching Skills																			•		•	•						•		
Aud/Vis. & Graphics														•	•		•			•	•	•						•		
Organiz. Structure																					•					•		•		
Tax Law	•	•	•	•	•	•	•	•		•			•								•	•								
S.E.C. Regulations	•												•								•									
Foreign Trade																		•												
Postal Regulations																														
O.S.H.A. Regulations									•														•				•			
Law Enforcement																						•								•
Transportation Regs.									•																					
Product Quality Regs.									•																					
Mfg. Process & Equip.																							•		•		•		•	
Industrial Eng.																														
Material Control																														
Transportation Mgmt.									•																					
Traffic Management																														
Education in Law																					•		•		•					
Educ. in Engineering																							•					•		•
Skilled Trades Know.																							•		•		•			•
Schematic/Blueprints																														
Education in Science															•	•	•	•	•		•	•								
Educ. in Medicine									•														•				•			
Health/Safety									•														•				•			
Lab. Technology																														

	MGMT INFO SVCS-GEN	Data Control	Computer Operations	Prog/Sys Analysis	Operations Research	PURCHASING-GEN	DISTRIB/INV CONT-GEN	Warehousing/Shipping	Traffic	Inv Plan & Control	Order Entry/Billing	Fleet Operations	ENGINEERING-GENERAL	COMMUNICATIONS SVCS	Telecommunications	Clerical Admin	Printing	RESEARCH & DEV-GEN	Technical Evaluation	Clinical Development	Regulatory Affairs	QUALITY ASSUR-GEN	Analytical Services	Quality Control	MANUFACTURING-GEN	Process Engineering	Production Planning	Production	Packaging	GENERAL MANAGEMENT
Accounting	•						•			•	•			•	•															•
Finance	•																													•
Economics	•			•			•			•	•							•	•	•										•
Insurance							•		•				•																	
Mathematics	•	•	•	•	•		•	•		•			•												•	•	•			
Statistics	•		•	•			•			•				•	•								•	•	•	•				
Clerical Skills	•	•	•	•	•	•	•	•	•	•	•		•	•	•	•	•	•	•	•	•	•	•	•	•	•		•		•
Data Processing		•	•	•			•			•	•	•		•	•												•			
Computer Science	•	•	•	•	•		•																							
Telecommunications	•		•																											
Tech. Product Know.				•	•		•			•								•	•	•	•	•	•	•	•	•		•	•	•
Field Sales Exper.																														•
Advertising																														
Marketing																		•	•	•										•
Psychology																														
Industrial Relations							•	•					•												•			•	•	•
Counseling																														
Government Relations																				•	•									•
Political Science																														
Personnel Admin.	•																													•
Oral/Written Commun	•	•	•	•	•	•	•	•	•	•	•	•	•	•	•	•	•	•	•	•	•	•	•	•	•	•	•	•	•	•
Multiple Languages							•							•	•															•
Negotiating Skills							•	•		•								•		•										•
Teaching Skills																														
Aud/Vis. & Graphics														•	•		•													
Organiz. Structure	•	•		•	•									•	•															•
Tax Law																														
S.E.C. Regulations																														•
Foreign Trade							•	•		•																				
Postal Regulations	•																								•			•		
O.S.H.A. Regulations													•												•		•			
Law Enforcement																														
Transportation Regs.							•	•	•																•			•		
Product Quality Regs.																		•	•	•	•	•	•	•	•		•			•
Mfg. Process & Equip.							•	•		•			•					•	•	•					•	•	•	•		
Industrial Eng.	•				•		•	•					•												•	•	•	•	•	
Material Control							•	•	•	•																				
Transportation Mgmt.							•	•	•			•																		
Traffic Management							•	•	•			•																		
Education in Law				•																										
Educ. in Engineering													•												•	•		•	•	
Skilled Trades Know.													•																	
Schematic/Blueprints													•												•	•				
Education in Science																		•	•	•	•	•	•	•	•	•				•
Educ. in Medicine																		•	•	•										
Health/Safety	•						•											•	•	•	•	•	•	•	•			•	•	
Lab. Technology																		•	•	•	•	•	•	•						

How to Prepare Management Progression Plans

Every organization must plan ahead to assure that the employee population has enough people with the necessary skills, education, experience, and interests to perform the work called for in the long-range business plan.

Who Is In Charge of Progression Plans

The people charged with the responsibility for manpower planning and development are
- every individual manager (for direct subordinates)
- specific executives
- groups of managers
- departments with such names as:
  - Human Resources Management
  - Training & Development
  - Manpower Planning
  - Personnel Development
  - Employee Selection
  - Employment
  - Career Planning
- the employee

Why Managers Collect Data on Career Aspirations from Employees

No matter how many departments are responsible for making personnel plans for the needs of the enterprise, the individual employee's input is vital to assure that the organization's plans are acceptable to the person expected to fulfill them.

While evaluations of employee future potential and developmental/improvement needs can (and will) be made without the knowledge of the affected employee, it is always preferable to encourage people to make their wishes known to the company. If employee desires or expectations are unreasonable or impossible, it is better to face the fact "up front" than to mislead an employee. In most situations, employee hopes are quite reasonable and potentially attainable in the organization. The company may well receive some surprises about employee ambitions that could lead the organization to proceed with developmental plans that would not have been considered without confirmation of employee interest.

As long as management knows employee intentions and aspirations, it can provide guidance and counseling for remedial, developmental and improvement actions that would qualify the employees as candidates for the kind of job they seek when an opening occurs.

Such information can be collected from various files and records or collected directly from employees and supervisors to be coordinated in a
- employee information inventory
- skills inventory
- human resource information system
- talent data bank
- internal candidate file

How a Typical Employee Information Inventory Works

A typical format follows, using the same codes for fields of work that appeared in the **Major Salaried Careers** section.

Employee Information Inventory

INSTRUCTIONS

A personnel inventory system has been established to provide coordinated information on employees for management "people decisions." An essential part of this computerized data bank will be provided by the individual employee. Other information will come from existing Personnel/ Payroll records and from line managers.

The attached sheet should be completed by you and submitted directly to _____ in the Personnel Development Department. You will periodically be asked to update this information in the future.

Instructions on how to fill out the form follow.

Name and Employee Number - Print your name (first name, middle initial, and last name) and enter your employee/payroll number (number must be accurate).

Education Completed - enter only schools from which you have graduated. Only one entry can be made for each educational level. A month and date of graduation may be approximate. Area of study should be as specific as possible, although the entry for high school area of study will typically be "general."

Name of the school should be the official, complete name of the institution: i.e., *Podunk Community College - Hinterland*, instead of *Dunk U.*

Degree in Process - Area of study should be as specific as possible, and the degree pursued should be the next degree expected. State the year you expect to complete that degree.

Non-Degree Education - Include any courses taken which have not and will not be credited towards a degree. Starting with the current year, enter the year you completed a course/seminar, its title, and the organization which conducted it. Be sure to include in-house Company programs; outside courses given by educational institutes, professional societies and training organizations; and special courses conducted by other employers. Also identify the organization which conducted the course/seminar (not the individual who taught the course or the organization who paid for it). Typical entries would be: 1983 - Managerial Grid - by Company; 1986 - Fortran IV - by IBM. ; 1988 - AAP Compliance - by National Manufacturers Association.

Foreign Language - List every modern language you can use and describe your proficiency. "High" indicates fluency in both written and oral communications; "Low" indicates you have limited ability to read/write or speak/understand the language.

Non-Company Field of Work and Organization Level - Specific and general fields of work and organization levels are coded for your selection. You are asked to indicate (1) fields where you have had previous experience before joining the Company, and (2) the highest organization level you have held in each field outside the Company. If you have held a number of organization levels in the same field, list the field once and report the highest level you have held. If you have roughly equal experience in all areas under a "general" field (in bold type), you may wish to make one entry under the "general" category instead of listing each specific field. Remember to use the code numbers rather than the words.

Future Career Interests - Select primary and secondary fields of work that represent your future career interests at this point in time and enter the code numbers. This section asks you to state a preference for future opportunities and in no way reflects on your feelings towards your present assignment. You make the choices and set your own priorities. Do not agonize over which field is primary and which is secondary; both entries will be recorded.

As soon as you have completed your form, review your entries for completeness and accuracy. Forward the completed inventory form in the enclosed envelope to _____ in the Personnel Development Department. If you have any questions, feel free to contact _____ at _____.

EMPLOYEE INFORMATION INVENTORY

NAME: _____ EMPLOYEE NO. _____

EDUCATION COMPLETED

	Date Graduated	Area of Study	School	City / State
S020 hs	_____	_____	_____	_____
S021 Assoc	_____	_____	_____	_____
S022 Bach	_____	_____	_____	_____
S023 Master	_____	_____	_____	_____
S024 Doctorate	_____	_____	_____	_____
S025 Medical	_____	_____	_____	_____
S026 Law	_____	_____	_____	_____

DEGREE IN PROCESS

S030 Area of Study: _____

Degree Pursued: Assoc $\boxed{1}$ Bach $\boxed{2}$ Master $\boxed{3}$ Doctorate $\boxed{4}$ Medical $\boxed{5}$ Law $\boxed{6}$

Year you expect to complete the degree: _____

NON-DEGREE EDUCATION S060			**FOREIGN LANGUAGE** S080			
Year Taken	Course / Seminar	Conducted by	Language	1. Hi	Proficiency 2. Med	3. Low
____	_____	_____	_____	___	___	___
____	_____	_____	_____	___	___	___
____	_____	_____	_____	___	___	___
____	_____	_____	_____	___	___	___
____	_____	_____	_____	___	___	___
____	_____	_____	_____	___	___	___
____	_____	_____	_____	___	___	___

FIELD OF WORK CODES

100100	**Finance-General**	100700	**Pers/Ind Rel-General**	101400	**Communication Svc-Gen**
100101	Auditing	100701	Employee Benefits	101401	Mail Services
100102	Financial Planning	100702	Industrial Relations	101402	Telecommunications
100103	Cost Accounting	100704	Employment	101601	Printing
100104	Systems & Procedures	100705	Safety/Health		
100105	General Accounting	100706	Training & Development	101700	**R & D-General**
100106	Tax	100707	Compensation	101701	Chemistry
100108	Payroll	100800	Security	101703	Pharmacol-Micro/Bact
100109	Insurance			101706	Physics
100120	Control Accounting	100900	**Mgmt Info Svcs-General**	101709	Flavor/Fragrance
100121	Credit	100902	Data Control	101730	Pharmacy
100122	Plant Accounting	100903	Computer Operations	101731	Radio/Pharmaceutical
100123	Treasury Operations	100905	Prog/Systems Analysis	101732	Radio/Chemistry
		100908	Operations Research	101733	Clinical Development
				101734	Regulatory Affairs
		101100	**Purchasing**	101736	Clinical Diagnosis
100400	**Sales/Mkt-General**				
100403	Marketing Research			101900	**Quality Assurance-Gen**
100404	Field Sales	101200	**Distr/Inv Cont-General**	101902	Analytical Services
100405	Product Management	101202	Warehousing/Shipping	101999	Quality Control
100408	International Sales	101203	Traffic		
100420	Customer Service	101208	Inv Planning & Control	102100	**Manufacturing-General**
100421	Sales Training	101209	Order Entry/Billing Cont	102101	Process Engineering
		101211	Fleet Operations	102102	Production Planning
				102106	Production
		101300	**Engineering-General**	102111	Packaging
100500	**Legal**	101303	Construction Eng.		
		101306	Maintenance Eng.	102200	**Other** _____
		101307	Utilities Engineering		
100600	**Public Rel/Advertising**	101308	Electrical Eng.	102300	**General Management**

ORGANIZATION LEVEL CODES

(0) Clerk   (1) Professional   (2) Supervisor   (3) Manager   (4) Director   (5) General Manager/Executive   (6) Corporate Officer

1. Use the above codes to indicate fields where you have had previous experience before joining Mallinckrodt, and the highest organization level you have held in that field. Place the one-digit organization-level code in the parentheses. For example, if you had a position in the past as an audit manager, you would indicate 100101 (3).

   Previous work experience (and organization-level) codes:

   _____ ( ), _____ ( ), _____ ( ), _____ ( ), _____ ( ), _____ ( )

2. Now you have an opportunity to indicate your career interests. This will assure that Management is aware of your interests when job openings occur. From the above codes, select two fields in which you are currently most interested and enter the codes below. You may express your interests by indicating either a major field of work, such as *100100* Finance-General, or a specific area within a major field, such as *100103* Cost Accounting. You are not restricted to the field where you presently work, but are encouraged to list any field where you would like to apply your skills. This represents your feelings at this point in time and will be updated on an annual basis.

   Primary field of interest _____

   Secondary field of interest _____

The information on such a form is easily custom designed for the needs of the organization and requested in a form that permits fast and convenient retrieval.

Typical reports that can be swiftly generated on a main-frame or personal computer include:

- which MBAs with supervisory experience in customer service and a stated interest in international sales are highly proficient in Spanish
- what kind of non-degree education courses (from all sources) have been attended most often by people with the rank of Director or higher who have expressed an interest in General Management positions
- who holds a bachelor's degree in a scientific discipline, has a past history of professional-level financial area work and seeks a career in Manufacturing
- what managers graduated from a certain university where company employment recruiters plan to visit and would like help from a graduate of that school

A data collection form like that is necessary if you want to collect and use information that is not otherwise already on file. It is also helpful to use when you wish to remind employees of the organization's vested interest in their career advancement, while simultaneously updating employee career information that may be out of date.

Where to Find Additional Reference Information on Employee Skills

Data already in other files are usually added to employee inventory information to provide a more complete picture. Official records of the employee's history with the organization will complement or confirm what the individuals may have volunteered about themselves. Information usually available from company files include

1. company personnel/payroll information
2. current and historical performance appraisal ratings
3. pay information, including recent raises
4. job titles and promotions
5. employment or assessment test data
6. work/school/military record verification data
7. in-house or company-sponsored training and education courses

The last piece of information added is the **Potential Assessment,** which is an estimate of the person's promotability.

When combined with other information in a consistent format, this will produce a dossier or data base of great value for predictions and plans for employee development.

A List of Criteria Used to Predict Job Performance Needs

Listed below are some commonly used dimensions of job performance. They are the skill or behavior areas that may be relevant to success in a given position. Such dimensions are popular measurement criteria for coaching, growth potential or career development and potential assessment appraisals.

Planning & Organizing	Problem Analysis
Management Control	Stress Tolerance
Use of Delegation	Interest in Self Development
Oral Communication Skills	Judgement
Oral Presentation Skills	Decisiveness
Written Communication Skills	Initiative
Listening Skills	Flexibility
Creativity	Independence
Work Standards	Range of Interest
Leadership	Salesmanship
Sensitivity	Tenacity
Cooperation	Foresight
Risk-Taking	Technical Knowledge
Impact	Energy

Warnings About the Use of Job Dimension Criteria

Before you use any of the above dimensions, be sure:
- they apply to the job;
- they are visible in work output results;
- they are defined in terms of specific observations rather than general "feelings";

▸ the employee has been notified of your expectations in each dimensional area, or (at least) you give feedback on the adequacy of ongoing performance in these areas.

Potential Assessments: How "The Crystal Ball" Is Read

Potential assessments are speculative estimates that range from pure guesses to tentative plans, based on current information and circumstances.

Management evaluations of the potential promotability of employees are usually made under strict conditions of absolute confidentiality, to assure frank and open discussion between managers. An additional reason for careful handling of **potential assessments** is the essentially subjective nature of the process, which deals with the prospective future rather than the more "objectively observable" past. And the use of subjective evaluation terms makes the validity of such hypothetical "what-if" appraisals all the more subject to legitimate criticism. It is important that the results of **potential assessments** are communicated to the subjects (if communicated at all) as current viewpoints, not as absolute guarantees of future action.

The Many Kinds of Information in Potential Assessments

Potential Assessments can include
□ the degree of readiness for immediate promotion
□ amount of time estimated for readiness for promotion
□ strengths and weaknesses in specific performance areas
□ the position for which the employee is currently best suited to serve as a possible successor, replacement or "back-up"
□ the highest position or organization level the person can be expected to reach, according to present performance
□ the position or level the organization would like to see the employee reach before the end of his/her career in the enterprise
□ the types of remedial/improvement/developmental actions necessary to qualify the employee for promotion
□ lateral moves which are either necessary or desirable, to broaden the employee's perspective and experience

Why the Tentative Nature of Potential Estimates Makes Managers Nervous

These estimates of career advancement potential are always theoretical projections based on subjective human opinions; they are highly tentative and subject to change. For example, it is quite routine to find that estimates of "the number of years needed before the employee is fully ready for move or promotion" are extremely pessimistic. Although a formal assessment may predict that three years will be required, a sudden opening six months later often sees that same person moved into it; the promotion may be technically "premature," but it is surprising how quickly employees can disprove management reservations about their qualifications when given the chance. As the old axiom goes, "No corporal ever looked like a sergeant until he got three stripes on his arm."

Whenever employers are unable to <u>guarantee</u> promotions or certain career advancement steps, they tend to refrain from announcing their projections to the employees, lest the tentative plans be considered commitments. Many executives would prefer to say nothing specific about advancement opportunities until they are confident they can deliver on their promises rather than prematurely outlining intentions whose failure to become reality may antagonize or distress the employee.

Ways to Show Confidence And Make It Contagious

Sharing information about their potential assessments with the employees is not always a risk; it can be an opportunity that will pay off in increased mutual trust and confidence.

Most managers and executives are quite aware of the tentative, temporary and situational nature of potential assessments (particularly when they have been making them for their own subordinates). Such people will not be misled by access to their own ratings; instead, it is far more likely that they will appreciate the information and place more trust in the integrity of their boss and the entire organization.

The best example of the ability of employees to cope with apparent disappointment may appear in how they handle <u>negative</u> future career potential assessments.

The Benefits of Sharing "Bad News" About Potential Judgments

It is quite possible and even common for a perfectly competent manager or executive to be considered un-promotable. Some superiors prefer to withhold such "negative" information from their subordinates, to protect against employee resentment, argument or other unproductive behavior that may interfere with the current performance that is quite acceptable in the present job. Unfortunately, that kind of protective behavior is rarely helpful to either the subordinate or the boss.

Failure to "level" about management's view of an employee's future potential denies the employee the very feedback necessary for corrective measures and positive future planning. Yes, a disappointed manager may leave if she is told she appears to have reached her ceiling; but she may leave anyway, if she is kept in the dark or allowed to believe that she has a bright future which never arrives.

There is another benefit to sharing bad news: it increases the probability that management will also share potential good news which is equally important for employees to know.

It is possible that a top performer who is considered a key candidate for quick promotion may become impatient and quit if she is not informed of her bright prospects. People cannot read minds, so it should not be suprising if they fail to accurately guess what management intentions are, when management has kept their plans secret. An open communications policy can prevent such unnecessary and undesirable negative events.

Even in a worst-case scenario, when management has nothing good to say about someone, there are good prospects that the "unpromotable" employee who is frankly told the consensus of top management will react in a positive manner. There are a number of ways that employees who are designated as "dead-ended" can respond. They can

- react negatively, sulk and fume, behave in such an unproductive and unprofessional manner that they are fired (asked to resign to "pursue other interests").
- quietly continue to work at a minimum performance level while actively seeking another job, leaving the company suddenly and without warning.
- begin efforts to remedy his defects and change management's opinion by demonstrating the desired proficiency and potential.
- accept the current opinion and wait for better times and other reviewers who will come to a more acceptable potential conclusion.
- openly begin a search for another job in a cooperative manner (taking her

time, while continuing to perform satisfactorily on the current job and actively assisting management to seek a qualified replacement for herself).

- express relief because he does not want any other/higher job than the one he now holds and had been concerned that admission of his "lack of ambition" would imperil his current job.
- arrange to take measures to encourage the development of subordinates for higher positions, assisting them to go around or "leap-frog" her position when qualified for promotion to a job for which she is not currently considered eligible.

You will note that only two of those options have a negative impact on the organization ... the vast majority of possible reactions are positive. And those two negative choices are somewhat unlikely to be expected from professionals, since they would have the effect of damaging their work records. In fact, the only time an employee would have (subjectively) good reason to so "hurt" the company by counterproductive behaviors would be if the company had demonstrated bad faith and treachery to the employee (i.e., by lying about future opportunities)!

Potential assessments are not only delicate; they are also vital for future manpower planning such as succession plans.

What You Need to Know About Succession Plans

Contingency plans showing conclusions about who should replace whom and the relative degrees of readiness are called

  ○ succession plans
  ○ replacement charts
  ○ manpower plans
  ○ human resource planning charts
  ○ management back-up plans

While these programs are increasingly computerized today, an example of a manual system using an organization chart format illustrates a fairly sophisticated approach (which can also be computerized).

HUMAN RESOURCES
PLANNING CHART

DIVISION _____
GROUP _____
DATE _____
SUBMITTED _____

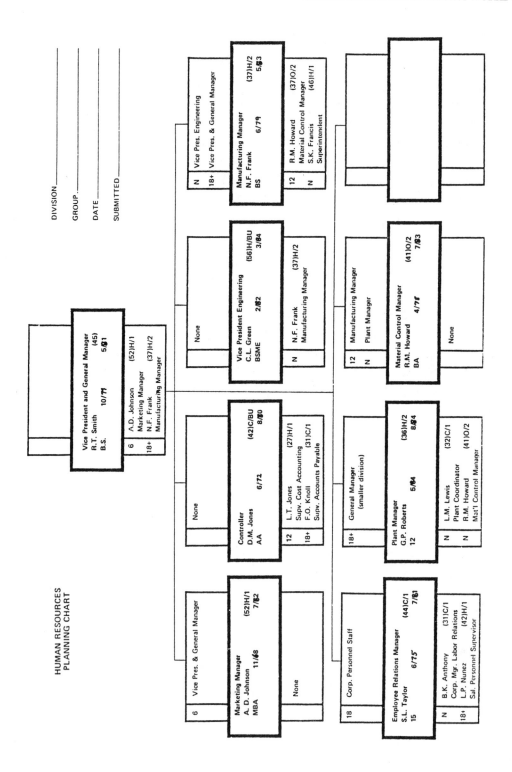

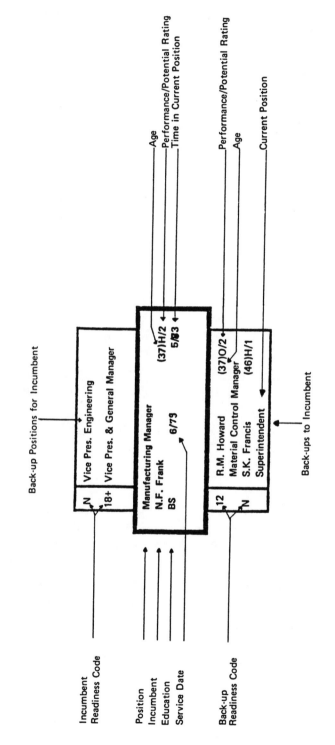

HUMAN RESOURCES PLANNING CHART

PERFORMANCE CODES

O = Outstanding performance
H = Highly effective performer
C = Competent performer

POTENTIAL CODES

2 = Two or more manager levels
1 = One manager level
PA = Senior professional/non-supervisory
BU = Being fully utilized

READINESS CODES

N = Ready now
6 = Ready in 6 months
12 = Ready in 12 months
18 = Ready in 18 months
18+ = Ready beyond 18 months

The types of instructions given to executives who conduct or participate in such succession planning meetings are illustrated next.

A Sample Policy on Human Resources Review Meetings

OBJECTIVES
The objective and purpose of the Human Resources Review Meetings is to:
1. Learn more about the current contribution of specific employees.
2. Understand why specific employees are considered to have or to lack advancement potential.
3. Identify talented employees within units who reside in low level or low visibility positions.
4. Examine the long-term effect of employee talent on the organizational structure of each unit.

REVIEW COMMITTEE
Those involved in the review of the Company's human resources should include:

Chairman of the Board, President, Vice President Human Resources, Corporate Director Personnel Development, all Group Personnel Directors, all Group Vice Presidents and unit executives on an individual basis. Each unit executive will lead the discussion about his or her people.

EMPLOYEES TO BE REVIEWED
Each unit executive will identify the key positions within his or her division. With the aid of Replacement Charts, the unit executive will discuss the position incumbent and possible replacements. (More detail is given in the Presentation Format section.) In addition to these employees, the unit executive may include in the Human Resources Review discussion other employees whose potential warrants the attention of the Review Committee.

PREPARATION ACTIVITIES
1. Human Resources Replacement Planning Charts must be completed for all positions from the executive through the manager level. Updated

performance and potential ratings must be included.
2. The unit executive should prepare to discuss the reasons for his or her estimates of
   - why an employee does or does not have advancement potential,
   - why a particular position is better than another for the employee,
   - why an employee is ready now or will be ready at some future date to assume the responsibilities of a new position, and
   - what the criteria were for the performance, potential, position and readiness judgements.
3. The unit executive and respective Group Personnel Director should discuss the long-range organizational structure of this unit as a function of the Five Year Plan.

PRESENTATION FORMAT
1. The unit executive will present each key position and:
   - Discuss the Incumbent, focusing on
     - current performance,
     - advancement potential, recommended position(s), and estimate of readiness time
     - reasons for these position recommendations and readiness estimates
     - significant/special skills; i.e. good administrator, has excellent interpersonal skills, communicates effectively, handles conflict well
   - Discuss Position Replacements
     - current job and performance rating
     - reason for being selected/designated as a replacement
     - rationale for readiness estimate
     - significant skills the individual possesses
2. After the presentation on each key position, the Review Committee members may want to
   - ask questions about details
   - make suggestions
   - discuss back-up candidates from other units
3. Discuss other employees not currently designated as back-ups or potential replacements whose potential warrants the attention of the Review Committee (particularly if their skills and abilities might be well utilized in

jobs that exist in other units).
4. Review Replacement Charts, concentrating on "holes" and positions where the incumbent is "blocking" an advancement/developmental path for others. Discuss plans and/or needs to fill "holes," to bypass "roadblocks" or to reduce the effects of any "blocking."
5. Discuss the long-range organizational structure of the unit (which is a function of the long-range plans of the unit and the Company) and future manpower/skill needs.

FOLLOW-UP

The Vice President of Personnel will summarize the Review Meetings to consolidate Review Committee conclusions on employee potentials into an updated report
☆ identifying the employees designated as primary and secondary back-ups for key positions
☆ listing jobs or performance areas where an adequate supply of replacements does not exist
☆ suggesting coordinated development plans for replacement candidates
☆ outlining plans to fill Replacement Chart "holes" and reduce the effect of unpromotable incumbents who "block" the progression/development of others.

Career Development Actions That Are Directed by the Company

The action plans followed by the organization to insure the continued vitality and success of personnel development efforts include
▫ Education
▫ On-the-job training
▫ Counseling
▫ Mentorship
▫ Transfers
▫ Promotions
▫ Reclassifications
▫ Special assignments
▫ Task force participation
▫ Research projects

◻ all the methods listed under **Training Methods** in the **Remedial Methods** chapter.

How Career Ladders Help People Climb Up the Organization

What Career Ladders Are and How They Work

Pre-established paths of progression within a job family of related positions called **Career Ladders** are one popular method of providing for predictable career development.

They are used most often to guide and regulate a smooth path of advancement from a "junior" to a "senior" position in a particular specialty area. Employees climb **career ladders** as they gain higher levels of experience, education, or skill (human capital) and/or qualify for more complex, responsible and important work (job content).

The steps of **career ladders** are precisely defined, to clearly communicate the requirements of each level and to assure that employees progress in title and pay along with opportunities to perform more valuable work.

Such ladders can be in technical, scientific, financial, administrative or craft fields: a career ladder can be constructed for any definable and related field of work where incumbents are expected and encouraged to move through a pre-ordained series of increasingly more valuable jobs. They are particularly useful within organizations that offer few opportunities for lateral (sideways on the org chart) transfers or promotions; the ladder progressions provide a periodic growth in employee status, pay, title and responsibility that might not otherwise be possible.

Career ladders that carry high pay and employment security for those who persevere can provide retention and protection against turnover by giving employees in key jobs a version of a "golden handcuff": the value of staying in the progressionary ladder can be so great that it reduces the attractiveness of other jobs.

That is also the exact defect of career ladders: they can "lock in" people to one particular job family. Employees may earn so much as senior computer programmers that they cannot afford to "step down" to move onto a lower-paying rung of another ladder or take a cut in status to retrain as a junior administrator. Other examples include teachers whose seniority ladders accelerate their pay in their first years so rapidly that by the time their administrative potentials are recognized, they cannot afford to move into management as assistant principals because of the lower pay; or craft workers whose hourly rate with overtime earns such a high income that they are reluctant to abandon the manual skills that earned them such success and instead become supervisors: in each case, the initial pay for the new job is less, even though the career advancement potentials are greater.

Be sensitive to the possibility that your formal progression practices may create conflicts with other objectives. Whenever policies and procedures violate the basic rules of effective performance management (i.e., *balance of consequences*), they will not operate in a fully effective manner.

What Career Ladders Look Like: Two Examples - Clerks and Editors

Career Ladder for Accounting Clerks

Title	Typical Tasks	Supervision	Education/Experience
Senior Accounting Clerk	keeps vital records, prepares final reports	exercises discretion under general supervision, directs and checks work of Intermed. & Jr. Clerks	Assoc. degree in Accounting or equivalent experience plus 6 years experience
Intermediate Accounting Clerk	reconciles accounts, posts to ledgers and balances, processes payments	follows standard procedures under immediate supervision	Assoc. degree in Accounting or equivalent experience plus 2 more years related experience
Junior Accounting Clerk	posts simple entries, processes routine payments, does filing	under close supervision	high school diploma or equivalent skills

Career Ladder for Publication Staff

Title	Typical Tasks	Supervision	Education/Experience
Managing Editor	approves all content, directs policy	under minimum supervision	Masters degree in Journalism or Liberal Arts or BA with equivalent experience plus over 8 years related experience
Editor	manages and edits a section	under general supervision	BA in Journalism or Liberal Arts or equivalent experience plus over 4 years related experience

Staff Writer	completes writing and editorial assignments	under immediate supervision	BA in Journalism or Liberal Arts or equivalent experience plus 2 years related experience
Editorial Assistant	collects research information, proofreads, writes simple articles	under close supervision	BA in Journalism or Liberal Arts or equivalent experience

How to Make Career Development Pay Dividends to the Organization

The Sad State of Employee Career Development Programs

Most organizations are not dedicated to personnel development. It is a prime example of conflicting or contradictory organizational messages, where the impartial observer is forced to the conclusion that either the actual practices fall far below the sincere intentions, or the company does not really believe that "our people are our most valuable resource."

Formal development programs within corporations and public employers tend to be purely defensive measures: enough to maintain minimum on-going training needs or to provide remedial actions to salvage an employee whose performance has slipped. There is a certain intense interest in manpower planning and management development, to the extent that adequate human resources will be available for growth and as back-ups for key positions; but few firms formally and officially

☆ reward managers who develop subordinates for advancement

☆ actively encourage employees to learn new skills not applicable to the job in the forseeable future

☆ encourage employees to pursue greater opportunities for career growth that would involve leaving the company

Some firms (and many excellent individuals) have the foresight to act against their own short term interest. They believe that happy ex-employees are better for the organization than frustrated ones who leave disappointed (or, even worse, who stay when they are disappointed).

But the deck is stacked against most managers who actively encourage their subordinates to perform with such excellence that they "outgrow" their current jobs.

How Supervisors Can Be Punished for Developing Good People

When a manager recommends a valuable subordinate for transfer or promotion,

- he loses one of his best workers;
- she must take time to recruit, select and train a replacement;
- unit productivity suffers in the meantime;
- an outside replacement capable of immediately filling the shoes of the departed expert may cost more and take a bigger bite out of department payroll than was originally budgeted;
- by year end, unit productivity is lower than expected and actual recruiting/payroll/training cost expenses are higher than planned;
- the manager receives a lower performance appraisal rating and gets a smaller raise.

How Supervisors Who Hide Good People Can Be Rewarded

On the other hand, the manager who hides her best people, only offering the dregs of the department for transfer or promotion, avoids all those negative consequences and gets a bigger raise. Of course, sooner or later, the high-performing subordinate will leave one way or another (physically or psychologically), but the manager will have gotten a few more years of output from them for her own benefit.

What Is Needed for Positive Employer/Employee Development

If organizations are truly sincere about the value of personnel development and employee career advancement for <u>all</u> rather than for only a select few, they will

- ★ assure that every manager's performance plan includes a requirement of subordinate development
- ★ provide contingency plans to protect "development managers" from budgetary and unit output damages caused by properly encouraging people to grow
- ★ evaluate and reward managers who nurture and develop the talents and potentials of employees
- ★ designate certain managers who have proven their aptitudes as "mentors," with a pay premium, special title/status and duties adjusted to allow

sufficient attention to special subordinate developmental activities
★ preserve and protect "mentors" from the "up or out syndrome," which would lead to their discharge if they do not constantly prove personal upward mobility (if they are not promotable, but can develop two promotable subordinates, they are twice as valuable staying where they are!)
★ make it abundantly clear that development is not an activity restricted to a separate staff department with that name in their title but a responsibility of all performance managers

Otherwise, the best people your organization develops will have more than adequate justification to flee to greener pastures. Some will, in any case; no one enterprise can make full use of all the talents of all its people all the time: but a reputation as an organization that constantly asks for the best its employees can offer and reciprocates by seeking the personal best for its employees is worth more than gold. It will attract better workers, retain them much longer and keep them as grateful admirers even after they leave.

Chapter 8:

PROVEN METHODS FOR EFFECTIVE RECRUITING AND EMPLOYMENT

The Steps to Build a Productive Work Team

Once the human resource needs for the future are known (the organization has gotten READY and taken AIM), then it is time for action, to FIRE towards the target of building a performance team for today and the future.

Building a team that can achieve organizational performance objectives involves recruitment, employment, search and selection. If these steps are done well, you will have a competent group of people who have the talent and ability to perform successfully. On the other hand, a poor recruitment and selection process will produce a motley crew who, despite all the good will in the world, might not be capable of filling your needs.

How to Begin the Search with a Needs Analysis

The search process starts with a needs analysis. Before you start "searching," "recruiting," "selecting" and "employing," be sure you know:
- [ ] what responsibilities, duties and tasks must be performed;
- [ ] the skills, training, aptitudes, attitudes and experiences that are both required and desired from candidates;
- [ ] details of the pay, working conditions, reporting relationships, opportunities, and other special features which may either attract or repel applicants.

Using a Hiring Requisition to Outline Search Criteria

Such information is detailed in a **Hiring Requisition** or **Employment Requisition**, although a summarized version may often appear on **Job Descriptions** or **Position Specifications**.

Sample Employment Requisition Form

Date submitted:_____ Earliest date needed:_____

Latest date needed:_____

Job title:_____ Pay Grade_____

Reports to:_____ Department_____

Budget charged_____

Candidates to be interviewed by _____

Overall job function:

_____

_____

_____

Requirements:

_____

_____

_____

Education:

Special certifications/licenses required:

Experience:

Other special requirements (technical/communication skills, test scores required, critical areas of knowledge, etc.):

Income: Start rate: _____   Current maximum:_____

Relocation expenses paid include: ☐ None ☐ All ☐ Some (specified below)

Have all current employees been eliminated as potentially qualified candidates? ☐ YES ☐ NO

Comments:

Recruitment sources:			Specify sources and cost limits:
Current employees	☐ YES	☐ NO	
Local advertising	☐ YES	☐ NO	

Regional advertising	☐ YES	☐ NO	
National advertising	☐ YES	☐ NO	
Search firm	☐ YES	☐ NO	
Employment agency	☐ YES	☐ NO	
Prof. assocs./networks	☐ YES	☐ NO	

Approved by: (Dept. Head) _____ (Date) _____
                (Director) _____ (Date) _____
                     (V.P.) _____ (Date) _____
             (Exec. V.P.) _____ (Date) _____

Additional Optional Data That Can Be Included on a Requisition

Other information is often added to the requisition form:
- Employment status type (Permanent or Temporary) and
  - ☐ Full time
  - ☐ Part Time
  - ☐ Summer
  - ☐ Co-op
- Hours or shift assignment
- Reason for opening (Addition or Replacement)
- Name of person replaced and why they left.
- Head-count control information
- Organization chart showing reporting relationships above and below
- Final disposition of the requisition
  - ○ Filled or unfilled, and when
  - ○ Who was hired, when and at what rate of pay
  - ○ Recruitment source for the candidate selected

How to Look Inside the Organization for Talent Before Going Outside

The immediate next step is to determine whether potential prospective candidates for the position already exist in the organization. If they do, you may want to review the search specifications to see if certain selection criteria should be added, deleted or changed in light of the possible availability of current employees for the new job.

The Reasons for Preferring Inside Candidates to Fill Openings

There are many advantages to transferring, promoting or reclassifying employees from inside the organization instead of hiring from outside. Current employees

- are known quantities, with proven skills and tested work records
- already possess inside knowledge about the enterprise
- typically require less orientation and training
- have directly relevant experience, gained and demonstrated under the eyes of reliable observers
- may have already voiced an interest in such a new opportunity
- have already earned a degree of management confidence
- can be less expensive and more effective than outside talent with paper credentials
- need to see proof that the firm really does promote from within and offer opportunities for advancement

Some search requirements that are designed to compensate for the lack of directly relevant work experience can be waived or altered for internal candidates.

The Reasons for Preferring Outside Candidates to Fill Openings

On the other hand, outside hiring can also bring certain advantages. External candidates

- are the only alternative when no internal candidates are ready
- can bring fresh viewpoints and new ideas
- permit the addition of qualifications and experience not held by current employees
- will always look good on paper compared to known employees who have invariably made a mistake at one time or another
- are less likely to repeat the behavior patterns of current employees (that can be either good or bad)

It is not uncommon to find hiring specifications for the same job created in two versions: one for internal candidates and one for people to be recruited from outside.

Four Methods for Finding Internal Candidates

Internal candidates can be identified by:

Succession plans	formal plans drafted by management and periodically updated, listing back-up candidates for key positions (*see the chapter on **Development***);
Skills inventory data bank	records of particular skills, abilities, education, experience, etc., held by current employees; often includes self-nomination information on job preferences, careers hopes, etc. (*see the chapter on **Development***);
Survey of managers	circulating a copy of the hiring specifications and job description to management members who can nominate people for consideration;
Job posting	announcements of position openings available to employees. A sample job posting policy follows.

A Complete Sample Job Posting Policy

POLICY STATEMENT
It is the policy of the Company that job vacancies and openings will be filled from within to the extent that qualified employees who desire promotion or transfer are available. This policy shall be announced to all employees.

PROCEDURE
A current report on job vacancies and new openings shall be posted by each local personnel representative, in a place offering maximum employee access, for a fixed period of time.

The report shall identify
- job title, department and location
- supervisor
- pay grade, salary classification or job value
- anticipated hiring rate
- contact person (normally the local personnel representative)

Employees with an interest in a posted position shall notify their personnel representative who will provide a copy of the position specifications (listed on the top portion of the employment requisition) prepared by supervisor and approved by the manager and the personnel executive of the hiring group.

If employees are still interested after examining the qualifications required and the job description (if available), they may submit themselves for consideration by completing an **Application for Promotion/Transfer** through their supervisor and personnel representative.

The local personnel representative shall forward the completed application to the personnel executive of the hiring group, who will

- review the applicant's qualifications with the hiring manager
- coordinate arrangements for an interview and any required testing
- provide feedback to the applicants and their supervisors
- assure that no outside hiring decision is made until all internal candidates have been eliminated and notified
- keep records of posting responses for personnel planning purposes

A Typical Application for Promotion/Transfer

Name_____ Date_____

Department_____ Division_____ Location_____

Present job_____ Pay grade_____ Time on job_____

Job sought_____ Requisition Number_____

Hiring department and division_____

I am requesting consideration for this open vacancy or new position.
I meet all of the following requirements:

- ☐ I have over six months service in my present job with the Company.
- ☐ My performance has met the required standards for the past year.
- ☐ I believe I meet all of the other qualifications listed for the opening.
- ☐ I understand that the final choice to fill the vacancy will be the person considered by management to possess the best qualifications for this job.

My qualifications are:

Employee signature_____ Date_____

Comments of present supervisor:

*Supervisor*_____ *Date*_____
*Manager*_____ *Date*_____

Comments of hiring manager:

*Interviewer*_____ *Date*_____
*Manager*_____ *Date*_____

A Standard Form to Use for Responses to Applicants

☐ This opening has been cancelled. We will retain your application in case the requisition is renewed.

☐ Your application was received too late for consideration.

☐ The information you provided on your qualifications does not indicate that you meet the minimum qualification requirements for this position. Specifically:

_____
_____
_____
_____

☐ This position is being filled from within our department.

☐ You have not been selected for the following reasons:

_____
_____
_____
_____

Signed_____ Title_____ Date_____

Why It Is Advisable to Search Inside First

Performance Management Tip

Always look inside before you search outside to fill a job opening.

While starting with an internal search does not mean that you must limit your search to internal candidates only, it does assure that you consider existing employees before you spend the money and time to seek outside ones.

If you allow employees to believe "the only way to get ahead around here is to quit and get re-hired," then you will probably encounter severe morale and turnover problems. Experience shows that the vast majority of employees sincerely appreciate being considered for a promotion even when they do not get it. Explanations of why they were passed over can focus on skill, training or remedial/developmental needs; that informs them of what they must do to have a better chance for advancement in the future and confirms that the company and their manager really cares.

Careful Steps for Implementing a Job Posting Plan

Those who have never had much experience with a good job posting program (and some who have) may have reservations about the process. While most effective performance managers see nothing wrong with speaking as frankly about job openings to current employees as they would with candidates from outside the organizations, there are certain problems and hazards that can inhibit or destroy a job posting program.

A Planning Method That Identifies and Prevents Problems

The method shown for coping with objections to (or problems with) a job posting program also illustrates a highly efficient proven method of <u>planning analysis</u> known as **Kepner-Tregoe** *Problem Solving and Decision Analysis* ©.

This application shows how an actual or potential problem can be anticipated and defined; each is then classified as to the degree of *Probability* that it may occur and the degree of *Seriousness* of the consequences of occurrence. What could go wrong? How probable is that (what is the likelihood that the potential problem will appear in reality? If it does happen, how serious could the consequences be (how severe are the ramifications of it coming true)?

The remedial plan is formed in two parts: how can we prevent it from happening through *Preventive Steps*; and if the preventive measures don't stop it, how can we cope with the effects through *Contingent Actions* which address what can be done to cushion the blow, to reduce the negative consequences and to provide corrective measures for the future.

Potential problems that are rated high in both the *Probability* that they will come true and the *Seriousness* of their consequences should get the highest priority for *Preventive* and *Contingent* or remedial actions. Next in priority should come those possible events that would be extremely serious but are less likely to happen. (Can you afford to fail to plan some kind of action to prevent or survive a disaster that would destroy your business ... even if it is fairly unlikely?) Lower priority goes to those problems that are likely to occur but where the consequences would only be annoying, at worse, and not a major threat. Last place is for problems that are both unlikely and relatively harmless.

A close look at how one can plan to solve, prevent and survive problems with a Job Posting program demonstrates the process.

A Detailed Potential Problem Analysis on Job Posting

Potential Problems	Probability	Seriousness	Preventive Step	Contingent Action
Can't hire experts from outside	High	High	Guarantee outside hire option if no qualified internal candidates found.	Unit Exec. may authorize outside search to begin before review of internals, but no new hires allowed before internals eliminated.
Managers feel their flexibility and authority is limited.	High	Medium	Explain procedures, resolve fears.	Exclude confidential or highly sensitive openings from program.
Rejected candidates argue that they are qualified.	High	Medium	Publish job specifications and selection criteria.	Confront conflict frankly and resolve. Management must manage.
Rejected candidates become demotivated.	High	Medium	Hold periodic career development discussions.	Rejection feedback includes communication of development needs and suggested programs.

Potential Problems	Probability	Seriousness	Preventive Step	Contingent Action
Managers exaggerate job requirements to eliminate internal candidates.	High	Medium	Sell benefits of reasonable criteria. Unit Exec. and Personnel must approve requisition.	Compensation Dept. will monitor job title & pay grade to match specs.
Managers & Personnel Reps. will spent more time screening, interviewing, counseling.	High	Medium	Sell benefits of such improved communications.	Provide interview training to increase efficiency and effectiveness.
Best people will move "prematurely," leaving old Manager short-handed.	Medium	Medium	Allow transition period. Set limits of frequency of job changes.	Give replacement priority and budget to depts. who lose someone thru promotion.
Depts. with low-pay or dead-end jobs will consistently lose their best people.	Medium	Medium	Establish vertical progression ladders.	Gear such jobs for fast replacement. Reward Managers who develop promotable employees.
Self-nomination is viewed with suspicion.	Medium	Medium	Assure managers that candidates must meet reasonable criteria.	Review and discuss reasonableness of expectations and criteria for selection.
Managers fear exposure of job grade values and duties.	Medium	Medium	Reaffirm management discretionary authority over job duties and explain how grade are assigned.	Tell policy, sell benefits, resolve individual anxieties.

Openings are not communicated uniformly or in time.	Medium	Medium	Use communications media offering wide and rapid distribution, such as computer mail or bulletin board.	Extend posting expiration dates where needed.
Turnover will get too high in depts. as people change jobs.	Low	Medium	Set limits on how often employees may change jobs.	Sell benefits (morale, incentive for better performance on current job, fewer quits to seek more advancement.)
Managers whose depts. post openings will be "pestered" by applicants and employment agencies.	Medium	Low	Restrict direct phone/personal access to Managers.	Managers are instructed to handle inquiries per policy and refer to Personnel.
Managers will "hide" jobs to avoid posting them and use consultants/ temporaries.	Low	Low	Install, communicate and enforce controls over outside services.	Resolve with individual offenders; offer help writing better hiring specs.

Methods to Recruit Employees from Outside

The process of recruiting and selecting a new employee gives the manager a chance to improve the performance potential of his or her department.

There are a tremendous number of people in the outside world who may be interested in your job, and a significantly smaller number who could perform it well. But finding enough reasonably competent candidates to give you a choice can be difficult.

Performance Management Tip

Seek candidates where they are found. Allocate your recruitment time and expenses to the areas which offer the highest probability of producing a viable competent candidate.

Where to Look for Qualified Job Candidates

Some of the sources of qualified people are
1. high schools
2. vocational institutes
3. government agencies
    - Federal and State employment services
    - vocational training agencies
    - rehabilitation agencies
4. colleges and universities
5. professional societies
6. trade associations
7. unions
8. customers and suppliers
9. conventions and meetings
10. outplacement organizations
11. employment agencies
12. search consultants
13. employee referrals
14. applicant files
15. "help-wanted" advertising

How to Deal with Geographic Factors That Can Affect Your Search

The "attractiveness" of a job opening varies according to the frame of reference of the candidates, which is strongly influenced by their experiences and expectations. Where people are coming from and where they are going can affect the search methods and the employment offer.

As the sample pages from the **1988 Annual Report (Geographic Reference of Costs, Wages, Salaries and Human Resource Statistics)** from the **Economic Research Institute** in Newport Beach, California, illustrate, there are many relative differences in how people from different parts of the country will see the same job offer.

Recruiters should note the differences in population, industry, types of employers, union influence, education, advertising media (particularly those newspapers offering Sunday editions, which are best for classified ad response), crime rates, starting salaries and cost factors. Such information, even when collected for an entire metropolitan area rather than for a specific suburb/industry/job, can be vital for a decision about where to search and what to advertise as an "advantage" that would attract qualified applicants to your location.

Sample Data on Geographic Differences that Influence Your Search

It is important to notice that salaries and living costs do not always relate each other. As covered later in the **Pay** chapter and illustrated in the sample data shown here, the relative "cost of living" in a given area does not necessarily predict the competitive entry rates or average salaries paid in that area.

Knowledge of such facts, and possession of the proof to back it up, can help assure a more effective recruiting process.

SPOKANE, WASHINGTON

Spokane is the economic center of the "Inland Empire," located on the Spokane River and flanked on the East by the Rocky Mountains.   Located in the central eastern area of Washington, it is adjacent to Idaho and within 100 miles of the Canadian border. The metro area has a population of 356,000.

The economy of Spokane depends upon agriculture and forestry products.   Food services, processing, mining, milling, and retail/wholesale distribution also play a role. Availability of cheap hydro-electric power generated by the Columbia River contributes greatly to Spokane's industrial success.

Employment by Industry

Construction	4.9
Finance, Insurance, Real Estate	5.9
Government	17.8
Light & Heavy Manufacturing	12.9
Retail & Wholesale Trade	27.7
Services	25.7
Transportation & Utilities	5.0

Major Employers

Sacred Heart Hospital	Kaiser Aluminum
Key Tronics	Deaconess Medical Center
ISC Systems Corporation	Cowles Publishing Compan
Columbia Lighting	Sun Runner Marine
Nortwest Alloys	Bayliner Marine

Organized Labor Influence
Percentage Union Employees/All Employees   39.6 %

Colleges & Universities

	Enrollment
Gonzaga University	3600
Whitworth College	1900
Spokane Community Colleges	20700
Eastern Washington State University	8100

Daily Newspapers

	Circulation
Spokesman Review	E - 227,000 S - 196,100
Spokane Chronicle	E - 117,000

Television Stations

	Ch	Affiliation
KREM	2	CBS
KXLY	4	ABC
KHQ	6	NBC
KAYU	28	NBC

Weather   Avg Temperature/Precipitation

	Minimum	Maximum	Rainfall	Snow
January	28.	31.	2.5	17.8
February	26.	39.	1.7	7.4
March	29.	46.	1.5	4.4
April	35.	57.	1.1	.5
May	43.	67.	1.5	.1
June	49.	74.	1.4	.0
July	55.	84.	.4	.0
August	54.	82.	.6	.0
September	47.	78.	.8	.0
October	37.	58.	1.4	.0
November	29.	42.	2.2	.0
December	24.	34.	2.4	.0
Extremes & Totals	20.	84.	17.5	30.2

Area Crime Rate

Robberies	85.5/100000	Homicides	3.5/100000
Rapes	19.9/100000	Assaults	185.4/100000

COMPARED TO THE U.S. NATIONAL AVERAGE

National Structure	* * *
Cost of Living	C C C
Salary & Wage Levels	S S S

Recruiting/Entry Level Salaries

Accounting Clerk	$	12813.	Accountant/Auditor $	18552.
Clerk Typist	$	11275.	Attorney	$ 29025.
Payroll/Pers Clerk	$	14817.	Buyer/Purchaser	$ 17189.
Receptionist/PBX	$	10990.	Personnel Manager	$ 22648.
Secretary	$	14025.	Programmer	$ 19504.
Word Processing Op	$	12319.	Sales Rep	$ 16299.

Housing Costs

Single 3 Bedroom, 2,000 sq ft Home	$	78630.
- estimated Mortgage Payment	$	633./month
- estimated Monthly Utilities	$	90./month
- estimated Annual Property Tax	$	977.
Estimated Comparable Rental	$	525./month

Hospital & Health Care

Average Daily Semiprivate Room Cost	$	272.
Average Total Hospital Cost Per Day	$	548.

Administrative Structures

	Cost of Living	Wage & Salary
Non Exempt	.875 x n + 90.	.782 x n + 1529.
Exempt Non Bonus	.860 x n + 330.	.879 x n + 4.
Exempt Bonus	.828 x n + 1335.	1.010 x n - 4179.

Cost of Living Analyses v U.S. Average Level

	7,000	15,600	32,000	50,000
Housing/Utilts	83.%	83.%	83.%	83.%
Taxes St/Fd/Pr	67.%	78.%	80.%	78.%
Consumables	90.%	90.%	90.%	90.%
Transportation	94.%	94.%	94.%	94.%
Services/Other	98.%	98.%	98.%	98.%
Total vs. U.S.	89.%	88.%	87.%	85.%

Estimated Workforce Demographics

Age 16-19	6.7 %	Age 20-40	42.8 %	Age 40 +	50.5 %
Caucasian	97.3 %	Black	1.3 %	Hispanic	1.4 %
	Male	61.6 %	Female	38.4 %	
		Unemployment	5.9 %		

Recommended Secondary School/Districts
Sacajawea JHS, Spokane   Mead, East Valley Dist 81

BOSTON, MASSACHUSETTS

Boston is called the "Hub of the Universe," and "Athens of America." Boston is located in north eastern Massachusetts, surrounded by the Neponset, Charles, Chelsea and Mystic rivers. Boston is the state capital and commercial center, and is fortunate to possess many sheltered harbors along the Atlantic coastline. The metro area population is approximately 570,000.

The extremely diversified economy of Boston depends upon high tech industries, shipbuilding, distribution, and trade. Boston's port handles many products including include residual fuel oil and limestone. Major manufactured products include industrial machinery, computers, ships, and processed foods.

Employment by Industry

Construction	5.0
Finance, Insurance, Real Estate	12.4
Government	.8
Light & Heavy Manufacturing	6.3
Retail & Wholesale Trade	29.3
Services	41.7
Transportation & Utilities	4.4

Major Employers

Digital Equipment Corp.	Sheraton Corp.
Raytheon Co.	Zayre Corp.
Stop & Shop Co.	

Organized Labor Influence

Percentage Union Employees/All Employees   18.1 %

Colleges & Universities

	Enrollment
Boston State College	11230
Boston State College	11230
Boston College	13545
Boston University	24292

Daily Newspapers — Circulation

Boston Globe	E - 512,000 S - 780,000
Boston Herald	D - 360,000 S - 308,000

Television Stations

	Ch	Affiliation
WBZ	4	NBC
WCVB	5	ABC
WNEV	7	CBS
WLVI	56	IND

Weather — Avg Temperature/Precipitation

	Minimum	Maximum	Rainfall	Snow
January	23.	36.	3.7	12.4
February	23.	38.	3.5	11.7
March	32.	45.	4.0	7.8
April	41.	56.	3.5	.7
May	50.	67.	3.5	.0
June	59.	77.	3.2	.0
July	65.	81.	2.7	.0
August	63.	79.	2.5	.0
September	57.	72.	3.2	.0
October	47.	63.	4.5	.0
November	39.	52.	4.2	.0
December	27.	39.	4.1	.0
Extremes & Totals	23.	81.	42.6	32.6

Area Crime Rate

Robberies	304.4/100000	Homicides	5.3/100000
Rapes	24.0/100000	Assaults	342.2/100000

29

COMPARED TO THE U.S. NATIONAL AVERAGE

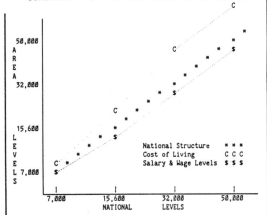

National Structure	* * *
Cost of Living	C C C
Salary & Wage Levels	$ $ $

Recruiting/Entry Level Salaries

Accounting Clerk	$ 14303.	Accountant/Auditor	$ 22310.
Clerk Typist	$ 12369.	Attorney	$ 32679.
Payroll/Pers Clerk	$ 16821.	Buyer/Purchaser	$ 20960.
Receptionist/PBX	$ 12010.	Personnel Manager	$ 26365.
Secretary	$ 15825.	Programmer	$ 23253.
Word Processing Op	$ 13681.	Sales Rep	$ 20079.

Housing Costs

Single 3 Bedroom, 2,000 sq ft Home	$ 257700.
- estimated Mortgage Payment	$ 2308./month
- estimated Monthly Utilities	$ 195./month
- estimated Annual Property Tax	$ 1222.
Estimated Comparable Rental	$ 1827./month

Hospital & Health Care

Average Daily Semiprivate Room Cost	$ 318.
Average Total Hospital Cost Per Day	$ 687.

Administrative Structures

	Cost of Living	Wage & Salary
Non Exempt	1.354 x n - 852.	.983 x n + 118.
Exempt Non Bonus	1.461 x n - 2519.	.998 x n - 112.
Exempt Bonus	1.501 x n - 3798.	1.000 x n - 196.

Cost of Living Analyses v U.S. Average Level

	7,000	15,600	32,000	50,000
Housing/Utilts	221.%	219.%	216.%	212.%
Taxes St/Fd/Pr	61.%	91.%	104.%	98.%
Consumables	102.%	101.%	100.%	98.%
Transportation	102.%	101.%	100.%	98.%
Services/Other	122.%	121.%	119.%	117.%
	-------	-------	-------	-------
Total vs. U.S.	123.%	130.%	138.%	143.%

Estimated Workforce Demographics

Age 16-19	5.9 %	Age 20-40	43.0 %	Age 40 +	51.1 %
Caucasian	91.8 %	Black	5.8 %	Hispanic	2.4 %
	Male 44.4 %		Female 55.6 %		
		Unemployment 5.8 %			

Recommended Secondary School/Districts

Acton-Boxborough HS, Acton   Rockland JHS, Rockland

Data Projected To: 3/15/88
Report Printed On: 3/ 7/88

Proven Procedures for Reviewing Resumes

Keep in mind that a resume, biography or *curriculum vitae* prepared by a job applicant is his or her sales pitch to the employer, stating all the best points and presenting what is hoped to be the very best picture of the applicant. If it is well done, it will be an "air-brushed" picture, magnifying the assets and minimizing the defects of the candidate.

A resume outlines what the applicant believes is the most favorable view of personal abilities, achievements, ambitions and potentials. It is not always what you, the employer, either want or need to know for your selection decision.

How to Make Maxium Use of the Employment Application

The standard information usually needed by the organization should be consistently covered in the employment application.

The employment application form has specific questions soliciting specific types of answers on subjects where the employer needs information before making a hiring decision. It should always be completed by applicants, to assure that the same vital questions are answered in the same complete manner by all applicants and employees.

A Sample Employment Application Form

APPLICATION FOR EMPLOYMENT

WE ARE AN EQUAL OPPORTUNITY EMPLOYER

PLEASE PRINT AND COMPLETE ALL SECTIONS OF THIS APPLICATION

Date _____   Social Security Number _____

Name _____   Telephone _____

Address _____

City, State, Zip Code _____

Position Applied For: _____

You are available to work: ☐ Full Time   ☐ Part Time   ☐ Temporary

Referred by: _____

Have you been employed with us before? ☐ YES ☐ NO **IF YES, WHEN** _____

Date of Birth (If under 18): _____

List any friends or relatives employed here: _____

Person to contact in case of emergency: (List name, address, and telephone number)

_____

Do you have any physical limitations which would place restrictions on your ability to work in the job for which you are applying? ☐ YES ☐ NO

If Yes, please explain: _____

Are you a U.S. citizen or an alien authorized to work in the U.S.? ☐ YES ☐ NO

EDUCATION

TYPE OF SCHOOL	NAME OF SCHOOL	CITY and STATE	GRADUATE?
High School			☐ Yes ☐ No
College/Univ.			☐ Yes ☐ No
Graduate Level			☐ Yes ☐ No
Business or Trade			☐ Yes ☐ No

Major course of study: _____

EMPLOYMENT HISTORY

Please account for all periods, beginning with your current or most recent employer.

Name of Employer:	**Employment Dates:**
Address: Street, City, State	**Telephone:**
Job Title:	**Name & Title of Supervisor:**
Income: Starting & Final:	**Reason for leaving:**

Name of Employer:	Employment Dates:
Address: Street, City, State	Telephone:
Job Title:	Name & Title of Supervisor:
Income: Starting & Final:	Reason for leaving:

Name of Employer:	Employment Dates:
Address: Street, City, State	Telephone:
Job Title:	Name & Title of Supervisor:
Income: Starting & Final:	Reason for leaving:

Please list any additional employment experience on a separate sheet of paper.

May we contact your present employer?   ☐ Yes   ☐ No

PERSONAL REFERENCES

Name _____   Telephone _____

Address _____

City, State, Zip Code _____

Name _____   Telephone _____

Address _____

City, State, Zip Code _____

Name _____   Telephone _____

Address _____

City, State, Zip Code _____

ACKNOWLEDGEMENTS AND AGREEMENTS

I, the undersigned, hereby apply for employment and certify that all information given on this application is true and complete to the best of my knowledge.

I understand that false statements, misrepresentation or omission of information will be sufficient cause for cancellation of consideration for employment or dismissal from the Company if I have already been employed.

I authorize all educational institutions, individuals, companies and their representatives to supply any information concerning my background, and I release them from any liability and responsibility arising from their doing so.

I agree to take a physical examination at any time, at the option of the Company, at no personal expense, to confirm an injury or illness resulting in absenteeism

or hampering my ability to perform. I also agree that the examining physician may disclose to the Company or its representatives the results of such examination.

I understand that my continued employment may be conditioned on the findings of this examination, if requested.

I understand that the Company can make no guarantee as to the number of hours that I may be assigned from week to week, and any reduction in hours can

affect my benefits. I also understand that I may be required to change days off and scheduled hours in order to continue my employment.

In consideration of my employment, I agree to conform to the rules of the Company and understand that my employment and compensation can be terminated,

with or without cause and without notice, at any time, at the option of the Company or myself. I understand that no one, other than the chief executive who

reports to the Board of Directors, has the authority to enter into any agreement for employment for any specified period of time, or to make any agreement contrary to the foregoing.

I have read and understand the above acknowledgements and agreements and recognize all of the above as conditions of employment.

SIGNATURE _____ **DATE** _____

FOR OFFICE USE ONLY

TO BE COMPLETED AT TIME OF HIRE, DOCUMENTING INITIAL TERMS:

Job Title: _____   **Effective Date:** _____

☐ **Full Time**   ☐ **Part Time**   **Rate of Pay: $** _____

Documents received: ☐ **Physical Exam Report**   ☐ **I-9 Form**

Supervisor's signature: _____

Approved by: _____

Additional Optional Elements for an Employment Application

The Employment Application may also include certain other questions or statements to assure that all necessary information was collected.

☐ more specific agreements to authorize reference checks
- with schools
- with former employers
- police record releases
- credit checks

☐ statement that the applicant is over 18 years old

☐ a non-compete or confidentiality agreement

- [ ] invitation to Vietnam Era Veterans and Disabled Veterans
- [ ] invitation to applicants to identify themselves as handicapped
- [ ] assurances that any part of the application will not be released beyond the hiring department
- [ ] any other names used
- [ ] whether a W-4 form (required by IRS for payroll withholding taxes) was completed
- [ ] whether an I-9 form (required of all employees by the new Immigration act) was completed
- [ ] other payroll data such as clock/i.d. number, budget charged, etc.
- [ ] other positions for which the applicant feels qualified
- [ ] how they came to apply (the recruitment source)
- [ ] military record
- [ ] and any other information considered valuable by the organization, after the question has been checked for legality

What to Do to Efficiently Screen Applicants

When you are faced with a large stack of paperwork from job applicants, separating the wheat from the chaff can be an imposing task; but it can be eased by a number of simple techniques.

The Key Principles of Employment Screening

A resume is a carefully posed picture that places the applicant in the most favorable light. An application form contains answers to the basic questions asked every person who wants employment. It is the screening process that determines whether further investigation is needed and whether an interview or series of interviews should be held, for further screening before an offer of employment is made and completed.

Reviewing employment candidates requires an investment of management time. To make sure that the time is used wisely, a series of steps should be taken to make the process most productive.

Most employment screening is a *heuristic* process: a method of empirical reasoning based on observation and experience rather than scientific theory; it relies on practical "rules of thumb" which have proven reliable in the past. While complex procedures and complicated tests can be used to make sure that every effort is made to identify all applicant qualifications, most organizations save such efforts for critical jobs which are extremely difficult to fill.

How to Sort Applicants According to Their Quality

Initial screening emphasizes the "negative approach."
- Applicants who clearly do not possess the vital qualification criteria are eliminated:
  - they are sent a "regret" letter thanking them for their interest;
  - the company sometimes promises to keep their resumes/applications for a period of time in case other openings offering a more suitable match between their qualifications and company needs might arise.
- Applicants who survived the first "cut" are again subjected to the winnowing process, sorting them into groups according to the apparent quality of their qualifications:
  - top candidates are identified and placed in one group;
  - ones who show great promise but where information is missing in some areas important for initial screening classification go into the second group;
  - those who appear to pass minimum standards but whose relative quality is otherwise questionable go into the last group.

How to Select Applicants for an Employment Interview

Interviews are scheduled and conducted with those applicants who have survived the initial elimination rounds, starting with those top candidates whose qualifications meet or exceed all requirements.

Procedures to Follow in the Actual Employment Interview

What to Do in the Interview

Handle the employment interview much as you would a **performance appraisal** or **counseling interview**. The INTERVIEW PLANNING GUIDE in the last chapter will be helpful.
  - TELL enough about the company and department to put the job opening in context

- o SELL the advantages of employment here (keep this short, since the candidate's presence is evidence of interest)
- o TELL what the major responsibilities and duties are
- o RESOLVE the candidate's suitability by **questions** and **probes** to explore past experience/training and how they would expect to handle the challenges of this job
- o **Listen** to the applicant and do not talk more than necessary to give and get vital information

What to Avoid Doing in the Interview

- **Avoid asking illegal questions** about sex, marital status, children, age, race, garnishments, arrest records, type of military discharge, religion or the health of a "qualified handicapped" applicant. There are a number of subjects where Federal, state and local legislation and court decisions prohibit or punish certain kinds of questions.

Subject	The Law Forbids Asking...	You Are Permitted to Ask...
Age	Birth date, age, high school graduation date, or to see birth certificate	Whether candidate is over legally-required minimum or maximum age
Knowledge	Legally restricted or confidential information about prior employers	Anything else
Criminal Record	Arrest record	Record of convictions that would directly affect ability to do the job
Credit Rating	Anything not relevant to ability to do the job	Anything that is directly relevant to ability to do the job
Disabilities	Anything not relevant to ability to do the job	Anything current that is directly relevant to ability to do the job
Marital or Family Status	Anything	Nothing
Military Service	Discharge status, unless it involves a relevant conviction	Type of job-related knowledge or experience gained
Race, Religion, Sex	Anything	Nothing
National Origin	Anything	Whether the candidate can legally work in the U.S.

- **Thank** the candidate for the opportunity to meet and discuss qualifications, but don't make any promise or commitment that you cannot guarantee. "We expect to schedule final interviews/make a final decision by _____," is best, if you can name a reasonable date.

How to Keep Interviews Consistent, for Comparisons

Be sure you get the same kind of information from all candidates you wish to consider for employment.

▷ if interview answers conclusively eliminate the candidate, you don't have to continue asking questions and noting responses

▷ record the interview findings, with all necessary detail, and your conclusions and recommendations in a standardized format (to assure that you can properly compare all candidates)

How to Continue the Process of Elimination

If an "ideal" candidate is not identified, follow up with the second group of applicants to either disqualify them or to qualify them for an interview. Follow the same interview process as above. Proceed to screen these candidates, sorting them into groups again, as done before.

If the second group is eliminated, move to the third group and repeat the screening process until you find a suitable person or conclude that none are worthy of a job offer.

What to Do When All Candidates Are Eliminated

If you get to a point when all candidates have been eliminated without finding even one who meets your standards, review:

- the efficiency of recruiting methods;
- the effectiveness of solicitation techniques;
- the adequacy of the pay, benefits and working conditions you offer;
- the clarity of your job description;
- whether the job specifications are reasonable (do viable candidates exist in sufficient number that you can find them);
- whether changes to the job description/specification should be made (along with any appropriate title, pay classification or hiring rate changes).

A Sample Applicant Interview Report Form

A standard form can be used to assure that all interviews are conducted in the same manner and to record interview results for later study and comparison.

Applicant Interview Report

On interview with _____ on _____ by _____ for the position of _____ in _____ .

QUALIFICATIONS	INTERVIEW FINDINGS	
Must Have:		
		□ Pass □ Fail
		□ Pass □ Fail
		□ Pass □ Fail
		□ Pass □ Fail
		□ Pass □ Fail
		□ Pass □ Fail
		□ Pass □ Fail

Prefer:	Weight	*Information gained in the interview is*	Score	Weight times Score

Total Weights		**Total of Each Weight times Each Score**		

As long as each applicant is rated and scored on same factors, using the same criteria, the same weights and the same scoring methods, this form will yield extremely useful comparative information.

How to Use the Applicant Interview Report

Must Have requirements would typically include such vital qualifications as <u>minimum</u> levels of essential technical knowledge, proven practical experience and an income expectation that does not greatly exceed what you can afford to offer.

Anyone who does not "pass" these minimum-requirement tests should not be seriously considered for the position unless changes occur that remove those major obstacles.

Prefer specifications list ideal qualifications or areas where the degree to which an applicant exceeds the **Must Have** minimum requirements is an important measure of their relative desirability as an employee.

> For example, the fact that a candidate has the minimum amount of technical knowledge (a Bachelors degree in engineering) means that they have passed the **Must Have** test. It is also quite important to know whether more than just the minimum is helpful. If so, the **Prefer** statement might read, "Prefer an advanced degree in engineering."

Weight The relative importance of preferences, things you want in a new hire (or transfer or promotion) candidate, should be clearly communicated in a consistent manner. Weights are best assigned on a scale no larger than one to ten, with a weight of ten (10) being the highest. You can also use a 1 to 5 scale or a smaller one, if you wish: but a weighting or scoring scale of 1 to 100 is too wide for consistent use; it becomes very difficult to make valid distinctions over a broad range of choices.

Score The interviewer should rate how well each candidate appears to match the ideal, using the same number scale for scores as for weights. If the applicant meets the highest standards in the qualification category, the highest rating would be put down as their score on that line.

Thus, if you want (**Prefer**) an advanced degree and the applicant has a Ph.D., you would note that fact on the *Information* line and score it at the maximum. If the applicant only has a Bachelors degree with marginal grades from a notoriously poor school, they might earn a minimum score of 1, while someone who meets the normal qualification standards (a B.S. with decent grades from a decent school) would get a 5.

The scores may be filled in after the interview, when you have had a chance to review your notes on the informational findings and confirm them (i.e., by checking a college transcript or getting a detailed reference report from a former supervisor).

Compute Weighted Scores   Once all qualification areas have been scored, the weight for each area is multiplied against the score for the area.

Total Weighted Scores   Those weighted scores for each qualification area are totalled to give you an overall score for the candidate.

Why You Should Investigate Final Candidates

Even the best employment interviewer can be wrong about a candidate. Interviewing is an inherently subjective activity which permits different conclusions to be drawn by different interviewers about the same person.

Remember that the interview is a brief meeting under extremely artificial and stressful conditions for the applicant (and sometimes for the interviewer, too). Investigation may be necessary to discover the actual past performance record of the candidate: past history will reveal much more about actual past and potential future performance than a brief interview. Together, interviews and investigations (which can include formal validated tests) are better than either one alone.

Relevant details of work history, educational history, technical credentials, etc., should be verified and confirmed if they are important to the hiring decision.

People always have a direction to their lives. It may not be apparent to you; it may not be obvious to them, either; it can change from time to time but usually is merely a refinement of a long-range goal: and it will show up in a good screening process that appraises employment potential. More aspects of this are covered in the **Remedial** and **Career** chapters. It is enough now to point out that before you can draw inferences from facts or come to conclusions about candidate suitability, you must know what the applicant seeks in order to decide whether the direction of the applicant matches the direction of the organization's job.

Investigation and analysis may lead you to revise or refine the information and scores on the **Applicant Interview Record.** Any such changes should be entered before you compare candidates.

How to Compare Candidates and Pick the Best

As long as the same areas are defined, weighted and scored in the same way, you then have a method of comparing the relative merit of each applicant who has been interviewed and investigated. It also has the additional advantage of allowing you to clearly identify the reasons one was rated higher than another, so you can focus on different perceptions perhaps held by other interviewers.

You can lay out the **Interview Records** of the applicants next to each other (or use a wide form showing the best candidates on one sheet) to compare total scores and the reasons for them.

How to Make a Formal Offer of Employment

After all necessary levels of management have been consulted and given the necessary approvals, the formal job offer should be made.

The Reasons for Documenting Job Offers

A formal job offer should be documented in your records and a letter confirming the terms and conditions of the offer sent to the successful candidate. This protects both employer and employee.

- It repeats the verbal information communicated in employment interviews.
- It clearly states the job title, starting pay and anticipated date for the new hire to report to work.
- It may ask for a similar written reply acknowledging acceptance, to confirm that the offer has been received and search activities can be ended.
- It gives the recruits the assurance that they can give notice to their current employer with another job safely in hand.

Why Expert Advice on Employment Procedures Should Be Followed

Employment Mistakes Are Easy to Make and Expensive to Correct

Many books have been written on the employment process itself, which is increasingly subject to governmental regulations whose violation can be extremely expensive to the organization and the individual supervisor. Even if no law is broken in the employment process, hiring decisions can still come back to haunt supervisors. Those who made the recommendation to hire a person who "didn't work out" are often blamed for poor judgment and faulted for wasting Company money on an incompetent new hire.

Experts Can Be Used to Support Generalists

The performance manager need not become an expert in employment. Unless hiring decisions are solely up to you or are a major component of your job, it should be enough for you to recognize and respect the expertise of others who are retained for their precise ability in those areas. Just like the company physician, they exist as specialized support resources to provide authoritative advice and guidance in certain areas.

Experts can save you time, trouble and money; but they are not responsible for doing your job. While the wise performance manager will respect the input and authority of specialized resources, he or she must work within the parameters set by others to accomplish the mission. The airline pilot relies on the air traffic controller for guidance, but it is the pilot who is ultimately accountable for flying the plane.

Why Employment Orientation Is Valuable and How to Do It

Employers are just as subject as employees to the old axiom that "you only get one chance to make a good first impression."

The way a company welcomes a new hire (or someone transferred/promoted from another unit) can have a permanent effect on the working relationship. If new workers get all important questions answered, at least discovering that answers exist with people available to give assistance, then they can start the new job with a certain peace of mind. If they are just thrown into the job with no orientation, they can become anxious, concerned, insecure, worried and confused.

A bad start can be overcome with much effort, but it is better to make remedial action unnecessary by starting right.

New employees should be given an introduction to general company activities, programs and procedures; and they should receive an orientation to the unique and specific unit or department they are joining.

A Sample Personnel Induction Checklist

The checklist that follows next shows what a Personnel Representative may be expected to do to welcome a new employee and assure that all necessary employment forms and procedures have been completed.

COMPLETE ON OR BEFORE FIRST DAY

PERSONNEL REPRESENTATIVE INDUCTION CHECKLIST

(To be placed in employee's personnel file)

EMPLOYEE NAME: _____ _____   DATE: _____

☐ Welcome

☐ Give <u>Employee Benefits Manual</u> to read for details on insured plans and benefit
   policies, such as:

   - How we work (hours, paydays, deductions)
   - Health insurance   • Travel insurance   • Holidays
   - Hospital insurance   • Sick leave   • Tuition aid
   - Dental insurance   • Death in family   • National Merit Scholarships
   - Long-term disability   • Voting   • Matching gifts
   - Retirement plan   • Military service   • Election/jury duty

☐ Ask new employee to read carefully and raise any questions they might have AT
   ANY TIME.

☐ Refer to company history in the front of the <u>Employee Benefits Manual</u> and hand out
   current description of divisions and products.

☐ Discuss non-discrimination policy.

FORMS TO BE COMPLETED AND RETURNED TO COMPENSATION DEPARTMENT

☐ Requisition   ☐ Pension

☐ Application   ☐ State withholding

☐ Blue Cross/Shield   ☐ Federal withholding

☐ Dental   ☐ United Way (optional)

☐ LTD   ☐ Employment agreement

☐ Life   ☐ Lunch ticket (if applicable)

☐ Physical exam   ☐ Guard office/badge card (if applicable)

_____   _____
Personnel Representative Signature   **Date**

Orientation Checklist for Supervisors

More detailed information on departmental procedures can be provided by the supervisor.

The importance of orientation for a "good start" is emphasized by a requirement that both managers and new employees document that the briefing has taken place and copies of the signed statement are placed in the new employee's personnel file.

COMPLETE ON FIRST DAY

ORIENTATION CHECKLIST FOR SUPERVISORS

NEW EMPLOYEE _____   START DATE _____

WELCOME

A Personnel Representative has covered the points listed on the other side.

☐ Explain overall department organization and its relationship to other activities of the company.

☐ Explain new employee's individual contribution to department objectives, discuss starting assignment in broad terms, and give copy of job description.

Explain performance standards ...

☐ Departmental training program(s)   ☐ Promotions
☐ Probation period   ☐ Attendance and punctuality
☐ Performance review   ☐ Handling confidential information
☐ Salary increases   ☐ Special behavior required
           (Employee should feel free to ask any questions)

Explain working conditions ...

☐ Hours of work, time sheets   ☐ Bulletin boards
☐ Breaks, lunch, rest periods   ☐ Lockers
☐ Overtime policy and requirements   ☐ Smoking
☐ Paydays and procedure for being paid   ☐ Parking
☐ Absence notification   ☐ Facility layout
☐ Safety/first-aid facilities   ☐ Use of employee entrance, elevators
☐ Housekeeping   ☐ Other _____
☐ Personal phone calls and mail

Introduce new employee to ...

☐ Manager(s) and other supervisors
☐ _____, who will help orient them
☐ Fellow workers
☐ Tour of the work area

_____   _____
Orientation conducted by/Date   **Signed copy received by new employee/Date**

Original – Personnel Representative
Copy – New Employee

Chapter 9:

HOW TO MAKE REWARD AND PAY DECISIONS THAT INCREASE PRODUCTIVITY

What Supervisors Should Know About the Types of Compensation

Reward and pay actions are SCORE and ADJUST elements of the performance management model. They provide **consequences** for actual performance results and **feedback** on the relative merit of accomplishments.

You do not have to become an expert in the technical details of compensation program design and implementation to be an effective performance manager; but you do have to understand how reward systems can help or hurt your efforts.

Rewards are a key element in any attempt to reinforce positive performance. "Compensation" is a term that covers all the rewards an employee receives as a consequence of employment. Some compensation is formal and some is informal.

What Is Meant by Formal Compensation

A List of Formal Reward Methods

- ☐ wages and salaries
- ☐ bonus
- ☐ fringe benefits
  - ○ pension
  - ○ unemployment insurance
  - ○ workers' compensation
  - ○ social security
  - ○ health insurance
  - ○ life insurance
  - ○ accident insurance
  - ○ disability insurance
  - ○ employee assistance programs
  - ○ other medical care

- ○ vacations
- ○ holidays
- ○ leaves of absence
- ○ tuition assistance
- ○ matching charitable contributions
- ○ credit unions
- ○ savings plans
- ☐ perquisites
  - ○ company car
  - ○ preferred working conditions
  - ○ reserved parking
  - ○ expense accounts
  - ○ supplemental benefits
  - ○ other employer services
- ☐ prizes, merchandise, travel
- ☐ professional memberships
- ☐ use of employer assets or equipment
- ☐ deferred compensation
- ☐ financial and estate planning
- ☐ day-care centers
- ☐ interest-free loans
- ☐ recreation facilities
- ☐ profit sharing
- ☐ gain-sharing
- ☐ stock options
- ☐ relocation expenses
- ☐ severance pay
- ☐ outplacement

Where Formal Rewards Fit in the Hierarchy of Needs

Formal compensation tends to be concentrated in pay and other forms of renumeration for expenses or items that would otherwise be purchased out of employee income. It is most effective in meeting basic human survival needs ... the physiological and safety needs which must be satisfied before motivations of a higher order can be expected to influence an individual. Further information on the *Hierarchy of Needs/Motivations* can be found in the seminal writings of A. H. Maslow.

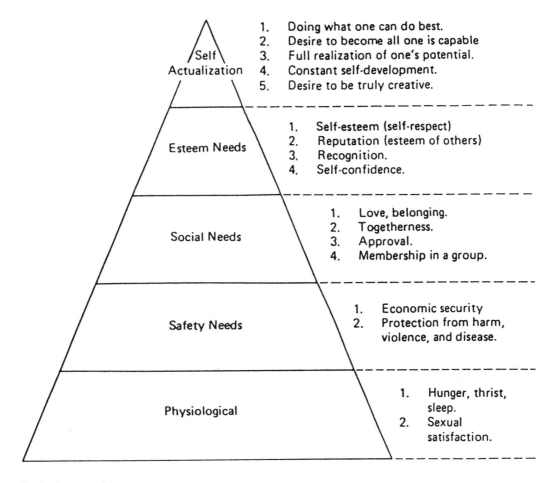

1. Doing what one can do best.
2. Desire to become all one is capable
3. Full realization of one's potential.
4. Constant self-development.
5. Desire to be truly creative.

1. Self-esteem (self-respect)
2. Reputation (esteem of others)
3. Recognition.
4. Self-confidence.

1. Love, belonging.
2. Togetherness.
3. Approval.
4. Membership in a group.

1. Economic security
2. Protection from harm, violence, and disease.

1. Hunger, thrist, sleep.
2. Sexual satisfaction.

Self Actualization

Esteem Needs

Social Needs

Safety Needs

Physiological

Basic Assumptions:
1. Man is a wanting animal.
2. Satisfied needs do not motivate behavior.
3. Needs and wants are arranged in a hierarchy of importance to the individual, but complete satisfaction of a lower need is not required before higher need satisfaction is demanded.

HIERARCHY OF NEEDS

Adapted from A. H. Maslow, "A Theory of Human Motivation," *Psychological Review*, vol. 50, 1943, pp. 370–96.

What Is Meant by Informal Compensation

There are also other types of "compensation" from work that are received by employees. These are rewards which are sought and valued (in various degrees) by people, who see them as benefits that can come from their work and further compensate for the "costs" of job performance. Even though informal rewards do not show up as payroll costs or appear on the financial balance sheets, they can be very powerful influences on employee behavior.

A List of Informal Rewards

- security
- support
- affiliation
- a sense of belonging
- peer support
- attention
- control
- power
- status
- recognition
- personal pride
- achievement

When Informal Rewards Are More Powerful Than Formal Ones

These informal compensation elements tend to satisfy the human motivational drives/needs found at the top of Maslow's hierarchy scale. They are most effective and powerful when the lower-order needs of health, food, shelter, safety and security have already been met. A starving man cannot become particularly excited at the opportunity to excel; first, he needs a full stomach. A woman raised in the years of the great depression may have such a strong anxiety about job security and a reliable income that she refuses to take a high-risk job that could make her famous.

Some of the informal rewards are consciously addressed by formal compensation schemes and some are not. In many cases, the informal rewards may be more attractive to the employee than the formal ones (see the **Reinforcement** section of the chapter on **Remedial Actions**). And it is not uncommon to find direct conflicts between the formal and informal systems, so that actions that win formal rewards by the organization cause losses in the informal compensation sought by the employee (and vice versa).

- A power-hungry supervisor may decline a hefty pay increase to a staff position that offers no outlet for his need to exercise direct authority over others.
- The worker paid on a piece-work basis may be forced to swallow her shame at the low quality of her output in order to meet quantity quotas.

How to Compensate People for Performance

Performance managers must be concerned with the effects **all** the compensation systems have on employee work behavior.

If efforts to produce good work results are not seen as "valued" by the employer, or if the person gets a stronger reinforcement from unproductive behavior, the manager inherits the problem.

Both formal and informal compensation systems operate as
- **feedback on plans and performance,**
- **communications,**
- **consequences of behavior,**
- **rewards,**
- **punishments.**

The Official Purposes of Compensation

The Conventional Reasons for Rewards

The usual statement given as the purpose of most compensation programs is:
1. to attract,
2. to retain,
3. and to motivate
competent employees.

That is an ambitious set of goals, particularly when compensation (in terms of payroll dollars) is always a significant cost expense to the organization; and exactly what will "attract, retain and motivate" different people is highly variable.

Needless to say, compensation efforts are not always successful. In fact, they can be quite destructive in their effect on performance management.

Some of the Ways Compensation Can Kill Performance

What Happens When the Wrong Message is Sent

As demonstrated in the **Diagnosis** chapter in the front of the book, compensation programs transmit messages about the organization's philosophies and policies. Sometimes, bureaucrats become so involved in refining and "improving" their compensation practices that they lose sight of the original intent of the program. When that happens, you find compensations programs that are designed for the comfort and convenience of their administrators while creating havoc throughout the rest of the organization.

Here are some examples.

Typical Performance Distortions Caused by the Wrong Compensation

When bureaucrats want...	They may require...	And the effect on performance managers may be...
to impress top management with their brilliance	compliance with an extremely complex compensation system	no one understands the system; it is confusing and unwieldy
to avoid conflict	senior executives such as the Chairman or President to approve every pay decision	line managers lose discretionary authority; approvals for raises take months
to limit payroll expenses so that results precisely match the budget	slavish and absolute compliance with budget projections made last year	proper rewards are denied when actual employee performance improves beyond original expectations
to make the compensation department a police function	an adversarial relationship between compensation and other departments	managers see compensation staff as the enemy and avoid consulting them for technical advice or needed assistance
to use a familiar pay scheme they learned at another firm	managers to follow and apply a reward system designed for a different industry	the "foreign" system doesn't fit the organization's unique needs and must be severely distorted and manipulated
to have a nice, neat compensation structure	every department and location must pay the same	units in different competitive labor markets pay too high or too low for the actual situation

When bureaucrats want...	They may require...	And the effect on performance managers may be...
to provide an immediate new solution to every compensation problem	new compensation programs are designed for every situation	there is no consistency or standard practice; programs overlap and conflict
to avoid unionization or employee complaints about favoritism	high compensation for all employees, based on seniority, and no merit systems	formal compensation is awarded without regard for performance, reducing incentives for achievement
to force a rapid improvement in Return on Investment	salary increases and bonuses will be based on short-term ROI improvement	executives sell off company assets and cut marketing, training and research; they get their money but cripple the firm

The motivations are sincere in every case; but the results can have negative effects on employee performance. It is easy for compensation "programs" to start running the company, instead of the company designing programs to efficiently meet overall goals and objectives. Before you know it, you may find your organization misallocating scarce payroll dollars, awarding benefits because of tradition, using methods that ignore operational realities and distributing rewards in ways that discourage the performance the organization needs.

Why Flat Pay Increases Are Hazardous

For example, regularly granting the same percentage of base salary to all "good" employees can be disastrous. If people holding the same or equal jobs have vastly different base salaries, the "equal percentage" of unequal base amounts yields disproportionate dollars to the employee with a higher base salary. In that case, even though job value and personal performance was equal, substantially more money goes to the "richer" employee, whose lead over the lower-paid employee increases. The gap between the two equal performers gets wider over time.

That is highly counter-productive, because it destroys motivation by denying incentive reinforcement to junior employees who greatly outperform more senior job peers. The obvious failure to maintain internal equity in pay also sends a bad message: it isn't performance that counts, but seniority. Those hard-working junior people may either "turn off" and start coasting or begin looking for another employer who pays for performance. And the senior people learn that big money comes their way no matter what they do.

Typical solutions to that problem are **merit increase grids** or **merit increase percentages applied to job values** rather than to base salaries. These and other advanced salary administration techniques are discussed later.

How to Overcome the Usual Problem with Salary Ranges

Salary ranges can give supervisors headaches when the permissable pay rates are inadequate for practical use. But with a little knowledge about the secrets of how they operate, a supervisor can easily overcome the usual handicaps.

Salary ranges are some of the most arbitrary systems designed by management bureaucrats. Intended to provide a minimum "floor" and maximum "ceiling" on wage and salary rates for job classes, each range is usually built around a single number that represents the competitive market rate or position value. Rather than identify a separate and unique number for every job in the company, each job is classified, for wage and salary administration purposes, into a pay grade with a range of permissable rates going from minimum to midpoint (or position value or average job rate, etc) to maximum. This process of approximation greatly simplifies the job comparisons and pay actions. It also introduces what can be a great amount of error when the minimum, the midpoint or the maximum are wrong for the job.

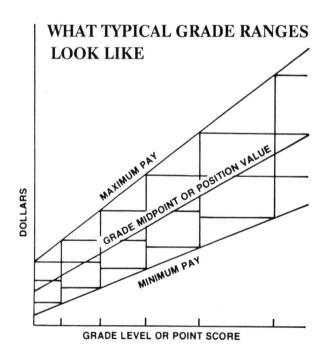

The most typical problem deals with the case when the range midpoint is fairly corrent (represents the approximate externally competitive and internally equitable pay rate for the job) but the minimum entry rate is wrong.

Most pay ranges are created with consistent distances between the minimums and the midpoint job values (usually from 15% to 25%), so that a conventional new hire brought into the job at the entry rate may be paid about 20% below the normal rate for a fully-qualified journeyman. The gap is supposed to provide room for variable pay based on performance, and it is generally wide enough to encompass the normal range of pay one expects to find between minimally and fully qualified workers in all the jobs assigned to that pay grade. But jobs whose average competitive values (midpoints) are the same should not necessarily have the same minimum entry rate!

Consider the case of a junior accountant and a senior technician. One is starting his professional career with a degree and little experience; the other is reaching the top of her technical career after many years of on-the-job experience. Assume that they both have the same average job value, based on surveys of competitive rates in the market and internal equity considerations at the firm.

The conventional salary range approach will assign both jobs to the same pay grade, because the value of journeyman work in both jobs is about the same; that would be correct in this case. In the typical range philosophy, both jobs will **also** have the same minimum and maximum pay rates; and that would be **wrong** in this case.

A junior accountant normally spends no more than three years in that position (if that long) before he is promoted to a full accountant position. It should not take a junior accountant more than two years to become fully qualified and eligible for the average job value (the midpoint or journeyman rate). On the other hand, a senior technician may be expected to spend many years (or the rest of her career) in that position, which demands enough room between the minimum entry rate, the fully-qualified midpoint rate and the maximim rate to provide for a long tenure during which the individual continues to receive pay increases.

Although the midpoint may be right for both jobs, the same entry rate will probably be "too low" for the junior accountant and "too high" for the senior technician. After all, if the midpoint rate is truly the amount of pay proper for a two-year junior accountant, there is no way that normal pay increases will close the 20% gap between entry rate and midpoint (even without taking compounding and periodic pay structure increases into account). Likewise, if the midpoint rate is correct for a typical ten-year senior technician, a 20% spread between entry rate and midpoint will be closed after seven or eight years of normal increases.

Periodic increases to the overall pay structure to reflect market changes further complicate the attempt to keep individual pay progression on a realistic schedule. The movement of individual pay from minimum starting rate to the market midpoint/target gets tougher when the numbers keep increasing: a 7% increase brings an employee only 3% closer to the job rate when pay structures and job rates go up 4% in response to market or internal value changes.

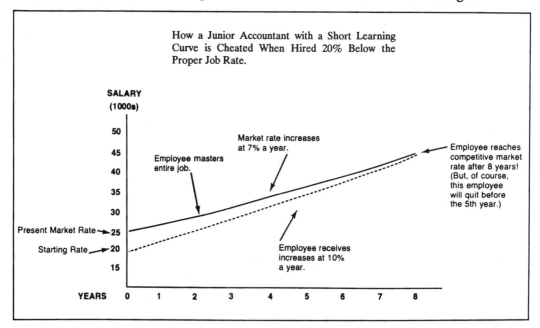

How a Junior Accountant with a Short Learning Curve is Cheated When Hired 20% Below the Proper Job Rate.

And if the midpoint actually does represent what other firms are paying for a journeyman, your worker who qualifies as a journeyman (or woman) may be sorely tempted to jump ship to one of the many others who will pay the standard rate to a competent professional right away. At the very least, failure to bring a good-working employee up to the "official" market rate by the normal length of time when he or she is truly fully qualified demonstrates bad faith to the worker. It also shows dishonesty or hypocricy, because the salary range system does not permit the proper pay progression it promises.

The solution to the problem of arbitrarily uniform wage and salary ranges is a strong renewed focus on the midpoint job value. If the firm truly intends to see all competent performers reach a certain "journeyman" rate in a reasonable length of time that matches the normal competitive practice, either the entry rate where they start or the increase amounts and periods must be adjusted to match normal reality. The simpler method is to alter minimum entry rates, so normal pay increases over the normal beginner-to-journeyman period will bring the competent individual up to the standard competitive/equitable rate in the proper number of years.

Further details of technical methods to deal with this problem are found in an extensive treatise by the author, **The Problem with Salary Ranges (and a Realistic Solution)** in the March, 1980, **Personnel Journal** (Costa Mesa, California). More information about how wage and salary ranges work is in a later section with that precise title.

Performance Management Tip

If you are stuck with a typical pay range program where the midpoint job values are correct but the minimum or maximum is too low for practical purposes, **scream like hell!**

In the first case, point out that the minimum entry rate is inadequate to attract or retain (much less motivate) competent workers and therefore must be increased, even if on an exception basis for this job only.

In the second case, emphasize the risk of destroying the incentive for a senior worker to continue improving or the danger of losing them to another firm which will not cut off pay progression because of an arbitrary and theoretical upper limit.

Make the argument that pay systems are supposed to serve operational objectives and not inhibit their attainment.

The Critical Pay Practices Under the Control of Supervisors

Most managers have relatively little to do with the selection, creation and design of compensation programs in general. Fringe benefits, in particular, are usually so dependent on highly complex actuarial and financial analyses that the average manager only sees their effect on self and subordinates. But base pay is another matter. Everyone gets it (unless you have a commission or piecework plan) and every people-manager must administer it.

The principal objectives of base pay programs are:
- internal equity
- external competitiveness/equity
- compliance with government regulations
- assuring a proper return on payroll investment (performance justifies cost)

Those and other pay program objectives are discussed in great detail in the

Compensation Audit sections of the **Diagnosis** chapter.

The most important aspects of base pay programs for the performance manager are:

job documentation	specifications or descriptions of job content
job evaluation	the method of placing a standard value on jobs, without reference to *who* performs the work
legal constraints	the laws and government regulations that require or prohibit certain pay actions
pay structures	how the rates of pay for various jobs compare to the rates at other enterprises
pay progression	how wages and salaries increase from the hiring rate through raises, promotions and adjustments
budgeting	estimating, guiding and controlling pay costs

How to Translate and Understand the Special Language Used for Pay

Before you explore the principal basic methods of pay management, you may wish to prepare by reviewing the unique language that is often applied to pay matters.

Human resource managers and compensation professionals in particular have learned the value of a unique vocabulary from observing how it has paid off in areas like data processing and engineering.

Many of the scientific, technical, statistical and professional terms used in personnel/compensation management are unfamiliar to the outsider. It can be extremely useful to have the definitions at your fingertips. Not only will the glossary that follows give you the meaning of the term used, but it will also make you aware of other methods and procedures which might not be used in your organization but are available for future improvements.

The definitions are adapted from a longer (and often different) **Glossary of Compensation Terms,** © 1989, by permission of the American Compensation Association.

Glossary of Compensation & Job Evaluation Terms

A PRIORI APPROACH An approach to job evaluation which emphasizes job responsibility features and is based on pre-defined factors that are considered to contribute to the worth of jobs. *A Priori* approaches are vulnerable to criticism of subjectivity or wishful thinking in the selection, weighting and scaling of job evaluation factors; but they may be valid to the extent that they accurately reflect the components of work value which the establishment, by policy, wishes to reward in a nondiscriminatory manner. An *A Priori* system which is "pre-packaged," with "canned" factors, scales, weights and values will impose the value system of the plan designer on the organization, whether it is appropriate or not. Users may experience relevance problems due to GIGO (garbage in, garbage out).

ANALYTICAL APPROACH The newest approach to job evaluation, using modern computerized statistical methods to test job content input (usually collected through **task inventories** or **job analysis** questionnaires to **test** potential factors and derive weights through **multiple linear regression** and **non-linear regression** analysis to best predict target pay rates. The *analytical approach* uses primary sources of job content information, uses questions custom designed to the actual needs and circumstances of the establishment, tests answers for factor use before creating final levels, scales and weights, and can assure that the pay rates predicted by the final evaluation model are both internally/externally equitable and nondiscriminatory. While the final results can be easier to administer, less subjective and more accurate, credible and consistent, it requires more expertise and time to create than **policy-capturing** or **a priori** approaches. It also must be revalidated whenever internal or external pay value relationships change, which can be **every year**, or at least whenever one job class (or bargaining unit) must be paid differently than when the original predictive plan was created.

BENCHMARK A standard with characteristics so detailed that other classifications can be compared as being above, below, or comparable to it. Most frequently in compensation, *benchmark* refers to a job, or group of jobs, used for making pay comparisons either within the organization or to comparable jobs outside the organization.

BONAFIDE OCCUPATIONAL QUALIFICATION (BFOQ) An exception to the restrictions of Title VII of the Civil Rights Act (1964) regarding discrimination on the basis of sex, religion and national origin. Thus, under certain conditions an employer may require a person of a specific sex, national origin, or religious affiliation to staff certain jobs. The intent of this provision is to specify that there are certain jobs for which race, sex or religion may be legitimate qualifications.

CLASSIFICATION METHOD OF JOB EVALUATION A method which compares jobs on a **whole job** basis. Predefined class descriptions are established for a series of **job classes** and a job is placed in whichever classification best describes it. Popular in public agencies and jurisdictions, in-depth **job analysis** (a listing of the tasks and qualifications required in job performance) is necessary. Examples include the Federal General Schedule.

CLASS OF POSITIONS A group of *positions*, regardless of location, that are alike enough in duties and responsibilities to be called the same descriptive title, to be given the same pay scale under similar conditions, and to require substantially the same qualifications.

COEFFICIENT OF DETERMINATION A measure of **predictive reliability**, defined as the correlation coefficient squared or r^2. Indexes the proportion of variation (see **variance**) in the predicted value that can be attributed to variation in the independent variable.

COMPA-RATIO The ratio of an actual pay rate (numerator) to a target rate (denominator), which is usually the position value, job rate or midpoint of the respective pay grade. *Compa-ratios* are used primarily to compare an individual's actual rate of pay to the midpoint or some other control point of the structure. It is most frequently used as an index of a person's relationship to the structure. In addition, *compa-ratios* can be calculated for a group of people, a department, or an entire organization.

COMPARABLE FACTORS Factors or common characteristics of jobs used to compare the relative value of different jobs. (see **Compensable Factor**).

COMPARABLE WORTH The doctrine that people should be paid according to the worth of the work to the establishment, without regard for the sex or race of the worker. Before disparate treatment of protected classes became an issue, this term was used for both external competitive comparisons and for internal equity decisions. Today, *Comparable Worth* goes beyond the traditional "pay equity" considerations. It focuses special attention on pay practices which may match the market or perpetuate past internal practices but thus create or perpetuate discrimination in the treatment of those holding female-dominated jobs whose content is **similar but not equal** to that of male-dominated jobs. *Comparable Worth* means that women should be paid the same as men, excepting allowable differences (i.e., seniority plans, merit plans, production-based pay plans, or different establishments or locations).

COMPENSABLE FACTOR Any factor used to provide a basis for judging job value in a job evaluation scheme. The most commonly employed *compensable factors* include measures of **skill and effort required, responsibility and working conditions.**

COMPENSABLE FACTOR DEGREE The level of a **compensable factor** exhibited by a job. Most job evaluation schemes involve **compensable factors** which are scaled in terms of 5 or 7 hierarchical levels or degrees.

CORRELATION   A statistical index that is employed to indicate the direction of movement and strength of association observed between two variables. The *correlation coefficient* takes on values from negative or minus 1.0 (indicating a perfect negative relationship ... when one variable goes up, the other always goes down) to plus 1.0 (indicating a perfect positive relationship ... when one variable goes up, the other always goes up). A *correlation* of zero indicates no relationship at all between two variables. *Correlation* does **not** indicate **how much** one variable moves when the other moves, but only whether they move together in some direction and the consistency of that joint movement; nor does *correlation* indicate cause and effect. For example, there is a high degree of positive *correlation* between the number of births in Des Moines, Iowa, and the rainfall in Bombay; but one does not cause the other.

DECISION BAND METHOD OF JOB EVALUATION (DBM) Measures the value of all jobs according to dimensions of *decision making* in various categories, with additional input on aspects of task variety/time/frequency, skills required, complexity, conditions, etc. Exclusively licensed by Arthur Young International, it is also known as "broadbanding," because it uses one principal or key factor to place jobs into one of six bands, which can be subdivided into pay grades. The **decision band method** places a heavy reliance on "decision-making responsibility," which may not be a valid criterion for pay in service organizations, particularly in the public sector.

DEVIATION   (See **Standard Deviation**)

DISTRIBUTION   (See **Skewed Distribution** and **Symmetric Distribution**.)

EXTERNAL EQUITY   A fairness criterion that influences an employer to pay a wage that corresponds to rates prevailing in outside markets for an employee's occupation. The precise level of *External Equity* is somewhat subjective and negotiable to the extent that the employer's pay rates permit the establishment to attract, retain and motivate competent workers. The minimum viable level of market competitiveness required by any policy decision regarding *external equity* must yield pay rates that attract and hold employees.

FACTOR COMPARISON METHOD OF JOB EVALUATION   A method in which jobs are compared against other jobs on the basis of how much of some desired factor they possess. It is a method in which jobs are ranked according to specific *factor comparison*: relative values for each of the number of factors of a job are established by direct comparison with the values established for the same factors on selected or key jobs.

FACTOR WEIGHT   A measure of the relative importance of a **compensable factor** in a job evaluation system.

FEDERAL EVALUATION SYSTEM (FES) The **point factor job evaluation** system designed in 1977 to replicate the existing GS (General Schedule) grade structure and currently limited to application for nonsupervisory GS jobs only. The *FES* is an **a priori** system created in a **policy-capturing** mode. Very few organizations require the amount of detail necessary for a **compensable factor** program like *FES*.

GEOGRAPHIC DIFFERENTIALS Pay variations established for the same job based on differences in the cost of living or the cost of labor between or among geographical areas. (**Note:** consumer prices or Consumer Price Index changes do not directly correspond with competitive wages or prevailing pay rates changes, even in the same geographic area.)

HAY PLAN A **point factor job evaluation system** that evaluates jobs with respect to "know-how," "problem-solving," and "accountability." It was designed for managerial jobs and is still used primarily for exempt and professional jobs.

INCUMBENT A person occupying and carrying out a job.

INTERNAL EQUITY A fairness criterion that influences an employer to set wage rates according to the relative value of each job to the organization. *Internal Equity* reflects value considerations that are unique to the specific establishment, beyond external market influences, and often explains why an employer deviates from a general market rate.

INTERVAL MEASUREMENTS Measurements in equal unit scales, where differences **do** indicate **how much difference** there is among values such as performance levels or job factor levels. The distance between adjacent units on an *interval measurement* scale is the same, irrespective of the magnitude of the adjacent scale units.

JOB A homogeneous cluster of work tasks, the completion of which serves an enduring purpose for the organization. Taken as a whole, the collection of tasks, duties and responsibilities constitutes the assignment for one or more individuals whose work is of the same nature and which requires the same skill/responsibility level. (A **position** is that precise and sometimes unique collection of *job* tasks assigned to a specific individual.)

JOB ANALYSIS A systematic study of the tasks making up a job, employee skills required to do the job, time and frequency factors, situation factors such as technology use, physical aspects, information flows, interpersonal and group interactions, and historical traditions associated with the job. *Job Analysis* provides the information needed to define jobs and conduct **job evaluation**.

JOB CONTENT EVALUATION METHOD Job evaluation methods such as the **point factor** method that concentrate on the actual content of a job in determining its relative value.

JOB DESCRIPTION A summary of the most important features of a **job** including the general nature of the work performed, specific task responsibilities, and employee characteristics (including skills) required to perform the job (these last characteristics are known as "job specifications"). A job description should describe and focus on the **job** itself and not on any specific individual incumbent who might fill the job.

JOB EVALUATION A process by which management determines the relative value and pay rate to be placed on various jobs within the organization. The end result of formal *job evaluation* consists of an assignment of jobs to pay grades or some other hierarchical index of job value.

JOB PRICING The practice of establishing wage rates for jobs within the organization, usually combining judgments regarding market value and internal job evaluation results.

LEAST SQUARES LINE In **regression analysis,** the line fitted to a **scatter plot** of coordinates that minimizes the squared **deviations** of coordinates around the line. Also known as the "line of best fit," it always runs through the point on the plot where the average value of the horizontal axis variable and the average value of the vertical axis variable intersect.

LINEAR REGRESSION A statistical technique that allows an analyst to build a mathematical model of a relationship between two variables. *Linear regression* assumes that the basic relationship between the two variables is linear in nature.

LOGARITHM The exponent of the power to which a fixed number must be raised to produce a given value. For example, the "common *logarithm*" of 1,000 is 3 (the power to which the most common fixed base number, 10, must be raised to produce 1,000).

MARKET PRICING A wage and salary setting policy that sets the rates to be paid for a job to the organization's best estimate of the going wage in the external market place for that job. It is a process that defines a job's worth solely by the going rate in the labor market (see **External Equity**).

MEAN (ARITHMETIC MEAN) A simple arithmetic average obtained by adding a series of numbers and then dividing the sum by the number of addends (items to be added) in the series.

MEDIAN The middle number in a numeric series ranked from high to low. When there is an even number of items ranked from high to low, the *median* is the average of the two middle items.

MODE The item or observation that occurs most frequently in a series of items.

MULTIPLE REGRESSION A statistical technique that allows an analyst to build a model of the joint impact of several X variables (often called independent variables) on a Y variable (often called the dependent variable). For example, in **regressed questionnaire** point factor systems, job evaluation factor scores would be independent X variables, while market benchmark pay would be the dependent Y variable. Thus, factor weights and point scores would be statistically set to predict actual competitive dollars or pay grades. Such "pay for points" is appropriate when the points are directly related to dollars; but unless *multiple regression* has been used to compute current point values, then the points will **not** correspond to precise dollars, even though they may reflect relative **ordinal** job value rank.

NOMINAL MEASUREMENTS Numeric identifiers or labels that merely signify discrete categories (for instance, *sex*), without implying quantitative differences. Examples include codes or labels that **do not** imply a relative value such as a social security number or the arbitrary numbering of companies in a salary survey.

NON-LINEAR REGRESSION A sophisticated form of advanced **regression analysis** that allows the analyst to build a model of a non-linear or curvilinear relationship between two variables.

NON-QUANTITATIVE JOB EVALUATION Any method of job evaluation that does not employ quantitative methods in the valuing of jobs. Examples of *non-quantitative job evaluation* methods include **classification** and **job ranking**.

ORDINAL MEASUREMENTS Indicate rankings without explaining the amount of difference between ranks. The numbers tell whether a level is higher than another, but not **how much** higher. Examples include alphabetic scales, numeric rankings or narrative labels like "maximum" and "minimum."

PAIRED COMPARISONS A technique that attempts to alleviate problems in the **ranking** method of job evaluation when many jobs are employed. In *paired comparisons*, each job is compared to every other job in pairwise fashion and the job of most value in each pairing is noted. The final score for a job is the number of times it is considered the most valuable in the pairs. Ranks are then created from these scores. The *paired comparison* technique becomes onerous, however, after a few jobs. For example, a ranking of 20 jobs would require that 190 paired comparisons be carried out.

PAY TREND LINE A line fitted to a **scatter plot** that treats pay as a function of job values. The most common technique for fitting a *pay trend line* is **regression analysis**.

POINT FACTOR METHOD OF JOB EVALUATION The most commonly used formal job evaluation technique; it employs the following steps:
1. **Compensable factors** are chosen that will be used to rate each job. These factors typically include job-required education and experience, physical effort, visual/mental demands, authority/freedom to act, responsibility for equipment or assets, responsibility for safety of others, supervisory responsibility, importance to (or impact on) the prime mission of the establishment, and working conditions.
2. Each **compensable factor** is scaled (most commonly 5 to 7 levels are defined) and weighted.
3. After each job is measured against each **compensable factor**, the total score is calculated for each job. The total evaluation point scores for each job are then used to establish a wage rate for each job or to place each job into pay grades defined by point spreads in the job evaluation system.

POLICY-CAPTURING An approach to job evaluation which emphasizes the need to predict existing wage rates. *Policy capturing* is based on the assumption that existing wage rates already properly reflect the correct and nondiscriminatory values of jobs to the organization. An evaluation system designed to capture the policy current at the time of design formalizes and freezes status quo relationships and will perpetuate any errors in the original wage classification program.

POLYNOMIAL REGRESSION A *regression* technique that fits a predicted equation to a predictive variable in a method that permits a curved line to be the result. While **linear regression** is a **straight** line that always passes through the average of both axes, *polynomial regression* develops a **curved** line that passes through these averages.

POSITION An opening or a **job** occupied by a specific employee. The precise and sometimes unique collection of job tasks assigned to a specific individual.

POSITION ANALYSIS QUESTIONNAIRE (PAQ) The *PAQ* is a job analysis technique that captures 187 aspects of a job. *PAQ* results can be regressed against market data to provide the dollar value of each level of each of these aspects. It is a **point factor** job evaluation system whose factors are particularly well suited to hourly wage jobs but less appropriate for professional, technical and management jobs.

POSITION CLASSIFICATION METHOD OF JOB EVALUATION
(See **CLASSIFICATION.**)

PREDICTIVE RELIABILITY (See **Coefficient of Determination.**)

QUANTITATIVE JOB EVALUATION Job evaluation systems that involve the use of numerical indices and analyses in the estimation of job value. The most common *quantitative* methods of job evaluation are the **point factor** method and the **factor comparison** method.

RANGE In a set of ordered data, the difference between the maximum value observed and the minimum value observed.

RANKING METHOD OF JOB EVALUATION The simplest form of job evaluation. A whole job, job-to-job comparison, resulting in an ordering of jobs from highest to lowest. *Ranking* methods include **market pricing, slotting,** and the replication of existing pay relationships (see **policy capturing**).

RATIO MEASUREMENTS Have all the characteristics of **interval measurements** plus an absolute zero. Salaries, percentages, years experience, and budget figures are examples of *ratio measurements* because they are numbers that indicate "how much" and at the same time where zero has a meaning. Since division by zero is not an acceptable mathematical operation, *ratio measurements* have certain computational limits.

REGRESSION ANALYSIS (See **Linear, Multiple, Non-linear, Stepwise** and **Polynomial Regression.**)

RELIABILITY The quality of a measuring device that determines how free the device is from common measurement errors. *Reliability* is an extremely important criterion for any evaluation measures, because it places an upper limit on **validity**.

SCATTER PLOT or **SCATTERGRAM** A mathematical technique designed to display a "picture" of a relationship between two variables. A *scattergram* is a plotting of coordinates simultaneously representing x (horizontal axis) and y (vertical axis) scores for a number of observations.

SLOTTING The act of folding or inserting a job into a category, grade, classification, or any other class defined by a job evaluation system. *Slotting* usually involves the subjective comparison of an un-evaluated job to some standard or **benchmark** job.

SKEWED DISTRIBUTION A *distribution* of data that is nonsymmetric, with a tail of extreme values in one direction. Usually a plot of frequency against another measure, such as age, showing that there are more cases at one extreme end than at the other and resulting in a trend line resembling a baseball cap.

STANDARD DEVIATION or STANDARD ERROR The amount by which all observations differed from the norm (the square root of the **variance**). *Standard error* measures one *standard deviation* either side of the line of prediction, in terms of dollars or percentages.

STEPWISE REGRESSION A form of **multiple linear regression** analysis which produces the predictive equations in a series of steps. It first selects the most predictive variable (usually on the basis of **correlation**), then adds other variables according to the increased accuracy they add **in combination** with other previously-selected predictive variables.

SYMMETRIC OR STANDARD DISTRIBUTION A *distribution* of data in which one half is the mirrored image of the other half. The point of symmetry is the **median,** which is also the **mode.** Because of the visual appearance of the trend line, the plot is also often described as a "bell-shaped curve."

STANDARD RATE The rate established for a job based on **job evaluations** and **job pricing** strategy.

STRUCTURED QUESTIONNAIRE Any *structured* paper and pencil device used to gather job information through indirect observation. (See **Task Inventory**).

TASK INVENTORY A structured questionnaire listing an entirety of potential tasks involved on a job. The responding incumbent simply identifies those tasks that apply to his or her job and may indicate any amounts or frequencies involved in carrying out those tasks. Job task information collected from the incumbent or immediate supervisor is considered to have come from the **primary source of job information**; any other source is considered a **secondary source.**

TIME SPAN OF DISCRETION The maximum period of time during which the use of *discretion* is authorized and expected without review of that discretion by a superior. *Time span of discretion* has been used as a non-economic definition of job value in Elliott Jacques' model of pay equity. As a job evaluation tool, the concept has been used more frequently in Great Britain than in the U.S. and is most applicable to management jobs. Although not particularly accurate in predicting precise pay, it is still one of the best of the "one-factor" job evaluation methods in establishments where discretion is the primary indicator of job value.

VALIDITY The quality of a measuring device that refers to its relevance. Is the measuring device actually measuring what it is intended to measure? This quality is extremely important for job evaluation as well for performance appraisal.

> **CONTENT VALIDITY** Involves the analysis of whether or not what is desired to be measured is actually successfully tested by the testing instrument and process of application.

> **CONSTRUCT VALIDITY** Measures how well the system retains its stability when in use.

> **CRITERION VALIDITY** The measure of such aspects as individual

compensable factor utility across all jobs.

FACE VALIDITY The determination of the relevance of a measuring device on the basis of "appearances" or "common sense" alone. Not a justifiable method for establishing the validity of a measuring device.

All the legitimate tests for validity involve the use of correlation and standard error analysis.

VARIANCE A measure of dispersion in interval or ratio data that is defined as the sum of the squared deviation of each observation from the mean.

WAGE CONTOUR A way of considering the external wage structure developed by labor economist John Dunlop. He defines a *wage contour* as a stable group of wage-determining units (for example, bargaining units, plants, or establishments) which are so linked together by a) similarity of product/service markets, b) resort to similar sources for labor, or c) common market organization or custom that they have common wage-making characteristics. As a practical matter, compensation planners must be accurate in correctly defining the contours in which they are hiring and competing.

WHOLE JOB METHODS OF JOB EVALUATION Methods of job evaluation that analyze the entire job in an effort to determine its relative value. No effort is made to break the job down into its components for the sake of job evaluation, nor are the criteria for comparison defined or standardized. While *whole job evaluation* is simple and requires no detailed documentation, it is highly superficial and subjective and cannot be directly traced to actual job content.

Methods of Job Documentation

Information about job content relevant to pay decisions can be collected in a number of ways. The most common are
1. job analysis
2. job specifications
3. job/position descriptions

How Job Analysis Gives Details on Work Content

Job Analysis is a detailed and structured collection of data about all the aspects of *skill, effort, responsibility* and *working conditions* that appear in the work duties and circumstances of the job.

It calls for clarifications of the nature and variety of the tasks, duties and work outputs; and it addresses the level of skill, training, complexity, authority and responsibility involved. Job analysis will ask questions about the *human capital* (the abilities typically required of each worker) and the *job content* (the work output results expected of each job-holder). A job analysis report would contain data about how many minutes a receptionist spends greeting each kind of visitor and would define the types of interactions and their consequences in great detail.

The information on job content comes from a number of sources.

Primary data sources are the people who actually perform or supervise the work. The input is provided through

- direct observation
- questionnaires
- personal interviews
- employment requisitions
- procedure manuals
- work plans
- other records of specific company job performance requirements

Secondary data sources are all other techniques which provide information that is not necessarily verified as specific to the precise and exact requirements of the job:

- general job descriptions
- comparison factors from pay surveys
- characteristics listed in the U.S. Department of Labor's *Dictionary of Occupational Titles* and other publications on standard job content
- help-wanted ads
- data on the prior work histories of incumbents

What Is Included in a Job Specification that Summarizes the Analysis

Job Specifications are summarized versions of **Job Analyses**. They usually contain less information than a job analysis report, but more information that a job description.

Job specifications tend to focus on specific elements of the required *skill, effort, responsibility* and *working conditions* that are needed for job evaluation and classification. Details of duties and task performance procedures are condensed and classified into categories common to a number of jobs throughout the organization. Standard terms or descriptions are used, to assist in the determination of the generic job title or pay classification. A job specification would outline the approximate percentage of time a receptionist spends dealing with different kinds of people and would summarize the types of contacts and their general importance.

POSITION SPECIFICATION

Name: Date:

Job Classification: Position Title:

Department: FLSA Status:

Office: Position Evaluation:

JOB REQUIREMENTS:

    Skill and knowledge required equivalent to:

    Working conditions/challenges/contacts:

    Responsibility:

    Management accountability:

    Special effort required:

                      Percent of time spent on routine work (   )

PRIMARY FUNCTION:

SPECIFIC DUTIES:

Prepared by: Signature: Date:

Approved by: Signature: Date:

How Job Descriptions Are Prepared for General Use: 13 Samples

Job Descriptions or **Position Descriptions** are standardized definitions of job content features shared by a certain job title. They document the type and range of duties, responsibilities, skills, working conditions, etc. common to the position, using the general criteria used to assign job titles and pay rates to different kinds of work.

Job descriptions establish the parameters for a title held by any number of individuals: as long as their duties and job requirements fall within the range described, their jobs may be considered comparable, even though precise details of tasks and the amount of time or effort spent in performing them may vary. A job description would state that a receptionist deals with people, without going into extensive detail about the number and kind of interactions with each particular kind of person they may encounter.

Samples of twelve clerical job descriptions and one for a plant manager are included to demonstrate typical formats and content styles. While these examples do not cover every acceptable method that can be used, they do illustrate the kind of information that is generally presented in a job description.

POSITION DESCRIPTION

Position Title: Receptionist (Gr. 2)

Incumbent: Exempt ☐

Reports to: Non-Exempt ☑

Division: Department:

Location: Date:

BASIC FUNCTION

Receives and processes visitors in a central
reception area.

SUPERVISION AND SCOPE

Follows detailed instructions or well-established
procedures. Requires tact, pleasant personality
and good appearance to establish positive image
of company, have knowledge of company organization,
personnel, and office locations. Does <u>not</u>
simultaneously operate a switchboard. Tasks are
simple, involving repetitive routine.

PRINCIPAL FUNCTIONAL RESPONSIBILITIES

Provides initial personal contact with visitors.
Greets and processes visitors. Issues appropriate
passes or badges as required. May maintain visitor
log. Directs visitors to proper office or locates
and informs proper employee of visitor's arrival.
May perform incidental work such as typing or
filing at work station.

POSITION DESCRIPTION

Position Title: File Clerk (Gr. 2)

Incumbent: Exempt ☐

Reports to: Non-Exempt ☑

Division: Department:

Location: Date:

BASIC FUNCTION

Performs file clerical work of a routine nature.

SUPERVISION AND SCOPE

Works under close supervision following detailed instructions or procedures. Entry level position requiring basic vocational skills but no previous experience.

PRINCIPAL FUNCTIONAL RESPONSIBILITIES

Files material according to detailed procedures.
Pulls files as requested, refiles returned material.
Maintains file system in a clean and orderly condition.
Removes and replaces obsolete matter.
Checks material for obvious errors or omissions and corrects.
Operates standard office machines.
May furnish information service or perform simple clerical tasks such as sorting, recording changes, posting information, and distributing material.

POSITION DESCRIPTION

Position Title: Junior Clerk (typist)

Incumbent: Exempt ☐

Reports to: Non-Exempt ☑

Division: Department:

Location: Date:

BASIC FUNCTION

Performs routine entry level office work of a general nature.

SUPERVISION AND SCOPE

Performs simple repetitive tasks under specific detailed instructions and close supervision. Work is routine, requiring proficient use of standard office machines and basic vocational skills (e.g., working knowledge of grammar, spelling, and typing layout) but little or no prior experience.

PRINCIPAL FUNCTIONAL RESPONSIBILITIES

Operates standard typewriter, adding machine, calculator, copy machine. Types routine letters, standardized reports, and similar work from rough draft or corrected copy. May type complex and difficult tabular reports that follow an established format. May keep simple records, do basic calculations, file and retrieve material and receive, sort and distribute mail in a work section. May transcribe from dictating machine.

POSITION DESCRIPTION

Position Title: Clerk (typist)   (Gr. 3)

Incumbent: Exempt ☐

Reports to: Non-Exempt ☑

Division: Department:

Location: Date:

BASIC FUNCTION

Performs wide variety of responsible clerical tasks of minor complexity.

SUPERVISION AND SCOPE

Follows established procedures under close supervision. Work requires some judgment in the selection and interpretation of data and a working knowledge of related work in other areas. Strong vocational skills (e.g., correct spelling, syllabication, punctuation, or technical/foreign word usage and proficient use of standard office machines) and 1-2 years of directly related experience required.

PRINCIPAL FUNCTIONAL RESPONSIBILITIES

Works/types from rough data/drafts where some judgment is required or where words are technical or unusual or in a foreign language. May type from dictaphone on a regular basis. Collects material as instructed and types/processes it into final form according to instructions or general routines. Keeps standard records and may set up and maintain files of directly related materials. Checks transactions for accuracy and completeness. Prepares standard reports, compiles statistical data, etc. May contact other departments to obtain information and reconcile routine discrepancies. May operate, at an entry level, specialized office machines requiring special technical training.

POSITION DESCRIPTION

Position Title: Stenographer   (Gr. 3)

Incumbent: Exempt ☐

Reports to: Non-Exempt ☑

Division: Department:

Location: Date:

BASIC FUNCTION

Takes dictation and performs secretarial and clerical duties for one or more professional personnel.

SUPERVISION AND SCOPE

Under close supervision, follows established practices and specific instructions. Work requires proficient stenographic speed and accuracy and a working knowledge of general business and office procedures. Entry level "secretarial" position for individual with strong vocational skills (shorthand, typing, etc.) who does not work solely for one manager.

PRINCIPAL FUNCTIONAL RESPONSIBILITIES

Takes and transcribes routine oral dictation.
Types data and performs associated clerical duties.
Obtains routine information from files, records data,
  maintains files, answers telephone, receives callers
  and takes messages.
May compose simple letters from instructions.
May provide general secretarial support to non-managers.

POSITION DESCRIPTION

Position Title: Senior Clerk (Gr. 5)

Incumbent: Exempt ☐

Reports to: Non-Exempt ☑

Division: Department:

Location: Date:

BASIC FUNCTION

Performs difficult and complex advanced clerical duties of a diversified or specialized nature.

SUPERVISION AND SCOPE

Under limited supervision, regularly exercises discretion and judgment to perform a wide variety of complex tasks under general instructions. Applies diversified principles and practices to unstructured work situations. Demands extensive in-depth knowledge of company procedures. Requires advanced specialized vocational skills (associate degree or 2 years training) and substantial work-related experience (4-5 years) in the particular field.

PRINCIPAL FUNCTIONAL RESPONSIBILITIES

Compiles complex data and processes into final form, where critical judgment and perfect accuracy is essential. Prepares and maintains complicated records and files, and regularly issues special reports demanding individual research and analysis. Regularly contacts professional/ management personnel in other departments and other companies to obtain information and reconcile difficult or sensitive problems. Plans own work within broad guidelines. May operate, at a senior level, specialized office machines requiring special technical training. Regularly directs or leads the work of others. Is able to assume duties of any junior person in department; may act as utility clerk.

POSITION DESCRIPTION

Position Title: Junior Accounting Clerk (Gr. 2)

Incumbent: Exempt ☐

Reports to: Non-Exempt ☑

Division: Department:

Location: Date:

BASIC FUNCTION

Performs routine entry level accounting clerical work.

SUPERVISION AND SCOPE

Work is closely supervised and of limited complexity and variety. Requires ability to follow detailed instructions or standard practice, operate adding machines and perform routine arithmetic calculations, but little or no prior experience required.

PRINCIPAL FUNCTIONAL RESPONSIBILITIES

Posts details of simple business transactions.
Verifies details and totals accounts.
Computes and records interest charges, refunds, etc. as needed.
Types and files records as required.
Checks accuracy and completeness of repetitive documents.
May compile simple reports and do related clerical work.

POSITION DESCRIPTION

Position Title: Accounting Clerk (Gr. 4)

Incumbent: Exempt ☐

Reports to: Non-Exempt ☑

Division: Department:

Location: Date:

BASIC FUNCTION

Performs intermediate level accounting clerical work.

SUPERVISION AND SCOPE

Under general supervision, performs variety of specialized, complicated tasks, generally of a non-repetitive
nature. Requires exercise of judgment in selecting
proper procedures to be applied from a variety of
prescribed methods. Requires advanced specialized vocational skills (associate degree) or intensive work-
related experience (2 years) at progessively more
responsible levels to understand general principles of
the specialized field. Must have in-depth knowledge of
related work in other departments.

PRINCIPAL FUNCTIONAL RESPONSIBILITIES

Posts, monitors, and controls transaction activity in
register or subsidiary ledgers. Verifies internal consistency, completeness, and mathematical accuracy of
accounting documents. Assigns prescribed accounting
distribution codes. Traces transactions through previous
accounting sequences to determine accuracy or locate
source of discrepancies. Analyze and reconcile activity
reflected in assigned general ledger accounts. Types,
files, does related clerical work as needed. May contact other departments to obtain information and
reconcile complicated discrepancies. Maintains files,
responds to inquiries.

POSITION DESCRIPTION

Position Title: Secretary (Gr. 4)

Incumbent: Exempt ☐

Reports to: Non-Exempt ☑

Division: Department:

Location: Date:

BASIC FUNCTION

Takes dictation and performs secretarial and clerical
duties for a manager.

SUPERVISION AND SCOPE

Under general supervision, performs basic secretarial
duties of a confidential nature for a manager. Work
requires strong vocational skills (shorthand, typing,
etc.) and 1-2 years specialized training/experience
in general business and office procedures, and ability
to perform a variety of dissimilar tasks with constantly
changing priorities.

PRINCIPAL FUNCTIONAL RESPONSIBILITIES

Types memos and letters using dictation, standard
   dictating equipment or from rough copy.
Sets up and maintains all related files and superior's
   calendar, schedules appointments, receives visitors,
   screens calls and mail, arranges travel, answers
   routine inquiries.
Prepares routine correspondence and reports.
Routes correspondence through organization.

POSITION DESCRIPTION

Position Title: Senior Secretary   (Gr. 5)

Incumbent: Exempt ☐

Reports to: Non-Exempt ☑

Division: Department:

Location: Date:

BASIC FUNCTION

Takes dictation and performs secretarial and clerical duties for a Director.

SUPERVISION AND SCOPE

Under general supervision, performs basic secretarial duties of a confidential nature of a Director. Work requires strong vocational skills (shorthand, typing, etc.) advanced specialized experience (including at least two years secretarial work in this Company) and ability to perform a variety of important, confidential, and complex tasks with constantly changing priorities.

PRINCIPAL FUNCTIONAL RESPONSIBILITIES

Types memos and letters using dictation, standard dictating equipment or from rough copy. Sets up and maintains all related files and superior's calendar, schedules appointments, receives visitors, screens calls and mail, arranges travel, answers routine inquiries. Prepares routine correspondence and reports. Routes correspondence through organization. Maintains continuity of operation in absence of supervisor. Assembles data for complex reports prepared by supervisor. Responsible for smooth flow of clerical work. May provide interpretations of superior's instructions and working directions to others.

POSITION DESCRIPTION

Position Title: Executive Secretary (Gr. 6)

Incumbent: Exempt ☐

Reports to: Non-Exempt ☑

Division: Department:

Location: Date:

BASIC FUNCTION

Takes dictation and performs secretarial and clerical duties for a General Manager.

SUPERVISION AND SCOPE

Under general supervision, performs basic secretarial duties of a confidential nature for a General Manager. Work requires strong vocational skills (shorthand, typing, etc.) advanced specialized experience (including at least five years secretarial work in this Company) and ability to perform a variety of important, confidential, and complex tasks with constantly changing priorities.

PRINCIPAL FUNCTIONAL RESPONSIBILITIES

Types memos and letters using dictation, standard dictating equipment or from rough copy. Sets up and maintains all related files and superior's calendar, schedules appointments, receives visitors, screens calls and mail, arranges travel answers routine inquiries. Prepares routine correspondence and reports. Routes correspondence through organization. Maintains continuity of operation in absence of supervisor. Assembles data for complex reports prepared by supervisor. Responsible for smooth flow of clerical work. May provide interpretations of superior's instructions and working directions to others.

POSITION DESCRIPTION

Position Title: Senior Executive Secretary (Gr. 7)

Incumbent: Exempt ☐

Reports to: Non-Exempt ☑

Division: Department:

Location: Date:

BASIC FUNCTION

Takes dictation and performs secretarial and clerical
duties for a Corporate Officer.

SUPERVISION AND SCOPE

Under general supervision, performs basic secretarial
duties of a confidential nature for a Corporate Officer.
Work requires strong vocational skills (shorthand,
typing, etc.) advanced specialized experience (including at least five years secretarial work in this Company)
and ability to perform a variety of important, confidential, and complex tasks with constantly changing
priorities.

PRINCIPAL FUNCTIONAL RESPONSIBILITIES

Types memos and letters using dictation, standard dictating equipment or from rough copy. Sets up and maintains all related files and superior's calendar,
schedules appointments, receives visitors, screens
calls and mail, arranges travel, answers routine inquiries. Prepares routine correspondence and reports.
Routes correspondence through organization. Maintains
continuity of operation in absence of supervisor.
Assembles data for complex reports prepared by supervisor. Responsible for smooth flow of clerical work.
May provide interpretations of superior's instructions
and working directions to others. Functions as liaison
for principal, resolving items of a non-technical
nature and investigating questionable areas. Prepares
correspondence on own initiative and makes minor
administrative decisions requiring wide knowledge of
company organizations, policies, and practices.

ASSEMBLY OPERATIONS, INC.

Position: PLANT MANAGER

Location: Local City Plants (2)

**Reports
to:**   President

Purpose: Provides management, direction and coordination of plant operations in carrying out production objectives consistent with quality requirements. Provides leadership and direction to plant personnel to insure high morale, efficiency, plant safety, and conformance to all Company personnel policies.

Principal Responsibilities:

1. Determines plant operating methods and procedures for two locations in accordance with overall Company policies and supervises the application of such policies to the production operations.

2. Coordinates the execution of production schedules based on sales requirements and capacity of plants.

3. Monitors all plant employee relations activities, reviews personnel needs, responds to recommendations of subordinates in personnel-related matters, and personally handles critical issues such as the employment of key staff and positive labor relations.

4. Controls quality, cost of production, material purchasing, and inventory control through appropriate supervisors.

5. Oversees the maintenance of buildings and equipment and plant security and protection.

6. Prepares operating budgets and monitors performance against budget.

7. Exercises primary responsibility for all activities directly related to production at both sites.

8. Any other activity as directed by the President.

Directly supervises the following positions:

Plant 1:

        Supervisor, Chemical Production
        Supervisor, Chemical Packaging
        Supervisor, Maintenance
        Supervisor, Pen Assembly
        Supervisor, Subcontracts
        Supervisor, Mop Manufacturing
        Shipping/Receiving Supervisor
        Secretary

Plant 2:

        Supervisor, Packaging
        Shipping/Receiving Supervisor

Indirectly supervises (through subordinates) all direct labor personnel, technical and clerical personnel, staff professionals and foremen engaged in support of production.

Qualifications: B.S. in physical sciences or equivalent. Minimum of 5 year's experience in manufacturing and production management, with demonstrated superior supervisory skills. Experience in chemical manufacturing and assembly operations strongly preferred.

How Job Evaluation Ranks Jobs for Pay

The Common Elements of All Job Evaluation Systems

Job evaluation is a process of comparing jobs so they can be ranked for pay purposes.

It always deals with the value of the job, the position, and the work that is done, rather than the value of the person performing the job. That is not always easy to do when you have a job or position that was custom designed around the talents and interests of one particular individual. Job evaluation provides information on the value of the work to the organization.

Every employer has a job evaluation system of some kind. As long as wages are paid to workers, a "value decision" has been made about the dollar amount the enterprise is willing to pay for that particular job. The types of job evaluation systems run the gamut from "whatever I have to pay" (a market comparison method) to point-factor plans with precise weights and negotiated pay rates determined by raw bargaining power.

Compensation professionals differ over whether job evaluation deals with

▷ only the internal organizational values a certain enterprise places on its jobs

▷ or a combination of the external market rates and the internal values unique to the enterprise.

It makes little difference, since job evaluation is absolutely useless to an organization if it produces pay rates that are insufficient to attract and retain (much less "motivate") competent employees. The *external market* plays an essential role in all compensation decisions and is particularly influential on base pay rates; but few people understand exactly what that role is.

Dispelling Myths About External Market Influences on Pay

Every employer **MUST** pay enough to attract and retain productive workers. But there is no one "magic number" for any job. It is extremely rare to find any two companies paying precisely the same rate for any two positions, no matter how their titles and content match. The external competitive "marketplace" for labor is highly variable (see **Pay Structures** later) and there is room for a great degree of choice in the exact amount of money a firm can pay for any job without suffering any damage.

However, there is a minimum rate, a salary floor, a threshold salary below which an employer cannot recruit or retain a competent employee. Yes, it varies from place to place, but it is very real. It is absolutely **vital** that an employer offer a pay amount that matches or exceeds the minimum entry rate or replacement cost for the job. If not, even the worst workers will be tempted to leave for higher pay anywhere else.

Once the minimum "market clearing rate" has been met or exceeded and the organization is assured that it can attract and retain competent people, the essential external "market" imperative has been satisfied. Beyond that point, most pay evaluation and classification decisions are made according to "internal" criteria that are unique to the enterprise. Job evaluation is the process of applying those unique organizational values so as to produce a job rank that influences *how high* above the "external competitive market" minimum rate the company will place the job.

Types of Job Evaluation Methods and Their Strengths and Weaknesses

All job evaluation methods produce a rank-ordering of jobs according to dollar value or pay classification.

They fall into two distinct categories: *Whole-Job* and *Factor* methods.

"Whole-Job" evaluation methods are non-quantitative. They do not use any intermediate statistics in the job comparison or evaluation process, other than a rank (ordinal data). They consider the "whole job" without precise measures of discrete job elements.

Non-quantitative "Whole Job" methods include:

Ranking: Jobs are ranked in order of their overall worth or value to the organization. *Market pricing* or *market comparison* is the most common ranking scheme, in which jobs are ranked in order of market pay survey results.

Advantages: simple and inexpensive.

Disadvantages: highly subjective; no specific or consistent standards for comparison ranking; likely to be influenced by the current pay of incumbents.

Classification: Broad descriptions are written specifying the types of jobs to be place in each of a number of pay grades; job specifications or descriptions are then compared to pay grade classification criteria or class specifications and the jobs placed into the most appropriate grades.

Advantages: relatively easy to use.

Disadvantages: inconsistent and inaccurate results; generic grade or class specs may not apply to certain jobs or show a job qualified for a number of different grades.

Slotting: Used in conjunction with the previous two methods. New jobs are compared to jobs already evaluated through "Whole Job" ranking or Classification and then inserted or "slotted" between jobs of greater or less worth, or placed beside jobs of similar overall worth. A matrix or guide chart may exist to standardize comparisons between job types.

Advantages: simple, fast and inexpensive.

Disadvantages: disregards the normal evaluation method used to rank the other jobs; introduces inconsistencies and errors to subsequent ranking decisions.

All non-quantitative "whole job" evaluation approaches share two major disadvantages: they are highly subjective (most appropriate in small firms where the evaluators know all jobs quite well) and imprecise (ranks are *ordinal* rather than *interval* measures ... they tell you a job is worth "more than one and less than another," but not **how much** more or less ... which you need for exact pay scales).

"Factor" evaluation methods use numeric (*nominal, interval or ratio*) codes or scores for each of a number of factors; they produce a precise numeric score for the total value of the job as the sum of the individual factor scores.

Quantitative "Factor" methods include:

Point Plans which apply a pre-selected number of compensable factors with fixed definitions and weights to jobs. Various levels or degrees within each factor are defined, along with their point values. The total of each job's point values for all factors is the score used for pay ranking.

> Advantages: well defined comparison standards make for greater objectivity and rater reliability; flexible; can cover a wide variety of jobs; highly credible and defensible.

> Disadvantages: if validated for the organization, costs time and money to develop; if "borrowed" from other firms, it may not reflect unique internal values; rigid factors, weights, terms and definitions may be out of date or inappropriate.

Factor Comparison methods start by selecting *benchmark* jobs and ranking them within a number of factors; a value scale of dollars or points is assigned to each factor and apportioned to each job by its rank within that factor. Other jobs are awarded the most appropriate factor scale values. Final total job value is the sum of the assigned factor point values.

> Advantages: highly valid if custom designed; uses defined factors; can be a *Policy Capturing* approach, assuring internal equity; suitable for large organizations.

> Disadvantages: validity and reliability depends on *benchmarks* and factors selected; requires sophisticated statistical analysis for optimal design; will perpetuate biased input; difficult to explain.

Regressed Questionnaire or **Job Component** methods emphasize custom application of statistical procedures to questionnaire responses about job content to *Capture Policy* or create a validated mathematical model of internal/external target pay values. A large selection of potential factors with various levels/degrees are applied, tested, statistically analyzed for usefulness and assigned weights and point values by the computer. The sum of factor level points equals job value.

> Advantages: highly objective, defensible, valid and reliable; factors are tested for reliability before final use; weights, values and points are

selected by computer statistical analysis for predictive accuracy and reliability; can be customized to unique external market or internal equity needs; allows employee self-rating without risk (computer throws out skewed responses); permits analysis and elimination of discriminatory or biased factors; can combine external/internal values. Disadvantages: complex to design; costs time and money; excessively precise for the needs of a small organization; requires regular update maintenance to retain advantages when internal or external conditions change.

All quantitative "factor" methods share disadvantages, to dramatically different degrees.

Their *points* always relate in some manner to dollars or pay grade; so when the external competitive market changes, the point values in the plans must change accordingly to retain whatever correspondence to reality they originally had. That eventually requires a revalidation of the plan rather than a simple formula change to boost point values, because while market value changes are relatively constant, they are rarely symmetrical (i.e., while all jobs usually increase in market value each year, different jobs increase at widely differing rates).

Point plans which have fixed factor choices and pre-set level language, weights and point values which cannot be changed are like one-size suits of clothes: they *might* fit today, but they won't when you grow or change. Customized **Factor Comparison** and **Regressed Questionnaire** point-factor approaches completely avoid the **Point Plan** problems of excessive rigidity, but only at the cost of regular plan revalidation or redesign every few years.

The Importance of Job Values to Performance Management

Some organizations and individual managers may question the need for **job values**. Particularly in small firms where each employee holds a unique job, management may see no purpose to ascribing a value to the **job** apart from the pay rate received by the individual job holder or *incumbent*.

There are many reasons why job values are quite important.

Failure to identify a frame of reference for job value creates serious problems and exposes you to many risks.

1. You lose track of competitive market realities. You may pay much more than you need (wasting scarce money) or much less than you should to attract, retain, and reward competent employees (stimulating resentment,

passive behavior, turnover, etc.).

2. You lack an objective frame of reference for internal equity. You open yourself to charges of bias, favoritism, power politics and discrimination; and you limit your ability to offer credible defenses against such charges.

3. You complicate all your pay decisions. Without a "standard rate" around which individuals with the same or equivalent jobs are paid (each varying from the "standard" or "job value" according to seniority, productivity or merit), each new hire, promotion or job change creates a pay crisis. And such crises will rarely be resolved in a consistent or manageable manner as long as no job values exist.

4. Merit pay or "pay for performance" becomes almost impossible. You need a norm or standard rate before you can credibly claim to pay more for better performers and less for poorer performers. "More" and "less" are comparative terms which require a base figure for comparison. . .i.e. , more or less than the STANDARD.

5. Basing all pay decisions on the actual base salaries of employees without reference to a standard job value creates special problems. Awards (bonuses or base increases) granted by applying a flat percentage to base pay tend to perpetuate past pay relationships and to ignore current performance realities.

   a. COMPOUNDING BASE SALARIES: Ten percent of a $40,000 salary yields twice the dollars of the same ten percent against a $20,000 salary. And if it is a base salary increase, the compounding effects will, over time, increase the lead position of the higher-paid person, despite equal or superior performance by a lower-paid peer in every year.

   b. MISALLOCATION OF PAYROLL: Without a job value as an objective control figure, scarce pay dollars flow to people who would otherwise be recognized as overpaid, in amounts disproportionate to their contributions. Meanwhile, better performers with lower base salaries get less in both relative and absolute terms.

   c. FORCED PERFORMANCE DISTRIBUTIONS: Pressure for financial controls may bring the suggestion that performance ratings be forced into a fixed distribution that guarantees budget compliance. Forcing Performance Rating distributions with quotas tends to destroy the credibility of merit programs and creates self-fulfilling prophesies which may not match reality. You no longer need to risk the hazards of "budgeting" Performance Appraisal Rating categories in order to assure that fixed reward percentages do not produce reward dollars that exceed the budget. Nor must you ever again be pressured to expend either more or less than the actual budgeted amount because of honest performance evaluations that deviate from what was anticipated at budget setting time (see page 363).

The Legal Constraints on Pay Actions

A long series of federal acts, executive orders, rules and regulations apply to pay decisions. And states and municipalities add their own laws and statutes, to create a list that is constantly growing.

A List of the Most Significant Pay Laws

Compensation and pay decisions are most seriously affected by a short list of legal factors:
- minimum wage regulations
- overtime laws
- non-discrimination legislation
- tax law
- pension regulations
- insurance requirements

The ones most often encountered by performance managers are the first few. Mistakes in decisions affecting minimum wages, overtime and equal pay can be expensive. If you doubt that you would ever make an error in those areas, you are invited to test your expertise.

A Test on the FLSA & EPA Regulations

THE FAIR LABOR STANDARDS ACT AND THE EQUAL PAY ACT

1. The Fair Labor Standards Act (the FLSA or the "Act") is enforced by:
   - A. The U. S. Bureau of Standards
   - B. The Wage and Hour Division of the U. S. Dept. of Labor
   - C. The Equal Employment Opportunity Commission
   - D. The Bureau of Labor and Statistics

2. An employer can change any of his nonexempt employees' status under the Act (i.e., make them "exempt" from the Act's premium pay requirements) by:
   - A. Paying them annual salaries in excess of $20,000
   - B. Significantly increasing the value of their employee benefits programs

C. Either of the above

D. Neither of the above

3. The "professional" exemption from the Fair Labor Standards Act is, in almost all cases, limited to persons holding four-year college degrees.

    A. True

    B. False

4. The record-keeping requirements of the Act mandate that the hours worked by nonexempt employees be recorded by a time clock.

    A. True

    B. False

5. A "workweek" as defined under the FLSA is a 168-hour period commencing at:

    A. 12:01 a.m. each Monday

    B. The start of Monday's "day" shift

    C. The employer's discretion

    D. None of the above

6. If your workweek starts at 12:01 a.m. on Monday, and a non-exempt secretary works eight hours on Monday, Tuesday and Wednesday, and works ten hours on Thursday, the "flexible forty" provisions of the Act would allow you to avoid paying

the employee any overtime premium provided, their next work day is only six hours and is the following:

    A. Friday or Saturday or Sunday

    B. Monday

    C. Either of the above

    D. Neither of the above

7. The current FLSA hourly minimum wage for covered nonagricultural employees is:

    A. $2.90

    B. $3.35

    C. $3.50

    D. $3.85

8. An exempt salaried employee who is scheduled to work a 40-hour work week has used all accrued vacation and sick leave. The employee has worked 8 hours on Monday, Tuesday, Wednesday and Thursday. On Friday, only 4 hours are worked. For that work week, the employer is required by law to pay the employee for _____ hours:

    A. 32

    B. 36

C. 40

9. If the same exempt salaried employee who has worked 32 hours and has used all approved time off decided to skip work on Friday, the employer is required by law to pay the employee for _____ hours during that work week:

A. 32

B. 36

C. 40

10. An employee who works from 9:00 a.m. to 5:30 p.m. Monday through Friday is asked to make an overnight business trip to another city. The trip requires him to leave his home at noon on Sunday for a 1:00 p.m. airline departure.
He arrives at the destination airport at 6:00 p.m., and arrives at the hotel at 7:00 p.m. What hours, if any, of travel time are considered as time worked?

A. 0 hours - no actual work was performed

B. 4.5 hours - from time of airline departure to the end of his normal work day

C. 5.0 hours - from time of airline departure to time of airline arrival

D. 5.5 hours - from time of departure from his home to the end of his normal work day

E. 7.0 hours - from time of departure from his home to time of arrival at the hotel

11. An employee with regular work hours from 9:00 a.m. to 5:00 p.m. is given a special one-day assignment in another city. She leaves her home in New York for an 8:00 a.m. flight to Pittsburgh.
The special assignment is completed at 4:00 p.m., and she arrives back in New York at 7:00 p.m. What hours, excluding usual meal time, are counted as hours worked?

A. From the time of departure from home to time of arrival at home

B. From the 8:00 a.m. flight departure time to the 7:00 p.m. arrival time

C. From the 8:00 a.m. flight departure time to 5:00 p.m.

D. From 9:00 a.m. to 5:00 p.m., the normal work schedule

12. Willful violations of the FLSA can lead to:

A. Suits for twice the amount of unpaid wages for a 3-year period

B. A $10,000 fine

C. Imprisonment

D. All of the above

13. Recovery of unpaid minimum and/or overtime wages may be achieved by any of the following mechanisms:
- Complaint resolution under the supervision of the cognizant Federal agency

- Litigation initiated by the Secretary of Labor
- Litigation initiated by an employee
    A. True
    B. False

14. A nonexempt employee who performs overtime work without the permission of his supervisor cannot claim premium pay for such work under the FLSA.
    A. True
    B. False

15. The language of the Act, and its interpretations by the relevant enforcement agency, could lead one to safely conclude that the exemptions from overtime pay requirements extend to:
    A. Virtually all Executive Secretaries and Administrative Assistants
    B. Computer Programmers earning more than $35,000 a year
    C. Either of the above
    D. Neither of the above

16. A nonexempt employee can legally forgo receipt of overtime pay in exchange for compensatory time off at some unspecified future date, such as an extra holiday or extended vacation, provided that the employee requests this exception in writing.
    A. True
    B. False

17. The Equal Pay Amendments to the Fair Labor Standards Act are enforced by:
    A. The Wage and Hour Division of the U. S. Dept. of Labor
    B. The Equal Employment Opportunity Commission
    C. The Women's Bureau of the U. S. Department of Labor
    D. The Office of the Solicitor General

18. A man hired to perform a job which is unique to that particular employer may still show a violation of the Equal Pay Act if he can prove:
    A. That his female predecessor was paid more than he is
    B. That his female predecessor, who performed the same job he does, was assigned to a higher pay grade than he is
    C. That the employer is paying him less than a female would demand to do similar work
    D. That female employees, doing jobs different from his which have similar overall worth to the organization, are paid more

19. An employer who is paying men more than women for performing the same job can avoid an Equal Pay Act violation by reducing the men's pay level to that of the women.

A. True

B. False

20. All of the following represent potential violations of the Equal Pay Amendments except:

A. Paying males more money for performing jobs requiring substantially equal levels of skill, effort, responsibility and working conditions as those required for lower-paid jobs performed by females

B. Paying females more money for performing the same job as males, where the income differential is not the result of a bona fide seniority or merit system

C. Paying females less than men for performing work which requires the same qualifications but which carries a lower value in the competitive market

D. Denying a promotion to a qualified female and filling the position with a less-qualified male

21. The Equal Pay Amendments prohibit pay differentials based exclusively on:

A. Race

B. National origin

C. Sex

D. All of the above

22. Which of the following is not a permissible basis for paying members of one sex more than the other, when both are doing the same jobs?

A. Job performance or "merit"

B. Length of service

C. Productivity

D. Labor market pay patterns

ANSWERS
THE FAIR LABOR STANDARDS ACT AND THE EQUAL PAY ACT

1. B	12. D
2. D	13. A
3. A	14. B
4. B	15. D
5. C	16. B
6. A	17. B
7. B	18. B
8. C	19. B
9. A	20. C

11. B   22. D

Number correct	Description
20 - 22	A "pro" who can design and administer wage and salary administration programs as an expert/authority
17 - 19	A competent practitioner who can handle almost any situation
14 - 16	A generally competent practitioner in need of additional information on non-standard cases
12 - 13	A neophyte who should research the law on each case to avoid problems
0 - 11	Here come de judge (see Question 12!)

How Overtime Exemption Rules Can Ruin Your Year

A short summary of the current (1989) Federal rules regulating the determination of whether an employee is legitimately "exempt" from required overtime at a rate of time and a half of the regular rate follows.

Not every employer is covered, but the vast majority of enterprises are affected by this little-known but important law.

New modifications to the **minimum wage**, held at $3.35 an hour since 1981, will affect the Fair Labor Standards Act minimum compensation standards for exemption and change the answer to question number seven.

Every manager with employees hired at or near the minimum wage and all who supervise people who do not receive time and a half overtime should satisfy themselves that they and their firm are in compliance with the current law.

TESTS FOR EXEMPTION OF EMPLOYEE FROM PROVISIONS OF FAIR LABOR STANDARDS ACT

NAME _____

DEPARTMENT _____ LOCATION _____ JOB TITLE _____ DATE _____

BASIS FOR EXEMPTION: ☐ EXECUTIVE ☐ ADMINISTRATIVE ☐ PROFESSIONAL

EXECUTIVE TEST

Long Test (Must qualify in <u>all</u> seven categories listed below)

1. _____ Management of an enterprise or a customarily recognized department or subdivision; and

2. _____ Customarily and regularly directs work of two or more employees; and

3. _____ Has authority to hire or fire employees, or whose recommendations are given particular weight; and

4. _____ Customarily and regularly exercises discretionary powers; and

5. _____ Devotes no more than 20% of weekly hours to work not closely related to above; and

6. _____ Compensated at a rate of not less than $155 per week; and

7. _____ Regularly paid on a salary basis not subject to reduction for quality or quantity of work.

Short Test

1. _____ Must qualify under the first two categories listed above; and

2. _____ Must be compensated at a rate of not less than $250 per week.

ADMINISTRATIVE TEST

Long Test (Must qualify in categories 1, 2, 4, 5, and 6 and one item in category 3)

1. _____ Performs office or non-manual field work directly related to management policies or general business operations; and

2. _____ Customarily and regularly exercises discretion and independent judgment; and

3. _____ Regularly and directly assists an employee employed in a <u>bona fide</u> executive or administrative capacity (Executive and Administrative Assistants); or

   _____ Performs specialized or technical work requiring special training experience or knowledge under only general supervison (Staff Assistants); or

   _____ Executes special assignments and tasks under only general supervision (Staff Representatives); and

4. _____ Devotes no more than 20% of weekly hours to work not directly or closely related to above; and

5. _____ Compensated at a rate of not less than $155 per week; and

6. _____ Regularly paid on a salary basis not subject to reduction for quality or quantity of work.

Short Test

1. _____ Must qualify under categories 1 and 2 above; and

2. _____ Compensated at a rate of not less than $250 per week.

PROFESSIONAL TEST

Long Test (Must qualify in categories 2, 3, 4, 5, and 6 and one item in category 1)

1. _____ Primary duty requiring knowledge of an advanced type in a field of science or learning customarily acquired by a prolonged course of specialized instruction and study; or

   _____ Original and creative in character, the results of which depend primarily on the invention, imagination or talent of employee; and

2. _____ Work requires consistent exercise of discretion and judgment in its performance; and

3. _____ Work predominantly intellectual and varied and is of a character that the output or results cannot be standardized in relation to time; and

4. _____ Devotes no more than 20% of weekly hours to work not closely related to the performance of work described in 1 through 3 above; and

5. _____ Compensated at a rate of not less than $170 per week; and

6. _____ Regularly paid on a salary basis, not subject to reduction for quality or quantity of work.

Short Test

1. _____ Must qualify under the second category and under either or both items in the first category shown above; and

2. _____ Compensated at a rate of not less than $250 per week.

APPROVALS

IMMEDIATE SUPERVISOR _____ DATE _____ INDUSTRIAL RELATIONS/PERSONNEL _____ DATE _____

NEXT HIGHER LEVEL _____ DATE _____

Employees can make anonymous complaints to the Wage and Hour Division of the U.S. Department of Labor; and they are protected by law from exposure or from retaliatory action.

Wage and hour law violations carry severe penalties. The enforcement branch is authorized to force you to open up all your payroll records, time cards, admission logs, etc., for their examination. And if they fail to find confirmation of the original complaint, they will probably find an error somewhere that will justify their inspection and bring you trouble and cost.

One can avoid such problems by communicating and enforcing a firm policy that:

- non-exempt employees (those who are eligible for overtime under the law) shall not work outside regular hours without advance permission of their supervisor
- all overtime hours worked must be reported by employees and paid by the company
- compensatory time off ("comp time") is offered as an alternative to overtime pay within the scope of the law (i.e., it can not normally be deferred to a different work week)
- supervisor-subordinate agreements or arrangements to evade compliance with the law ("don't turn in the overtime for this project and I'll do you a favor later") are strictly forbidden: employees still retain the right to file a complaint and the law permits no waiver of payment

How to Understand Modern Equal Pay Issues

Before 1963, it was legal for employers to openly discriminate against women in wages and working conditions. The Equal Pay Act of 1963 and the Title VII of the Civil Rights Act of 1964, as amended by the Equal Employment Opportunity Act of 1972, changed all that. Later legislation added Vietnam veterans, the aged (ages 40-70,) and the handicapped to the long list of groups now considered *protected classes* under Federal law.

At present, employers may not discriminate in compensation because of

- race
- color
- religion
- sex
- national origin

The Equal Pay Act amended the Fair Labor Standards Act to require that men and women performing equal work must receive equal pay. Section 6(d) reads:

> No employer... shall discriminate... between employees on the basis of sex by paying wages to employees... at a rate less than the rate at which he pays wages to employees of the opposite sex... for equal work on jobs the performance of which requires equal skill, effort, and responsibility, and which are performed under similar working conditions, except where payment is made pursuant to (i) a seniority system; (ii) a merit system; (iii) a system which measures earnings by quantity, quality, or production; or (iv) a differential based on any other factor other than sex...

The Civil Rights Act extended this protection to minorities. Other laws require that written personnel policies must expressly indicate no discrimination on account of sex and guarantee women and men equal opportunities for overtime and apprenticeship rates.

So the previously legal pay discrimination is now illegal. But the effects of that past history remain.

Women and men doing *the same* work were to be paid the same: so employers gradually accelerated the pay for women to the same level as their equal-performing male co-workers ... but only if they held the same job as the men.

The new legislation only required equal pay for *the same* work. Employers were not required to **correct** the historically depressed pay rates for jobs held **only** by women; if no men held a low-paying "female" job in a given enterprise, the employer could not be charged with paying men more than women for that same job. So the most dramatic improvement in wages to women occurred in "integrated" jobs held by both men and women in each company, where discrepancies in pay between men and women holding the same jobs were obvious and required to be corrected.

That progress is still uneven. In 1981, the American Compensation Association conducted a survey of member pay using a **regressed questionnaire** job evaluation approach. They found that when the variables of age, experience, education, number of jobs, position level, organizational type and company size were accounted for, women earned 14.3% less than their male peers.

While that is a great improvement over the past, it was still quite embarrassing to find that even the female executives in charge of pay programs had not achieved pay equity almost twenty years after the new legislation. Of course, it is possible that women compensation professionals merely perform at a level below that of men; but that is highly doubtful. Needless to say, the ACA never repeated that same survey format.

The results of surveys and studies today show that when all variables of human capital and work content are held constant, women still earn somewhat less than men with the same skills and work/education history who hold jobs with the same duties, responsibilities, and working conditions.

The differences range from 20% to 1%, depending on the male/female ratio in the job. A mathematical formula was derived to predict the sex-based pay differential by Don Treiman, a professor of sociology who headed the National Research Council (National Academy of Sciences) authoritative 1981 report, *Women, Work, and Wages: Equal Pay for Jobs of Equal Value* for the Equal Employment Opportunity Commission. The fewer women in a given job, the more female wages approximate that of the men; the higher the proportion of women in the job, the greater the difference between their wages and the wages of the men. A female controller typically earns about the same as a man; but a female secretary typically earns far less than the few men in the profession.

How Job Evaluation Often Causes Underpayment to Women

Society does seem to depreciate and underpay "women's work," just as it did "black jobs." The proof of "underpayment" often comes from job evaluation, which compares work content to come to a conclusion about pay value. It is common to see that a job evaluation plan that accurately reflects both the external competitive market rate and the internally equitable ("felt fair") pay rate for jobs dominated by men always produces a job evaluation/pay rate that is "too high" for women. The employer does not have to pay that much to get a qualified female or minority worker; and the pay rate yielded by the "male" evaluation plan is inappropriately high for the traditional internal job value structure of the enterprise.

The values ascribed by the open market and internal company culture to "male work" are simply higher than the values for the same skills, education, experience, responsibility, effort, etc., in "women's work." There is a certain logic in this. If you want to abide by the competitive marketplace and pay as other employers do, you are subtly discouraged from paying

- senior bookkeepers as much as junior accountants, when the women bookkeepers are more competent and more valuable than young male accountants, who are more plentiful and must be trained by the female bookkeepers

- registered nurses as much as truck drivers, when RNs are more vital, more skilled, more essential to a health service function (and harder to recruit) than drivers who nevertheless have a higher wage expectation
- executive secretaries as much as beginning shipping clerks
- laundry workers as much as custodians
- baby-sitters as much as grass-cutters

because the surveys show that jobs dominated by women have **always** earned less.

Of course. There was absolutely no requirement for employers to pay the same for *similar* or *comparable* work, but only for *the same work*. Canadian law is more liberal in this respect than U.S. law: in Canada, *equal work* means *work of equal value* to the employer as measured by the evaluation scheme of the particular employer rather than precisely the same tasks, duties, responsibilities and titles.

So in the U.S., there are few legal remedies for women, minorities or other protected classes who are segregated into jobs with lower pay than conventional "male" work. Market surveys continue to show their pay as low and compensation professionals continue to design and install pay plans that parallel the market surveys, thus perpetuating discrimination that is improper but legal.

That situation creates an incentive for employers to segregate women in certain jobs which traditionally pay less than they would if men did the work: the company can get the same output at less cost. And it leads to separate job evaluation and pay plans which have one set of values for male work and another (lower) set of values for women's work.

The employer must pay at or above the minimum market clearing rate for women's work as well as for men's or it will not attract or retain female workers. But there is usually a strong tendency to pay well above the minimum and the average for male jobs while keeping women tightly clustered near the bottom of their scale or restricted to a pay grade with a more narrow range between the minimum and the maximum rates.

All this can create anger and frustration among the women and other protected classes who are so victimized. That brings stress and conflict to the performance manager who inherits the dissatisfaction of workers with company pay and progression programs.

What to Do About Comparable Worth and Pay Equity in Your Organization

The performance manager must be prepared to deal with employee perceptions of unfair and inconsistent pay practices.

All employers compare the worth of jobs within their enterprises and between enterprises (through market surveys), so the **Comparable Worth** of a job is whatever the organization decides it will pay. Whether that determination of "worth" is fair and meets a proper standard of **Pay Equity** is the real question.

The equity of pay is a relative matter, best applied within the employing enterprise rather than between different firms. As long as the pay rates for women and other protected classes are established and administered according to the same rules used for men (and those rules do not single out protected classes for inferior treatment, which is called *systemic discrimination*), then the pay system that compares job worth is probably equitable. It may be "cheap"; but that is a pay structure decision quite within the rights of management to make: as long as all jobs are paid "below the market average but above the minimum" without regard to the sex, race, age, etc., of the incumbents, it is both legal and fair.

Pay equity disputes can be best avoided if the company

- maintains a fully integrated job population, so that no job titles or classes are dominated by women or other protected groups
- has one job evaluation plan or method for all jobs in the entire enterprise, so the pay scales for all work is established according to the same rules;
- designs and implements the pay plan in an open manner, using job content information from employees
- validates the pay plan for the enterprise where it is to be used, assuring that any adverse impact on protected classes can be justified as a matter of business necessity
- publicizes and communicates the evaluation method, the factors and weights, so the natural tendency to suspect foul play when information is withheld can be overcome
- has an appeals mechanism for the review of decisions which may involve exceptions beyond the scope of the normal rules
- conducts regular reviews of the evaluation plan and its application, to confirm continued validity and reliability
- periodically tests plan administration and pay results for undue or disparate impact on protected classes
- makes sure that "market" arguments used to defend higher pay for male jobs are not merely smokescreens for perpetuation historical discrimination (i.e.,

high rates for men due to higher replacement costs are valid, but moving male salaries far above their grade minimums while keeping female pay close to the bottom of their grades suggests discrimination)

    □ uses trained people to evaluate and classify jobs

Despite antiquated arguments by reactionaries who would like to see women restricted to "children, kitchen and church" (which was one of Adolf Hitler's campaign promises), women have a permanent and major presence in the workplace. In fact, when you consider all the groups covered under the blanket of "protected classes," the majority of workers are female, minority, over age 40, handicapped, or veteran. These groups want to make a contribution and want to be treated as well as the next person.

The demands of people seeking **pay equity** are rarely unreasonable. The hysterical accusations that fair pay within individual companies actually means a single pay plan for all employers, imposed by the national government, are without foundation. "Straw man" arguments, designed to attribute outrageous motives to those who seek correction of historical inequities, are pure demagoguery. In over twenty years of compensation practice and close dealings with the most rabid proponents of "equal pay for equal work," the author has never heard a pay equity supporter suggest such a silly idea. It is enough that each enterprise should value and pay its workers according its own unique system, as long as that system is not biased against protected classes.

Further details on the actual ambitions of pay equity supporters can be found in *JOB EVALUATION: A Tool for Pay Equity*, 1987, by the National Committee on Pay Equity, 1201 16th Street, N.W., Suite 422, Washington, DC 20036.

How Pay Structures Influence Wages and Salaries

While all employers compete in the open market for workers, no two enterprises pay the exact same rates.

The Difference between Economic Theory About Market Pay and the Reality

In classical economic terms, there is no absolute *equilibrium point* for pay: no "correct" number which everyone must pay for any particular job. When the supply of applicants increases, the salaries paid to incumbents do not fall; and when the supply of applicants declines, salaries do not notably increase. Pay scales are relatively *inelastic* and the traditional economic penalties for the misapplication of resources do not apply.

Firms that pay high wages rarely go out of business for that reason. If prosperity falters, companies prefer to lay off people before they cut pay. And firms that pay low wages do not find it impossible to attract and retain productive employees.

Wage and salary surveys for comparable jobs show that variety in pay between employers is the rule instead of the exception. Fervent claims that pay is determined solely by "the market" are deceptive. Wages and salaries are actually set in a complicated management decision making process that takes many factors into account; and the competitive marketplace is only one factor, whose imperative is merely "thou shalt pay enough to get and hold thy workers."

Examples of What Market Surveys Will Reveal

The **Executive Comp** example shows how information from different surveys can be examined.

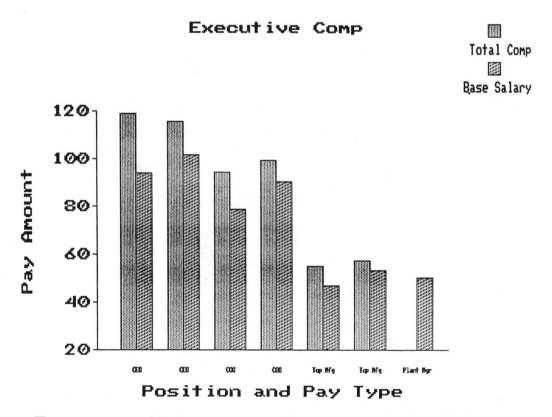

Two surveys provide data on competitive compensation for Chief Executive

Officer (CEO), Chief Operating Officer (COO) and the Top Manufacturing Executive (Top Mfg).

The **Maintenance** example shows the hourly rates of pay for the custodian/light maintenance function at nine different organizations. Some pay different rates according to seniority or experience in *steps*, while others have only a single pay rate for all incumbents.

If the company studying the market data concluded that it only wanted to match the lowest pay rate in the survey, it would pay $7 an hour; a rough "average competitive" median rate would be $9.80 an hour; and $12 an hour would place their pay above the highest rate reported in the survey sample.

Maintenance

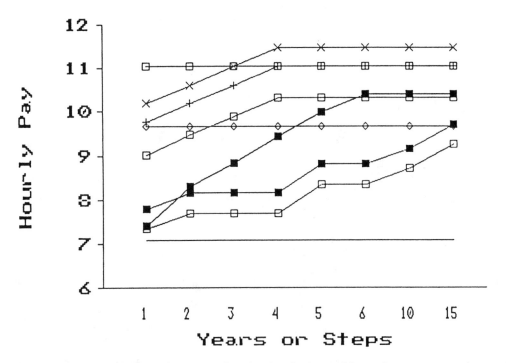

Pay structures define the organization's choice of how its pay practices will relate to the practices of others.

Other Influences on Pay Structures

Other factors that carry more weight than the average practices of other employers include:
1. union pressure
2. internal equity
3. the relative importance of the job to the employer
4. financial ability to pay
5. unique industry circumstances
6. company size and profitability
7. geographic location
8. major differences in job content from the norm
9. the philosophy of the employer

Market pay surveys cannot account for all these factors, which vary among all employers. It is no surprise that no two surveys yield the same pay results for any one job.

Market data is merely used as a reference point around which each company deliberately deviates when it sets actual pay structures, rates, and practices.

Pay structures are usually represented by Salary/Pay Grades, Job Values or Position Standards. Structures are created to show a hierarchy of *job values* which relate in some manner to the target rate used by the employer (which can be a survey average, median, lowest/highest rate, etc.).

A Typical Pay Structure

The typical pay structure illustration example shows a structure created by a *line of best fit* approach. The pay structure line is computed by *regression analysis* to cut through and between the average pay rates in the labor market. This usually involves a *least squares* statistical analysis; but a pencil line drawn free-hand will often do almost as well.

The pay structure example (reprinted from *Elements of Sound Base Pay Administration* with the permission of the **American Compensation Association,** Scottsdale, Arizona; Copyright 1988) demonstrates how the line formed by the polynomial equation $y = a + bx$ does not touch any target point precisely; it would produce a pay rate below some target rates and above others. But that is good enough for administrative use.

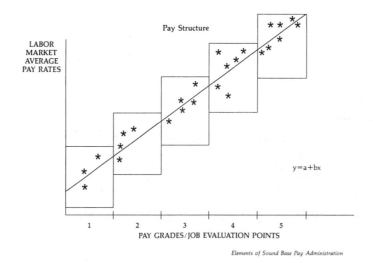

Elements of Sound Base Pay Administration

How Wage & Salary Grade Ranges Work to Police Pay Practices

Pay grades are administrative devices used to simplify compensation decisions and policies. They also exist as guidelines to accomplish organizational objectives of cost control, external competitiveness and internal equity.

As illustrated in the earlier section on **How to Overcome the Usual Problem with Salary Ranges,** they set limits on permissible pay rates for jobs grouped together according to their standard or "average" value. Positions or jobs with similar values to the organization (based on the unique balance of external competitiveness and internal equity selected by the employer) are classified into grades with pre-established minimum and maximum limits.

Grade range **minimums** define the lowest permissible pay rate within a grade. No incumbent should be paid less than the minimum, because it is the figure below which the company does not expect to be able to hire competent people for the job. The assumption is that people willing to work below the range minimum will either be incompetent (unable to command the lowest wage accepted by qualified workers) or will become upset (when they discover that they were short-changed and all their co-workers ... even those with fewer credentials ... earn more than they do).

Minimums serve a cost control purpose: to assure that managers will hire qualified candidates. The minimums also exist to create consistent internal equity between job holders (incumbents) and to start new people at rates that promise to meet competitive standards in the employment marketplace, both for hiring beginners and for retaining and motivating journeymen/women. As treated earlier, hiring a new worker at an excessively low starting rate can interfere with the intended pay progression plan that should bring the beginner up to the fully qualified rate over a reasonable period of time. Failure to hire at the proper entry rate will eventually cost money, disrupt internal equity (thus hurting morale and productivity) and destroy pay competitiveness (which creates turnover as well as low morale and reduced motivation).

Jobs are usually sorted/classified into grades and appropriately assigned ranges according to how close the job value comes to the grade range **midpoint** (or control point, standard job value, or fully-qualified rate), which falls between the range minimum and maximum. All jobs assigned to a given range are treated as though they are all worth precisely the same amount. That target figure usually represents how much a fully qualified and proven job performer can normally expect to earn, on the average.

The actual pay of job holders/incumbents within each grade are expected to vary around the standard midpoint value according to sustained performance. In a seniority system, where performance is assumed to increase with time on the job, job seniority sets range position. In a merit system, a consistent history of superior work results should produce higher merit increases which accelerate personal pay faster for the better performer.

New hires with minimal credentials and unknown potential, as well as consistently marginal performers, should be paid below the fully-qualified job rate/midpoint, while proven experts with a long established record of achievement should earn pay above the norm and up to the maximum for the job.

A range **maximum** is the highest rate that can be paid to any person whose job is classified in that grade. It states the upper limit placed by the organization on the value of the job. Maximums establish a ceiling on the finite value of the job, no matter how talented the person who holds the job may be. Once a person reaches the maximum rate in the assigned grade range, he or she is usually prohibited from further pay raises in that job until the maximum is raised in response to pay structure changes caused by market/internal value increases.

The cost control aspects of range maximums are obvious. In most organizations, managers must fight long and hard to win a pay increase for an employee that takes the salary over the maximum limit. Employers may permit exceptions in special circumstances, but they are generally quite reluctant to violate the standard rules, fearing that any precedent will open the door to unlimited and uncontrollable pay escalation far beyond reasonable limits.

Many (if not most) grade ranges are symmetrical, with the same percentage distance between minimums and midpoints as between midpoints and maximums, and with the same percentage between the midpoints of successive grades. Such nice neat uniformity is purely theoretical, based only on the preference of the designer; there is absolutely no logical reason beyond the desire for conceptual/visual beauty for grade ranges to be so constructed.

Reality tends to be more messy than neat, more inconsistent than uniform; so don't be surprised if scientifically designed wage and salary grade ranges just don't work very well in actual practice. Their very consistency and uniformity may stifle their practical utility.

For example, the distance between grade range minimums and maximums should reflect the range of anticipated actual salaries for jobs in the grade. The minimum and maximum should encompass the externally competitive and internally equitable distribution of pay. But some grades will contain jobs with a tighter distribution than others: jobs whose pay rates do not vary much at all. So the same minimum/maximum spread is not necessarily appropriate for all grades.

Entry-level clerical jobs, for instance, have relatively little value to the employer and are usually classified in the lowest grades, in line with their market value. Incumbents typically have limited experience, apply few skills, are quickly trained and easily replaced; their learning curve is short and the value of improved performance in the same low-level job is very limited. Indeed, the workers are neither expected nor encouraged to make a career out of the entry clerical job; management expects them to either quit or be promoted to more valuable (and thus higher-graded) positions within a few years. The range of pay from minimum to maximum should be very small for such jobs.

The same dynamics exist for entry-level professional jobs which are merely the first step towards progression into more valuable, higher-graded jobs.

In contrast, grades that contain senior professionals and mid-level managers must provide pay rates for jobs that have considerable value to the company. Incumbents have variable experience and skills, require many years to master their jobs, are not easily replaced, and may spend the remainer of their careers in the same job. The range of pay from minimum to maximum should be wide for such jobs.

It is obvious that the same min-max range spread (even when stated as a percentage rather than in dollars) should not be applied to all these jobs.

If the midpoint (standard job value) of a clerical job is correct but the range around it is very wide, the minimum entry rates may be too low to be realistic. Likewise, an excessively high clerical pay range maximum will permit salary increases far beyond the productive value of the jobs.

Symmetrical grades can create similar problems for professional and management jobs whose pay reality (in market or internal terms) does not match the theoretical grade range model. Some jobs with similar normal/average dollar values have a very long learning curve, while other jobs placed in the same grade call for immediate "journeyman" status and a short tenure followed by quick promotion to another job. In such cases, one job requires a pay range that permits a long time for progression from the minimum entry rate to the standard fully-qualified rate, while the other job requires a pay range that permits the starting rate to be very close to the standard job value and keeps the maximum pay for the job low enough that marginal performers and unpromotable people are not allowed to siphon off scarce payroll dollars.

Supervisors and managers can fight ineffective grade range programs with practical suggestions.

☐ Grade ranges can be tapered to reflect the proper distribution of actual wages and saleries in each grade. As a later example shows, the min-max spread of each grade range can be increased for each successive grade: the lowest clerical jobs may have a 10% spread from minimum entry to maximum ceiling; the spread increases until professional jobs have a 30% range; middle management positions would have a 50% range; and top executive positions could have minimums and maximums that are much farther apart, to allow for wide variations in individual merit.

☐ Position values (otherwise known as job values, standard rates, midpoints, etc.) can be located somewhere in the range besides the exact statistical middle. There is absolutely no practical reason for arbitrarily decreeing that all grade ranges must be created so that the minimum and maximum is always equidistant from the fully-qualified job rate.

☐ Standard company grade ranges can be modified by exception for certain jobs which demand slightly different treatment from the others in the same grade. This practice, known as **pegging**, involves setting a precise dollar value for one job that differs from the norm applied to other jobs in the same grade, usually to avoid salary compression. Also, **shadow ranges** can be constructed as subsets within normal grades to define the special min-max limits that will be applied to one of the jobs in the grade: that lets you administer pay for the exceptional job in a modified manner without having to create an entire new grade. One job may be given a lower minimum entry rate, due to excess market supply or longer in-place job tenure; another can be granted a higher maximum than the other jobs in the same grade because the incumbent is truly irreplaceable.

Further details discussing grade range practices and technical options to overcome special problems can be found in the author's March, 1984, **Personnel Journal** article, "Everything You Need to Know About Salary Ranges" and

Richard I. Henderson's text, "Compensation Management: Rewarding Performance" (Fourth Edition, copyright 1985 by *Reston Publishing Co. Inc., a Prentice Hall company, Reston, VA.*).

What to Do About Geographic Pay Differences

As illustrated and discussed earlier in the **Recruitment** chapter, different geographic pay patterns can be so drastically different that an employer with wide-spread operations may find it quite desirable to adjust pay rates to reflect the local reality.

The U.S. government is the largest example of an employer who ignores geographic pay differences. Pay rates and scales are the same everywhere, with few exceptions; but pressure is growing for more exceptions, because the uniform pay program is unrealistic. Federal service has become the employment of last resort in high-pay areas like New York City, Los Angeles, etc., while the same government pay rate attracts much more qualified applicants in rural areas of the deep South where comparable jobs are paid much less by other employers. As federal budget economies reduce the money available to keep government salaries competitive in even low-pay areas, the relative advantages of a single national rate structure are being outweighed by the practical problems of getting competent workers to take a cut in pay to serve the public.

The proper way to deal with large differences in competitive employee replacement costs between areas is to pay the rates necessary to attract and retain people in each locale. *Cost of Living* data are relevant to relocation costs but not very predictive of actual wages and salaries.

Enterprises that want to retain consistency in their job evaluation and pay classification methods while still offering realistic wages and salaries in different employment markets find *pay zones* the best compromise. As shown in the exhibit, the same job values (expressed as grades, steps or evaluation points) carry different dollar amounts according to the competitive pay zone.

A Grade 5 job which earns $15,000 on the national average:
- earns about $13,000 in Brownsville TX; so it goes into Zone A for the lowest-pay areas, which would include areas like Allentown PA, Knoxville TN, Laramie WY and Lafayette LA.
- earns about $14,000 in Baltimore MD; that matches Zone B for areas slightly below the national norm, such as Rochester NY, Springfield IL, Colorado Springs CO, etc.
- earns the national average of $15,000 in Madison WI, which would be Zone

C for areas that pay close to the norm, like Provo UT, Oklahoma City OK, Washington DC and Gainsville FL.

- earns around $16,200 in Dallas TX, which fits Zone D for those cities notably above the national average like Gary IN, Chicago IL and Newark NJ.
- earns around $17,500 in Manhattan NY, which is Zone E for super-high pay areas, which include San Francisco CA, Honolulu HI and Anchorage AL.

The zones are wide enough to cover all areas variations. The zones are constructed so that cities or areas are grouped together with enough distance between adjoining zone cut-off points (the maximum and minimum boundaries of each zone) that it is unlikely that changes in relative pay rates will require a city to be moved into a new pay zone for a few years.

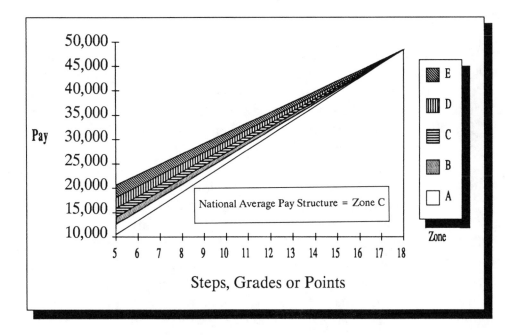

Explanations of the Various Methods for Pay Progression

Pay progression methods demonstrate an organization's value system by showing what it pays for.

Pay for Membership or Merit

Some enterprises pay for membership rather than individual merit.

When there are limits on the permissible extremes of possible performance, so that everyone in a certain job must perform in a narrow range with little possible variation, it makes sense to pay all members approximately the same rate. Examples include:

- assembly line workers who are tied to the line speed and must all adjust production to a coordinated level and pace
- the initial professional jobs for engineers shortly after graduation, as they are introduced to practical job applications for their education and paid on a *maturity curve* based on the number of years since their degree
- work teams who perform as a unit where the relative merit of individuals is subordinated to their effectiveness as a group, such as firefighters and military ranks

Military organizations pay by rank and seniority, with few differences for individual proficiency within the same rank/seniority levels. Police, fire, and public safety units do much the same. Such organizations find the retention of competent members far more important than variable renumeration for individual excellence. No military or quasi-military organization is completely comfortable with "heroes." They prefer steady team members whose behavior can be predicted. Heroes tend to expose themselves and others to risk. In hazardous trades, it is usually considered preferable to maintain a high level of minimum employee competence and discourage (or provide little incentive for) members to take actions that are spectacular only if they succeed and usually end in disaster if attempted by ordinary people under normal conditions.

Groups involved in emergency response or public safety work also spend most of their time "getting ready"; training, practicing, sharpening skills that may be suddenly needed. Dramatic ACTION in their professional specialty may be infrequent and rare, so there is a high degree of potential boredom that can lead to frustration and dissatisfaction. To compensate for that syndrome, both literally and figuratively, pay rates may be high to provide more retention than is possible through the intrinsic satisfaction provided by the work alone.

Academic institutions, regulated industries, and political bodies also find pay for membership easier to administer than individual merit pay.

Pay for Merit

To have a successful merit pay system in any industry, certain conditions are necessary.

- Performance objectives that serve the organizational mission must be defined for every position. Workers must know precisely what they are supposed to accomplish, so they can AIM, plan and ACT properly.

- Standards of desired performance output must be set and communicated in advance. There must be mutual understanding of what results are expected and how people can get feedback for SCORING and ADJUSTMENT of their work behavior.

- Performance standards should be relatively consistent among comparable jobs. Positions with the same job title or in the same job class should have common general characteristics or the equivalent value to the organization.

- Special expectations, common to such jobs which require unique results from different positions, must be defined (e.g., while all Associate Professors of English have common duties, one must specialize in Victorian literature while another covers Creative Writing).

- It must be possible to observe and measure individual work output results that can be attributed to the efforts of each employee. If management can't identify who did what, they can't validly recognize individual merit.

- Employees must be able to be held accountable for the results of their work. Circumstances beyond the control of the worker should not be permitted to influence individual merit decisions.

- Workers must receive good feedback so they can SCORE and ADJUST their performance, correct their AIM, and ACT appropriately.

- Performance measures must be objective, valid and reliable so each employee can be evaluated on legitimate criteria. Subjective traits that are irrelevant to work quality should not be used.

- Differences in the range of performance possible from individuals must be large enough to be noticed and important enough to be worthy of differential consequences. *Don't sweat the small stuff that doesn't count.*

- Supervisors must be adequately trained in performance review and appraisal methods. They must know the basics of performance management and how to evaluate employee performance.

- Supervisors and other appraisers must be willing to provide frank, honest, and credible feedback and evaluations to subordinates.

- There must be sufficient mutual trust between supervisors and subordinates that a performance appraisal and merit pay decision is accepted as fair.

- The merit system must not pit employees in competition against each other but against their own personal job objectives. Merit plans that encourage rivalry among peers can destroy group spirit, damage team cooperation and sabotage the attainment of unit objectives. **Never** install a merit system that reinforces destructive behavior by rewarding people who undercut the performance of their co-workers.

- There must be a firm comitment to pay the financial cost of a merit program.

  - Better performers must get higher pay.
  - Pay ranges must be wide enough to permit significant pay differences between employees with varying sustained performance levels who hold the same basic job.
  - If general employee performance greatly exceeds original expectations, the merit budget should be increased to allow appropriately greater rewards for the improved financial results. And vice-versa. There is not much true "merit" in a merit budget that is spent as planned despite major changes in the meritorious performance of the employees.

- Current pay rates and structures must meet reasonable standards of external competitiveness and internal equity. If the organization barely pays enough to retain competent people, then the "merit pay" may improve retention but will not be very effective as an incentive for better work.

These conditions are difficult to meet even in private industry, where management has far more control over operations and finances than in the public sector. Failure to meet some criteria will limit the effectiveness of a merit pay program. Failure to meet many of the conditions will make merit pay either impossible or undesirable.

Although the concept of merit pay based on individual performance is popular in America and consistent with capitalistic philosophical principles, it is not universally appropriate at all times and in all places. For example, few public school systems can meet many of the essential preconditions for a merit pay program. And even many politicians who call for merit pay for others have successfully resisted its imposition on their incomes.

Whenever the minimum standards for admission to the work class are high and there is little opportunity for variable personal merit to be accurately and credibly measured, pay for membership, experience, or seniority is popular. Some merit pay may be added for such jobs, but the major burden of compensation progression is wisely reserved for other methods when the conditions for merit pay are not favorable.

Pay Progression Methods, Discussed and Demonstrated

The progression of individual employee pay through a pay grade or range can take place in a number of ways.
- general increases
- cost of living increases
- promotional increases
- step progression
- merit increases
- adjustments

General Increases

The very simplest are **General** or **Across-the-Board Increases**. Equal dollar amounts or percentages of current salary are granted to all members of an eligible group.

Cost of Living Increases

General increases that are tied to a **cost-of-living** index are typically awarded in the amount of a certain number of cents per hour for changes in the Consumer Price Index published by the U.S. government.

Formal Cost of Living Adjustments (known as COLAs) are usually found only in contracts and labor agreements. They are tied to a government price index figure that measures the rate of change in the cost of buying certain specific goods and services in a given location. There is no one-for-one correspondence between increases in the index and in pay, but a formula. A typical COLA clause formula would produce a 6% pay increase (computed in cents per hour) from a 10% increase in the Consumer Price Index (computed as the ratio of today's prices to the prices for the specific market basket of goods and services in the base year).

Cost of living adjustments always go up, never down. They are seen as entitlements which increase wages and salaries without any personal responsibility from workers, and are therefore jealously guarded by those diminishing numbers who still receive them.

The scientific connection between "cost of living" figures and pay is tenuous, at best. No research has ever established any significant positive predictive correlation relationship between cost of living and salary, except in those occupations where wage increases have historically been tied to the Consumer Price Index.

National price costs, which are preferred for most COLA programs, rarely have much application to the wages of individual employees who live in areas where local prices ...and wages... are far different from the national norm. As noted earlier, local wages and prices often show opposite conclusions. There are many cities like Dallas and Houston where wages are above the national average while living costs are below average. And there are cities like Boston and Baltimore where living costs are far above the national norm while pay rates languish around or below the average. Even in New York City, there are tremendous differences between the cost of living for Manhattan workers who **actually live** in Queens, Brooklyn, Long Island and Scarsdale.

The information in living-cost reports is therefore usually not particularly relevant to the typical worker. The most authoritative data on living costs comes from government (and a few private) surveys of the cost of certain limited items in certain limited locations. If someone does not live in the survey area and does not regularly buy the exact goods and services surveyed, then that person has not experienced the living costs measured by the survey.

And, even if a worker has suffered higher living costs, why should that be the measure of the value of their work to the employer? Very few people expect to get a raise **because** they moved into a more expensive house and thus voluntarily increased the cost of supporting their enhanced lifestyle. People who demand that their pay be raised because "living costs" increase are the same ones who would look shocked if you suggested that their pay should be reduced when their living costs go down.

While employers can be forced into accepting a cost of living pay policy as the only alternative to a crippling work stoppage, the vast majority prefer to follow the more sensible method of basing pay on competitive rates in the area, modified by internal equity considerations. Those who follow the labor market can be assured that if the living costs in a given area actually do rise to a level that affects pay, that will become evident when they recruit new workers; and it will be documented and confirmed in salary budgeting and pay planning surveys long before competitive labor pressures result in pay rate increases.

More information on this little-understood subject is covered in the author's article, "**Cost of Living Increases**: A Legal Euphemism for Lifestyle Choices ," **Personnel Journal**, Costa Mesa, California; November, 1984.

Step and Merit Increases

A series of charts illustrating **step** and **merit** increase methods from the American Compensation Association/American Society for Personnel

Administration *Elements of Sound Base Pay Administration* are analyzed next.

Comments on the relative advantages and disadvantages of each method have been added to demonstrate what a performance manager can expect from each.

B–1

Step Increases—Separate Performance Tracks

Performance Level	Minimum	12 Months	12 Months	12 Months	12 Months	Performance Zone Maximum	(Source of Zone Maximum)
1	$960	$1,056	$1,152	$1,248	$1,344	$1,440	(Range Maximum)
2	$960	$1,032	$1,104	$1,176	$1,248	$1,320	(Midpoint ÷ 10%)
3	$960	$1,008	$1,056	$1,104	$1,152	$1,200	(Range Midpoint)

Advantages	Disadvantages
Defines dollar amounts.	Does not communicate increase %.
Larger increases for improved performance.	Relatively smaller increases for sustained high performance.
Improved performer can reach max.	Perceived inequity: no advantage for consistently high performer compared to formerly poor performer who suddenly gets high rating.
If performance drops, increase drops.	Slight performance slippage is punished excessively, with no increase possible if already at the Zone Maximum.
Increase dollars can be allocated to keep proper pay differential between old and new employees.	Increase amounts must be revised annually to reflect market changes.
Track Table is customized to fit the proper pay progression for a specific job.	Different Track Tables must be constructed for different jobs.

B–2

Step Increase
Performance Tracks, Plus Timing Differences

Performance Level	Minimum	Step 1	Step 2	Step 3	Step 4	Performance Zone Maximum
1	$960	$1,056 (6 mos.)	$1,152 (6 mos.)	$1,248 (9 mos.)	$1,344 (9 mos.)	$1,440 (12 mos.)
2	$960	$1,032 (6 mos.)	$1,104 (9 mos.)	$1,176 (12 mos.)	$1,248 (12 mos.)	$1,320 (12 mos.)
3	$960	$1,008 (12 mos.)	$1,056 (12 mos.)	$1,104 (12 mos.)	$1,152 (12 mos.)	$1,200 (12 mos.)

Advantages

Same as B–1

Faster increases, with compounding, for better performance.

Originally low performers will never earn as much as fast as consistently high performers.

Disadvantages

Same as B–1

Variable timing requires more frequent reviews, not always followed by raises.

An originally-low performer may get stuck on a 12-mo. review cycle and miss faster increases when the 12-mo. review shows he/she was eligible for a 6 or 9-mo. increase

B–3

Merit Increase Guidelines—Fixed Timeframe

Performance Rating	Fixed Increase Amount	or	Discretionary Increase Range
Outstanding	11%		10-12%
Consistently Exceeds Standards	9%		7-10%
Consistently Meets Standards	7%		5-7%
Occasionally Meets Standards	5%		0-5%

<u>Advantages</u>

Communicates % increase.

Allows limited management discretion.

Consistently high performers will earn large amounts due to compounding.

Extremely simple to communicate and apply.

<u>Disadvantages</u>

Does not specify dollar amounts.

A poorer performer can earn as much as a better performer, if discretionary ranges overlap between ratings.

Creates in-range distribution spread: higher-paid (or more senior) employees will receive increasingly greater dollar amounts than lower-paid (or more junior) employees.

Over time, high-performing junior employees will never catch up to lower-performing senior employees.

Extremely difficult to replace this approach with one that will decelerate increases for "overpaid" employees.

B–4

Merit Increase Guidelines—Fixed Timeframe

Performance Rating	Fixed Increase Amount	or	Discretionary Increase Range
Outstanding	11%		10-12%
Consistently Exceeds Standards	9%		7-10%
Consistently Meets Standards	7%		5-7%
Occasionally Meets Standards	5%		0-5%

Advantages

Appears as simple as B–3.

All increases granted once a year.

Communicates % increase.

Dollar increase amounts will be the same for all employees with the same performance ratings and grade midpoints regardless of their current pay amounts.

Increase rates, as a percentage of current pay, will be higher for better performers whose current pay is low and lower for poorer performers whose current pay is high.

Allows limited management discretion.

Very easy to budget precisely.

Disadvantages

Actually more complex than B–3, and often more difficult to explain.

Impossible to grant increases more rapidly than annually.

Employees may not understand why % increase is applied to grade midpoint.

Higher paid employees may complain that their current pay increases at a lower % than that of more junior employees.

Provides a purely symmetrical reward structure.

A poorer performer can earn same midpoint percentage as a better performer (and a higher % increase to current pay) if discretionary increase percentages overlap between ratings.

B–5

Merit Increase Based On Quartiles—Fixed Timeframe

Position In Range Before Increase

Performance Rating	1st Quartile Or Below	2nd Quartile	3rd Quartile	4th Quartile
Outstanding	x + 8%*	x + 6%	x + 4%	To Maximum
Consistently Exceeds Standards	x + 6%	x + 4%	x ÷ 2%	x%
Consistently Meets Standards	x + 4%	x + 2%	x%	No Increase
Meets Standards Occasionally	To Minimum If Below	No Increase	No Increase	No Increase

*x = Range movement for current increase period

Advantages	Disadvantages
Clarifies precise amount of net increase after competitive grade range adjustment.	Communication of precise competitive grade range adjustment amount may lead employees to perceive that as COLA and dispute it as inadequate.
Increases granted once a year; all employees earn at least grade minimum.	Best performers may lose motivation if rewards granted only once a year.
Communicates % applied to current pay.	Employees with same rating and same quarterly position will receive same %, but those with higher base pay will get larger dollar amounts.
Accelerates pay of high performers whose current pay is low and decelerates pay increase rate of those earning over midpoint.	Consistently high-performing and high-paid senior employees will complain of inequity . . . their increase rate will be lower than more junior employees with lower performance ratings.

B–6

Merit Increase Guidelines—Variable Timing

Position In Range Before Increase

Performance Rating	1st Quartile	2nd Quartile	3rd Quartile	4th Quartile
Outstanding	x + 8% (6-9 months)	x + 6% (9-12 months)	x + 4% (12 months)	To Maximum (12-15 months)
Consistently Exceeds Standards	x + 6% (6-9 months)	x + 4% (10-12 months)	x + 2% (12-15 months)	x% (15-18 months)
Consistently Meets Standards	x + 4% (9-12 months)	x + 2% (12 months)	x% (12-15 months)	No Increase
Meets Standards Occasionally	To Minimum If Below	No Increase	No Increase	No Increase

<table>
<tr><th style="text-align:center">Advantages</th><th style="text-align:center">Disadvantages</th></tr>
</table>

Advantages	Disadvantages
Clarifies precise amount of new increase after competitive grade range adjustment.	Communication of precise competitive grade range adjustment amount may lead employees to perceive that as COLA and dispute it as inadequate.
Communicates % applied to current pay.	Employees with same rating and same quarterly position will receive same %, but those with higher base pay will get larger dollar amounts.
Accelerates pay of high performers whose current pay is low and decelerates pay increase rate of those earning over midpoint.	Consistently high-performing and high-paid senior employees will complain of inequity . . . their increase rate will be lower than more junior employees with lower performance ratings.
Faster increases, with resulting compounding advantage for higher-performing employees.	Requires frequent reviews to assure high-performers eligible for earlier increases are identified. All reviews will not result in increases.
Slower increases for employees over midpoint will limit exesssive pay problems.	Good or superior performers may lose motivation if no increase received in over a year.
Annual payroll costs can be reduced by ability to budget no increases in a current year for some senior employees.	Rapidly changing competitive market conditions may create a situation where one-year range movement can seriously disrupt salary budgets and increase plans based on 15-18 mo. increases.

B–7

SALARY INCREASE GUIDECHART

WHEN THE PERCENTAGE OF POSITION VALUE IS

AND WHEN THE PERFORMANCE APPRAISAL IS		75%	80%	85%	90%	95%	100%	105%	110%	115%	120%	125%
1	Performance results consistently meet and frequently exceed the desired results.	20% 6M	19% 8M	18% 10M	17% 10M	16% 12M	15% 12M	13% 12M	11% 12M	9% 14M	7% 16M	6% 18M
2	Performance results consistently meet, occasionally exceed and seldom fall short of desired results.	15% 8M	14% 10M	13% 10M	12% 12M	11% 12M	10% 12M	9% 12M	7% 12M	6% 14M	5% 16M	
3	Performance results normally meet, rarely exceed, and occasionally fall short of desired results.	11% 10M	10% 12M	9% 12M	8% 12M	7% 12M	6% 12M	5% 12M	4% 14M			
4	Performance results sometimes meet, seldom exceed, and often fall short of desired results.	8% 12M	7% 12M	6% 12M	5% 12M	4% 12M						
5	Performance results occasionally meet desired results—improvement is needed.											

This chart is designed to provide guidance for normal salary recommendations, as determined by management and competitive trends. These recommendations are subject to revision in response to changing competitive practices or government action. Please note that this is a "guidechart"; variance from suggested increase percentages is expected.

Advantages

Same as B–6, except a) it does not define the precise amount of grade adjustment; (b) nonsymmetrical increase %'s may be used.

Disadvantages

Same as B–6 except a) employees will not be told the precise amount of grade adjustment.

How to Choose Between the Two Increase Timing Options: Simultaneous or Anniversary

Wage and salary increases can be given at different times for different reasons and with different effects.

The performance manager should review the pros and cons of each alternative to better understand the consequences of each approach.

THE TIMING OF SALARY INCREASES

The Pros and Cons of Same-Time v. Variable-Interval Increases

Same-time pros & cons

ADVANTAGES of Same-Time Increases

Simultaneous increases discourage employees from seeking or expecting increases at other times.

Easy to plan and budget increases right before action time. Little possibility of performance change before increases are granted.

Cash flow is easily predicted and controlled. Known, fixed cost.

Simple to administer either manually or on computer.

Offers greater probability of consistency in performance appraisals, communications, and reward treatment.

Permits all increases to be based on the same full fiscal-year results.

Performance appraisal gets high visibility and attention at the same time throughout the firm.

DISADVANTAGES of Same-Time

Large one-time cash flow cost.

Everyone compares amounts or percentages of increase at the same time. Stimulates inequity complaints.

Variable pros & cons

ADVANTAGES of Variable-Interval

Variable-timed increases occur on anniversary of hire or promotion and are therefore personalized.

By varying the interval, can reward closer to occasion of the best work.

Can change or alter reward intervals for reasons of individual merit, range caps or company finances.

Can adjust increase amounts or intervals at any time during the year to reflect new circumstances.

Reduces employee tendency to compare increases (they occur at different times under different conditions).

Develops good management performance appraisal habits (appraisals are done constantly through the year).

Can "close out pay accounts" of those promoted/transferred to new departments.

DISADVANTAGES of Variable-Interval

Hard to plan, budget and control. Total cost is often unknown.

The need to guess future performance may result in self-fulfilling prophesies or forced distributions that ignore actual merit.

High probability that supervisors may be afraid to differentiate between employees who will compare and challenge decisions.

Supervisors may allocate increases in a biased or inconsistent manner.

Supervisors tend to compare employee personalities rather than work output during evaluations.

Supervisors may abuse the merit system because of budget limits.

Those who do their best work just before increase time may receive inappropriately larger rewards.

Employees may expect or demand increases at any time.

Little incentive to stay or improve performance right after "the day." No more rewards for another year.

Individual performance review periods may overlap or not fit fiscal year cycles.

Difficult to administer manually.

Same-Time Pay Plan

THE PERFORMANCE-BASED DISTRIBUTION OF SAME-TIME MERIT OR BONUS AWARDS

Here is a new and fool-proof method for the same-time distribution of a fixed merit or bonus fund pool in a variable manner consistent with performance incentives and budget limits.

It overcomes all the usual problems encountered in trying to:
1. Grant rewards proportional to performance;
2. Eliminate the prejudicial effect of current salary on rewards;
3. Stay within budget even when other factors change;
4. Avoid forced performance distribution systems.

Organizations that grant merit increases (or bonuses) to employees at the same time will receive the greatest benefit from this method. It has a more limited application when increases are given on anniversary dates or at times that vary by individual throughout the year.

There are four steps to the process, which is implemented at the end of the performance period under review.

STEP 1

THE PERFORMANCE RATING DETERMINED FROM A PERFORMANCE APPRAISAL IS CONVERTED INTO PERFORMANCE UNITS.

Table 1 illustrates how any ordinal, alphabetic or adjectival summary Performance Ratings can be translated into interval numeric values called "Performance Units" which incorporate state of the art reward theory. The table has a minimum threshold below which reward units are not granted, so the lowest performance ratings earn no reward, while the Performance Unit values ascend in ever-larger increments as performance exceeds normal expectations.

TABLE 1
FOR THE CONVERSION OF PERFORMANCE RATINGS TO PERFORMANCE UNITS

PERFORMANCE RATING CATEGORY DESCRIPTIONS			PERFORMANCE UNITS
(Ordinal)	(Alphabetic)	(Adjectival)	
5	A	Outstanding	14
4	B	Excellent	9
3	C	Good	6
2	D	Fair	4
1	F	Poor	0

Table 1 is used in the example identified as Exhibit A.

TABLE 2
FOR THE CONVERSION OF PERFORMANCE RANKS TO PERFORMANCE UNITS

PERFORMANCE RANK	ADJECTIVE	PERFORMANCE UNITS
90-100th %ile	Outstanding	6
70-89th %ile	Excellent	3.5
30-69th %ile	Good	2
10-29th %ile	Marginal	1
1-9th %ile	Inadequate	0

Table 2 shows how a rank-order approach to performance ratings, using percentile bands, can also be applied.

Some organizations prefer a "totem pole" appraisal method that simply ranks all employees from the top to the bottom, from the best down to the worst, from the most valuable to the least valuable, etc., without the need for semantically-loaded adjectives. (N.B.: if you do use adjectives, never use the term "average" to describe performance).

As individual achievement of work results rises above maintenance levels and exceeds competent levels, the number of performance reward units increases in an upward-curving manner that provides greater incentive and reinforcement for further improvement. For example, "Poor" work results are not worthy of reward because they do not meet minimum acceptable standards, while "Fair" performance earns the lowest reward; to go from "Fair" to "Good" is not worth as much as to go from "Good" to "Excellent," and the greatest incentive reward is for those who go from "Excellent" to "Outstanding."

STEP 2

THE PERFORMANCE UNITS GENERATED FROM EACH PERFOR-MANCE RATING ARE MULTIPLIED BY THE POSITION VALUE OF THE INDIVIDUAL'S JOB TO PRODUCE PAY UNITS.

Position Value may also be known as "job value," "grade midpoint," "control point," "fully qualified rate," or whatever other term is used in the organization to signify the value of the job rather than the value of the person holding it.

Basing the reward distribution on Position Value rather than on actual salary serves the same purpose as a merit increase grid using range position or comp-ratio. All such approaches are designed to modify same-performance-level increase rates to prevent past salary history from prejudicing current rewards. If flat percentages are applied to the base salaries of incumbents, it will perpetuate and exacerbate "once low, always low" and "once high, always high" internal pay relationships.

This method instead bases payouts on the job value. Thus, when employees have the same Performance Ratings and the same job values, the salary growth of low-paid individuals is accelerated while the salary growth of high-paid individuals is decelerated. This is vital, to permit high- performing new people to gradually catch up with more senior peers who are content to coast on their past laurels.

The Performance Units and these new Pay Units are the basic reward units.

Once the next step has been completed (computation of the Budget Factor), Performance Units are multiplied by the Budget Factor to produce the proper increase percentage which, when applied to individual Position Value, will produce individual merit or bonus dollars that will always add up to the exact total of the budget pool. Likewise, Pay Units multiplied by the Budget Factor will yield the precise merit or bonus dollars necessary to expend the total budget pool.

STEP 3

THE BUDGET FACTOR IS COMPUTED BY DIVIDING THE TOTAL BUDGET POOL BY THE SUM OF INDIVIDUAL PAY UNITS (THE

PRODUCTS OF EACH INDIVIDUAL'S POSITION VALUE TIMES THEIR PERFORMANCE UNITS).

The value of the resulting Budget Factor is the value of each Pay Unit in dollars and the value of each Performance Unit as a percentage of Position Value.

The value of the Budget Factor in a given year will thus vary according to the performance of the individuals, the values of their jobs and the size of the total budget pool to be distributed.

STEP 4

DISTRIBUTE THE MERIT INCREASES OR BONUS AWARDS, DESCRIBING THE REWARD IN TERMS OF PERCENTAGE OF POSITION VALUE AND/OR PERCENTAGE OF BASE SALARY.

Although most employees tend to compare rewards in terms of percentage of base salary, it is important for them to recognize that their rewards are affected by the value of their jobs as well as by the size of their base salary. Under this process, two individuals in the same position with the same performance will receive the same dollars; that reward will be exactly equal as a percent of Position Value, but it could be different as a percent of each individual's base salary.

CONCLUSION

This reward allocation program is self-adjusting as well as motivationally appropriate. It allows you to distribute funds according to the actual circumstances that exist at the end of the year but which could not have been accurately predicted at the beginning of the year, such as:

- larger or smaller budget pools;
- unpredictable or changed job values and base salaries;
- unknown or not-normally-distributed **Performance Ratings**.

The Performance Unit table assures that awards will be distributed in a manner proportional to merit and consistent with modern motivational principles.

Forcing Performance Rating distributions with quotas tends to destroy the credibility of merit programs and creates self-fufilling prophesies which may not match reality. You no longer need to risk the hazards of "budgeting" Performance Appraisal Rating categories in order to assure that fixed reward percentages do not produce reward dollars that exceed the budget. Nor must you ever again be pressured to expend either more or less than the actual budgeted amount because of honest performance evaluations that deviate from what was anticipated at budget-setting time.

This flexible allocation system will always fit the budget precisely while simultaneously distributing rewards which vary according to actual personal performance and job value.

EXHIBIT A

SAMPLE BUDGET DISTRIBUTION WORKSHEET

Where the Budget Pool is fixed at 6% of Total Position Values or 5.58% of Total Base Salaries ($71 K).

($ in 000s)

Job Title	Base Salary	Position Value	(STEP 1) Perf. Rating	(STEP 2) Perf. Units	Pay Units	Award $	(. . . STEP 4 . . . . .) Award as a % of Position Value	Award as a % of Base Salary
Exec. VP	$145	$130	5/A/Outstd	14	1820	$12.7	9.8%	8.8%
Sr. VP - Admin.	$110	$110	4/B/Exclnt	9	990	$ 6.9	6.3%	6.3%
Sr. VP - Operations	$120	$110	3/C/Good	6	660	$ 4.6	4.2%	3.8%
Sr. VP - Planning	$ 90	$110	2/D/Fair	4	440	$ 3.1	2.8%	3.4%
VP - Data Processing	$ 93	$ 95	1/F/Poor	0	0	$ 0.0	0.0%	0.0%
VP - Production	$ 87	$ 95	5/A/Outstd	14	1330	$ 9.3	9.8%	10.7%
VP - Finance	$ 83	$ 89	4/B/Exclnt	9	801	$ 5.6	6.3%	6.8%
VP - Engineering	$ 89	$ 89	4/B/Exclnt	9	801	$ 5.6	6.3%	6.3%
VP - Communications	$ 92	$ 85	4/B/Exclnt	9	765	$ 5.3	6.2%	5.8%
VP - Legal	$ 72	$ 75	4/B/Exclnt	9	675	$ 4.7	6.3%	6.5%
Asst. VP	$ 68	$ 65	3/C/Good	6	390	$ 2.7	4.2%	4.0%
Asst. VP	$ 60	$ 65	5/A/Outstd	14	910	$ 6.4	9.8%	10.7%
VP - Human Resources	$ 74	$ 65	4/B/Exclnt	9	585	$ 4.1	6.3%	5.5%
	$1273	$1183			10167	$71.0		

(STEP 3)

Budget Factor = Total Budget ÷ Total Pay Units = Budget Factor

$$\frac{71}{10167} \div = .00698$$

Individual Award as a ratio of Position Value = Individual Performance Units x Budget Factor

Individual Award $ = Individual Pay Units x Budget Factor

Sample Pay Policies that Give Specific Guidance

Good pay policies provide guidance to the performance manager. They
- maintain proper management consistency in compliance with company policies
- anticipate problems and provide preventive/contingent measures
- explain the logic and rationale behind procedures
- leave room for managerial discretion in areas where rigid policies and procedures are unnecessary

The samples that follow reflect a great deal of careful thought about how hiring rates, promotions, transfers and ajustments will affect the performance of employees.

One special feature of this enterprise's pay program is their use of *entry rate* as their measure of *job value*. Most firms use a labor market average or grade midpoint as the job or position target pay value. Here, this rapidly-growing organization found little relevance to the average rates paid by more staid, longer established companies.

They found that the *entry rate* or minimum hiring rate below which they could not find qualified applicants was far more useful as a reference guide for salary administration. With the market clearing rate or *entry rate* as the basis of comparison for each job's value, they were able to
- ▷ assure adequate hiring rates
- ▷ respond more swiftly to employment marketplace changes
- ▷ remind managers of the replacement cost of employees
- ▷ win stronger executive support for pay progression methods adequate to keep the pay of more senior employees ahead of accelerating hiring rates that would otherwise have caused *salary compression*
- ▷ ignore the "average" because neither the firm nor its employees wished to be average (a subtle but positive semantic point)
- ▷ permit variable range maximums or "caps" to job pay, leaving it up to management to justify whether a long-service senior employee is really worth 50% more than the cost of a qualified replacement

The major effect the reader will see is a slightly different meaning to *comp-ratio* (or *compa-ratio*) references. In all pay structure schemes, a comp-ratio of 1.00 represents a case where the actual salary and the job value are identical; 1.05 means that the employee's salary is 5% higher than the target job value; and .95 shows the employee being paid almost up to the target job value. It works the same way here, but the target job value in this example is not the average competitive rate but the minimum **entry rate**.

In this example, where the job value equals the current minimum hiring/entry rate, a comp-ratio of 1.00 means the employee is earning the lowest rate that would be offered a new hire; and a .95 comp-ratio means that they are working for less than the company expects to have to pay for a brand-new person from the outside.

How to Pay New Hires

RULE: New hires must meet all job requirements specified in the Position Description and should be paid at or above (depending on qualifications) the Entry Rate for the job.

EXCEPTION: If job peers (current employees who perform competently in identical or equivalent jobs) are paid below the Entry Rate, new hires may initially be paid below the Entry Rate for reasons of internal equity.

PRACTICE:

A) The proper hiring rate is the Entry Rate, in most cases. Hiring rates that vary from the Entry Rate are authorized only in cases when candidates for employment exceed the job requirements or when special internal equity factors intervene, as specified below.

To determine whether the proper hiring rate should be higher than the Entry Rate, assess the length of time it should take the new hire to learn the job well enough to perform it adequately. Consider the job demands (per Factor D: Learning Time) and the qualifications of the Job candidate. Then the hiring rate would normally fall within the proper comp-ratio (C/R) indicated for people with such qualifications.

Remember that (in our company) comp-ratio (C/R) represents the actual starting salary divided by the Entry Rate, which is the foundation of our salary administrations system. So if you offer a starting salary of $210 a week and the Entry Rate for that job is $200 a week, the comp-ratio (C/R) is 210 divided by 200 = 1.05

Factor D (Learning Time)	C/R for new hire with minimum qualifications	C/R for new hire with maximum qualifications
1. (one month or less)	1.00	1.00-1.01
2. (1 to 3 months)	1.00-1.015	1.01-1.02
3. (3 to 6 months)	1.00-1.02	1.03-1.04
4. (6 mo. to 1 year)	1.00-1.03	1.05-1.07
5. (1 to 2 years)	1.00-1.05	1.08-1.11
6. (2 to 4 years)	1.00-1.08	1.12-1.20
7. (more than 4 years)	1.00-1.12	1.13-1.30

B) Determine whether internal equity requires temporary hiring rates below the Entry Rate, until such time as all employees can be brought up above their Entry Rates.

Are job peers (current employees in equivalent jobs) paid above the Entry Rate?

If YES, then Maximum Hire Rate = Entry Rate times C/R.

If NO, then Maximum Hire Rate = Salary of lowest-paid job peer times C/R

EXAMPLE 1

A) The best candidate meets minimum entry requirements (per Factor A: Education and Experience) of a job that normally requires 6 months to one year of on-the-job learning here for adequate performance of all job duties and responsibilities.

A Learning Time requirement of 6 mo. to 1 year warrants a comp-ratio of 1.00 to 1.03 for a new hire with minimum qualifications.

B) All job peers are paid above the Entry Rate, so the proper hiring rate is Entry Rate times C/R.

GUIDELINE: New Hire Rate = from 1.00 to 1.03 of the Entry Rate.

EXAMPLE 2

A) The best candidate greatly exceeds the minimum entry requirements of a job that normally requires 1-2 years of on-the-job learning here for adequate performance of all job duties and responsibilities.

A learning Time requirement of 1-2 years authorizes a C/R of 1.09 for a new hire with minimum qualifications and a C/R of 1,12 for a new hire with maximum qualifications. Since this candidate has qualifications which are somewhere between the minimum and maximum, his or her C/R should be between 1.10 and 1.11.

B) All job peers are paid above the Entry Rate, so the proper hiring rate is Entry Rate times C/R.

GUIDELINE: New Hire Rate = from 1.10 to 1.11 of the Entry Rate.

EXAMPLE 3

A) The best candidate somewhat exceeds minimum entry requirements of a job that normally requires 2-4 years of on-the-job learning at here for adequate performance of all job duties and responsibilities.

Learning Time for this job and qualifications of this candidate suggest a C/R of 1.04 to 1.08.

B) Some job peers (all competent performers) are paid below the Entry Rate; so the proper hiring rate is the salary of the lowest-paid job peer times C/R.

GUIDELINE: New Hire Rate = 1.06 of salary of lowest-paid job peer.

How to Pay Someone Who Is Promoted

RULE: A promotion is the official delegation of significantly greater responsibilities to an employee. A promotion occurs when an employee is assigned to a new job whose value (Entry Rate) is at least 5% higher than the value of the previous position held by the employee.

         Upon promotion, the employee will receive whatever merit increase was accrued from the old position and will be considered for a promotional increase to bring his or her salary into line with the proper value of the new job.

SPECIAL NOTES:

1. A title change is not necessarily a promotion. The test of a promotion is at least a 5% increase in job value due to new duties or responsibilities, without regard for title.

2. Late recognition that an employee's position description is out of date and that their job was therefore incorrectly evaluated too low in the past may call for an Adjustment, but that is not a Promotion (see Adjustment).

RULE: Promotional increases shall be computed after accrued merit increases are granted and shall normally be the amount required to bring the employee's salary up to the Entry Rate of the new job or 5% of base salary (whichever is greater).

EXCEPTION: If, after the accrued merit increase from the old job, the base salary of the promoted employee already substantially exceeds the proper pay level for established performers in the new job (new job peers), a promotional increase may not be granted.

PRACTICE:

A) Is the Entry Rate of the new job at least 5% higher than the Entry Rate of the old job?

If NO, **Stop!** The job change may require an Adjustment, but it is not a Promotion.

If YES, then continue to B.

B) Apply the merit increase accrued from performance in the old job to the employee's base salary. Does the new base salary of the promoted employee, after the accrued merit increase, exceed either the Entry Rate of the new job or the actual salary of the lowest-paid competent job peer?

C) If NO, **go to C-1.**

If YES, will the promoted employee be immediately more effective in the new job than the lowest-paid new-job peer?

If YES, **go to C-1.**

If NO, **Stop!** No promotional increase is due. The accrued merit increase from the old job is adequate to place the promoted employee's salary at the proper level in the new job. (No further pay action is required.)

C-1) Compute the Standard Promotional Increase: the difference between the Entry Rate of the new job and the base salary of the promoted employee after the accrued merit increase.

D) Does the Standard Promotional Increase exceed 5% of the promoted employee's base salary after the accrued merit increase?

If YES, **go to E.**

If NO, the Promotional Increase shall be equal to 5% of base salary after merit (continue to E.)

E) Add the Promotional Increase to the promoted employee's new base salary after the accrued merit increase, to derive the proposed new salary in the new job.

EXAMPLE 1

A) An employee is moved from a job whose Entry Rate is $10,000 to a new job with an Entry Rate of $11,000. The Entry Rate of the new job is more than 5% higher than the Entry Rate of the old job (actually 10% higher), so it is a promotion.

B) The employee was making $10,000 and performing at a level that would warrant a 10% merit increase for one year's work when he was promoted only 6 months after his last increase.

Accrued merit = 10% x 1/2 year = 5% of old Entry Rate = $500 New Base Salary = old base ($10,000) + accrued merit ($500) = $10,500.

C) New Base Salary ($10,500) does not exceed either the Entry Rate of the new job ($11,000) or the actual salary of the lowest- paid competent peer. The Standard Promotional Increase is therefore the difference between the new and old Entry Rates, which is $11,000 - $10,000 = $1,000.

D) The Standard Promotional Increase of $1,000 is greater than 5% of the new base salary (5% of $10,000 is $500); so the Promotional Increase should be $1,000.

E) The Proposed New Salary in the new job is new base salary ($10,500) + $1,000 = $11,500.

EXAMPLE 2

A) An employee is making $20,000 in a job whose Entry Rate is $18,000 when she is given a new job with an Entry Rate of $20,500. The Entry Rate of the new job is more than 5% higher than the Entry Rate of the old job (actually 13.9% higher), so it is a promotion.

B) The employee was performing at a level that would warrant a 12% merit increase for one year's work when she was promoted 9 months after her last increase.

Accrued merit = 12% x ¾ year = 9% of old Entry Rate = $1,620. New Base Salary = old base ($20,000) + accrued merit ($1,620) = $21,620.

C) New Base Salary ($21,620) exceeds the Entry Rate of the new job, which is $20,500.

The promoted employee is not expected to be more effective in her new job than peers; so no promotional increase is due.

EXAMPLE 3

A) An employee making $14,000 is reassigned from a $15,000 job to a $16,000 job, two weeks after her last merit increase. The new job's Entry Rate is 6.7% higher than that of the old job, so it is a promotion.

B) Since the last merit increase was only two weeks ago, there is no accrued merit to be applied from the old job.

C) The employee's New Base Salary (still $14,000) is far below the Entry Rate of the new job and the salary of the lowest-paid new-job peer. A Standard Promotional Increase of 14.3% ($2,000) is needed to bring the promoted employee up to the Entry Rate of the new job.

D) The Standard Promotional Increase of 14.3% is more than 5% of the employee's base salary after accrued merit, so 14.3% ($2,000) is the proper Promotional Increase amount.

E) The promoted employee's new salary of $16,000 bring her up to the new Entry Rate: but she is expected to perform on the new job at a level just below that of 2-year incumbents who are earning around $17,000; and the department plans to hire a less qualified person for the same job next month, at the $16,000 Entry Rate.

Although the Promotion was correctly handled, an additional salary Adjustment may also be appropriate to maintain internal equity. If the promoted employee is truly more valuable in this job than a minimally qualified new hire earning $16,000, while less valuable than 2-year veterans earning $17,000, then her proper pay in the new job should be around $16,500 (3% above the Entry Rate). *See the section on Adjustments for more details.*

How to Make a Pay Adjustment

RULE: All employees should be paid in relation to
1. the value of their jobs (shown by Entry Rate), and
2. their personal performance (merit).

Normal merit increase practices should accelerate the salary growth of high-performing employees who are being paid at or even below their job's Entry Rate. Thus, over a period of time, better performers will move rapidly to a healthy lead position over new hires and less-competent peers.

However, there will be rare cases when an examination of individual employee pay compared to job value and merit performance shows that the employee is being paid inappropriately low.

This is particularly important if actual hiring practices show that minimally-qualified new hires cannot be found to start work at the rate of pay being received by an experienced competent employee.

The next most common case is when a competent veteran employee, due to historical underpayment, is found to be earning a salary that is over the Entry Rate, but barely more than inexperienced new hires or less-capable peers. A good rule of thumb is that a good performer should be earning 3% over the Entry Rate for each year of competent performance on the job: i.e., a four-year veteran should be earning about 112% of the Entry Rate, and a two-year employee should be paid around 1.06 times the Entry Rate. If the employee's actual pay is far out of line with this general guideline, a Salary Adjustment may be necessary to correct the problem and to provide internal equity and/or external competitiveness.

Although Salary Adjustments are generally made at the same time as merit or promotional increases (when it is most likely that past mistakes will be noticed), Adjustments are special ADDITIONS to normal merit or promotional actions, designed to "make the employee whole" before normal merit or promotional policies are applied. Adjustments are required **only** when normal merit or promotional policies will not bring the employee up to the proper pay level within a reasonable period of time.

EXAMPLE 1

Sally was hired into a low-level clerical job years ago. Since then, she has gradually assumed far greater responsibilities than her original job description contained. Today, her updated job description is far different than the job description of other people with the same job title. Her boss, and her boss's boss, both agree that her actual function is very different from that of her former peers who hold the same title; they also agree that her actual duties and responsibilities are necessary to the organization. She is still being paid as a low-level clerk, although a new job evaluation of her actual duties shows that she should be paid 15% more just to bring her up to the Entry Rate for the work she is doing. And she is performing at a level that a new hire could not be expected to reach for two years, at least.

> GUIDELINE: An Adjustment of 21% is called for (15% to bring her to the Entry Rate and 6% for proper positioning above the new hire rate). Even if a title change is made to clearly identify her actual function, the title change and increase are title RECLASSIFICATIONS and salary ADJUSTMENTS rather than a promotion. There is no promotion because no new duties are being assumed; the actual reality of her true job is merely being belatedly recognized.

EXAMPLE 2

George is in the same circumstances as Sally (above), except that he has been doing extra work beyond the parameters of his job description without the knowledge or permission of his supervisors. Now that they recognize that he has actually been doing more important work than his job description requires, they appreciate it; but they do not wish to change his job description from its original form. They want George to give his "old" job first priority, while continuing to assist in occasional more-important duties. They want him to focus on his regular job but are reluctant to discourage him from showing initiative in areas that are not supposed to be his responsibility.

> GUIDELINE: As long as George is being properly paid (which means highly paid for meritorious performance beyond the minimum value of his true job), no adjustment is due. He is officially assigned to a low-level job, so his job value should be low; but his actual salary should be relatively high due to personal merit. If and when his supervisors decide to formally delegate him the greater responsibilities he appears competent to exercise,

then he will be eligible for a Promotion.

EXAMPLE 3

Ruth was hired at a bargain rate. Desperate for a job, she came on board at a pay rate far below normal levels for her initial job. Since then, despite top merit increases and one promotion, her salary still lags the Entry Rate by 20% and is 25% below the salaries of her peers who hold the same job and perform at the same level. For years, she has earned less than the new hires in her job category, whom she routinely trains and out-performs.

> GUIDELINE: The Adjustment procedure exists to correct historical mistakes and to provide internal equity when normal merit and promotional practices are inadequate. An Adjustment of 22-25% is in order, to place her pay above that of less-capable new hires and close to her properly-paid peers.

A Complete Sample of Typical Salary Budget Instructions

A typical set of salary budget instructions for a large corporation will show a more conventional and less detailed approach to pay policies.

October 1, 19XX

To: Supervision

From: Compensation Manager

Subject: 19XX Salary Budget Forecasts

Attached are the 19XX merit increase guidelines, salary ranges and budgeting instructions for your use in budgeting 19XX salary increases for your employees. The Salary Forecast Budget Sheets have been sent to each division Chief Executive for appropriate distribution. You will receive your budget sheets from them after they have removed their copies and made any preliminary recommendations.

If you have any questions regarding the guidelines or budgeting procedures, please call.

Attachment

19XX Salary Budgeting Instructions

1. General - the 19XX merit budget is 8% annualized and 5% for 19XX for each division and the corporation. Both exempt and non-exempt salary ranges have been adjusted by 6% effective January 1, 19XX.

The attached Merit Increase Guidelines for 19XX suggest a range of percent increase based on performance level. The actual percent increase an employee receives may be larger or smaller than the guidelines, however, the average of 8% annualized and 5% for 19XX for merit increases for each division must be adhered to in order to stay within budget.

Budget only for merit increases and known promotions. Otherwise promotions and adjustments should be processed and approved as they become necessary throughout the year and are not part of the merit budget.

A performance appraisal must be given at least annually for all salaried employees and each salary increase must be based on the **actual** performance level of the employee, as observed and documented for the period. NOTE: although budgets are set according to projected performance expectations, it is not uncommon for actual employee performance to vary from the projection, particularly when you must "guess" how performance will be more than a year from now.

2. Completion Date - Salary Budget Forecast worksheets have been given to each Chief Executive, who will distribute them as appropriate. All Salary Budget Forecasts must be returned to the Compensation Department in final approved form no later than November 15, 19XX. January 1, 19XX increases will be prepared for distribution to supervisors by December 1, 19XX, if we receive the worksheets in time.

3. **Effective Date of Information** - The cut-off for the information on the Salary Budget Forecast was September 30, 19XX. Increases that were not fully approved by that date will not be shown in the employees' salary increase histories or in their year-end base salaries. Those increases should be added to the worksheets. Salary increases budgeted for October through December, 19XX are shown as budgeted and included in the year-end salaries. If there are changes to these increases, it should be noted on the worksheet.

4. **Salary Budget Forecast Forms** - We are using a five part form. The last copy should be removed and used as a worksheet by the supervisor or manager to develop the budget forecast. The supervisor or manager should retain this copy for his or her files. The final budgeted increases should be typed on the remaining sheets and returned to the Compensation Department. After the budgets are approved, distribution of the remaining four copies of the form will be as follows: Compensation Department; Controller's Division; and the originating division's Chief Executive and Controller.

5. **Supervisory Increases** - Supervisors will, in most cases, be shown on two budget sheets. A supervisor will be shown on the budget sheet for his or her own expense account along with his or her people and with his or her current salary. Any increases forecasted for 19XX should not be shown on that sheet. The supervisor's manager will receive a sheet that shows only his or her subordinate supervisors. The manager should show the appropriate 19XX salary increase on that sheet.

6. **Forecasted Salary Increases** - Following a review of each employee's performance, use the attached 19XX merit guidelines to determine the recommended salary increases for budgeting.

REMEMBER: THIS IS ONLY A FORECAST OF PERFORMANCE AND SALARY INCREASE. EACH SALARY INCREASE SHOULD BE REVIEWED VERY CAREFULLY AT THE TIME OF SALARY REVIEW AND SHOULD BE BASED ON PERFORMANCE AT THAT TIME.

The forecasted increase should be rounded to the nearest five dollars of monthly salary for non-exempt employees and annual salary for exempt employees. Enter in the appropriate columns of the salary budget worksheets the following information regarding the forecasted salary increase:

- effective date (all merit increases should be on the first of the month). The interval should be calculated from the last regular merit increase, or promotional increase if it was a combination of promotion and merit;

- amount of the increase (monthly and annual);

- number of months since the previous increase (exclude special adjustments or promotions, if they did not include an increment for accrued merit) or, for new employees the date of employment;

- type of increase: M-merit.

- performance appraisal rating on which the merit increase is based.

- total increase amount is the actual cost of the increase to be incurred during 19XX, e.g. a $1200 annual increase effective on 7/1/XX will cost $600 during 19XX.

Increases for newly hired or promoted employees and forecasted hires should be budgeted for merit increases assuming satisfactory performance. The amount of the increase can be adjusted at the time it is processed based on the actual performance level at that time.

Non-exempt employees below their new range minimums on January 1, 19XX, should receive their increases as of that date to bring their salaries within their new ranges. Non-exempt employees in the bottom $\frac{1}{3}$ of their salary ranges may be eligible for two increases during the budget year. Exempt employees below their new range minimums should be budgeted for regular merit increases no later than July 1, to bring them within their salary range.

7. **Vacancies and Additions** - Any approved but unfilled vacancies and/or additional personnel must be shown on the budget sheets under the appropriate account. Include the title, grade, projected employment date, and projected salary.

19XX

MERIT INCREASE GUIDELINES

Generally speaking, performance appraisals should be conducted annually. Annual salary reviews should be based on that appraisal consistent with the following schedule. Each recommended increase must be accompanied by the performance appraisal.

Exempt	Non-Exempt
Outstanding 10-12%	Outstanding 9-11%
Exceptional 8-10%	Exceptional 7-9%
Satisfactory 6-8%	Satisfactory 5-7%

It is anticipated that there will be few merit increases allowed at less than a 12 month interval, with the exception of the early increase program, and as individuals move higher in their salary range, the interval between increases will increase to 15-18 months.

Early Increase Program

New exempt employees or newly promoted exempt employees, in the bottom third of the range of grades 10, 11 or 12, should be considered for a salary increase after 6 months and 12 months service, and annually thereafter.

Non-exempt employees who are in the bottom third of the range should be considered for a salary increase every six months until they are out of the bottom third. The amount of increase should be roughly half of the guideline rate for a 12-month increase.

What a Traditional Grade/Range Pay System Looks Like

The traditional formal pay grades and ranges illustrated here are highly symmetrical around the *midpoint* which represents job value.

They are also separated into two parts: one set of grades for hourly non-exempt employees who are legally entitled to time and one-half overtime; and another higher set of grades and job values for people exempt from the legal requirement for overtime. This was done in the past supposedly because of the loss of overtime pay experienced by people who move from hourly wages or salaries in *non-exempt* jobs to salaried professional, administrative, executive or sales jobs, where the precise job duties meet the **Fair Labor Standards Act** tests to permit the employer to eliminate overtime pay.

As a matter of fact, most major employers today do offer overtime (sometimes on a *straight-time* rather than time and one-half basis) to exempt employees working in close contact with hourly people. The extra overtime pay voluntarily offered by the employer beyond legal requirements has the effect of

- encouraging hourly workers to become exempt supervisors without a loss in total compensation

- satisfying organizational perceptions of *internal equity* in pay between supervisors and subordinates

- reducing the need for a large job value differential between exempt and non-exempt job classes

An additional historical reason for a big jump between the highest non-exempt job job value and the lowest exempt job value was the simple fact that non-exempt hourly clerks tended to be women with low job values, while the first ranks in "management" or professional jobs tended to be males who were traditionally paid more despite having less or little more skill, experience, training, and so on. The rapid influx of women into professional and managerial ranks has changed that situation so that there is little market justification for a wide chasm between the highest clerical and the lowest supervisory job. It is now more common to see an overlap between separate exempt and non-exempt pay grades, with the highest non-exempt technician or hourly specialist able to earn far more than the lowest level of exempt professionals.

Non-Exempt Monthly Salary Ranges

Grade	Bottom ⅓ Minimum		Middle ⅓ Midpoint		Top ⅓ Maximum
1	581	678	726	774	871
2	639	745	799	852	958
3	703	820	878	937	1,054
4	773	902	966	1,031	1,160
5	850	992	1,063	1,134	1,276
6	935	1,091	1,169	1,247	1,403

Grade	Bottom ⅓ Minimum		Middle ⅓ Midpoint	Top ⅓ Maximum	
7	1,029	1,200	1,286	1,372	1,543
8	1,132	1,320	1,415	1,509	1,698
9	1,245	1,452	1,556	1,660	1,867

Exempt Annual Salary Ranges

Grade	Bottom ⅓ Minimum		Middle ⅓ Midpoint	Top ⅓ Maximum	
10	16,320	19,040	20,400	21,760	24,480
11	17,952	20,944	22,440	23,936	26,928
12	19,747	23,038	24,684	26,330	29,621
13	21,722	25,342	27,152	28,963	32,583
14	23,894	27,876	29,868	31,859	35,841
15	26,284	30,664	32,854	35,045	39,425
16	28,912	33,731	36,140	38,549	43,368
17	31,803	37,104	39,754	42,404	47,705
18	34,983	40,814	43,729	46,644	52,475
19	38,482	44,895	48,102	51,309	57,723
20	42,330	49,385	52,912	56,440	63,495
21	46,563	54,323	58,204	62,084	69,844
22	51,219	59,756	64,024	68,292	76,829
23	56,341	65,731	70,426	75,121	84,512
24	61,975	72,304	77,469	82,634	92,963
25	68,173	79,535	85,216	90,897	102,259

What a More Modern Pay Grade/Range System Looks Like

A more modern grade structure has one set of pay grades for all jobs in the enterprise. This simplifies administration and avoids some of the negative employee relations that comes from having "segregated" pay classes that suggest barriers between hourly labor and salaried management.

The change from manual labor to "knowledge" work has blurred some of the old distinctions between labor and management. Even the term "salaried" has undergone an evolution: the increase in service workers paid by timesheets rather than "punching a clock" has led to more people being paid a relatively fixed monthly "salary" just like management, even though the wages of clerks and technicians legally must be computed on an hourly basis to assure compliance with federal overtime law.

One set of pay grades emphasizes the kind of smooth progression employees seek and companies want to offer (or at least want employees to believe is available).

The modern sample also abandons the traditional pay range symmetry in favor of a more realistic philosophy.

The value of employees in jobs that start at the minimum wage level does not increase much: the "worth" of file clerk duties after two years of experience is not much greater than after six months. People are expected to be promoted out of low-value, low-maximum range jobs before many years have passed.

As the normal learning curve for job proficiency gets longer, the distance between minimum entry rates, job values and range maximums increase. This permits more variation in hiring rates and merit pay, taking into account the greater differences in individual employee performance and the higher economic value of the performance of those jobs to the employer.

Also, the job values are not "midpoints" but standard rates representing the pay of the normal fully qualified incumbent in the competitive marketplace. The job values are set at levels consistent with the normal time progression of a competent worker from minimum qualification to the "fully-functional journeyman" level for the kind of job. The more valuable the job, the longer the time/distance for movement from beginner to master of the entire job. As in the real world, there is a lot more room for pay growth above the standard rate than between the midpoint and the job value. The tabular and graphic displays show how valuable senior specialists can be retained by pay far above the normal rate suitable for "average" performers.

Chapter 10:

HOW TO HANDLE DISCIPLINE, TERMINATION AND EXIT INTERVIEWS

In every organization, there are certain actions that cannot be permitted. Behaviors that violate the minimum standards of behavior required of all employees must not be condoned or ignored.

The Role of Discipline in the Performance Cycle

Discipline is an ADJUST step in the performance cycle. It is **communication feedback** that applies negative **reinforcement** after preventive **planning** and **remedial** methods such as **counseling** have proven unsuccessful. Discipline applied as **punishment** provides a negative weight to the **balance of consequences** foreseen by employees when they consider their choices of action.

An organization is a group of people working together towards a common goal. Those members whose behaviors
- endanger the safety of others
- threaten the attainment of vital goals
- are incompatible with organizational needs and expectations

may be subjected to disciplinary action up to and including separation from employment.

Discipline is defined by **Webster's New World Dictionary** (Copyright ©1980, **Simon & Schuster**) as
1. a system of rules; or
2. treatment that corrects or punishes behavior.

Ideally, discipline should be applied to shape positive behavior. Prior chapters emphasized that aspect of *discipline* as a coherent system of rewards and inducements, with the punishment aspect reserved to this chapter.

Punitive discipline is not the most effective way to prevent, correct or remedy performance deficiencies. It is primarily reserved as a negative feedback measure for willful employee actions which, if repeated, seriously imperil the organization and its members.

In the work environment, discipline:

- cannot be fully successful unless it is voluntarily accepted by the workers at all levels;
- involves careful discretionary judgment in its application;
- is directed against the behavior, not against the person;
- is intended to change the performance action rather than the personality of the performer;
- must be designed and periodically reviewed to assure that it actually helps achieve the prime mission goals and objectives of the enterprise;
- should be fair, appropriate and progressive.

Why Punishment Is More a Remedy for the Organization than for the Individual

Punishment always comes too late to give maximum remedial assistance to the one who receives it; its primary purpose is to remove the offender from the unit and to give a public warning (a feedback communication on the consequences of negative behavior) to others who may be deterred from the same course of action. It may be a remedy to remove the threat that the organization would otherwise continue to suffer from the "bad behavior" of a given individual, but it cannot "cure" the offender as well as cooperative **remedial methods**.

Termination, the ultimate organizational disciplinary step, is a recognition of mutual failure.

The Four Major Penalty Levels in Progressive Discipline

Serious problems in employee performance are normally addressed in a series of steps that involve increasingly and *progressively* severe consequences which are appropriate to the risk the organization suffers from the improper employee action.

The short sequence of penalties under a "progressive disciplinary" procedure is:

1. oral warning
2. written warning
3. suspension or disciplinary layoff
4. discharge

The Eight Steps To Take for Effective Progressive Discipline

A more detailed analysis of the entire sequence for progressive discipline shows the intermediate steps, using terms already covered in this workbook.

1. Give normal communication to the employee (a TELL activity)
2. Provide periodic appraisal, review and feedback
   a. TELL what results are desired
   b. TELL what was actually observed
   c. RESOLVE why the discrepancy occurred and how to correct it
   d. SELL the benefits of proper performance
   e. PLAN actions to remedy the problem, PREVENT recurrence, etc.
   f. RESOLVE what will be done by the manager and the employee to correct the problem, get feedback on results, monitor improvement and provide consequences of behavior
3. Apply the appropriate special remedial actions
   a. counseling
   b. coaching
   c. training
   d. practice
   e. clarify expectations
   f. remove obstacles
   g. improve feedback
   h. change consequences
   i. other remedial/corrective/improvement actions
4. Give an emphatic verbal warning
5. Deliver a formal written reprimand or written warning
6. Impose a disciplinary layoff or suspension
7. Place the employee on formal probation
8. Discharge

Each step clarifies the desired performance, investigates the causes of the problem, communicates what must be done to correct the deficiency and makes the consequences of continued "undesirable behavior" clear to the subject.

The process is far more involved than a simple "three strikes and you are out" approach. While that may be sufficient in some cases, some offenses are so grievous that "two strikes" are too many to allow: your policies should specify the types of behavior that will bring immediate discharge, such as unauthorized possession of a firearm on the premises. Likewise, reporting to work one minute late on three occasions in a year is generally not enough to justify summary discharge after the third tardiness.

A Detailed Checklist for Applying Discipline

- ❏ Be sure the employee knows what is wanted or what the rule is.
- ❏ Check the facts of the case. Investigate before jumping to conclusions.
  - ○ determine whether you might exhibit a personal bias
  - ○ ask the employee to report his or her observations
    - explain the reason for the interview
    - solicit information on their viewpoint
    - be considerate of the individual's feelings
    - remain neutral, do not argue and do not pass judgment until all facts are clearly established
    - listen, question and probe
    - let the employee have their say
  - ○ collect information from others involved
  - ○ review the views and motives of others involved
  - ○ document findings, separating confirmed facts from allegations
- ❏ Confirm your authority to take disciplinary action.
- ❏ Consider the seriousness of the improper employee action and make sure your response is appropriate and authorized.
- ❏ Review the employee's past performance record, work history, length of service, behavior habits, demonstrated attitude, etc.
- ❏ Be consistent, considering the circumstances.
- ❏ Do not delay taking action after it has been decided what must be done; be as prompt and timely as possible.
- ❏ Conduct a private disciplinary counseling session.
  - ○ explain the measure to be taken and why, being
    - specific
    - frank and honest
    - tactful
    - open and receptive to employee comments
  - ○ state your expectations for improvement
  - ○ warn of the consequences of continued improper action
  - ○ encourage the employee that the desired improvement will restore a positive management view
- ❏ If you must condemn anything, condemn the action, not the person.
- ❏ Apply discipline in private. Public criticism lowers the effectiveness of

management corrective efforts and turns the process itself into an embarrassing and humiliating personal insult.
- Never be abusive, profane, sarcastic or rude.
- **Document** and file the record of disciplinary action as required for
   - non-discriminatory compliance
   - relevant evidence for future actions should the misconduct be repeated before your "statute of limitations" expires
   - proof of proper and consistent disciplinary process
- Once the deficiency or misconduct has been corrected and/or the formal disciplinary action has been completed, don't "ride" or "nag" the worker who has been disciplined.

How a Point/Demerit System Provides Progressive Discipline

The next exhibit illustrates a disciplinary policy that classifies work rules in a formal schedule. It emphasizes the negative, specifying "disciplinary points" as a measure for progressive action. The actions that constitute grievous offenses versus minor mistakes are clearly defined, along with a process that erases past "demerits" over time while still assuring that employees who consistently violate even minor work rules will be constrained from repetition (or face termination).

Designed for the fire department of a large community, it has a number of unique features. This fire district disciplinary schedule is:
- extremely formal (for application to both union and management);
- harsh on activities that might threaten public safety or public confidence in firefighters or medical emergency personnel;
- more specific than most in its control of employee interactions (male and female fire district employees live and sleep in integrated quarters while on duty);
- geared to the precise working environment of the enterprise.

It shows how the value system of the organization (why it exists and what is most important to it) can, will and should affect the disciplinary system.

A Detailed Policy for Disciplinary Points

Each offense specified in the Disciplinary Policies carries a number of Disciplinary **Points** which provide a simple, clear and fair method of progressive discipline.

Ten Points Means Termination

Only four offenses are so grievous that they always result in 10 points, which means immediate termination.

The accumulation of 10 (ten) active disciplinary points will result in automatic termination for misconduct. Employee appeal rights will be respected.

Two Points Expire Each Year

Any employee balance of accumulated disciplinary points will be reduced by 2 (two) points a year (measured from the date of the first offense which earned disciplinary points). The written reprimand forms (the **Record of Disciplinary Action** form) shall be removed from employee files and destroyed after the same number of years as the number of points earned by the offense.

For example,

If a 2-point offense is committed on June 1, 1990, the two points remain on the employee's balance until they are subtracted from that employee's total balance of accumulated disciplinary points on June 1, 1991. The **Record of Disciplinary Action** form for the offense remains in the employee's file until June 1, 1992 (two years after the date of the two-point offense), when it should be removed and destroyed.

Likewise, the points from a more serious 6-point offense will be reduced to zero in three years if no other offenses are committed, while the reprimand form will be destroyed after SIX years.

An employee who commits a series of offenses will see his or her point balance go down by 2 (two) points every year after the date of the first offense.

To illustrate...

A 6-point offense is committed on January 1, 1990, and a separate 2-point offense on March 1, 1990. That makes a total of 8 active disciplinary points on March 1, 1990. Another 2-point offense before January 1, 1991, will bring the total active points to 10 and result in immediate termination (subject to normal appeal and grievance procedures).

But as of January 1 of each year thereafter, the accumulated total of active disciplinary points for that employee will be reduced by two; so the 8 active points in effect in March, 1990, will be totally erased in 4 years (on January 1, 1994, if the employee commits no further offenses).

DISCIPLINARY ACTIONS CLASSIFIED BY SEVERITY OF OFFENSE

The following policies do not, in any way, invalidate employee rights under law or under a current ordinance.

According to the Fire District Board of Directors, the following offenses shall be documented by a formal written reprimand and shall carry the following penalty:

TEN (10) POINTS AND IMMEDIATE DISCHARGE FOR ...

Code   Offense

D.1 Refusal to follow established required procedures or direct orders dealing with the protection of public life or property.

D.2 Possession or use of any controlled substance while on duty, except for prescription drugs taken with supervisor knowledge.

D.3 Drinking liquor or any alcoholic beverage while on duty.

D.4 Leaving the duty station during work hours without supervisor permission.

D.5 Theft.

TEN (10) POINTS AND IMMEDIATE DISCHARGE FOR THE FOLLOWING (unless the Board determines that significant extenuating circumstances do not justify summary dismissal, in which case the action will bring a minimum penalty of EIGHT (8) POINTS AND A TERMINATION WARNING. WITH EIGHT (8) POINTS, THERE IS ALSO THE OPTION, BASED UPON THE SPECIFIC CIRCUMSTANCES, OF A LAYOFF.)

Code   Offense

C.1 Intentional misuse or removal from District premises without proper authorization of District records, documents, property or confidential information of any nature.

C.2 Concerted or deliberate restriction of work output ... either a slowdown of own work or delaying/interfering with other workers.

C.3 Unauthorized deliberate destruction or damage of property, tools, machines or equipment.

C.4 Immoral conduct or indecency while on duty or while wearing attire that identifies the employee as a member of the Fire District.

C.5 Unauthorized statements or communications which detract from or misrepresent the official policies and practices of the District.

Code   Offense

C.6 Abusive or threatening language or behavior towards the public while on duty or while wearing attire that identifies the employee as a member of the Fire District.

C.7 Willfully falsifying an application for District employment, work reports, or any other work-related data requested by the District.

C.8 Fighting on District premises.

C.9 Refusing to acknowledge receipt of a written reprimand.

SIX (6) POINTS FOR ...

Code   Offense

B.1 Refusing to obey orders of supervisors dealing with work or supervisors' duties.

B.2 Refusing to properly exercise any command responsibilities of your position.

B.3 Refusing to follow the chain of command in an official business situation.

B.4 Failure to report to duty station ready to begin work at starting time without supervisor's prior authorization.

B.5 Unexcused absence.

B.6 Violation of established safety rules or District safety practices.

B.7 Speeding in a non-emergency situation or careless driving of equipment.

B.8 Neglect or mishandling of a District machine or other equipment.

B.9 Violation or conviction of any Federal, State, County or municipal statute, ordinance or regulation that might reduce any employee's ability to perform District duties.

B.10 Violation or conviction of any Federal, State, County or municipal statute, ordinance or regulation that might diminish public trust and confidence in District personnel.

B.11 Organizational or promotional activities for any group without permission of the Board of Directors while on duty, or on District premises, or while wearing attire that identifies the employee as a member of the Fire District.

TWO (2) POINTS FOR ...

Code   Offense

A.1 Smoking on duty outside the fire station without supervisor authorization.

A.2 When identification badges or uniforms are required: failure to wear them properly on duty, or misrepresenting rank or identity.

A.3 Smoking on District premises except in designated areas or with supervisor authorization.

A.4 Unauthorized distribution of written literature or printed matter of any description while on duty or in uniform.

A.5 Horseplay or throwing things while not engaged in authorized sports activity.

A.6 Creating or contributing to unsanitary conditions.

A.7 Allowing unauthorized personnel to enter the work area or operate District machines, tools or other equipment without supervisor permission.

A.8 Posting or removal of notices, signs or writing in any form on any bulletin boards or other surfaces on District property without management permission.

A.9 Obscene, abusive language, the spreading of rumors, or gossip which reflects discredit on District personnel.

A.10 Threatening, intimidating or coercing fellow employees while on duty.

A.11 Gambling for money or any other wagering while on duty or on District premises.

A.12 Unauthorized operation of District machines, tools or equipment.

A.13 Transporting unauthorized personnel in District trucks or automobiles.

A.14 Failure to maintain the security of the District uniform in your care, with the result that any offense under these rules is performed by someone wearing any of your uniform attire that identifies the person as an employee.

A.15 Reporting to work under the influence of intoxicants so that one is not considered able to perform at normal safe levels. (**Employee will also be sent home immediately and his or her pay will be docked for the cost of the replacement's wages.**)

How to Document and Record Disciplinary Steps (CYA)

Written documentation of disciplinary actions are always essential. They are not only necessary to CYA (Cover Your [exposed posterior]), but also to

- ☐ remind managers that disciplinary actions must be taken according to specific guidelines
- ☐ confirm the facts on which the action was based
- ☐ show that an impartial and fair investigation was conducted
- ☐ verify that the employee act was an offense against a previously communicated work rule
- ☐ collect and report relevant historical information on past related offenses
- ☐ determine the application of any progressive disciplinary policy
- ☐ specify the action to be taken
- ☐ permit the review of the action by senior executives before irreversible steps are taken
- ☐ prove that the information about the action and its implications were communicated to the offender

How to Create and Use a Discipline Form to Guide Action

A sample disciplinary form drawn from the earlier policy illustrates how you can put together your own form to remind you of all the information that needs to be documented and the steps that must be taken to comply with the official disciplinary policy.

RECORD OF DISCIPLINARY ACTION

Employee: _____   **Date of offense:** _____

If covered in Employee Manual, circle appropriate Work Rule Group:
A   B   C   D

Details of Offense:
_____

_____

_____
_____
_____
_____

For Group C violations, circle whether the infraction is the: First, Second, Third, Fourth, or Other.
if "Other," describe circumstances.

_____

If covered under Group D, Attendance Standards:
Cite the number of incidents of absence/tardiness and the time period covered:

_____

Action Taken/To Be Taken: _____

_____	_____
Immediate Supervisor	Date
_____	_____
Next Management Level	Date

"I have seen this Record of Disciplinary Action. My signature does not necessarily mean that I agree with this charge, but only that I acknowledge receipt of it."

_____	_____
Employee Signature	Date

(Written employee comments are encouraged and will be attached to this form, if provided.)

How to Design and Complete a Remedial Performance Plan

Every discussion about a serious employee performance deficiency should involve a **remedial performance plan** in which both manager and subordinate reach a common understanding on what must happen next.

The employee deficiency is defined, with the emphasis placed on the *correct* performance that is desired and the shortfall between actual and desired output. Do not dwell all the *wrong* ways to perform: there are usually a great number of ways to go wrong, and much fewer ways to produce the right result. Focus on desired results.

The remedial plan requires commitment by the employee who must produce the results, along with the supervisor's approval of who will do what when and how. An employee who refuses to make any suggestions about remedial actions may merely be confused and uncertain. But one who refuses to accept or implement any reasonable remedial prescriptions may be rejecting the right of managment to establish standards of performance; that is a quick route to termination, unless the employee's standards happen to be much higher than those of management.

The presence of a legitimate remedial plan keeps the disciplinary actions from becoming purely punitive; every effort is made to correct and improve employee performance to acceptable levels.

What to Do When It Is Termination Time

Once an irrevocable decision for termination has been reached by *either* the employer or the employee, management must take action
1. to plan for a replacement or reassign duties
2. to collect company property
3. to preclude employee access to confidential or privileged data
4. to provide information on termination rights and procedures to the departing employee
5. to review the person's opinions about the employer

How to Decide When the Offender Should Leave Work

Formal termination policies show a wide degree of variety in how and when *ex*-employees are sent home permanently.

What Can Happen in Worst-Case Scenarios

Some firms initiate the separation process the minute either party decides the employment relationship will be terminated. People fired for flagrant misconduct are not surprised to be ordered off the premises forever. But good workers who resign voluntarily may also receive a quick escort to the exit door. A friendly notice by an employee that they intend to quit in the future may be met with a command to leave immediately.

There are many legitimate business reasons for such apparently harsh treatment. While it is not always justified, some managers fear that employees who are leaving the organization will

lose interest in continued job performance	Their minds will be elsewhere, thinking about the new job, distracted and unable to give full attention to the duties they are leaving. Their sense of dedication, mission and work urgency will suffer. They are essentially uncontrollable, as well, no longer as responsive to either rewards or punishments as before.
harm the morale of the employee group left behind	A fired worker may become an angry and disgruntled "lame duck" who spreads dissension. A happy voluntary resignee who is moving to a "better" job may call attention to the defects of the employer and brag about the better pay, salary, opportunities, etc., of the new job. Their joyful anticipation at leaving may tempt others to seek other jobs. If quitting is seen as contagious, employers may try to isolate, quarantine or ostracize the potential source of infection.
inhibit the initiative or productivity of their replacements	The helpful advice and training of an "old hand" can be an undue influence against fresh viewpoints and new ideas by a replacement. If trained by the previous incumbent, new trainees might adopt the prejudices and rigid methods of their predecessors without challenge or question. Also, the attitude of a trainer who is planning to quit may not be the most conducive to positive enthusiasm in the new worker.
become a security risk	When someone plans to move to a competitor, a prudent manager may decide to remove them from a position where they would have access to secret company information which they might unconsciously

or deliberately leak to their new employer. Departing employees with customer contact responsibilities might praise your competitor, criticize your products or services or otherwise endanger continued business.

The Way to Make Positive Separations: How to Fire with Minimal Pain on Either Side

Performance managers are advised to exercise **great care** and much caution about negative assumptions about the attitudes and possible behaviors of departing employees. People tend to fulfill the expectations of those they respect. If you treat people as though they are unreliable, you create a *self-fulfilling prophesy* and encourage the very behavior you want to avoid.

Unless you have strong and good information to conclude that there is a high risk to be run by keeping a departing employee on the job until their separation date, with a high probability of serious negative consequences (see the **Potential Problem Analysis** under **Job Posting** in the **Recruiting** chapter), do not assume the worst.

Most employees can be relied on to behave just as dependably before they leave as they did before the termination decision was reached. The way the performance manager handles the termination process can even improve employee output during the final period.

There are many advantages to keeping departing workers on the job until their last available day. People who are leaving voluntarily (or at least without resentment) often demonstrate

a new burst of enthusiasm	The same psychological lift that accompanies a decision to leave often unleashes a fresh wave of energy and revitalizes their pride and productive drive. The last days may see their very best work done, when they feel free to achieve.
increased loyalty and respect	Most people who voluntarily quit when their employer wants them to stay feel a deep and true emotion of gratitude to the firm that has fed them, developed their skills and helped them qualify for the "better" job they have found. When the employer demonstrates trust, that show of faith will

communicate positive expectations and create memories of a decent employer which earns and deserves respect. Happy ex-employees who have "graduated" from your ranks are wonderful ambassadors of good will for your organization.

a test lesson for others

If the firm makes a practice of "canning" people who give notice, sending them home like criminals, then those who plan to leave in the future will quickly learn to give minimum notice or none at all. It is highly preferable to encourage employees to notify the employer when they intend to leave, so you can retain the option of keeping them on the job and take the necessary actions to prepare a replacement for their duties. A pattern of punitive actions towards people who "play fair" with the employer will only inspire distrust, resentment and hostility, as well as destroying any incentive for people to be honest with the company.

better ways to do their jobs

With no threat to job security (having already decided to depart), the old incumbent will often suggest new and improved methods of job performance for their replacement. The insights and experience of the veteran can be critical to the success of a new worker, particularly in highly technical jobs.

Helpful Termination Policies and Checklists

A precise list of all the elements to be covered for the separation process that ends in formal employment termination is recommended for the purpose of consistency and legal/policy compliance. It is easy to forget something that will come back to haunt you.

When a clear policy has been written down and distributed, with a checklist to assure completeness, the task becomes much easier, as the example shows.

A Sample Employee Termination Worksheet

To: Personnel Department

From: _____ Date: _____

C O N F I D E N T I A L

IMPORTANT: Pay will continue until termination information is submitted to Personnel.

This form completed on (date)_____ by (name)_____.

Employee Name:_____ Payroll Number:_____

Address:_____

Date Hired:_____

Last Day Worked (*see below*):_____

Number of Days Vacation Due:_____

Termination Initiated by: □ Employee   □ Management   □ Mutual

Amount of Notice: On _____, □ Employee   □ Manager gave _____ weeks _____ months notice.

(Attach notice, if given in writing.)

Reason for Termination: (Use code from next page) _____

Exit Interview Form Attached? □ Yes   □ No

See Policy for Handling Terminations of Salaried Personnel for guidance on details about termination pay.

Details: (*Attach copy of exit interview form and add any pertinent information not on form.*)

Last day worked and date notice was given may be two different dates. We must know both dates to properly determine amount of pay in lieu of notice due and the effective date of separation.

A List of Reasons for Termination

"REASON FOR TERMINATION" CODES

1. Voluntary Resignation
   a. Other employment, for pay
   b. Other employment, for advancement
   c. Other employment, for pay and advancement
   d. Other employment, miscellaneous
   e. Education
   f. Domestic
   g. Health
   h. Relocation
   i. Other
   j. Self-employment
   k. End temporary assignment
2. Resignation to Avoid Discharge
   a. Resigned in anticipation of a request by management
   b. Forced resignation; submitted resignation after request by management
3. Discharge
   a. for Performance
   b. for Cause (misconduct)
   c. Other
4. Retirement
   a. Regular
   b. Early
5. Long-Term Disability
   a. Long Term Disability
6. Force Reduction
   a. Temporary Force Reduction
   b. Permanent Force Reduction
7. Lay-Off
   a. Subject to Recall
   b. Not Subject to Recall
8. Death
   a. Natural Death
   b. Accidental Death
9. Leave of Absence

    a. Military
    b. Maternity
    c. Paternity
    d. Sabbatical (Educational/Developmental)
    e. Authorized Personal Leave
    f. Emergency Compassionate Leave

A Complete Termination Policy

POLICY FOR HANDLING TERMINATIONS
OF SALARIED PERSONNEL
Effective xx/yy/zz

Voluntary Resignations -

Employees are normally expected to give two weeks notice prior to the effective date of their resignation.

- It is at the company's option if the employee is to continue on his job for the two week notice period.
- When the company elects for the employee not to remain on his job for the notice period, the employee will still continue on the payroll and receive his normal salary plus benefit coverage until the end of the two week notice period.
- The employee will receive pay for any earned but unused vacation left at the time of his termination. This unused vacation time will not extend the effective date of the termination but will be considered a lump sum payment in lieu of vacation. *(See note below.)*

Involuntary Terminations -

- When the company elects to terminate an employee, the following notice time, or pay in lieu of, will be given:

Non-Exempt employees	2 weeks
Exempt employees	1 month

Important Point: Discharge should be preceded by warning/counseling interviews, summarized in writing, so that the employee knows his/her status and has a chance to correct the performance deficiency.

- If notice time is given, the employee continues on the payroll and receives the normal salary plus benefit coverage until the end of the appropriate period.

- If pay in lieu of notice is to be given, the employee remains on the payroll until the last day of the notice period with benefit coverage continuing through the period.
- The employee will receive a lump sum severance payment based on length of service in accordance with the attached schedule.
- Any earned but unused vacation time will be handled by a lump sum payment. This unused vacation time will not extend the effective date of the termination but will be considered a lump sum payment in lieu of vacation. *Note: the company's severance and vacation pay policies are not required by any law but are required to be consistently applied as a matter of formal internal policy.*

Forced Resignations -

- When an employee is given the option to resign from his employment with the company or be discharged, the provisions covering involuntary terminations shall apply. The decision to terminate the employee must be definite so that if the employee fails to resign, then discharge is certain.

Discharge for Cause -

- When there has been a flagrant violation of rules or ethics and the employee is terminated for misconduct, the notice time and severance pay provisions shall be waived and only payment for earned but unused vacation will be made.

Final Pay -

- An employee's final pay will not be released until his or her expense account has been cleared and all monies owed to the company have been paid. When necessary, any remaining monies owed the company will be deducted from the employee's final pay before payment is made.
- All company property such as automobile, time cards, keys, access codes, hospital record cards, sample material, manuals, books, attache cases, credit cards, etc., must be returned before final payment is made.
- Final pay will include the following items when applicable:
  - Salary for the last period worked.
  - Pay in lieu of notice time given or worked.
  - Severance pay according to the policy schedule.

○ Pay in lieu of earned but unused vacation time.
○ Refund of employee's payments plus interest to the retirement income plan (unless vesting privileges apply).

Procedural Approvals -
- The Corporate Personnel Department should be consulted before final actions/commitments are made. Any deviation from these procedures must have the prior approval of the Director of Personnel, General Manager, Group Executive, and Vice President of Personnel.

A Detailed Severance Pay Schedule

If Years of Service with the Company since the most recent date of hire are	Severance Pay at base pay rate is equal to (see below) months pay
0 - 1	¼
1 - 2	½
2 - 3	¾
3 - 4	¾
4 - 5	1
5 - 6	1
6 - 7	1 ¼
7 - 8	1 ½
8 - 9	1 ¾
9 - 10	2
10 - 11	2 ¼
11 - 12	2 ½
12 - 13	2 ½
13 - 14	3
14 - 15	3
15 - 16	3 ½
16 - 17	3 ½
17 - 18	4

18 - 19	4
19 - 20	4 ½
20 - 21	4 ½
21 - 22	5
22 - 23	5
23 - 24	5 ½
24 - 25	5 ½
25 - 26	6
Over 26	6

How to Use Outplacement to Ease the Termination Shock

When someone loses a job through involuntary action initiated by the employer, such as a layoff, reduction in force (RIF), job elimination, discharge, etc., they go through the same five stages of reaction of loss experienced by people who lose a loved one or learn of a fatal illness:

1. denial
2. anger
3. bargaining
4. depression
5. acceptance

Much of the pain and suffering that comes with loss of a job can be minimized by a formal outplacement program that assists terminated employees to find another job or career. It can be handled by in-house experts (usually in the Employment or Personnel Departments) or contracted to outside agencies and professional outplacement firms which operate on both local and national scales.

Many employers have found that assisting employees who have been terminated for reasons other than "cause" (grievous offenses) is good business practice.

1. When managers know that terminated employees will be helped to find another job or otherwise eased through the separation process, they are more willing to make the tough decision to let someone go. Even when the economic reasons are overwhelming, many managers hesitate out of worthy personal concern for the well-being of those let go. Such delays in swift

corrective action caused by pangs of conscience actually make the eventual terminations more necessary, harder, more numerous and more difficult for the victims. The knowledge that support mechanisms exist will often help, just as the knowledge that the patient feels no pain makes it easier for the surgeon to operate.

2. Terminated employees who receive assistance in finding other jobs
   - are protected against loss of income or career
   - experience less trauma in the transition
   - draw less unemployment compensation (paid for by the employer)
   - exhibit a more positive attitude towards the past employer

3. Employees who remain in the enterprise see the outplacement program as a positive proof that the company really cares about its people. They are assured that they will be treated fairly and not abandoned. They show less anxiety about their own job security and exhibit fewer counterproductive reactions to company financial problems, feeling free to do their best work without as much distraction and task interference from personal concern about their fate.

How to Use Exit Interviews to Make Future Improvements

When someone leaves the organization, you have an opportunity to learn what they thought about their experiences with your firm.

Why You Need to Know What Departing Employees Can Tell You

Formal exit interviews are valuable because they:
1. document how various people perceived the organization;
2. provide information on **all** the reasons why someone is leaving;
3. expose problem areas that can be addressed to prevent additional undesired turnover;
4. give the employee's view of
   - management policies and practices,
   - job content,
   - compensation,
   - training and development opportunities,
   - supervision, and
   - fellow employees;

5. allow employees a safe chance to "sound off" with either praise or criticism, to vent any strong emotions and to leave in a better state of mind;
6. confirm the success or failure of performance management methods.

The Special Importance of Understanding Why People Quit

No one leaves a job for only ONE reason. Although your official termination record form may only have room for a single reason for termination, there are always more than just one. If people actually only considered pay and advancement in their choice of jobs, there would be constant and rapid turnover in every organization as all employees jumped from company to company every time they located a higher pay rate or a more attractive career prospect.

As discussed in the **Informal Compensation** section of the **Reward** chapter, there are many motivations that lead people to stick with a job despite regular exposure to opportunities to earn a few more dollars or gain a nicer title elsewhere. Other employers offering more money and a better title only become overwhelmingly irresistible to people when their view of their current organization leads them to believe that

- current income is inadequate and unlikely to rise sufficiently soon
- career advancement is slow or non-existent
- they do not like their supervisor(s) and/or co-workers
- they are overqualified and/or bored with the job duties
- the work is beyond their capabilities
- the work location/hours/conditions are unfavorable
- job security is lacking
- the organizational culture is not compatible with personal or professional preferences
- they do not receive a sense of pride from their work
- there is an insufficient feeling of accomplishment, growth or challenge
- they do not get enough recognition for personal achievements
- they are not treated fairly
- they are uncomfortable with organizational goals, objectives or policies

There are as many reasons for leaving a firm as there are individuals who work.

Most people can (and do) deal with shortcomings in a number of such areas.

It is rare to find any employee who can sincerely say that their job is absolutely perfect and incapable of improvement. People live and work in an imperfect world; but there is a point beyond which each person cannot any longer accept the accumulated "imperfections" on the current job.

A number of "compensation" elements that retain employees must fall below the minimally acceptable level before anyone voluntarily leaves the organization. How many and which ones are most important is up to the individual. Some people will accept 10% less pay to work close to home; others will commute long distances and put up with many undesirable working conditions because the job is exciting. The one common fact is that no one quits over only one **reward** element. A number of "motivational factors" must lose their effectiveness before an employee willingly accepts the stress of changing jobs.

The best way to get full information on the precise mix of motivation elements that led to the resignation of a competent employee is to conduct an exit interview that identifies all the reasons.

When to Conduct Exit Interviews

There are two good times to conduct exit interviews: when the employee is undergoing the termination process; and a few months later, when the employee's perspective may undergo a change.

When leaving, employees may be rather unwilling to speak frankly or freely about their true opinions and feelings, for fear of a bad reference report. The reason given for leaving (if the termination is voluntary) is usually "for a job offering more opportunity and better pay." That answer is quite safe and socially acceptable. It does not antagonize or "burn bridges" and probably contains some truth, since everyone can find a "better job paying more" if they look long enough.

A few months later (or even a year later), ex-employee observations about the old organization are likely to be less detailed and current but more valid and objective. They will be less concerned about what you will think or say about them (if they are employed on a new job at that time) and they will have new experiences since leaving that may affect their observations about "the old job." Once some time has passed and their initial feelings on termination day have faded, you may receive far different comments that in their initial exit interview.

While exit interviews conducted when the person is leaving are easier to arrange in person, a post-partum follow-up by telephone much later will confirm or modify the initial interview responses. Such validity checking is important if the organization wishes to make use of exit interview comments for effective preventive/remedial actions.

What Information to Seek in the Exit Interview

How to Create a Consistent Exit Interview Format (and a Sample Form)
Employee Name _____ Job Title _____ Date _____
Unit/Department/Location _____
Supervisor _____ Hired _____
Termination Date _____
Reason for Leaving (as understood by Supervisor):

_____

Employee Comments on:
1. Job duties

   _____

2. Working conditions

   _____

3. Compensation (pay and fringe benefits)

   _____

4. Training received

   _____

5. Advancement opportunities

   _____

6. Other Management policies/practices

   _____

7. Fellow employees

   _____

8. Treatment by Supervisor(s)

   _____

9. What Supervisor(s) think of you as a worker

   _____

10. How your last Supervisor compares to previous ones

    _____

11. What circumstances would have to change for you to continue working here?

    _____

12. New employer:_____

New job title:_____ New salary: $_____

Interviewer's evaluation of the reasons for leaving

Exit Interview Conducted by _____ □ Initial □
Subsequent

Special Features You May Want to Add to An Exit Interview Form

Other features of an exit interview form can include:
- Any questions you feel would be useful can be asked.
- Coded responses to questions consistently asked can be computerized for centralized review and trend analysis.
- Departing employees and ex-employees should be assured that they are not required to answer every question.
- Confidentiality should be guaranteed.
- For greater objectivity and less "threat" to the subject, a Personnel specialist or manager other than the immediate supervisor should conduct the exit interview.
- If controversial information is disclosed, other managers from Personnel or in the chain of command should repeat the interview.

Chapter 11:

THE PERFORMANCE MANAGER'S TOOL KIT

How to Use the Tool Kit as a Source of Samples and Techniques

This final chapter contains a potpourri of extra policies, program applications, forms and optional techniques for your reference. You will find a minimum amount of theoretical discussion and a maximum number of practical "how-to" tools.

Some vital techniques, such as the INTERVIEW PLANNING GUIDE, properly belong in this final section because they are practical instruments whose use could not be restricted to only one chapter: they are important tools that can be used in any number of performance management areas.

One long example, a sample Personnel Policy Manual, and a short Generic Bonus Plan were placed here because they summarize many of the principles and techniques discussed throughout the book. In addition, their inclusion in the earlier text chapters could also have been unnecessary, irrelevant, redundant or boring to many readers.

The extensive section on PERFORMANCE APPRAISAL FORMS provides a comprehensive overview of various "good" appraisal methods, complete with brief analyses and sample formats for the more sophisticated people-manager who wants to begin experimenting from a running start.

Sample Employee Personnel Policy Manual

EMPLOYEE MANUAL FOR
YOUR ORGANIZATION

Effective August 1, 1988

<u>WELCOME</u>

We welcome you as a new member of the Organization. The part you will play as an employee is an important one, as we can only be as strong as the individual members of our team.

We know that during your first days of employment, you will have questions regarding our company and its policies. The purpose of this handbook is to answer some of those questions, to inform you about our company, to explain some of the working conditions and the many benefits you will enjoy as a member of our team. We urge you to read your handbook carefully and to keep it in a safe place for future reference. Should you have any questions regarding the contents of this handbook, your supervisor or personnel services will be happy to respond.

The Organization is a .... organization which was created .... It is incorporated under the laws of the State of ....

Its aim and objectives are to ....

EMPLOYMENT POLICIES

NONDISCRIMINATION

The Organization is an equal opportunity employer and affirmatively accepts, supports, and practices the concepts of nondiscrimination pertaining to, but not limited to: recruitment, hiring, compensation, training, transfer and promotion, benefits and all other terms and conditions of employment regardless of race, color, religion, sex, age, national origin, handicap, or veteran status.

ORIENTATION

You will be provided an orientation to our facilities, your co-workers, and your position by your supervisor, who will also be responsible for your on-the-job training. If you have any questions, please ask them of your supervisor.

PROBATIONARY PERIOD

The first ninety (90) days of employment is a probationary period for all employees. This period is to permit an employee time to adjust to a new environment and to allow management an opportunity to observe and judge the employee's ability to perform the full range of job requirements.

During this period, your job performance will be evaluated by your supervisor. You and your supervisor will have the opportunity to formally discuss your job performance upon completion of this period.

The probationary period may be extended with the written approval of the

Personnel Director if it is determined that unusual circumstances have produced sufficient cause for an extension.

EMPLOYEE CLASSIFICATIONS

Because of the nature of our organization, we have two employee categories: (1) Staff, which includes supervisors and office personnel, and (2) Production personnel.

All employees experience a training period which may vary from 4 weeks to 13 weeks. While employees are in training, they are paid the minimum wage in compliance with the Wage and Hour Law.

The following employee classifications are used:

REGULAR FULL-TIME: Normally and consistently scheduled to work a 40-hour week.

REGULAR PART-TIME: Normally and consistently scheduled to work less than a 40-hour week.

TEMPORARY: Hired to work for a limited, specified period of time regardless of the number of hours worked.

PROBATIONARY: See explanation under Probationary period.

WORK HOURS

The time you are to be on the job will be assigned by management. As a production organization, our hours of peak employee needs vary. Therefore, your hours, days off, etc., will be scheduled to accommodate our daily staffing and workload requirements.

While we cannot guarantee specific hours of work, we will try to keep your hours as consistent as possible. Your cooperation with the schedule is necessary.

Generally, production personnel will be scheduled to work from 7:00 a.m. to 3:30 p.m., Monday through Friday. Changes in hours for production purposes will be assigned by management.

TIMEKEEPING

All supervisors will keep a daily record on each employee in their department. The time you begin and end work will be recorded on the time card, along with your production and rate. At the end of your scheduled work week, you will be expected to sign your card.

COMPENSATION

PAY PERIODS

Our pay period is seven days long. It begins every Monday at 12:01 a.m. and ends the following Sunday at 12:00 midnight. There are fifty-two pay periods in a calendar year.

PAY PROCEDURE

Paydays are every Friday and cover time worked during the previous week. You will receive your paycheck from your supervisor or someone designated to give out checks. Any problem regarding your pay should be directed to your supervisor who will report any error to Payroll. If there is a discrepancy, the necessary adjustments will be made.

If you are absent on payday, your check will be held until it is picked up by you or someone who has been authorized by you. This can be done by signing an authorization letter advising Payroll who may receive your check. The authorization letter will be filed in your job folder and considered valid until you change it. No check will be mailed, unless you send a letter of authorization to us.

PAYROLL DEDUCTIONS

Those deductions required by law are withheld from your check each pay period. They include federal income tax, state income tax, social security (FICA), city tax for City residents, and any legal wage garnishment.

Other deductions require your written authorization. Examples include deductions for transfer to your savings account and payment for employee purchases.

OVERTIME

For proper salary administration and labor law compliance, each employee must be classified for payroll records as either "exempt" or "non-exempt" on the basis of whether certain tests relating to duties and responsibilities in the job assigned are met.

"Exempt" means exempt from the overtime requirements of the current Federal Fair Labor Standards Act. Employees who are "non-exempt" are eligible for overtime pay under certain conditions.

Accurate records of hours worked must be maintained on all employees who are non-exempt. These records are required by government regulations.

An employee who is non-exempt is paid at a rate of one and one-half times the regular rate of pay for all hours actually worked in excess of 40 hours in a workweek.

Hours paid that are not actual hours worked are not included in the overtime provision. Hours which may be paid which are not actual hours worked include, but are not limited to, vacation, funeral leave and holidays.

EMPLOYEE BENEFITS

HOLIDAYS

Holiday pay is based on the following:

Full time employees who work a minimum of forty (40) hours a week will be paid holiday pay based on eight (8) hours per holiday.

Employees who work thirty-two (32) hours per week will be paid holiday pay based on eight-tenths of eight hours (6.4 hours per holiday).

Employees who work twenty-four (24) hours per week will be paid holiday pay based on six-tenths of eight hours (4.8 hours per holiday).

To receive holiday pay, the following rules apply:

1. You must have worked a minimum of forty (40) hours within thirty (30) calendar days prior to the holiday and,

2. You must work the last scheduled day prior to the holiday and the first scheduled day after the holiday, with the last scheduled work day not more than four (4) working days prior to the holiday and the first scheduled work day not more than four (4) working days after the holidays.

The following are recognized as **paid holidays**:

New Year's Day

Martin Luther King's Birthday

Memorial Day

Independence Day

Labor Day

Veterans' Day

Thanksgiving Day

Friday following Thanksgiving

Christmas Eve

Christmas Day

A holiday which falls on Saturday or Sunday will be observed on the day it is observed by the federal government. If you cannot work a scheduled day before or after the holiday, a written excuse in advance to your supervisor may entitle you to holiday pay. The final decision will be at the discretion of the Personnel Director.

LEAVE OF ABSENCE

While leaves of absence are not encouraged, we understand there may be times when you need to be away from work for more than one week, excluding vacation time. The circumstances must be of a medical, military, or very serious personal nature for a leave to be considered valid.

Employees with more than six (6) months of continuous service with the Organization may request a leave of absence. Should the requested leave of absence be granted, the following conditions apply:

1. The time away from work will be without pay.

2. There will be no break in service with the company.

3. A leave of absence may not exceed thirty (30) calendar days. If the absence is due to illness, the leave may be extended up to an additional thirty (30) calendar days. Medical evidence satisfactory to the Organization will be required.

4. Should you fail to return to work on the agreed upon date, you will be considered to have resigned without notice.

5. Upon your return to work, the company will make every reasonable attempt to reinstate you to your position or to a comparable one. This will depend

on what positions are available at the time of your return to work.

6. The company cannot in any way guarantee placement upon your return to work.

7. Any special circumstances such as hospital/medical or life insurance premiums will be covered separately.

A request for a leave of absence must be made in writing as far in advance as possible. The final approval/disapproval of your request will be made by the Personnel Director.

VACATION

Vacation accrual is based on the number of full months of service completed.

Earned vacation is calculated by a mathematical model, using base hours. The number of base hours is determined by subtracting paid holidays, vacation and an established number of absences.

Earned vacation is calculated at the rate of .047829 x base hours actually worked during a month. For a full-time employee, monthly base hours are 139.33 (or 1672 annually), which equates to earned vacation of 80 hours over a 12-month period.

Employees with five consecutive years of service, who have earned <u>full</u> vacations in each of those 5 years, may qualify for additional vacation time. For a full-time employee, vacation accrues at the rate of .0717435 x monthly base hours, or 120 hours over a 12-month period.

Employees with 10 consecutive years of service, who have earned full vacations in each of those ten years, may qualify for additional vacation time. For a full-time employee, vacation accrues at the rate of .095658 x monthly base hours, or 160 hours over a 12-month period.

Earned vacation will accrue, but cannot be taken, during the first 90 days of employment. Vacation time may be taken only after it has been earned and must be taken within the 12- month period following accrual.

Vacation must be scheduled in advance and approved by the supervisor. In case of scheduling conflicts, seniority of requesters will be given consideration.

Payment in lieu of vacation will not be made except in unusual circumstances and only with the approval of the Personnel Director. Vacation time off with pay will not be counted as hours worked for purposes of computing overtime pay. Vacation time which has been earned but not used will be paid upon termination of employment, but not to exceed one year's accrual.

EXCUSED ABSENCES

The company recognizes a need to be absent from work for short periods of time. If you are a full-time employee (40 hours a week), you are eligible for the following excused absences with pay:

FUNERAL LEAVE

If a death occurs in your immediate family, up to 3 scheduled work days may be taken off with pay. One day must be the day of the funeral. Immediate family is defined as the employee's spouse, child, parent, brother, sister, grandparent or grandchild.

To attend a funeral home service or burial, one scheduled work day may be taken with pay upon the death of a close relative. A close relative includes aunt, uncle, niece, nephew, cousin, in-laws, etc.

Verification of the reason for the absence is required prior to granting pay for funeral leave. Proof of relationship may be required. Time off with pay for funeral leave will not be counted as hours worked in computing overtime pay.

JURY DUTY

If you are called for jury duty, you will receive your regular straight-time pay. The maximum number of days for jury duty with pay from the Organization is 10 days annually.

If called for jury duty, notify your supervisor and provide a copy of the court's notice to serve immediately upon receipt of the notice.

If you should have to serve less than a full day, you are expected to return to work. Time spent on jury duty is not counted as hours worked for the purpose of computing overtime pay.

MILITARY LEAVE

Short-term: Employees who are members of the State National Guard or of any reserve component of the armed forces of the United States are entitled to a leave of absence. Upon return to work, you will be paid the difference between your regular base wages and your military pay.

The maximum period of reimbursement is 10 work days annually.

Before base wages are paid, you must file an official order from the appropriate military authority with the Organization.

Long-term: An employee who enlists, is drafted, or is called to active duty should notify the Organization immediately and will be granted an unpaid absence in accordance with federal guidelines.

INSURANCE BENEFITS

The following summary descriptions of the medical and life insurance plans are not intended to modify or in any way replace the controlling descriptions contained in the group insurance certificates. Please consult the certificates of coverage for specific issues or information which may be subject to periodic revision.

All employees regularly scheduled to work a minimum of 30 hours a week are eligible to enroll in the Organization's plans covering medical and life insurance.

Coverage is effective the beginning of the month following 60 days of continuous employment, providing the employee is at work on that date. The effective date of coverage is not changed if that date is a holiday or a regularly scheduled day off. In such case, however, the employee must have worked the last regularly scheduled day and not be disabled.

If there is a lay-off due to a shortage of work, the Organization will pay the premium for medical insurance for the employee for the first month. If the lay-off is for two consecutive months, the Organization will pay the premium, but the employee must repay the second month's premium through payroll deduction upon return to work. If the lay-off exceeds two months, you will have the opportunity to remain, at your own expense, in the program for a specified period of time. If you choose not to remain in the program, your health insurance will be cancelled.

In certain instances, you have a right to choose continuation of coverage if you lose your group health coverage because of a reduction in your hours of work or the termination of your employment. Continued coverage for a specific period of time may also be applicable for family members in the event of death, divorce, legal separation, medicare eligibility or loss of dependent status due to age. In such cases, you would be responsible for the payment of monthly premiums.

MAJOR MEDICAL PLAN

A medical plan with coverage for a broad range of expenses is available to employees who regularly work a minimum of 30 hours a week.

The plan is designed to provide security for you and your eligible dependents by protecting you from the high cost of medical care.

The majority of the cost for the eligible employee is paid by the Organization. You may cover the cost for your eligible dependents through payroll deduction.

Eligible Dependents

Eligible dependents include: your spouse, and your unmarried child less than 25 years of age who depends on you for more than 50% of his or her support and maintenance and who may be claimed as an exemption on your federal income tax.

Summary of Benefits

After an insured individual has met a calendar year deductible of $100, the insurance company will pay 80% of reasonable and customary expenses covered under the plan. The maximum number of deductibles per calendar year for any family is 3.

The maximum annual out-of-pocket coinsurance payable by any one individual is $580, with certain exclusions listed below. For a family, the annual out-of-pocket limit (same exclusions) is $1,740.

The program **requires, prior to hospital admission, pre-admission authorization from the insurance company.** If your physician does not obtain pre-admission authorization, benefit payments will be reduced by 25%.

Certain out-patient surgical services and pre-admission testing is paid at 100% after the annual deductible has been met. Employee cost for a prescription is only $3. If a generic brand is used, the cost is only $1. The first $500 of expenses is covered for an accidental injury. Consult your Group Insurance booklet for details and time restrictions.

Exclusions to the Co-insurance Percentage Listed Above

There are maximum benefit amounts for the care or treatment of the following:

1. Mental illness or nervous disorders

2. Alcoholism, chemical dependency or drug addiction

3. Vertebra, spine, back and neck

Claims Processing

Once the calendar year deductible has been met, insurance claims should be submitted to Personnel Services for processing.

LIFE INSURANCE

A group life insurance program is available for employees who regularly work a minimum of 30 hours a week.

Life insurance coverage is in the amount of $15,000. It is supplemented by accidental death and dismemberment coverage in the amount of $15,000.

The majority of the cost of the program is paid by the Organization. The remainder of the cost, in the amount of $1.00 a month, is paid by the employee through payroll deduction.

The amount of life insurance coverage is reduced by 35% at age 65, and coverage is terminated at age 70.

RETIREMENT PLAN

To help meet your financial needs after retirement, the Organization contributes to a plan which covers employees who:

- have completed one year of service, and,
- work a minimum of 1,000 hours during the year, and,
- have attained the age of 21

Each plan year, the Organization makes contributions to the plan on behalf of eligible employees equal to 6% of the employee's earnings for that plan year below $7,800, and 10% of the employee's earnings over $7,800.

The plan year is a 12-month period beginning on January 1. For retirement contribution purposes, as described above, "earnings" means your regular basic pay, and excludes overtime and all other forms of extra compensation.

The plan provides the following **vesting** schedule:

Years of Service	Vested %
less than 4	0%
4	40%
5	50%
6	60%
7	70%
8	80%
9	90%
10	100%

For vesting purposes only, service is counted from age 18.

You may elect to contribute, on a tax-deferred basis, up to 15% of your gross earnings to the plan.

Note: This brief summary description of the plan is not intended to modify or in any way replace the provisions of the plan. The retirement plan itself may be amended or modified at any time, and the legal text and provisions of the retirement plan will govern.

TAX DEFERRED ANNUITY PLAN

The Organization provides employees the opportunity to defer a portion of their income without having to pay federal or state taxes on such income until it is actually received. This program is available only to employees of tax-exempt organizations, and the Organization administers a program of payroll deduction for employees in accordance with the governing federal rules and regulations.

WORKERS' COMPENSATION

Any on-the-job accident, injury or illness must be reported to your supervisor immediately.

The Organization carries Workers' Compensation insurance in compliance with state law. The insurance is designed to provide financial assistance to employees who are injured or who become ill as a result of their employment.

It is the policy of the Organization to comply with the state law and to aid any employee whose injury or illness is determined to be compensable under the provisions of the State's Workers' Compensation Act.

The Organization pays for all costs associated with providing the coverage, and the insurance carrier makes all payments and decisions pertaining to compensable illnesses or injuries.

SAVINGS PLAN

A savings plan, using payroll deduction, is available to all employees. An initial deposit of $50 is required to open an account. Questions regarding balances or withdrawals are to be made to the financial institution holding the account.

If your individual circumstances allow, the Organization encourages you to use a payroll deduction for your savings.

PURCHASES

Employees may purchase, through payroll deduction, any item sold by the Organization. Purchases are made through the office and merchandise should be picked up there.

LOANS

At the discretion of the Personnel Director, up to two loans a year, with certain limitations, may be granted to an employee in an emergency situation. Loans are available only to employees who are actively at work at the time of the emergency. Loans must be repaid within 8 weeks by weekly payroll deductions. If a loan is not repaid within 8 weeks, the full balance will be due the following week.

LUNCHROOM

A lunchroom with a refrigerator and microwave oven is provided for your use. Consumption of food or beverages in any other part of the plant or office is a violation of the health and safety code and is not permitted.

LOCKERS

A locker for your personal articles will be provided upon request by your supervisor. It is your responsibility to keep your locker clean and closed. If you provide a lock for it, a duplicate key must be filed in the office.

POCKET CHANGE

Change can be obtained from office personnel during the morning break each work day.

EMPLOYEE PARKING

Ample parking is available on the company parking lot.

PICTURES

From time to time, there are guided tours of our facilities. Occasionally, media will take general group pictures for news articles for the purpose of helping the Organization generate public response to its goals. If you do not wish to have your picture taken, you may sign a statement explaining the reason, and it will be placed in your job folder. The Organization will make every effort to protect your privacy when requested, but it does reserve the right for publication.

<u>WORK RULES</u>

The following work rules are published so that all employees will know what is considered unacceptable conduct and to ensure the consistent application of discipline for any violation of these rules. The company views disciplinary procedures as steps taken for progressive, corrective purposes. The following rules are designed to ensure a smooth-running organization in the best interest of all employees, the company, and our customers. They do not, in any way, invalidate employee rights.

The offenses and disciplinary actions listed below are not all-inclusive. Any unacceptable conduct, though not specifically covered by these rules, may result in disciplinary action.

Repeated violation of the same rule, violation of more than one rule in a single act, or violations of different rules at different times shall be cause for accelerated or compound disciplinary action. Disciplinary notice will be given to the employee where appropriate.

GROUP A

A violation of a Group A rule is considered so serious that it will result in immediate discharge.

   1. Engaging in any unlawful conduct on company premises, or engaging in any

unlawful conduct off company premises which affects the employee's relationship to fellow employees.

2. Willfully falsifying attendance records, employment application, reason for absence, or any work-related data.

3. Smoking in designated unauthorized areas.

4. Entering place of employment outside of working hours without permission.

5. Theft from the company, employees, or customers.

6. Reporting to work under the influence of intoxicants.

7. Unauthorized possession or use of alcoholic beverages on company premises at any time.

8. Possession, use or sale of any controlled substance on company premises (except for use of prescription drugs taken with supervisory knowledge).

9. Intentionally misusing, destroying or damaging any company property, vehicle or equipment, or the property of any employee.

10. Unauthorized removal of company records from the premises or unauthorized release of any confidential information.

11. Carrying or possession of firearms or weapons of any kind while on duty.

12. Failure to provide acceptable and sufficient reason for an absence of three (3) days or more.

13. Engaging in any hazardous or unsafe conduct which results in injury or damage of any kind.

14. Refusal to obey specific working instructions of supervisor.

15. Sexual harassment.

16. Performing work for or engaging in any other unauthorized affiliation with a competitor of the company.

17. Entering or exiting the building through unauthorized areas.

GROUP B

A violation of a Group B rule will be handled on a two-step basis as follows:

First infraction: A 3-day suspension without pay.

Second infraction: Discharge

1. Quitting work before the scheduled end of shift without supervisory permission, or exceeding specified time for lunch and/or breaks.

2. Leaving place of employment during working hours without supervisory permission.

3. Acting in a discourteous, threatening or abusive manner.

4. Using any unlabeled product or container in the plant.

5. Sleeping during normal working hours.

6. Engaging in any hazardous or unsafe conduct.

7. Engaging in a fight of any kind on company premises.

8. Unauthorized operation of tools, machinery, or equipment.

GROUP C

A violation of a GROUP C rule will be handled on a four step basis as follows:

First infraction: Written warning

Second infraction: Final written warning

Third infraction: A 3-day suspension without pay

Fourth infraction: Discharge

1. Negligence or carelessness in work performance.

2. Failure to notify supervisor of absence or tardiness prior to the start of the scheduled workshift. (See termination policy regarding failure to notify supervisor for 3 consecutive scheduled shifts.)

3. Failure to promptly report an accident or injury.

4. Failure to properly perform assigned duties.

5. Failure to maintain cleanliness and neatness in individual work area.

6. Failure to comply with company safety practices and policies.

7. Inability or unwillingness to work harmoniously with others.

8. Leaving work area during working time without authorization.

9. Unauthorized gambling on company premises.

EMPLOYEE CONDUCT

PERSONAL BUSINESS ON COMPANY TIME

We ask that you limit any telephone calls to those of an emergency nature, and keep "small talk" to a minimum.

The company's letterhead and other supplies may not be used for anything other than Organization business.

GARNISHMENTS

The Organization cannot refuse to honor legal garnishments. A garnishment is a court order requiring the Organization to withhold a sum of money from an employee's paycheck. We must follow legal procedures in withholding the appropriate amount for repayment of a debt incurred.

When an employee's income is garnished, the Organization incurs costs in the paperwork and time required to comply with the order of the court. A garnishment is viewed as an extremely serious matter, and an employee may be discharged by the Organization if garnishments from two different sources are received within a twelve-month period.

MEDICATION

No medication will be dispensed by the office unless a written notification is filed in your personnel file. Your signature is required before medicine will be administered.

TELEPHONE CALLS AND MESSAGES

Employees may not make or receive personal telephone calls during working hours. Only emergency messages will be forwarded to you through the office. A pay phone is provided in the lobby for you to make outgoing calls, but only during coffee and lunch breaks. Please show courtesy to your fellow employees by keeping your calls as brief as possible so that others may use the phone.

SEXUAL HARASSMENT

All employees have the right to work in an environment free from sexual harassment by other employees or customers. If you are subject to or witness any form of sexual harassment, you should present a signed statement describing the incident to a member of management. The incident will be reviewed and appropriate action will be taken. An employee who is guilty of sexual harassment will be subject to disciplinary action.

COMPANY TOOLS

When you start each new assignment, you will be given the necessary tools. Please take care of them and see that they are returned in good condition at the end of your work period.

PHYSICAL EXAMINATIONS

Physical examination reports should be dated for the current year, signed by a licensed physician and submitted to the Organization no later than the end of September of each year. A new employee should submit a report the first day of work.

FIRE DRILLS

Fire drills may be held at any time. Your supervisor will tell you what to do and where the exits are from your work station. When a long sustained bell alarm is sounded, you must immediately leave your work station and report to a supervisor on the outside of the building.

SAFETY AND HEALTH

We are concerned with the safety of our employees. Safety throughout the Organization involves the individual effort of each employee. It is your responsibility to help by working safely at all times. This includes making sure your work area is neat and clean. Do not place boxes or other supplies in aisles or stack them in an unsafe manner.

Any conditions which you feel are unsafe should be immediately reported to management. Should an accident occur, notify management immediately.

You should be familiar with the location and use of all fire extinguishers within the building. If you are not, ask management for instructions.

EMPLOYEE ENTRANCE AND EXIT

All employees must leave and enter the building through the designated area at all times. Failure to comply with this rule will be considered sufficient cause for dismissal.

The Interview Planning Guide

This worksheet will help you plan and conduct performance appraisal interviews. Use it as a guide before, during and after the interview, and you will develop confidence in your ability to conduct effective performance reviews.

PLANNING GUIDE	COUNSELING NOTES
A. PREPARE FOR THE INTERVIEW A-1. **Get Information** (Review employee data: background and work history; past performance appraisals and other personnel records).	Name of Employee _____ Position _____ Employed _____ Time on Job: _____ Last review on _____ <u>NOTES:</u>
A-2. **Determine Interview Objectives** (Write the three or four main objectives to be achieved during this interview).	The objectives I want to achieve during this interview are: (be specific).
A-3. **Develop a Plan to Achieve Interview Objectives**	The main areas to be discussed are: (list these areas as **questions** to be asked and answered; consider having the employee prepare his or her ideas from the same list)
A-4. **Consider Your Own Attitudes)** Get into the right state of mind.	Answer: Do I believe that *I should do unto others as I would have them do unto me*? Yes No (Do **not** hold the interview until your answer is "yes.")
A-5. **Select the Right Time and Place**	I have arranged to have this interview as follows:

(Arrange for uninterrupted privacy).

1. Interview Date _____
2. Time for interview is from _____ to _____
3. Place and location _____
4. Time & place verified with employee? Yes No
5. Arranged for phone calls/visitors to be handled during interview time? Yes No

Plans made by _____ on _____

B. CONDUCTING THE INTERVIEW

Opening remarks and statement of purpose:

B-1. Get to the Point

(Tell the purpose of the interview; don't overdo small talk; emphasize the need for two-way discussion; remember, the employee is more nervous than you).

B-2. Be Natural

(Create an atmosphere of open communication for mutual understanding; consider how well you know the employee; be yourself and don't put on airs).

B-3. Exchange Information – Be Helpful and Understanding

(Raise each question in turn; let the employee respond first; give information they ask for or need; note areas of agreement before offering different opinions).

The key questions for discussion (see A-2 and A-3), in sequential order, are:

B-4. Listen – Encourage the Employee to Talk

(Be patient and non-judgmental; respect their feelings and opinions; discover their perceptions; acknowledge their viewpoints, let them vent frustrations or anxieties; reserve your disagreements on any point until employee has finished).

Use active listening techniques; be attentive; "play back" their comments.

B-5. **Level With the Employee**

(After exploring their thoughts, share your observations and conclusions; be frank and honest...people want to know where they stand; you are the boss, so you don't have to argue or debate).

B-6. **Explain Any Improvements Needed in the Work – Not in the Person**

Ask questions on how work output results can be improved: (Suggest specific observable examples of job results that are desired or expected – not personality traits).

(Again, ask employee for opinions and suggestions first; note areas of agreement; discuss any differences of opinion sincerely and sympathetically; ask how you can help employee do better).

B-7. **Establish Goals for the Future – Develop a Mutual Plan**

Goals set to be achieved by the next review are: (List statements that are objective, specific and measurable in terms of quality, quantity, time or cost)

(Set goals that will improve present employee job performance and career growth opportunities; establish performance standards and measurement methods...they don't have to be numbers, just results both parties can recognize).

(Get employee involved in developing a mutually-understood plan).

Note: If this portion of the interview involves a long-range Development Plan, both you and the employee may want some time to think about it carefully before documenting it. A wrap-up session later may be a good idea.

B-8. Seek Acceptance and Commitment

(Ask for the employee's ideas on steps both of you can take to achieve the goals established).

(Work out the specific improvement actions to be taken).

(List which items are the employee's responsibility and which are yours – some things will require your support and periodic feedback).

(Agree on dates to check on progress and review results).

List the specific steps and dates to accomplish the goals:

(a) What the employee will do; (b) What you will do.

B-9. Close on a Constructive Note

(Review the interview – check on mutual understanding).

(Tell how the discussion has helped **you**; offer to remain available for help in the future).

Check and confirm employee understanding – document promises you both have made.

C. AFTER THE INTERVIEW

C-1. Follow up and keep promises

C-2. Seek feedback from the employee on progress; also periodically review and provide feedback to employee.

Notes on subjects and dates for follow-up:

C-3. Evaluate the Appraisal interview Itself

Were interview objectives achieved?

What went well and why?

What could have been improved and how?

Did the employee do at least **half** of the talking?

   Why? Why not?

What attitude did the employee show at the end of the interview?

Notes on the interview process itself:

Generic Bonus Plan

BONUS PLAN FOR TWO SUPERVISORS

Purpose: To provide an appropriate reward to key supervisory positions for positive Company performance results, an incentive for effective leadership and control in various units, and special reinforcement for close cooperation and mutual support between all units through a recognition of joint destiny and a share in overall Company success.

Eligibility: Supervisors employed for the full bonus period.

Bonus Pool: Funded by Company income after other costs and expenses; while the number of eligible participants is two, the size of the total bonus pool shall not exceed ...

A. $10,000 when at year-end, overall production volume at the Company has risen by over 10%, labor costs per unit produced have fallen by over 2%, and production schedules have been met within quality standards;

B. $5,000 when at year-end, overall production volume at the Company has risen by 5% or more, labor costs per unit produced have fallen, and production schedules have been met within quality standards;

C. $2,000 when at year-end, the overall production volume at the Company has been maintained, labor costs per unit produced have been maintained, and any failure to meet production schedules within quality standards did not threaten or create a financial loss and resulted from causes not under the control or influence of the eligible employees.

If the number of eligible participants increases, the bonus pool fund amounts will increase proportionally: i.e., if four supervisors (twice as many as are in the initial plan) become eligible for the plan, the A, B and C bonus pools will double.

Performance Feedback: The Manager shall notify the eligible Supervisors of the precise performance objectives, establish a feedback system so they can reliably track their personal performance, their unit performance and the overall Company performance against those objectives, and shall inform them of any developments or circumstances which might reduce the potential bonus pool fund or their potential share.

Distribution of Bonus Pool: The entire bonus pool (if any) shall be totally distributed as soon as practical after the end of the bonus period. The bonus pool shall be divided and distributed according to the number of total performance units assigned to the eligible employees at the sole discretion of the Manager, using the following standards to measure the individual Supervisor's performance results: 2 performance units for Outstanding performance, 1 performance unit for Good performance and 0 units for Poor performance.

Supervisor Bonus Pool Criteria Sheet

Has production volume increased over 10%?	☐ Yes	☐ No
Have labor costs per unit declined over 2%?	☐ Yes	☐ No
Were production schedules met?	☐ Yes	☐ No
Were quality standards maintained?	☐ Yes	☐ No

A. If all the above answers are "Yes," the bonus pool = $10,000. Otherwise, continue ...

Has production volume increased over 5%?	☐ Yes	☐ No
Have labor costs per unit produced declined?	☐ Yes	☐ No
Were production schedules met?	☐ Yes	☐ No
Were quality standards maintained?	☐ Yes	☐ No

B. If all the above answers are "Yes," the bonus pool = $5,000. Otherwise, continue ...

Has production volume been acceptably maintained?	☐ Yes	☐ No
Have labor costs per unit stayed acceptable?	☐ Yes	☐ No
Was production adequate under the circumstances?	☐ Yes	☐ No
Were quality standards maintained?	☐ Yes	☐ No

C. If all the above answers are "Yes," the bonus pool = $2,000. Otherwise, there will be no bonus pool for plant Supervisors.

Supervisor Performance Evaluation Criteria
(apply to each individual Supervisor)

Units	Individual Supervisor's Performance Results
2	*Outstanding* - actual results far exceeded all expectations; the Supervisor also met professional development objectives for self and subordinates, encouraging upward mobility potential and providing management back-up;
1	*Good* - actual results met expectations; also, professional development activities effectively improved personal and subordinate management skills;
0	*Poor* - actual results did not meet expectations.

Bonus Distribution Worksheet

Step 1 ... apply the Supervisor Performance Evaluation Criteria, determine individual performance units and total them.

Supervisor: _____ Performance Units:

Supervisor: _____ Performance Units:

Total Performance Units:

Step 2 ... divide bonus pool by total performance units to get the value of each performance unit.

Pool of $ divided by   total perf. units = $ unit value

Step 3 ... multiply each Supervisor's performance units times the dollar value of each performance unit to get the individual bonus award amounts.

Supervisor: Perf Units: x $ = $

Supervisor: Perf Units: x $ = $

Total Bonus Awards = $

Step 4 ... confirm that total bonus awards equal the total bonus pool amount.

Example: If all the criteria for bonus pool fund A are met and $10,000 is available for distribution, and Employee X is rated "Outstanding" (2 performance units) while Employee Y is rated "Good" (1 performance unit), then the $10,000 bonus fund is divided by the 3 total performance units, with Employee X receiving $6,666.66 and Employee Y getting the remaining $3,333.33. The most senior plant Supervisor will get the odd penny.

If both Employees performed at the same level of effectiveness, both would receive the same bonus, no matter what fund level.

DISCUSSION

Bonus Philosophy

Maintenance of high production volume, acceptable production costs and quality standards are vital, essential and primary requirements. Failure to meet minimum standards in those areas threatens the very existence of the Company. No bonus pool shall be funded for any fiscal year in which production volume falls below 81% of the target or in which quality standards (for production or safety) are not met.

If one unit fails, the entire organization suffers. Therefore, the size of the bonus pool for Supervisors depends on the success of all units. Supervisors, even though they direct different units, share a common destiny and are expected to act in a spirit of cooperation and mutual assistance; so it is only proper that they be eligible for special rewards based on that group performance. The size of the bonus "pie" depends on total Company performance. The size of each Supervisor's "slice" of that pie depends on their management of the assets under their control: see the Individual Supervisor's Performance Results for further details.

Supervisors are held accountable for the results of the decisions they are authorized to make and eligible for bonus reward for effective management that produces desired outcomes.

If original operating plans or budgets are officially changed, the evaluation of performance under this bonus plan shall be based on the most current plans or budgets.

There are some circumstances under which failure to achieve production or budget goals are not attributable to Supervisors. Bonus pool C exists to permit a bonus after "excusable" failures caused by things like: acts of God, such as a tornado whose effects could not have been minimized by reasonable preventive measures; management decisions which change original plans and create new operating circumstances; client contract cancellations not due to Company actions which invalidate earlier production targets or related goals. Such factors are not under the control of Supervisors. The minimum bonus pool may be distributed if the Manager finds it feasible and decides that failure to meet goals was caused by such extraordinary factors.

Most factors fall under the control of Supervisors, for the purposes of this plan. The loss of a key subordinate will not disrupt operations if cross-training and back-up planning has taken place. Careful monitoring of quality control procedures and reports should assure low product reject rates. Contingency plans should exist to deal with manpower scheduling problems, to head off supply and inventory shortages, to provide alternative transportation sources in the event of delivery problems, etc. In other words, the failure to prudently prepare for potentially less-than-perfect performance by others is not "excusable" in terms of this bonus plan.

Periodic Feedback

The Manager shall ...

1. notify Supervisors of the precise performance objectives in each area for bonus evaluation (while it is expected that production and quality standards shall be created with the input and participation with Supervisors, the manager shall be the final authority over the precise objectives).

2. keep Supervisors informed on their actual progress against the specific objectives, through regular discussions confirming mutual understandings of operational results.

3. inform Supervisors whenever results in any area threaten overall organization success or the proper formation of the bonus pool. Since Supervisors share in their joint success or failure, they shall be notified of any potential or actual problems in other areas as well as their own.

Samples of Performance Appraisal Forms, With Analyses

The following pages contain **examples** of various Performance Appraisal forms and worksheets, preceded by comments on their special features, advantages and disadvantages. Their application and appropriateness depends on your unique circumstances.

Each sample Appraisal or Evaluation form:

- defines the general area or category of work that is being evaluated,

- describes the type of output or work results that are expected,

- asks for a rating in each area/category,

- and asks for a summary evaluation or final appraisal score.

Some forms are checksheets, while others are narrative. Some ask for weights, while others either assume that all appraisal categories carry equal importance or do not specify the weighting scheme. There are general forms with appraisal approaches that can be used for any and all jobs, one that was designed for a medical environment and one that was designed for a top executive. Some are broad and simple; some are more detailed and complex. Versions that cover both current performance and career development are included, with variations showing a number of different rating scales and process approaches.

The Performance Appraisal rating forms are followed by a series of typical worksheets for:

- Employee Self-Appraisal

- Performance Ratings

- Analysis of Results Against Objectives

- Bonus Recommendations

- Accountability Management (for Performance Objective Planning)

- Improvement and Development Planning.

The samples illustrate the range of options you have. All these examples were designed for organizations that had slightly different agendas; but all follow the same principles documented in the preceding pages, except as noted.

The ancient form below has been expanded and updated for illustration and amusement about the defects of the "checklist" approach to performance appraisal.

Performance Appraisal Checklist

A light-hearted example of a behaviorally-anchored checklist

PERFORMANCE APPRAISAL of _____

For each measurement area, check the appropriate box to the right describing performance results.

GRADING SCALE → ON ↓	Far exceeds job requirements	Exceeds job requirements	Meets job requirements	Needs some improvement	Does not meet minimum requirements
QUALITY	Leaps tall buildings with a single bound.☐	Needs running start to leap over tall buildings. ☐	Can leap over a short building or a medium one with no spires. ☐	Crashes into buildings when jumping. ☐	Cannot recognize buildings at all. ☐
TIMELINESS	Is faster than a speeding bullet.☐	Is as fast as a speeding bullet.☐	Not quite as fast as a speeding bullet.☐	Would you believe as fast as a slow bullet?☐	Wounds self with bullets when trying to shoot.☐
INITIATIVE	Is stronger than a locomotive.☐	Is stronger than a bull elephant.☐	Is stronger than a bull.☐	Shoots the bull.☐	Smells like a bull.☐
ADAPTABILITY	Walks on water consistently.☐	Walks on water in emergencies.☐	Washes with water.☐	Floats in water.☐	Passes water in emergencies.☐
COMMUNICATION	Talks with God.☐	Talks with the angels.☐	Talks to himself.☐	Argues with himself.☐	Loses arguments with self.☐
PROMOTABILITY	Related to the big boss.☐	Dating the big boss.☐	Looks like the boss.☐	Attends corporate affairs.☐	Had affair with my spouse.☐
SUMMARY EVALUATION	Is Christopher Reeves.☐	Is Steve Reeves.☐	Is Arnold Schwartzenegger.☐	Is Steve Martin.☐	Is Peewee Herman.☐

Yes, it specifies areas to be evaluated, but:

- they may not be relevant;

- they may carry different levels of importance (weight) between jobs;

- neither performance expectations (requirements) nor actual results are specified or reported;

- it appears extremely subjective.

The next checklist is far more useful and defensible. It specifies what was expected, requires comments on observed results and asks for simple rating judgments.

The more specific the performance expectations, the easier the appraisal. Note that very few rating categories are used. Evaluators are not required to differentiate between large numbers of obscure rating categories. There is no need to risk your credibility by trying to explain why an employee is *very good* but not quite *extremely good*, when no one can really see the difference. Such fine, precise shadings of judgment may be more important for salary administration than for performance appraisal. Don't let the needs of one system destroy the integrity of the other ... pay variations can easily be defended without artificially distorting the performance appraisal process.

The advantage of a checksheet format is that it requires all supervisors to review employees along the same dimensions (categories) of performance results.

The disadvantages of checksheets were listed before the "Superman" form. Checksheets tend to be overly universal and excessively rigid.

Performance Appraisal Form

PERFORMANCE APPRAISAL of _____

CATEGORY	EXPECTED PERFORMANCE	COMMENTS on actual work results	RATING
Work Habits	Punctual, never absent without notice; helpful and cooperative; demonstrate professional attitude and behavior at all times		□ Poor □ Good □ Excellent
Quantity	Handle work volume; keep current, avoid backlogs		□ Poor □ Good □ Excellent
Quality	Accurate, complete and neat work results; dedicated to excellence; show initiative		□ Poor □ Good □ Excellent
Time	Meet time deadlines, due dates, complete assignments promptly, keep work current and on schedule		□ Poor □ Good □ Excellent
Cost	Demonstrate sensitivity to costs, avoid waste; take action to increase revenue and reduce expenses		□ Poor □ Good □ Excellent
Professional Growth	Improve abilities and knowledge; seek out and apply new methods and techniques		□ Poor □ Good □ Excellent
Special Assignments	Perform other duties as specified.		□ Poor □ Good □ Excellent

Significant Strengths: *(what the employee does best...the most valuable attributes demonstrated on the job)*	
Weaknesses: *(areas where performance is poor or where substantial improvement is needed to meet job requirements...)*	

SUMMARY EVALUATION = □ **Poor** □ **Good** □ **Excellent**

Date _____ Signature _____

Date _____ Signature _____

Employee signature merely acknowledges receipt. Add any comments here or on the back:

The **Medical Office Performance Appraisal Form** and its generic version, the General Performance Appraisal Form, both illustrate a fairly "universal" format with some sophisticated features. Each form:

- identifies the sources of information about performance adequacy;

- defines specific standards for each performance rating level;

- has only three rating categories (equivalent to *super*, *ok*, and *lousy*) to simplify judgments;

- asks for weights, so ratings in vital categories can carry the proper importance in the summary appraisal;

- explains the process to determine a weighted final summary appraisal score.

Its weaknesses are:

- does not show the details of observed work behaviors which must be contained on a supplemental worksheet, if done at all;

- does not have space for an analysis of employee corrective or developmental needs;

- may require some modifications to defined **responsibility areas, performance indicators** and **standards** before they could be used for different jobs.

Medical Office Performance Appraisal Form

PERFORMANCE APPRAISAL of _____

RESPONSIBILITY AREA	PERFORMANCE INDICATORS (sources of information)	STANDARDS (for rating work quality)	RATING (2,1 or 0)	x WEIGHT (1-3)	= SCORE
Work Habits	Attendance, punctuality, compliance with office dress and behavior code, degree of dedication to work	Placed job first = excellent = 2, On time, tended to business = ok = 1, Neglected work or violated codes = poor = 0		x	=
Patient Care	Feedback from doctors, patients and their families	Frequently praised = good = 2, No comments = ok = 1, Received many complaints = poor = 0		x	=
Quantity of Work	Perceptions and reports of doctors and other staff members	Excellent = 2, Satisfactory = 1, Poor = 0		x	=
Quality of Work	Accuracy, completeness and anticipation of doctor's needs	Excellent = 2, Satisfactory = 1, Poor = 0		x	=
Time Management	Ability to meet time deadlines, due dates and keep calendar schedules	Always ahead of schedule = good = 2, Always on schedule = ok = 1, Late = poor = 0		x	=
Professional Development	Interest and ability in seeking out and applying new methods and techniques	Showed initiative and mastered new skills = 2, Maintained competent skill level = 1, Did not learn new skills needed on the job = 0		x	=
Perform Special Assigned Duties	Opinions of doctors and feedback from outside observers like suppliers or hospital staff	Exceeded expectations = excellent = 2, Met expectations = good = 1, Did not meet expectations = poor = 0		x	=
Contribute to Office Profit	Financial results of employee's actions and decisions	Far above plan = good = 2, On target = ok = 1, Below plan = poor = 0		x	=
FIRST STEP TO COMPUTE THE FINAL SCORE:		Multiply each RATING by its WEIGHT, then total the WEIGHTS and total the SCORES.		TOTL.WT.	TOTL.SC.
SECOND STEP TO COMPUTE THE FINAL SCORE:		Divide the TOTAL SCORE (TOTL.SC.) by the TOTAL WEIGHT (TOTL.WT.) to get the FINAL SCORE.	FINAL SCORE =		

Date _____ Signature _____

Date _____ Signature _____

Date _____ Signature _____

Employee signature merely acknowledges receipt. Add any comments here or on the back:

General Performance Appraisal Form

PERFORMANCE APPRAISAL of _____ **Date** ____

RESPONSIBILITY AREA	PERFORMANCE INDICATORS (sources of information)	STANDARDS (for rating work quality)	RATING (2,1 or 0)	x WEIGHT (1-3)	= SCORE
Work Habits	Attendance, punctuality, compliance with office dress and behavior code, degree of dedication to work	Placed job first = excellent = 2, On time, tended to business = ok = 1, Neglected work or violated codes = poor = 0		x	=
Dealing with Others	Feedback from managers, clients, peers and impartial observers	Frequently praised = good = 2, No comments = ok = 1, Received many complaints = poor = 0		x	=
Quantity of Work	Perceptions and reports of managers and other staff members	Excellent = 2, Satisfactory = 1, Poor = 0		x	=
Quality of Work	Accuracy, completeness and anticipation of Company's needs	Excellent = 2, Satisfactory = 1, Poor = 0		x	=
Time Management	Ability to meet time deadlines, due dates and keep calendar schedules in line with proper priorities	Always ahead of schedule = good = 2, Always on schedule = ok = 1, Late = poor = 0		x	=
Professional Development	Interest and ability in seeking out and applying better methods and techniques	Showed initiative and mastered new skills = 2, Maintained competent skill level = 1, Did not learn new skills needed on the job = 0		x	=
Perform Special Assigned Duties	Observations of managers and feedback from other staff or outside observers like clients or suppliers	Exceeded expectations = excellent = 2, Met expectations = good = 1, Did not meet expectations = poor = 0		x	=
Contribute to Company Profit	Financial results of employee's actions and decisions	Far above plan = good = 2, On target = ok = 1, Below plan = poor = 0		x	=
FIRST STEP TO COMPUTE THE FINAL SCORE:	Multiply each RATING by its WEIGHT, then total the WEIGHTS and total the SCORES.			TOTL.WT.	TOTL.SC.
SECOND STEP TO COMPUTE THE FINAL SCORE:	Divide the TOTAL SCORE (TOTL.SC.) by the TOTAL WEIGHT (TOTL.WT.) to get the FINAL SCORE.		FINAL SCORE =		

Date _____ Signature _____

Date _____ Signature _____

Date _____ Signature _____

Employee signature merely acknowledges receipt. Add any comments here or on the back:

The form for **GENERAL MANAGER** is more individualized than the previous sample, and has the same strengths with fewer weaknesses.

It contains more performance indicators and illustrates the wide range of ways that performance standards can be defined.

Some standards are specified, some are not; some are general, some are numeric, some are subjective and some are simply unspecified.

PERFORMANCE MANAGEMENT FORM FOR <u>GENERAL MANAGER</u>

Performance Appraisal of _____

RESPONSIBILITY AREAS	PERFORMANCE INDICATORS	STANDARDS (good=2, ok=1, poor=0)	RATING (2,1 or 0)	x WEIGHT (1-5)	= SCORE
Implement documented policies approved by the Board	Board of Directors opinions on quality, time and cost of implementation	Better than expected = good = 2, As expected = ok = 1, Below expectations = poor = 0		x	=
Maintain production schedules	Production reports to Executive Committee	Ahead of schedule = good = 2, On schedule = ok = 1, Behind schedule = poor = 0		x	=
Production Services	Efficiency of services provided at the required Volume levels	Maintained services with few interruptions = good = 2, Many breakdowns and interruptions = poor = 0		x	=
Recommend effective new methods and policies	Board/Executive Committee acceptance of new methods & policies and success in use	All recommendations accepted = good = 2, Some recommendations accepted = ok = 1, No recommendations accepted = poor = 0		x	=
Technical Rules	Legal compliance	Followed governmental rules and regulations = good = 2, Allowed operations which violated laws = poor = 0		x	=
Records and Reports	Presentation quality, completeness and accuracy	(Standards to be set by Board)		x	=
Finances - Budget	Spending	Under budget = good = 2, On budget = ok = 1, Over budget = poor = 0		x	=
Finances - Investments	Investments are timely, judicious and profitable	Always = good = 2, Frequently = ok = 1, Never = poor = 0		x	=
Finances - General	Audit Results from outside examiners	Excellent = 2, Satisfactory = 1, Poor = 0		x	=
Employee Training and Supervision	Employee knowledge and performance as demonstrated by their work results	Exceeded expectations = 2, Met expectations = 1, Did not meet minimum requirements = 0		x	=
Employee Appraisal	Employee feedback	Employees were told where they stand = good = 2, Had to ask = poor = 0		x	=
Employee Morale	Employee complaints	No complaints = good = 2, Complaints were few or not valid = ok = 1, Employees filed many written complaints = poor = 0		x	=
Employee Retention	Number of employees quitting and reasons for turnover	Best stayed = good = 2, Good people left due to action of GM = poor = 0		x	=
Special Project - Self Improvement	Fulfillment of plan to attend seminars, study management films, join management group, take classes	Met plan = good = 2, Did not meet plan = poor = 0		x	=
Special Project - Delegation	Fulfillment of plan to train backups, to delegate responsibilities and show confidence in employees	Better than plan = good = 2, Met plan = ok = 1, Did not meet plan = poor = 0		x	=
Other duties specified in writing by Board	Board's opinion	(To be set when projects assigned)		x	=

TO COMPUTE THE FINAL SCORE: FIRST STEP	Multiply each RATING by its WEIGHT, then total the WEIGHTS and total the SCORES.	TOTL.WT.	TOTL.SC.
TO COMPUTE THE FINAL SCORE: SECOND STEP	Divide the TOTAL SCORE (TOTL.SC.) by the TOTAL WEIGHT (TOTL.WT.) to get the FINAL SCORE.	FINAL =	SCORE

Date _____ Signature _____

Date _____ Signature _____

Employee signature merely acknowledges receipt. Add any comments here or on the back:

The PERFORMANCE EVALUATION form on the following pages is a classic modern narrative appraisal form for the evaluation of professional, managerial and executive personnel. Its special advantages are that it:

▷ reminds the supervisor to confirm that job duties have not changed since current performance expectations were communicated;

▷ offers the employee an optional opportunity for voluntary self-appraisal;

▷ can be used in a Management By Objectives (MBO) environment;

▷ asks not self-appraisal;

▷ asks not just **what** actual results were, but also **why** they occurred (to explain what was due to employee efforts and what was beyond their control or influence);

▷ specifies certain evaluation categories to be appraised in all cases, leaving others open for discretionary definition and inclusion;

▷ calls for remedial actions or corrective steps where needed;

▷ requires both parties to agree on who must do what by when in an improvement/development plan.

Its major defect is the absence of Legal Compliance (EEO, Affirmative Action, overtime law, etc.) issues as a category where all supervisors and management personnel have important responsibilities that should be appraised. As long as that subject is covered among the optional objectives, however, the absence of such a pre-printed category is not necessarily dangerous.

PERFORMANCE EVALUATION

Name: _____ Date Hired: _____

Position Title: _____ Time on Job: _____

Division/Department: _____ Date of Review: _____

1.   Attach copy of current position specification, signed by both employee and employee's supervisor.

                              Attached [ ]

      Does the attached position specification contain any substantial changes that might affect position value?   [ ] Yes   [ ] No

      Did the employee choose to complete a Performance and Development Review Sheet?
                          [ ]   Yes (attached)   [ ]   No

2.   PERFORMANCE REVIEW

      A.   In order of importance, state the specific objectives the employee was expected to achieve (refer to Objectives Worksheet) and describe the actual results. If appropriate, comment on "why" actual results differ from planned results.

      OBJECTIVE   ACTUAL RESULTS   WHY

OBJECTIVE   ACTUAL RESULTS   WHY

B.   All supervisory, and some nonsupervisory, employees have responsibilities in the following areas. Where appropriate, describe objectives, actual results, and "why" comments in these areas.

Employee Development: (Training, coaching, evaluating performance and preparing for promotion)

3.   SPECIAL CONSIDERATIONS

Include any relevant facts regarding special contributions (such as patents awarded, unexpected discoveries made, honors bestowed, internal commendations received, etc).

4.   AREAS OF STRENGTH AND NEED FOR DEVELOPMENT

Based on performance, demonstrated skills, interest, potential and general observations, describe the strengths and needs this employee shows in job skills and behavior.

               STRENGTHS   NEEDS*

*   See Section 6.

5.   PERFORMANCE RATING

Based on this information, the employee's overall performance since the last evaluation can best be described as:

1.   Consistently exceeds all job requirements and performance standards.   [ ]

2.   Fulfills job requirements and meets performance standards.   [ ]

3.   Does not meet job requirements or meet performance standards.   [ ]
      (*Note:* this rating requires a follow-up review within three months. Refer to Guidelines for Improving Unsatisfactory Performance. In addition, consult with the Personnel Department for assistance in establishing corrective action.

               OVERALL SUMMARY RATING (circle one) is   1   2   3

6. IMPROVEMENT/DEVELOPMENT PLANS

Based on performance, interests and organizational needs, identify areas for improvement or development. Describe the action plans for each area and establish a target date for completion. Specify what the employee will do and what the supervisor will do to assist the employee. If this information is recorded in some other format, attaching a copy will be sufficient.

Each Area of NEED described in Section 4 must be addressed here.

IMPROVEMENT OR DEVELOPMENT AREA	*ACTION PLANS* *Employee will:*	*Supervisor will:*	*TARGET DATE*

SIGNATURES

(Employee's signature merely indicates that the evaluation has been reviewed.)

_____   _____
Employee   Date

_____   _____
Supervisor/Reviewer   Date

_____   _____
Secondary Reviewer   Date

COMMENTS

Original to be sent to Personnel Department. Copies to be retained by employee and supervisor.

The following two **Performance & Development Report**s are minor variations on the same theme, reflecting older methods which carry some risk.

Both forms use more rating categories, which can complicate appraisal judgments; but the different rating levels are carefully defined in terms of job standards. Both call for a summary appraisal of overall performance based on position standards that are not specified. The relative importance of the various **accountabilities** or result categories is not stated, and the summary can be based on an unexplained set of priorities.

The first form:

- uses SUMMARY APPRAISAL language that mixes past performance and future potential (the top ratings for immediate past performance are reserved for promotable employees, even though they may not have done the best work);

- evaluates personality traits for DEVELOPMENT purposes, opening the door for irrelevance, subjectivity, stereotyping, bias, confusion and inconsistency.

PERFORMANCE & DEVELOPMENT REPORT

NAME _____ DATE OF HIRE _____

PRESENT POSITION_____ DATE ASSIGNED_____

DEPT._____

COMPANY_____

DATE OF LAST   DATE OF THIS   DATE DISCUSSED
APPRAISAL_____   APPRAISAL _____ WITH INDIVIDUAL _____

PREPARED
BY _____ DATE _____

REVIEWED
BY _____ DATE _____

REVIEWED
BY _____ DATE _____

C O N F I D E N T I A L

PART I - PERFORMANCE

A. PERFORMANCE REVIEW: (NOTE: IF ACCOUNTABILITY MANAGEMENT WORKSHEET IS USED, OMIT THIS SECTION)

1. ACCOMPLISHMENT OF ACCOUNTABILITIES: Describe the results achieved by the employee against each of the accountabilities of the position. Consider quantity, quality, cost, and timeliness. State facts and figures where possible.

2. PERSONAL OBJECTIVES AND SPECIAL ASSIGNMENTS not covered above:

B. SUMMARY APPRAISAL: Place a horizontal line at the level best describing your over-all assessment of the employee.

DISTINGUISHED:	A TRULY OUTSTANDING PERFORMER HAVING <u>HIGH</u> POTENTIAL FOR <u>RAPID</u> ADVANCEMENT. ACCOMPLISHMENTS AND SKILLS <u>FAR</u> EXCEED THE STANDARDS OF THE POSITION.
EXCELLENT:	AN OUTSTANDING PERFORMER WHOSE ACCOMPLISHMENTS AND SKILLS SUBSTANTIALLY EXCEED STANDARDS OF THE POSITION (USUALLY WITH GOOD POTENTIAL FOR ADVANCEMENT).
VERY GOOD:	PERFORMANCE CLEARLY EXCEEDS STANDARDS OF THE POSITION.
GOOD:	PERFORMANCE IS AT OR NEAR STANDARDS OF THE POSITION.
ADEQUATE:	PERFORMANCE IS AT MINIMALLY ACCEPTABLE LIMITS.
UNSATISFACTORY:	PERFORMANCE IS BELOW ACCEPTABLE LIMITS.

PART II DEVELOPMENT

A. PERSONAL DEVELOPMENT PROFILE: Select the rating most accurately describing <u>your personal</u> assessment of the individual in terms of each of the applicable factors listed below. Your judgments, though subjective, provide the best source for identifying training and development needs.

EXCELLENT - FAR EXCEEDS REQUIREMENTS

VERY GOOD - CLEARLY EXCEEDS REQUIREMENTS

GOOD - FULLY MEETS REQUIREMENTS

ADEQUATE - MEETS MINIMUM REQUIREMENTS

UNSATISFACTORY - PROBLEM AREA

1. TOTAL KNOWLEDGE:	THE SUM TOTAL IN DEPTH AND BREADTH OF ALL WORK-RELATED KNOWLEDGE HOWEVER ACQUIRED.						
2. PROBLEM SOLVING SKILLS:	ABILITY TO COPE WITH PROBLEM SITUATIONS OF VARYING DEGREES OF COMPLEXITY OR CHALLENGE. INCLUDES SKILL IN INTERPRETATION OF FACTS AND ASSUMPTIONS TO ARRIVE AT LOGICAL SOLUTIONS.						
3. CREATIVITY:	TALENT FOR FINDING BETTER WAYS OF DOING THINGS; GENERATING NEW CONCEPTS, APPROACHES, METHODS OR APPLICATIONS.						
4. COMMUNICATION SKILLS:	RELEVANCE AND CLARITY OF WRITTEN AND ORAL EXPRESSION; EFFECTIVENESS IN EXCHANGING IDEAS AND INFORMATION WITH OTHERS.						
5. PERSONAL MOTIVATION:	THE TOTAL DEMAND THE INDIVIDUAL PLACES ON HIMSELF TO ACCOMPLISH, INFLUENCE OR OTHERWISE ACHIEVE RESULTS						
6. EMOTIONAL ADJUSTMENT:	ABILITY TO ADJUST READILY TO CHANGING CIRCUMSTANCES, TO BE INTELLECTUALLY RATIONAL DURING CRISES AND PERSONAL CONFLICTS, AND TO BE CALM UNDER PRESSURE.						
7. PLANNING:	THINKING THROUGH WHAT HAS TO BE DONE. INCLUDES SETTING OBJECTIVES, ESTABLISHING PRIORITIES, ALLOCATING RESOURCES, AND ANTICIPATING FUTURE REQUIREMENTS.						
8. ORGANIZING:	ESTABLISHING ORGANIZATIONAL REQUIREMENTS, DEFINING AND DELEGATING POSITION DUTIES AND RESPONSIBILITIES, AND ASSIGNING STAFF TO APPROPRIATE POSITIONS.						
9. CONTROLLING:	MEASURING AND REGULATING RESULTS. INCLUDES DEVELOPING STANDARDS, REPORTING, EVALUATING RESULTS AND TAKING GORRECTIVE ACTION.						
10. LEADERSHIP:	MOTIVATING OTHERS TO TAKE EFFECTIVE ACTION.						

WHAT DO YOU PROPOSE TO DO, OR RECOMMEND BE DONE, BASED ON THE ABOVE?

B. PROMOTABILITY: (To be completed if Summary Appraisal, Section I-B, is 'Very Good' or higher)

TO WHAT POSITIONS	DIV. OR DEPT.	READY WHEN	AVAILABLE WHEN	DEGREE OF RISK		
				NONE	MINIMAL	MODERATE

This second **Performance & Development Report** is a bit better than the previous one, although it is not particularly sophisticated.

```
+---------------------------+
|                           |
|    PERFORMANCE &          |
|    DEVELOPMENT            |
|    REPORT                 |
|                           |
+---------------------------+
```

NAME _____ DATE OF HIRE _____

PRESENT POSITION _____ DATE ASSIGNED _____

DEPT./DIV. _____

LOCATION _____

DATE OF LAST
APPRAISAL _____

DATE OF THIS   PREPARED
APPRAISAL _____ BY _____ DATE _____

                      REVIEWED
                      BY _____ DATE _____

                      REVIEWED
                      BY _____ DATE _____

C O N F I D E N T I A L

A. ACCOMPLISHMENT OF ACCOUNTABILITIES: Refer to the accountabilities or responsibilities listed in the Position Analysis or Description. Write in the identifying phrases for each accountability and your assessment of how well the individual has performed each accountability.

Specific Accountability

No.	Identifying Phrase	Rating
1		Comment
2		Comment
3		Comment
4		Comment
5		Comment
6		Comment
7		Comment
8		Comment

B. SUMMARY APPRAISAL: Overall job performance during the appraisal period.

☐ PERFORMANCE RESULTS CONSISTENTLY MEET AND FREQUENTLY EXCEED THE STANDARDS OF THE POSITION.

☐ PERFORMANCE RESULTS CONSISTENTLY MEET STANDARDS OF THE POSITION. OCCASIONALLY EXCEEDS BUT SELDOM FALLS SHORT OF DESIRED RESULTS.

☐ PERFORMANCE RESULTS NORMALLY MEET BUT RARELY EXCEED THE STANDARDS OF THE POSITION. OCCASIONALLY FALLS SHORT OF DESIRED RESULTS.

☐ PERFORMANCE RESULTS SOMETIMES MEET STANDARDS OF THE POSITION BUT LACK CONSISTENCY. SELDOM EXCEEDS AND OFTEN FALLS SHORT OF DESIRED RESULTS.

☐ PERFORMANCE RESULTS MEET STANDARDS OF THE POSITION ONLY OCCASIONALLY. PERFORMANCE IMPROVEMENT NEEDED.

C. PROMOTABILITY: Indicate the employee's potential for advancement at this time.

☐   READY FOR ADDITIONAL RESPONSIBILITY AT THIS TIME.

☐   HAS POTENTIAL FOR INCREASED RESPONSIBILITY IN THE NEAR FUTURE.

☐   REQUIRES CONTINUED DEVELOPMENT BEFORE CONSIDERATION FOR ADDITIONAL RESPONSIBILITY.

☐   HAS REACHED THE MAXIMUM LIMITS OF RESPONSIBILITY AND DEVELOPMENT.

COMMENTS:

D. DEVELOPMENT: Consider the employee's development needs in terms of:

☐ IMPROVED PERFORMANCE IN THE PRESENT POSITION AND/OR   ☐ PREPARATION FOR A POSITION OF GREATER RESPONSIBILITY.

RECOMMEND SPECIFIC ACTIONS THAT YOU BELIEVE WILL IMPROVE PERFORMANCE/POTENTIAL TO ACCOMPLISH THE ABOVE:

ADDITIONAL COMMENTS:

Two different versions of employee self-appraisal forms, both titled PERFORMANCE AND DEVELOPMENT REVIEW: EMPLOYEE WORK-SHEET, follow.

They ask the employee to discuss his or her perceptions about the job and their performance.

The first pages are essentially the same; but there are significant differences on the second page of each version.

The first worksheet has a back page that focuses on a self-evaluation of skills. It specifies different skill areas and asks for ratings.

A small amount of space is allowed for future career interests.

PERFORMANCE AND DEVELOPMENT REVIEW: EMPLOYEE WORKSHEET

NAME: _____ TITLE: _____

> *The appraisal process is intended to help both you and the organization. Completing this worksheet and returning it to your supervisor will contribute to your appraisal in two ways: (1) it will ensure that your viewpoints are understood; and (2) it will help make the performance and development review discussion more productive.*

SECTION ONE—JOB RESPONSIBILITIES: Describe your job as you see it in terms of key responsibilities. Other words meaning about the same are: result areas, major goals, primary duties, or important functions. Here are some questions to help you identify the key responsibilities of your job: What important results are expected of you? What does your supervisor emphasize? On what things do you spend a lot of time and effort?

_____
_____
_____
_____
_____
_____
_____

SECTION TWO—MAJOR CONTRIBUTIONS: Review each job responsibility and note any major contributions you have made. These may include an important problem solved, successful implementation of a new idea, an improvement in your job, or accomplishment of a particularly difficult to achieve objective or assignment.

_____
_____
_____
_____
_____
_____
_____
_____
_____

SECTION THREE—PERFORMANCE DIFFICULTIES: Since we all have some difficulties with particular aspects of our jobs, review your job responsibilities or areas of expected results, and note trouble areas, things that have happened to make you less effective than you could be, or things that you attempted that did not work out to your satisfaction.

_____
_____
_____
_____
_____
_____
_____
_____
_____

SECTION FOUR—SKILLS EVALUATION: Your performance is generally dependent on your skills. Look over the list of skills and evaluate how they contribute to your performance. Evaluate according to: *(1) Very proficient in this area, probably more than the job requires; (2) Proficiency is a good match to the job's demands; (3) Need to develop more in this area to be effective; (4) Not a high priority skill for this job.* Don't feel that you have to be good in, or rate yourself in, all skill areas.

BUSINESS SKILLS

1. **Problem Analysis:** _____

   Identifying problems, analyzing the causes and solutions of problems.

2. **Decision Making:** _____

   Making judgments after analysis of available information; responding with a timely and effective decision.

3. **Planning:** _____

   Your own work, work of others; direction of the business, priorities.

4. **Organizing/Coordinating:** _____

   Your own work, work of others, deciding time, place and sequence of activities.

5. **Control:** _____

   Setting standards; evaluating quality, following-up for results.

6. **Innovation:** _____

   By modifying or adapting existing designs, procedures, methods: by new direction, new approaches.

COMMUNICATION SKILLS

7. **Oral:** _____

   Speaking clearly and precisely in a one-on-one or small group situation.

8. **Written:** _____

   Presenting written ideas in a clear and concise manner.

9. **Presentation:** _____

   Orally presenting information and ideas in a clear, concise and convincing manner.

10. **Listening:** _____

    Understanding what has been said; probing for better understanding.

PEOPLE SKILLS

11. **Sensitivity:** _____

    To own impact on others, to needs of others; to consequences of actions, to timing, etc.

12. **Developing Subordinates:** _____

    Identifying needs, appraising, coaching and counseling.

13. **Handling Conflict:** _____

    Performing effectively in spite of stress, conflict or pressure.

14. **Persuading:** _____

    Influencing others in favor of an idea, product or point of view.

15. **Consulting:** _____

    Serving as a source of "technical" information, providing ideas to define, clarify or develop programs, procedures or plans.

16. **Interviewing:** _____

    Gathering and evaluating information about individuals, situations, etc.

TECHNICAL

17. **Job Content:** _____

    Knowing the technical and professional aspects of the job.

OTHERS

18. _____ _____

19. _____ _____

20. _____ _____

SECTION FIVE—CAREER INTERESTS: Think about your future. Describe what, if any, other position or function you would like to pursue. What do you see as your next career "move"?

_____

_____

_____

_____

_____

_____

This second self-appraisal worksheet allows narrative responses about perceived improvement needs. It does not specify "standard" skill categories to be used by all employees.

No special provision has been made on this form for an employee declaration of future career interests; but that can be added quite easily.

PERFORMANCE AND DEVELOPMENT REVIEW: EMPLOYEE WORKSHEET

NAME: _____ TITLE: _____

> *The appraisal process is intended to help both you and the organization. Completing this worksheet and returning it to your supervisor will contribute to your appraisal in two ways: (1) it will ensure that your viewpoints are understood; and (2) it will help make the performance and development review discussion more productive.*

SECTION ONE—JOB RESPONSIBILITIES: Describe your job as you see it in terms of key responsibilities. Other words meaning about the same are: result areas, major goals, primary duties, or important functions. Here are some questions to help you identify the key responsibilities of your job: What important results are expected of you? What does your supervisor emphasize? On what things do you spend a lot of time and effort?

_____
_____
_____
_____
_____
_____
_____

SECTION TWO—MAJOR CONTRIBUTIONS: Review each job responsibility and note any major contributions you have made. These may include an important problem solved, successful implementation of a new idea, an improvement in your job, or accomplishment of a particularly difficult to achieve objective or assignment.

_____
_____
_____
_____
_____
_____
_____
_____
_____
_____
_____

SECTION THREE—PERFORMANCE DIFFICULTIES: Since we all have some difficulties with particular aspects of our jobs, review each job responsibility and note trouble areas, things that happened that made you less effective than you could be.

_____
_____
_____
_____
_____
_____
_____
_____
_____
_____
_____
_____

SECTION FOUR—IMPROVEMENT PLANS: Now you can begin to develop sound action plans based on your thoughts about job responsibilities, contributions and performance difficulties. As you develop plans, use these guidelines:

    —   Concentrate on Performance Improvement in your current position by increasing your effectiveness or removing performance difficulties.

    —   Be specific enough so that you will know when you have improved.

    —   Development improvement plans around on-the-job activities and/or educational activities.

You and your supervisor should spend ample time developing these plans during the appraisal discussion. Take some time now to note any specific ideas you have regarding performance improvement.

_____
_____
_____
_____
_____
_____
_____
_____
_____
_____
_____
_____
_____
_____

The BONUS PERFORMANCE APPRAISAL SUMMARY SHEET shows a worksheet that can be used for any type of appraisal ... salary, performance, counseling, etc.

It refers directly to details documented on subsidiary worksheets, which are illustrated on later pages.

BONUS PERFORMANCE APPRAISAL
SUMMARY SHEET

Name _____   Title _____

Unit _____   Department _____

Performance Appraisal Conducted by _____   Date _____

Reviewed by _____   Date _____

Reviewed by _____   Date _____

...Details of [] Overall Category Performance Ratings
        [] Analysis of Results Against Objectives
                                    are attached.

BONUS SCORE COMPUTATION

GOAL CATEGORY	OVERALL CATEGORY PERFORMANCE RATING	CATEGORY WEIGHT
	÷	
	═══	═══

Total Overall Category
Performance Ratings ÷   Total Category Weights   =   Bonus Score

The OVERALL CATEGORY PERFORMANCE RATING WORKSHEET has space for almost every type of information the most expert performance manager might want to communicate to the employee at the **beginning** of the performance period, long before the actual results have been observed.

It assures that the employee clearly understands what is expected, the weight (relative importance) of each goal or objective, and how the supervisor will determine the level of performance. With such information, employees can monitor their own performance, getting direct feedback about performance adequacy during the year and always knowing where they stand.

This worksheet is time-sensitive. If priorities change, weights must change. If goals or objectives are modified by management decree or external circumstances during the year, this worksheet should be revised accordingly. It must be a real and living performance plan that flexes and changes in line with real expectations and which is clearly understood by both boss and subordinate.

OVERALL CATEGORY PERFORMANCE RATING WORKSHEET

GOAL CATEGORY	CATEGORY WEIGHT	PERFORMANCE AREA	PERF. OBJECTIVES	STANDARDS OF PERFORMANCE	Obj. Weight	Obj. Rating	Wtd. Obj. Score

Total Obj. Weights

Total Wtd. Obj. Scores

Overall Category Performance Rating =

Total Wtd. Obj. Scores _____ divided by

Total Obj. Weights _____ = _____ times

Category Weight _____ = _____ .

The PERFORMANCE APPRAISAL WORKSHEET can be used for any job.

It is a worksheet for documenting actual observations at the **end** of the performance period just prior to making a summary evaluation decision.

If the final appraisal form does not have sufficient space for detailed comments that vary by employee and by job, this kind of worksheet is invaluable as an attachment.

PERFORMANCE APPRAISAL WORKSHEET
FOR ANALYSIS OF RESULTS AGAINST OBJECTIVES

Area	Objective	Performance Indicators*	Results	Comments	Rating

*sources of information on quality, quantity, time and/or cost results which can be compared to expectations for performance appraisal.

The REMEDIAL ACTION PLAN is extremely useful for all kinds of actions intended to correct a deficiency, to improve performance or to develop new skills.

It is not restricted to "bad" performers, but can be used to communicate and document developmental/promotional needs.

The form calls for specific actions, and asks for a clear definition of *who* must do *what* by *when*. That means that the supervisor must accept responsibility for certain actions like planning, guidance, feedback, review, and support.

An important element is the line that asks for a statement of the consequences (if any) of non-compliance with the plan. This could be vital to prevent claims of misunderstanding after the fact.

A pyschological contract is signed by both employee and supervisor, showing mutual commitment to the plan.

And finally, it calls for an evaluation of results and a confirmation of understanding by the employee.

Remedial Action Plan

For _____ on _____

This plan was initiated by the ☐ Supervisor ☐ Employee.

The purpose of this plan is ☐ to correct a performance deficiency on the current job

      ☐ which detracts from overall competence

      ☐ which left work results below acceptable levels

      ☐ which threatens continued employment

☐ to improve employee performance

      ☐ in important areas of the current job

      ☐ for the demands of a specific future assignment

      ☐ to levels that might qualify the employee for advancement

☐ to enhance general employee development and growth potential

      ☐ to retain employment in a changing workplace

      ☐ to improve skills and abilities for other jobs

      ☐ to learn and demonstrate new skills and abilities

Area of Skill or Ability Needing Improvement	Specific Actions Needed to Achieve and Demonstrate Improvement	Who Must Act	By *(Date)*	Evaluation of Results

Target Date for Evaluation of Results: _____

Failure to achieve Remedial Plan objectives will result in: _____

_____

I, _____, the Employee, commit myself to this course of action on *(Date)*

I, _____, the Supervisor, commit myself to support the Employee in this course of action on *(Date)*

Reviewed and approved by the next level of management: _____ on *(Date)*

RESULTS EVALUATED AFTER THE TARGET DATE BY
Supervisor _____ on *(Date)*   Manager _____ on *(Date)*
EVALUATION ACKNOWLEDGED AS "UNDERSTOOD" BY   Employee _____ on *(Date)*

Why Certain Common Methods and Forms Were Excluded as Dangerous or Defective

Certain traditional performance appraisal forms have deliberately **not** been included as samples in this workbook. Such forms were excluded because they are very bad examples that can mislead, confuse, complicate, etc., your job as a supervisor.

For instance:

■ trait-based performance dimensions (a list like the Boy Scout code) have little relationship to job content or actual performance, are highly subjective opinions of inputs rather than output results, invite bias and abuse, etc.;

■ management by pure numbers is impractical and ineffective for most firms;

■ formats that measure limited numbers and types of behaviors that do not cover all essential behaviors of the job have been avoided, as much as possible, and identified as dangerous when used in samples;

■ examples of forced rankings of employees (the "totem pole" approach), where people are compared to each other and placed in sequential order of value by section, department, division, etc., have been omitted as generally inappropriate;

☐ while the negotiation process required for a "totem pole" gives supervisors great insight into top management perceptions, it seriously undercuts employee morale by pitting one against the other rather than encouraging group cooperation ...

☐ instead of rating people by their performance against their own job expectations, they are forced to compete against other people whose job performance is unknown to them ...

☐ it creates rivalry, antagonism, suspicion of favoritism, and is extremely difficult to explain ...

☐ the ranking results are often used for layoffs and terminations, resulting in employee anxiety and supervisor reluctance to rank people low ...

☐ the process confuses long-term career potential and short-term actual performance (the best people in both categories may not be the same) ...

☐ it results in an arbitrary measure of the person's relative overall value to the organization rather than a report on the adequacy of their recent performance.

■ employee reviews of supervisors, where subordinates evaluate the performance of their boss, are useful feedback for perspective, can improve self-knowledge for personal growth and may indicate the level of employee satisfaction with supervisors, but any employee reviews of supervisors should not replace management reviews of supervisors;

   ○ subordinates may lack the information and training to validly rate the results for which their boss is held accountable ...

   ○ employees may be highly satisfied with a supervisor whose work results fall far below the reasonable expectations set by upper management ...

   ○ employee attititudes towards the supervisor might change if they knew how their boss behaved in closed sessions with the big boss ...

   ○ the supervisor works for (and reports to) top management and is accountable to them, rather than to his or her immediate subordinates.

■ peer reviews, where employees rate each other's performance, suffer from many of the same weaknesses.

The author has taken care to include the "better" forms; but a decision on what is "precisely the best" for your needs depends on your unique and ever-changing circumstances. At least, now you have a much better idea of the range of options available to you, why they exist and the relative advantages and disadvantages of each.

INDEX